LAWRENCE R. KOLLER'S
SHOTS AT WHITETAILS

A DEER HUNTING CLASSIC

EDITOR

PATRICK DURKIN

MANAGING EDITOR

JENNIFER PILLATH

COVER ART BY

MICHAEL SIEVE

DRAWINGS BY

RUTH A. PILLATH

Book design by Allen West, Krause Publications.

Cover Credits:
Front cover painting: "Play the Wind" by Michael Sieve;
courtesy of Wild Wings, Lake City, Minn.
Back cover photo: Ross Hubbard

Published by

 **krause publications**
The World's Largest Hobby and Collectibles Publisher

700 E. State St. • Iola, WI 54990-0001

Please call or write for our free catalog of publications. Our toll-free number to
place an order or to obtain a free catalog is (800) 258-0929. Please use our regular
business telephone (715) 445-2214 for editorial comment and further information.
Library of Congress Catalog Number: 00-101583
ISBN: 0-87341-865-4
Printed in the United States of America

To
ALMA, my wife
whose great fund of tolerance and wisdom
befits her admirably for existence
with a hunter and angler.

"The first pink rays of sunrise bathing the top of the ridge above stirred me from my reverie. It was time now to get up on that ridge and look for my buck. Behind the little school ran a low ridge, gently sloping upward to meet the big ridge that I felt should be the resting place of at least a few deer. Slowly, reluctantly, fearful of making any sound that might break the spell of silence, I began the climb."
— Larry Koller
Chapter 5, *Shots at Whitetails*

IV   SHOTS AT WHITETAILS

An Introduction

Some time in 1971, as a recently enrolled member of the Outdoor Life Book Club, I ordered *Shots at Whitetails* by Lawrence R. Koller. There is a saying that says the pen is a long hand from the grave, and *Shots at Whitetails* proved that to me. Koller had been dead nearly four years before I read this, his first book. With *Shots at Whitetails*, Koller — as much as any person — helped spark my longtime fascination with deer and deer hunting.

Like many deer hunters who grew up during the 1950s, '60s and early '70s, I also give Koller credit for much of my early knowledge and appreciation of whitetails and deer rifles. He wrote about rifles, whitetails and deer hunting with such entertaining insight and passion that I found myself looking over his shoulder when he shot his first forkhorn with a .25/20, when he killed a buck during an early-morning rain while his companions slept in, and when he encountered a bundled up old-timer who didn't know the difference between "still-hunting" and "stand-hunting."

Koller also got me interested — at least for a time — in finding an old Enfield, Mauser or Springfield military bolt-action and sporterizing it. While I never have acquired one of these classic rifles, I still fantasize about a time in the future when I'll have time to take one of these old guns to the basement workbench and get creative.

Koller and *Shots at Whitetails* also boosted my confidence when I began hunting whitetails with a bow and arrow. Back in my youth, we were still shooting recurves, wooden arrows and one-piece broadheads. In fact, until the mid-1970s and the sky-rocketing popularity of compound bows, many people thought bow-hunting for deer was so gallant and hopeless that it was considered noble, almost romantic. Although Koller didn't dwell on bow-hunting in *Shots at Whitetails*, he made clear his respect for archers and archery equipment. So, when friends and brothers scoffed at my early bow-hunting efforts, I simply retreated to my room and reread Koller's words to refresh my confidence.

Now, as a middle-aged adult, I realize how lucky I was to be able to read *Shots at Whitetails* in my formative years as a deer hunter. It has long bothered me that this book was out of print for most of the recent renaissance in white-tailed deer hunting. It seems ironic, maybe even shameful, that a book that had done so much to promote and elevate white-tailed deer hunting in North America was mostly out of public view from the late 1970s until 2000. At least one full generation of deer hunters was allowed to go afield without benefit of reading this book.

Granted, some hunters will see that *Shots at Whitetails* was written in 1948 and think, "What can I learn from a book that doesn't include tactics on calling, rattling, scent usage, lunar theories, interpreting scrapes or hunting rub lines?" Plenty. Chief among this book's virtues is Koller's appreciation of whitetails. While deer hunting has changed somewhat in recent years, especially in terms of equipment, the whitetail remains just as fascinating and probably more elusive.

As legendary gun writer Jack O'Connor wrote in his 1970 introduction to *Shots at Whitetails*: "The whitetail is still the furtive, wary, four-legged genius he was (in 1948). If anything, the race is considerably smarter. These lovely deer seem to get shrewder every year."

I also worry sometimes that many of today's deer hunters haven't learned what deer hunting is supposed to be about. What would Koller think of all the innovations in gear and hunting strategies that have come along since he died in 1967? Koller thoroughly knew his era's firearms, ammunition, clothing, cooking, taxidermy and deer-hunting tactics. But there was no "whitetail industry" during his lifetime. When he died, the mass commercialization of deer hunting was still at least 10 years from take-off. I wonder what Koller would have thought of our preoccupation with scent control, scents, lures, GPS units, deer decoys, fiber-optic sights and the myriad camouflage patterns that people like me enjoy using.

In *Shots at Whitetails*, we do learn of his clear dislike for hunting from trees. Koller considered it foolish and dangerous, and surely couldn't have envisioned a time when 80 percent of deer hunters spend most of their time aloft. Would he have changed his opinion if he could have tried some of today's safe, comfortable models that make tree-stand hunting safer and more productive than ever? Maybe. Then again, like most serious still-hunters, then or now, Koller didn't relish stand-hunting, period. So maybe he could never look at some modern contrivances objectively. Those who hunted with him remember he seldom took a stand during a drive, preferring to let others take advantage of sitting on the deer's favorite escape routes.

Although Koller knew the technical side of deer hunting equipment, he also knew that knowledge of the deer itself was most important to every hunter's success and enjoyment. Even so, before his unexpected death at age 54 cut short his plans, he had intended to revise the chapters in *Shots at Whitetails* that dealt with guns, ammunition and gunsmithing; and open, peep and telescopic sights.

At one point in planning this third edition of *Shots at Whitetails*, I fleetingly thought about scrapping Koller's chapters on sights, gunsmithing and taxidermy. After all, many of the items and techniques he mentioned are obsolete. And even today's deer-specific magazines struggle to keep up with all the new rifles, slug guns, muzzleloaders, bows, shotguns, ammunition and broadheads. I'm confident in stating that the computer field is the only industry today that changes its core products more rapidly.

The more I thought about it, though, the more it seemed sacrilegious to omit any of Koller's original chapters from this edition. If nothing else, Koller's original text makes us better appreciate deer hunting during his era. At least one generation of deer hunters has already grown up assuming riflescopes and compound bows have always been part of the deer woods. Maybe we'll better appreciate deer hunting's heritage if we can envision a time when men argued whether peep sights or open buckhorn sights were better for deer hunting.

On the other hand, it's also interesting to realize that not much changed in shotguns and slugs for deer hunting between Koller's era and the late 1980s. Koller would probably have been shocked to find most hunters in the mid-

1980s were hunting with virtually the same technology available when he wrote *Shots at Whitetails* in 1948. In fact, not until the mid-1990s did deer hunters see dramatic improvements in shotgun-slug technology, even though rifled barrels were widely available by the end of the 1980s. I guess a charitable person would say better late than never. And even though many shotgun-deer hunters continue to hunt whitetails with '40s-era slugs and guns, today's shot-gunning deer hunters have far better options. They can choose from a variety of bolt-action, semiautomatic and pump-action slug guns with fully rifled barrels. And from these guns they can fire slugs that accurately deliver more energy at 125 yards than traditional loads offer at the muzzle.

Furthermore, although changes in rifles and rifle ammo evolved much more quickly and consistently than on the shotgun side, it's hard to claim those changes have been as dramatic. Today's rifle bullets are more diverse, consistent and reliable than those of Koller's era, yet I struggle to argue that modern deer rifles are noticeably more deadly and reliable. And although we have more choices in rifle stocks, lengths, weights and calibers, that speaks more of a big menu for a wider variety of tastes than noticeable in-field performance.

By the time the second edition of *Shots at Whitetails* was printed in 1970, many of the rifles and calibers Koller discussed were dying fast. The .250/3000 Savage cartridge was nearly dead, and the .30 and .32 Remington rimless cartridges were ancient history. The Remington Model 141 pump-action rifle and the Remington Model 81 autoloader had been replaced by the Remington Model 760 pump and Model 742 automatic. In turn, they were replaced by the Model 7600 and Model 7400, respectively. And while the .303 Savage is now part of deer hunting's rich history, we're still loving the .30-06 and have steadily broadened and embraced a growing list of newer calibers, such as the .243 and .270 Winchester, the .280 and 7mm-08 Remington, and the .308 Winchester, to name a few.

And although their numbers aren't large, many deer hunters today cling to various magnum calibers. With that in mind, I've long enjoyed this section from O'Connor's 1970 introduction:

"Larry Koller and I were in perfect agreement about deer rifles and their use. We both agreed that the hunter killed deer, or any other game for that matter, not by excessive power, not by blinding velocity, but by putting into the right spot a bullet that has been properly constructed to open quickly against the light resistance offered by the fragile and lightly constructed body of the average whitetail. We also agreed that of the various factors in killing power, the most important was a hunter who didn't get buck fever and who could shoot well enough to hit. Larry Koller also said that the man who could shoot well enough to keep his shots in an 8-inch circle at 50 yards shot well enough for most whitetail hunting."

I've also enjoyed this observation by O'Connor, possibly because I agree with the words but often practice otherwise:

"Since this book was written, American hunters have come down with a bad case of 'magnumitis.' All manner of powerful, high-velocity, hard-kicking magnum cartridges have been introduced. None of these has any place in the hunting of whitetails. They are unnecessarily powerful; rifles for them are too heavy; and their recoil is disconcerting. For whitetails, no one needs more power than that afforded by the .308 or, for that matter, by the .35 Remington or the .30/30."

While it's impossible to argue with O'Connor and Koller about the actual necessity of magnums for deer hunting, they do overlook one thing: Some deer hunters like them for another important reason — because they're there. I've shot various magnums the past half-dozen years, figuring that anyone who can handle a 12-gauge slug gun has nothing to fear from most magnum rifles. And if the magnum somehow increases a deer hunter's confidence and he harnesses the extra power expertly, why criticize the choice? This seems even more true in today's era when considering most magnum-toters do their deer hunting from stands, where solid rests are often part of the design and portability of a heavy rifle is a secondary consideration.

O'Connor also noted that *Shots at Whitetails* appeared before the postwar boom in riflescopes got under way. He wrote: "Since that time, the scope has become the No. 1 hunting sight, so much so that probably 99 out of 100 whitetail hunters who take their hunting and equipment seriously now use telescopic sights. ... Material on specific models of scopes in *Shots at Whitetails* is, of course, obsolete. Of all the scopes mentioned, the only one still manufactured is the excellent Weaver K2.5, and it has been vastly improved since 1948. The companies that made Noske and Maxwell Smith scopes are no more, as is the firm that made the Norman Ford Texan."

Of course, today's deer hunters have far more options in riflescopes than they did in 1970, and like nearly everything else in deer hunting equipment, the models are continually changing. In fact the once-famous Redfield scopes have come and gone since *Shots at Whitetails* was written, but that company still makes rings and bases. At risk of offending through omission, companies like Bausch & Lomb, Burris, Leica, Leupold, Millett, Nikon, Pentax, Simmons, Swarovski, Tasco, Weaver and Zeiss are competing robustly for the deer hunter's attention in 2000. Again, though, menu size is the most staggering change we enjoy today. The technology in riflescopes has not changed dramatically since O'Connor wrote his introduction, at least — again — not to the degree obvious in shotgunning for deer.

O'Connor's thoughts on the virtues of low-power riflescopes for whitetail hunting in brush and forest remain highly relevant. But even though low-power variables in the 1.5-4.5X, 1.5-6X or 2-7X range are most appropriate for hunting whitetails, the 3-9X variables seem to draw the most attention from consumers. To be fair, though, that might be quibbling these days because of the popularity of stand-hunting over still-hunting, and the fact that even bigger variables have many virtues. As O'Connor said: "a good scope with a quickly seen reticle like a heavy cross-wire makes accurate shooting possible in light too poor for iron sights to be used at all. ... The hunting scope also has the curious quality of enabling the user to 'see through' brush. A deer completely or largely indistinguishable with the naked eye can be made out through the glass."

Today's scopes, almost universally, are absolutely waterproof and can be carried worry-free even in rain. While most still require a lens cover for hunting in rain, modern coatings transmit more light and some make the exterior glass much more fog-resistant.

Perhaps most gratifying in recent years is the growing popularity of telescopic sights for shotgun deer hunters. This trend is likely to keep growing for years to come as more hunters realize scopes allow them to take full advantage of their shotgun's improved accuracy and down-range performance.

Today, as in O'Connor's time, most scopes for whitetail hunting are held on by solid bridge-type mounts screwed to the top of the rifle's receiver. These models are strong, streamlined and handsome. And while several companies offer see-through mounts, most serious whitetail hunters choose permanent mounts or detachable models. The latter are especially popular with muzzle-loading-hunters, a group of fanatics nearly unheard of during Koller's era.

Finally, despite the incredible wealth of knowledge Koller presents on equipment and gunsmithing in *Shots at Whitetails*, let's keep an important fact uppermost: This book is by far more concerned with white-tailed deer and deer hunting. If it were primarily about gear and repairs, *Shots at Whitetails* wouldn't have even been reprinted in 1970, let alone today.

It's Koller's insights into whitetails and the world in which they live that keep his book so strikingly relevant. It's ironic, for instance, to read his thoughts on the troubles that deer overpopulation presented in some regions during the late 1940s. Obviously, suburban deer herds were causing concerns long before anyone scheduled university workshops to discuss the issue.

It's also humbling to hear Koller discuss at length the important role hunters play in keeping deer herds in line with their habitat. Scientific deer management isn't a recent development, despite how stubbornly some deer hunting families resist it. Koller was in step with the scientific community, and less concerned about fitting in with the barbershop biologists who refuse, for example, to shoot an antlerless deer. Koller thought it crucial for hunters to view whitetails, and themselves, as connected parts of the environments they share. He knew his trees and plants, and understood how they, too, connect with the other plants and animals of the forest and woodlot. Only by under-standing the whitetail's world and the hunter's responsibilities in managing these deer can we fully appreciate the animal itself.

Just in case anyone reads *Shots at Whitetails* without understanding Koller's purpose in writing it, he ends his book with these paragraphs:

"My aim in presenting this work is not only to help deer hunters take their trophy, but to implant in them some of my unbounded admiration for these wonderful animals. I hope this book helps you find success in a soul-filling sport whose rewards lie deeper in the heart than the filling of a license.

I shall forever wonder how close I came to the mark."

Larry, your shots hit just as true today as they did in '48. While the equip-ment has changed and an entire industry now revolves around the whitetail, the whitetail itself remains as elusive and fascinating as ever.

Somehow, though, I doubt that would surprise you.

— PATRICK DURKIN
Editor, *Deer & Deer Hunting* magazine
June 2000

An Appreciation:
Koller's Legacy Lives On

If it were possible for *Shots at Whitetails* to have two dedications — with one, of course, permanently reserved for Lawrence R. Koller's wife, Alma — the other would read something like: "To all white-tailed deer hunters who appreciate a good story as much as straight facts and in-depth information on all aspects of deer and deer hunting."

It's with extreme pride and an odd sense of inevitable inspiration that *Deer & Deer Hunting* magazine brings *Shots at Whitetails* back into print for North America's white-tailed deer hunters. It was this 1948 book, Koller's first, that helped inspire the founders of *D&DH* to publish in 1977 the world's first magazine devoted exclusively to hunting white-tailed deer.

The magazine's co-founders and co-owners — Al Hofacker, Jack Brauer and later, Rob Wegner — were all huge fans of *Shots at Whitetails*. They took some direction straight from Koller's teaching methods, striving to make their magazine informative as well as entertaining. Soon after launching *D&DH*, the motto the trio chose for their magazine was: "Practical and Comprehensive Information for White-Tailed Deer Hunters." Coincidentally, in his 1948 foreword to *Shots at Whitetails*, Clayton B. Seagears of the New York State Conservation Department wrote a similar thought: "In our decidedly humble opinion, (*Shots at Whitetails*) is the most practical and comprehensive work on the white-tailed deer and its byproducts ever written."

Hofacker chuckled in surprise when asked in May 2000 if the *D&DH* brain-trust had subtly honored Koller by choosing such a similar phrase to describe the magazine's purpose. "No, I really wasn't aware of that," he said. "That's news to me."

During the last quarter of the 1900s, *D&DH* made frequent references to *Shots at Whitetails*, including a Wegner-penned feature article on Koller in its November 1997 issue. Without fail, those references spurred letters, e-mails and phone calls to the magazine from readers who wanted to know where they could buy a copy of the classic book. The magazine's readers understood and appreciated Koller's broad, in-depth knowledge about nature, whitetails, hunting and firearms, and they wished to learn more from him — and about him.

Shots at Whitetails Returns

Unfortunately, until now, all we could do was refer Koller's many admirers to various outlets that specialize in out-of-print books. Those of us lucky enough to have our own copy of *Shots at Whitetails* — some of us clinging to these rare prizes since our childhood — weren't about to loan or sell them. Sure, we'd make Xerox copies of certain sections of the book and mail the copies to friends or writers, but the original book never left our sight for more than a few minutes.

Finally, we took the hint and decided to try reprinting the book. We tracked down Paul Koller, Larry's last surviving offspring. Paul owns the copyright to *Shots at Whitetails*, and agreed with us that it was time to reacquaint the continent's deer hunters with one of the most knowledgeable all-around hunters and teachers of the 1900s. Although Larry Koller had no formal schooling in the sciences or teaching, he had a natural ability to take information, assemble it in logical and sensible order, and then pass it along to those willing to learn.

Koller's teaching talents were evident to those who knew him, with or without his prolific writings. Just ask any member of the Eden Falls Hunting and Fishing Club, which Koller helped form in the late 1940s. The club controlled about 3,000 acres that was owned and run by Abe Wexler and his family, and it remains active today, not far from the original campsite in the Neversink River Gorge. (The club even maintains a Web site: www.edenfalls.com.)

Ernie Thiesing of Monticello, N.Y., joined the club in 1961 and remembers Koller as an intense hunter who never stopped learning, teaching and observing everything that went on in the deer woods.

"He was a natural teacher and an unselfish hunter," Thiesing said. "Larry loved to teach you everything he knew about the woods, and explain how hunters should handle themselves in the woods. He never missed a deer season, and when he was here, he ran the drives. He knew these mountains very well and he knew where the deer would go. He would tell you where to sit and why you should sit there, and then he would go help on the drive. We could never get Larry to sit down. He always had to be one of the drivers."

Running the drives was no simple task. Koller-run drives usually involved about three or four drivers to get the deer moving, and 10 to 15 standers to cover saddles, runways, overlooks and creek crossings. Everyone knew their responsibilities. And just to make sure there was no confusion, Koller and camp members tacked numbers onto trees to designate the various stand sites.

Vic Perruna of Spring Valley, N.Y., became part of the Eden Falls camp in the early 1950s. Perruna ran a restaurant and Koller — a gourmet cook himself — was a frequent customer. Perruna has never forgotten how Koller helped him become a better hunter.

"He was an unbelievable hunter and an excellent teacher," Perruna said. "He built a moving deer target for the camp so everyone could practice. He was always doing things like that. Always helping out. He was always here."

Thiesing and Perruna also recall Koller's impressive shooting skills in the deer woods.

"He was a great shot, an incredible shot," Perruna said.

"If you were with him during a hunt, he always let you take the first shot," Thiesing added. "Part of that might have been that he was just so good with a rifle. He knew if you missed, he could make the shot when the deer tried to get away."

Koller, the Still-Hunter

One reason Koller was such an excellent shot and tactical expert in deer drives was that he devoted countless hours to still-hunting whitetails. Still-hunting, more so than stand-hunting, often requires lightning-quick decisions and nearly instinctive shooting skills to spot, aim and drop a deer before it can flee.

Thiesing recalled that while Koller was always a big part of the weekend and Thanksgiving hunts with the group, he often returned or stayed behind "when things petered out" to still-hunt by himself. If Koller planned to hunt on the far side of the Neversink River, he would pack a small lunch and be gone for the day.

"He really liked to be out there on his own," Thiesing said. "He enjoyed trying to get a deer by himself when no one else was around."

Koller, the Shooting Instructor

Perruna recalled how Koller took time to teach Perruna's four sons how to shoot, and how greatly Koller emphasized firearms safety.

Thiesing agreed. "He had a great deal of respect for firearms and never stopped stressing safe gun-handling."

Koller also helped teach Thiesing's children, Chris and Mary Anne, how to shoot.

"When we came here in the summers, it was like having an entire cadre of uncles, and Larry was one of them," Mary Anne said. "I remember how he was real strict about gun safety. With Larry, you could screw up in nearly everything else, but you could never mess up with guns."

Paul Koller also remembers an important rule his father enforced during deer season: You didn't fire your rifle unless it was aimed at a deer.

"I remember one time I shot a raccoon. I made a good shot," Paul said. "My dad wasn't impressed. He smacked me pretty good for doing that. We were there to hunt deer, not raccoons."

Koller, the Parental Paradox

Interestingly, while Larry Koller often went out of his way to be a good hunting companion and instructor for friends and their children, he didn't consistently demonstrate the same attention and affection with his own children. Such paradox isn't unique to Koller, of course. Most of us can think of many adults, maybe even ourselves, who do everything possible for friends and coworkers, but seemingly neglect or take for granted their responsibilities at home.

Even so, we shouldn't think the family isn't affected by this often-stressful detachment. Paul Koller recalls a weekend when his father promised to begin his shooting instruction.

"I was about 9 or 10 years old," Paul said. "We drove up to camp, and I kind of assumed we would get out the .22 on Saturday morning and start shooting. Well, Saturday came and went, and so did Sunday morning. Finally, on Sunday afternoon he gave me a box of .22 shells, and told me to take the rifle out back and start shooting. That's how he taught *me* to shoot. I just shot and shot and shot.

"That was pretty much how he taught me to fly-fish, too. He had me watch him from a distance, and then I was on my own. Learning for me was a matter of doing, listening and observing. That was probably how he had learned, too."

Paul also recalls that his father didn't take him, his older brother, Larry Jr., or his older sister, Ann Elizabeth, under his wing and teach them woodcraft and deer hunting skills.

"No, he didn't really hunt with us," Paul said. "He would bring me and my brother to camp sometimes, but back in those days the kids were always the drivers. That's the only reason we were in camp."

At risk of rationalizing, we should also remember that deer camps back in the mid 1900s were often different from what we've come to expect in recent years. For one thing, when Koller's camp first got organized in the late 1940s, family participation wasn't the club's main purpose. Women weren't invited along to hunt and fish. The club members came by themselves, and family members were only invited onto the grounds for the club's annual summer picnics. The men-only approach gradually eased over time.

We should also remember that from the 1940s through 1960s, deer hunters were more worried about the future of deer populations, not declining numbers of hunters. During that era, deer numbers were rising, but not as fast as hunter numbers. Such concerns were voiced by Clayton Seagears in the 1948 foreword to *Shots at Whitetails*, who worried that the supply of deer could not keep up with the rising demand of a growing hunter population. Since the 1980s, of course, the whitetail population has been booming across most of its range, and by the early 1990s, many states were worried about long-term declines in hunter numbers. To counteract those predictions, states and the hunting industry have been promoting more family participation.

Whether such social differences explain everything or not, Paul said deer season wasn't a big family-participation tradition for the Kollers during his childhood. Paul remembers his father as a hard-nosed disciplinarian who struck first and, maybe, asked questions later. Paul also openly discusses the fact that his father often drank heavily, and that alcohol was a longtime problem throughout his family, including himself. Paul, who turned 57 in July 2000, has outlived his older siblings, and has lived longer than anyone from the family's last two generations.

"Alcohol killed nearly everyone in my family, and it almost killed me," he said matter-of-factly.

A Student of Relevant Detail

During Larry Koller's relatively short life, however, his intense drive helped him become a widely recognized expert in deer hunting the Catskill Mountains. No detail concerning rifles, deer, terrain or people seemed to escape his notice. And he didn't seem to dwell on details that weren't critical to his hunting success. While he paid attention to deer tracks, deer biology, wind direction and weather conditions, he spent little effort analyzing rubs, scrapes, possible lunar influences and other more recent points of interest. As primarily a rifle-hunting still-hunter and drive-master, Koller was more concerned with stealth, woods vision, reliable rifles, efficient sights, shooting skills and familiarity with terrain. Seldom did he take a stand and wait for a deer to come by on its own.

As a result, Koller immersed himself in the minutia of rifles, sights, landscape, hunting clothing, cooking and tanning, and even the tendencies of hunting companions. He knew who could be relied on to cover escape routes that offered tricky shots, and who to place on stands where the shots weren't so difficult. While companions knew he could be impatient and demanding, they respected his skill, versatility and knowledge.

Readers of *Shots at Whitetails* might be amazed by the many details Koller offers on how to get a deer out of the woods. It might be impossible to appreciate those fine points and the various techniques unless a person regularly hunts the Catskills. This picturesque region features steep ridges, dense alder thickets and stately pines and hemlocks. One feature that might stand out even more strikingly to visitors, however, is its rock-strewn limestone landscape that makes dragging deer a constant struggle. Sometimes the easiest way to move a deer is to get it off the ground, and Koller was practiced in the various methods.

Conclusion

No matter where you hunt whitetails, it's impossible to read *Shots at Whitetails* without becoming not only a better hunter, but also a better student of deer and deer hunting. Koller sincerely loved the whitetail and made the animal one of his year-round, life-long interests.

Perhaps best of all, Koller could relay his passion to others through the written word. He was not only a masterful teacher but also a gifted storyteller who could make his readers envision every colorful detail he described. It's hardly unique that people who read *Shots at Whitetails* in the early 1970s can still recall anecdotes from Koller's book.

In fact, here's a guarantee: If this is the first time you've read *Shots at Whitetails*, years from now you'll recall in vivid detail Koller's conversation with boys who visit his gunshop to buy cartridges, customers who nearly ruin their rifles with excessive care, a buck that continually eludes hunters by leaping off a sheer rock shelf, camp guests who forsake their healthy diet for Koller's cooking, or the hunting companion who surprises two trespassers trying to make off with his buck.

Also guaranteed: You'll never again look at a deer's throat patch without thinking, "That was Koller's favorite target when he lined up the peep sights on his .30-40 Krag."

Quite simply, Koller's teaching method of instructing while entertaining has already passed the test of time. Through *Shots at Whitetails*, he will long be teaching his myriad lessons to many generations of North American deer hunters.

— PATRICK DURKIN
Editor, *Deer & Deer Hunting* magazine
June 2000

Foreword

There are exceedingly few people who can (1) consistently outsmart a particular buck deer, (2) collect it with either a really good bow or rifle of his own manufacture, (3) properly dress and butcher the carcass, (4) concoct palatable dishes therefrom and (5) expertly mount the remains.

Larry Koller can. Furthermore, he can write entertainingly of the whole operation. That last just about puts Larry in a class by himself. It puts this book in a class by itself, too, for in our decidedly humble opinion it is the most practical and comprehensive work on the white-tailed deer and its byproducts ever written. It should be standard for a long time to come.

There's one thing wrong with Larry's book: It's too enlightening.

Readers of *Shots at Whitetails* are bound to come out the other end more efficient hunters. Thus, the deer lose. That is bad. For under the current hunting system, there'll come a day when there'll be too many hunters to harvest too few deer. Then bong will go the gong proclaiming a deer-bank holiday.

Here's what we mean: In 1932, New York State had about 68,000 licensed deer hunters. In 1948 — only 16 years later — an army of more than 300,000 licensed deer hunters took to the tall timber.

To be sure, the nation's whitetail population has been increasing, too, simply by extending its range. Again using New York as an example, the legal deer-hunting territory in that state increased nearly 100 percent in the past 20 years, while its take of deer increased 150 percent. But the increase in the number of Empire State hunters was nearly 300 percent during that same period. Also, the carrying capacity of the nation's white-tailed deer range has been reached, or even exceeded, through much of the land.

So maybe we should consider a book like this too enlightening, although, of course, Larry Koller himself is as good a conservationist as he is a hunter. In any event, the book is bound to contribute substantially to the pleasure of the hunter, whether he gets a deer or not. That is good.

This is Larry Koller's first book. It is easy to predict that the public will not permit it to be his last.

CLAYTON B. SEAGEARS
Director of Conservation Education
New York State Conservation Department
Delmar, New York, 1948

Table of Contents

PART 1

The Sport of Deer Hunting

CHAPTER 1

Perspectives

Way in the days when old Dan'l Boone and Cooper's Leatherstocking roamed the timbered ridges and valleys of the country's great Alleghenies, the white-tailed deer was the support on which our pioneer forebears extended the Western frontiers. They looked to the whitetail for their fresh meat, always easily available to these skilled riflemen and woodsmen. Its dark red flesh formed the basis of their daily menus, varied only by occasional squirrel, grouse, wild turkey or fish. But the deer was always first choice, for it meant to them a maximum in food with the least expenditure of precious powder and ball.

Its tough, pliable skin clothed the settler in soft, warm garments — shirts, trousers, moccasins and even cap — clothed him almost entirely from head to foot. Sinews were used for laces and threads, bones went to make soap and needles; even antlers were fitted to knives and other simple tools, just as today. On long trips of exploration into new country where game might be scarce, no pioneer would be without his buckskin pack of "jerky" — smoked venison, hard as rock but capable of sustaining life for long periods in the wilderness. Even for more or less permanent camps sun-dried deer hides, coarsely thatched with their heavy hair, kept a waterproof roof over the settlers' heads.

Truly then, we can understand how much heavier would have been the burden of exploration and settling of new wilderness regions had the white-tailed deer not been a permanent and prolific resident of the forests.

Today, hundreds of years after the Mayflower first touched the rocky Eastern coast, we still have with us, keeping rapid pace with our growing civilization, white-tailed deer. These have not gone the way of many other vanished or vanishing Americans, and we must gratefully thank the Maker of All Things for bestowing on us so abundantly these splendid game animals in ever-increasing numbers.

The Adaptive Whitetail

Obviously, it is true that wise conservation measures and the never-ending search for new methods and ideas among our various state game commissions have made the present-day abundance of whitetails possible. Equally true is it that no other native game animal or bird has responded so well to intelligent conservation.

Encroaching civilization and the machine workings of man have failed miserably to daunt the spirit, and will to live, in the whitetail. Indeed, he thrives on these, it seems, growing more cunning with each generation, until now he puts to shame the sagacity of his pioneer-days ancestors. This deer lives and survives almost in the midst of the hum of cars and planes, raising its spindly legged, spotted family in the best whitetail manner, well able to outwit all but the most careful sportsman.

Yes, if any of you who read this would gaze into the setting sun from the top of that great monument of stone and steel in mid-Manhattan, the Empire State Building, your eye would encompass lands now sheltering hundreds of wild white-tailed deer, living now as they have before, a placid, almost abundant existence. Few elements disturb them other than the week or two each year when red-capped sportsmen take to the outdoors for that biggest of annual hunting events, the open season.

These magic words stir many thousands of hunters every fall. Year after year finds the number increasing, and their degree of success increasing in proportion — indicating that the whitetail is not only the most popular of our bigger game, but the most suited to sustain the casualties of heavy hunting in the thickly populated metropolitan areas.

Increasing Numbers of Hunters

During the past few seasons, the licenses issued to New York state hunters alone have virtually doubled and doubled again. All other states where deer are hunted also show this tremendous increase in hunting pressure, particularly since the return of service men. It is, of course, fortunate that not every hunter kills his buck. Certainly there would be few left for posterity should this condition exist for a few years. There will ever be a high percentage of hunters who simply go deer hunting with little thought to the game as a specialized sport. This group will never menace our deer supply. Bucks they kill can be charged to Lady Luck.

On the other hand, there is an increasing number of sportsmen who have a sincere desire to learn enough about deer hunting to enable them to see their buck and dispatch it humanely with a well-directed shot. The thousands of wounded deer that are never recovered each year show a dead loss on the sportsman's ledger — not to mention the harried conservation officials. High quality sportsmanship demands of the hunter that he attain the prerequisite skill in hunting and shooting to make such losses each season a negligible factor. But careful checking of deer taken against licenses issued each season shows that less than one hunter in every 10 is successful in bagging his buck.

Attention to almost assumptive detail often means the difference between the deer hunter and one who goes deer hunting. And, oddly enough, few of our good hunters ever stop to analyze just why they happen to return year after year with the proper spoils of the hunt. All too often it is a single detail that makes or breaks the whole season's setup for the shooter.

Failure to Prepare

During the season of '39, I spent a few days in deer hunting with a comparatively new deer hunter. This chap had already killed his first buck — and with a single shot — so I couldn't classify him as a greenhorn. He wasn't quite satisfied with his rifle though, after his first year in the woods, and in the spring and summer of 1939 I made some changes for him. First I built a new stock and equipped the rifle, a Krag, with ramp front sight and aperture rear. We loaded plenty of shells and fired all of them at targets and woodchucks during this off season, until he had reached the point of proficiency where a target the size of a deer offered no difficulties.

Our third or fourth day in the woods gave him a wonderful shot at a big buck; a standing, broadside shot at not over 20 yards, with the deer totally unaware of his precarious position. At the report the buck reared high, reversed his field and abruptly vanished in the laurels, in complete possession of his remarkable faculties, and body and mind perfectly intact; in a word, a complete miss.

My partner's story was sad, but brief. He had raised his rifle, squinted through the aperture, and could see only a dark, indistinct background filling the circle. The buck stood so close that he completely filled the area encompassed by the peephole. He couldn't tell whether his front sight was resting on trees, brush or deer. If it were on the deer he couldn't tell just where, so he lowered his rifle and tried again, with the same result, and then once more. At last in desperation he threw the rifle to shoulder and fired blindly in the general direction of his game. Net result was a bullet passing somewhere under the buck's body where it promptly cut off a small poplar on the far side of the deer.

The obvious answer to this maddening situation was simply this: He had unconsciously closed his left eye in squinting through his rear sight, shutting off the clear picture of his target and sight that he most certainly would have clearly seen had this left eye been open. His training in my hands had been in two-eye shooting, but under the stress of sighting at the all-important buck, he reverted to his days with a BB gun. Here the accepted mode of sighting, outlined graphically in Saturday-afternoon "horse operas," is to close tightly the left eye and leave the whole job of watching sights and target to one eye.

I wonder just how many bucks are missed each year for this one single reason. It seems such a simple detail, yet in my experience I know of at least 10 deer missed or "creased" because sights could not clearly be seen in dim light against dark backgrounds, with the dark gray-brown of the buck's body subtly merging into shadows, sights and trees. In this situation, two good eyes would have had trouble enough in directing the sights to the proper spot.

Common Cause of Failure

This business of sights being out of adjustment on deer rifles is one of the most common causes of hunting failures each season. An almost incredible number of deer shooters, beginners and experienced alike, do not know how to adjust their rifle sights; and with many of these same shooters, rifle sights could be far out of line without the hunter's knowledge.

Several years ago a close friend of mine — an excellent wing shot, by the way — decided to hunt and kill his deer with the rifle rather than use the scattergun and buckshot with which he had managed to kill a couple of nice bucks. Acting on my suggestion he bought a Savage model 99 K in .300 caliber, one of the best models this outfit turned out, at least from the standpoint of price, and certainly a highly effective weapon for Eastern white-tailed deer hunting.

This sportsman wasn't a rifle shot in any sense, so he spent a number of days afield with the new weapon, potting at 'chucks, crows, stones and what not, at all possible ranges. Just a day or two before the season opened, he went out to get an hour or so of last-minute practice, just to reassure himself of his abilities. During this last outing, and after burning up most of his available ammunition, he decided to do some long-range work as a finale.

Directly across the little valley where he finally decided to take his last lesson stood a large white rock on the opposite hillside, offering a conspicuous target at a range of 600 to 700 yards.

His first shots, of course, dropped far short, so he started to move up the rear sight by adjusting the step elevator. At last he began hitting his target with the elevator raised to its highest notch. After firing his last cartridge and noting the satisfying spurt of white dust appear from the rock, he was well convinced of his prowess as a deer shooter, at least on a target the size of a deer.

Opening day found him standing the first drive, full of confidence and expectation. Appropriately enough, this first drive pushed out a fine buck directly toward him, offering a perfect standing shot at not over 50 yards. Still full of confidence, he held for the neck and squeezed off, but to his great surprise the buck showed no change in attitude whatever, but calmly began to walk along a small ridge of ground. Friend shooter then went completely haywire and dumped shot after shot at the buck, hoping only to hit him somewhere.

Emptying his rifle, he still had time to reload completely and finish this rapid-fire round before the deer had passed from sight, still apparently much unconcerned, and injured in nothing more than feelings. Close examination of the ground covered by this buck revealed no indications of a hit, not even a hair, so this hunter headed right back to camp and offered his rifle for sale promptly at a bargain price of $5.

Fortunately for him, all of his hunting pals were also his friends and none of them would take advantage of his generous offer under the circumstances. One of the more curious individuals in this group decided to look over the rifle carefully to determine, perhaps, "if the barrel was bent." No, the barrel was in perfect condition, but his rear sight was still carefully and tightly placed in the highest step of the elevator. None of the dozen-odd shots had passed even as close as 6 inches over the buck's back, with the sight in this position. The hunter had merely forgotten to drop his sight down to its normal position after his long-range target practice.

So much for sighting failures. We could talk about dozens of incidents where almost tiny details in sights and sighting have made a hunting trip a complete failure, so far as game is concerned, but these two will suffice.

Malfunctioning Firearms

Next in order of prominence is the malfunction of firearms. Firing pins break, actions jam, rifles won't fire or safeties confuse the shooter. Many of these functional troubles lie with the shooter alone and not with the maker of the arm. They may be caused by faulty loading, abuse of rifle mechanisms, or improper cleaning or lubrication. Most of these troubles can be avoided if the shooter is careful and well-informed.

Cold-weather misfires are common and usually the result of excessive lubrication with heavy oil or gun grease. A few years back, in the middle of an unusually cold season, a deer hunter dropped into the shop with a new rifle of Remington design and make, a slide-action repeater. He loudly complained the rifle wouldn't fire at all early in the morning, but seemed to work pretty well later in the day. He added, also very loudly, that the d—cd thing had robbed him of at least two bucks within the past two days.

Without comment, I dismounted the action and removed the breech block, a little task that had certainly never been done since this hunter had owned the rifle. The entire action was drowned in a heavy grease that proved to be vaseline. In reply to my question, he blandly stated that he thought it was a good idea to keep his guns well greased, inside and out, so he had melted a large jar of vaseline and poured it into the action. It goes without saying that the early-morning cold had almost solidified the grease throughout the action, slowing down the spring and firing pin action to the point where it failed to strike the cartridge with a hard-enough blow to fire it. Added to this was the danger of grease running into the chamber and barrel, likely resulting in a blown-up action if the rifle were fired in this condition.

Proper cleaning with gasoline and a little lubrication with a light oil put the weapon in perfect shape for the woods, and as far as I know this hunter had no further trouble with the bucks.

Telling of Tales and Safety Factors

Perhaps no single sport produces such a fund of improbable stories as deer hunting, unless it be that of Ike Walton. And even with this tough competition, deer-hunting tall tales and alibis surely make a great showing. The tragic part of this situation is that deer-hunting tales need not be taken with such a large grain of salt as fishing stories, because in most cases they hold closely to facts. In deer hunting, not only the big ones get away — there is no distinction of size. Bucks big and small get away, time after time, for no apparently sound reason. But such is deer hunting; and the fraternity increases year after year, regardless of the supposed danger hazard and the low average of successful sportsmen.

Safety in the woods is an important factor. No, not safety from the wrath of ferocious deer, although now and then a dying buck plants a sharp hoof somewhere on his captor's person. Rather, safety for the hunters from brother sportsmen, who sometimes, in their zeal to outshine their partners, mistake a red cap for a huge rack of antlers.

This little matter of danger in connection with deer hunting, while it must be considered, is highly overemphasized. Some hunters of small game won't even consider the grand sport of deer hunting because of the "danger" from their brethren. As a matter of cold fact, during the season of 1939 in New York state over 149,000 deer hunters took to the field and forest, and of this number only five were killed. In the same year in the same state, pheasant and duck hunting alone produced almost twice the number of fatalities — and no sportsman would ever consider pheasant or duck shooting dangerous to the hunter. These 1939 figures for New York state average out pretty well nationwide for the years since that date. Small-game hunting produces fully as many accidents each year, but of course there is a somewhat larger number of small-game hunters.[1]

This writer believes the automobile is a much more deadly weapon than the deer hunter's rifle, and the risk of a single Sunday-afternoon drive on our big highways is far greater than the slight risk involved in a whole season of deer hunting. Yet not one of us, sportsmen or otherwise, would consider driving exclusively on back roads or giving up driving cars altogether just to avoid being killed.

Good drivers are careful drivers, and seldom cause accidents or suffer injury in their cars. The same goes for deer hunters, with the possibilities of injury or death still far on the credit side of the ledger. Foolishness or carelessness in the woods reaps its own reward in bullets, but most of it can be avoided.

On our last deer drive of the 1940 season one of our bunch — a rookie hunter, incidentally — carried a 12-gauge shotgun well-charged with big buckshot. We placed this chap well within the line of drivers to forestall any chance of his straying in strange country, and the drive went forward in good style. All was going well, the drive was almost completed, with the drivers only a matter of 200 yards from the standers. At this choice moment a grouse elected to flush wildly out in front of our shotgun bearer, and he just couldn't resist throwing his two loads of buckshot at the bird, even though the season was closed on grouse.

His buckshot swept the line of standers tommy-gun fashion, narrowly missing three of them and coming a bit too close for comfort to the others. I can't quite remember what became of this chap, but he must have stopped running at least by this late date.

All of these are deer-hunting problems, plus the failure of certain hunters to find and see deer even in country thoroughly populated with whitetails. The still-hunter has many factors to consider in his hunting; the club member who participates in deer drives exclusively also has an equal weight of details instinctively to remember. But the grasping of these details is only a matter of a little instruction and much practical application.

Obligations to the Whitetail

More wounded deer should be recovered than are taken each year to date; fewer of these fine animals should be wounded, to stagger off into swamps and thickets and die slowly and miserably, alone, without comfort, not knowing why; with festering wounds, tongue and throat

[1] *Deer hunting is far safer today, despite much higher numbers of deer hunters. In Wisconsin, for example, nearly 700,000 deer hunters went afield in that state's November 1999 firearms season, and only two died of gunshot wounds.*

slowly burning for water they cannot reach; with fever gradually consuming their great strength and vitality, and their blood slowly flowing to the forest floor, taking with it the final spark of vigor.

These white-tailed deer are warm-blooded creatures, like ourselves. They must feel pain to much the same degree, perhaps even more, because of their extreme sensitivity. If we must kill them, let it be quickly and cleanly, without excuses. Paradoxical though it might seem, a sportsman, to enjoy his sport, must kill that which he admires. He must possess it, fondle it, show it to his friends; and to possess he must kill. No one can object to this, for it is the way of nature; but in the name of this mother of all wild things, it should be a sudden, painless death.

The Author's Purpose

It will be the privilege and purpose of this writer in succeeding chapters to carry the deer hunter through the many details associated with hunting the whitetail. We'll need to know a few of its life habits and queer traits, as they affect the hunter; its food, growth and mating practices. Methods of the still-hunter and group hunting will be detailed, and definite information on proper weapons and loads must be discussed.

Of all the deer hunter's equipment, his weapon is, to him, the most important; it forms the connecting link between himself and his game. Many, many thousands of pages have been written about rifles and ammunition, much of it highly technical, some of it practical. Modern developments in weapons and loads have made it difficult for the deer hunter to sift this information to get the facts that he needs.

The deer hunter is largely not a rifle crank. He doesn't have the time or interest to devote to careful study of ballistics and energies, and after wading through masses of trajectories and new calibers, he throws up his hands and decides to stick by his old .30-30. He doesn't know and doesn't care whether a Special .296 Magnum Flash is more effective on deer than an old .45-70 soft-coal burner. What he does want to know is how new developments in rifles, calibers and bullet designs are going to make it easier for him to bag his buck next season up in the spruce thickets of the Adirondacks.

His rifle sights, too, play a vital part, as the directing agent for the striking force of his bullet. It is still a fact that the only shot that counts is the shot that hits ... And to this we must add, the right spot. Sights must be selected to suit individual variances in vision, type of backgrounds and cover to be hunted, and the shooter's own capabilities.

To these ends, this book on white-tailed deer will be devoted: that one or two points will be added to each hunter's store of woodcraft and knowledge, enabling him, perhaps, to add just one more buck to his list of lifetime deer-hunting experiences; that after the thrill of the supreme moment, when his game is down, he will be better prepared to bring out his game, properly dressed and ready for its last preparation — the banquet table. His trophy, too, he can prepare and mount with his own hands, making it ready to dominate gracefully his den or office, bringing back the ever-recurrent thrill of that grand day when the Red Gods smiled down on him at last.

More than this no one writer can expect: that he may again renew the urge to seek the white-tailed deer in the often-disappointed hunter; that he may drop one hint, even only one, that will effect a clean kill instead of a crippled and lost animal; and that in the final analysis he may gently stir a better appreciation of the great joys of deer hunting in the hearts of the novice and the old-timer alike.

If any or all of these aims are realized, then the labor in preparation of these succeeding chapters, plus the delights of this writer in setting them forth, will be amply rewarded to the end of his own deer-hunting days.

CHAPTER 2

The Whitetail At Home

Regretfully, we turned away from the river to begin the two-mile return trip to our starting place at the bridge. We had been trout fishing, Earl and I, since early morning, wading and whipping the clear, boulder-studded waters of that most majestic of Catskill streams — the Neversink.

The bright sun of mid-May had passed the peak of its ascent, to swing slowly toward the lofty ridges above Kitchen Eddy, bathing the valley slopes and their freshly budding hardwoods in an ever-growing golden light. Again it was a new spring and trout-time in Oakland Valley, and we had made our first foray up the river in the hope the heavier browns would be ready to slash viciously at a big wet fly cast over the deep, rollicking runs. Odd that I cannot remember how many trout we caught or just how big was the heaviest; but I distinctly recall our meeting with the new fawn.

We had climbed out of the river at the head end of Long Eddy. Reluctantly, shoes and waders had been stripped off and light moccasins taken from our wading vests. Our weary legs welcomed the change from rushing rapids and heavy hobnails to the featherlight footwear springing our stride down the woods trail. As we swung down the bottomlands it was easy to see the reawakening of the forest with the coming of the new season. A vigorous odor of new, living, growing things filled our nostrils; the soft zephyr of a southern breeze swayed the tips of hemlock and poplar ever so gently. Bell-shaped blooms of dog-tooth violet poked above the snow-flattened dead leaves of a past fall, lone blooms on a bare forest floor save for an occasional bit of pale pink hepatica. The reedy, flutelike song of a hermit thrush filled the cathedral arches of big timber, now and then complemented by the rising crescendo of a drumming cock-grouse.

The New Fawn

Perhaps the lethargic drowsiness of the late afternoon and the ear-filling roar of the river had dulled my senses of more acute perception. Certainly it was not until my companion, bringing up the rear, had hissed sharply, then again, that I became aware of the tiny new deer lying by the trail. We had passed almost through a little glade in the small hemlocks when Earl had signaled. Turning, I discovered him pointing to the little bed of rooster-head ferns that lay between us and just off the trail. Momentarily I expected to find a coiled rattlesnake, just out of winter hibernation, and for an instant I failed to discern the white-spotted red coat from the sun-speckled dead leaves and winter-browned ferns covering the ground.

There, lying hidden from a casual gaze, lay an infant member of nature's most interesting and admirable family, the white-tailed deer. It crouched snugly in its bed of tender ferns, tiny, dime-sized shining hoofs peeping out from under a delicately slender body, a well-molded head, with its lucent baby-pink ears laid back along a sleek neck, fully extended and pressed flat to the ground. Here the mother doe had left it in hiding while she fed along the river flats on tender new buds, and here it would remain, protected by nature's coloring, until she returned. I marveled at the rich red-brown shade of its coat; admired still more the blanket of scattered pure white spots covering its back and flanks, as though a heavy fall of outsized, puffy snowflakes had suddenly descended, then just as quickly stopped.

The miniature deer showed no fear, but a faint twitching of the moist nose, the overly bright gleam of its dark eyes, revealed the hidden inner conflict between its instinctive fear of the man-animal and the knowledge that to lie quietly hidden would be the best security. At once I was overcome by the urge to creep up to this little fawn, snatch it into my arms, then, when its struggles had subsided, to put its tiny hoofs again to earth and send it off to the white birch and laurel thickets of its home. Many times before I had touched a white-tailed deer, and known that mine was the first human hand ever to do so; but never had I been able then to say, "Off to the woods again and be more heedful of your mortal enemy!"

Although I tried, I didn't catch this little fawn. My clutching fingers grasped only dead leaves as the spotted form came quickly to life, bounding in a flash from the ground, then swerving off on wobbly legs to disappear within the thick hemlock screen. We could hear its tiny hoofs pattering through the dead leaves and the swish of hemlocks as it brushed by, long after it had melted from view. For many moments we both stared after it, charmed first by its appearance then astounded at its sudden departure.

Development to Maturity

Often during the years that followed this incident have I wondered what became of the little fawn. How interesting it would have been to be able to follow its development through the years! Perhaps from this little spotted wood-nymph evolved a heavily antlered, broad-chested and thick-necked buck, a lord over all the deer tribe in the valley and the scourge of the younger spikes and forkhorns. Or the infant might have retained much of its sleek, delicate lines, its slender neck and neatly modeled head, to become a mature doe, the bearer of all the hunters' future venison and trophies.

Few people are privileged to find a newborn fawn. Were it not that the writer is a trout fisherman as well as a hunter, there would be but little opportunity to see the little ones in their home forests. But it is during this time of rising trout, fresh green leaves and early wild flowers that the doe retires to the seclusion of heavy thickets to bring forth a spindly legged, dainty new deer or, as more often happens, a pair. Fortunately for fawns, the deer country of the East and North harbors few natural enemies at this critical period, so for the first few months after birth, the little deer lead a placid, frolicking existence. They nurse at the mother doe's flanks for several weeks and then experimentally begin to nip at tender young buds and leaves.

When Jack Frost begins his landscape painting, the fawn has his new coat. The white-flecked, fiery brown hair is shed, never to return, and in its place comes a tawny-gray winter coat of coarser, hollow hair to give insulating warmth against the chill winds of autumn and the icy blasts of dead winter. At this time the little bucks will have small skull buttons but, as a rule, no antlers. With the coming of the next spring the antler buds begin to form: downy blood-filled finger-size bulbs that by the next early fall will be hardened to small, sharp spikes. From now on the young buck must be on the alert for hunters — in most areas he is legal game. And the young does, in some sections, will have given birth to their first single fawn by sometime in the latter part of the spring; most does will have it a year later. Thus the life cycle continues, season after season, with few disturbing elements other than the autumn meetings with red-capped Nimrods and the lean, hungry days of late winter.

The white-tailed deer is far and away our most important larger game animal. With surprising tenacity and amazing fecundity, he has populated a great portion of our rolling hills and mountain lands; his forward-sweeping antlers and broad, white undercoated tail will be found flashing through much of our Eastern area, wherever food and cover are to his liking. He is as much at home in the dense wilderness of the Adirondacks, in northern Maine, and in Michigan's Upper Peninsula as he is within a few miles of New York City's boundaries. No other large game animal has the admirable versatility to so adjust itself to varying conditions of weather and environment. He is numerous in Florida swamp country and in the rocky ridges of northern Vermont, in the muskegs of Canada and in the southern tier farming belt of New York.

In fact, the whitetail's ever-increasing abundance is a conservation headache in a dozen states. Herds have so increased in certain areas that they have eaten themselves out of house and home. Under these conditions, far from being rare, the deer starve during the severe winter months to die off by hundreds and thousands. Conservation workers are constantly harried by the nightmare of too many deer in some sections and comparative scarcity, so far as hunting pressure is concerned, in other areas.

The Whitetail as a Trophy

As a trophy, the whitetail leaves nothing to be desired. Cannily outwitting all but the best (and luckiest) hunters — many times, it seems, by divine guidance — when finally taken he should be highly prized. His dark red flesh is a table delicacy when properly handled and prepared;

his tough, pliable hide makes the softest of gloves and outer garments; the head, with its neat antlers, becomes a favorite decoration for the hunter's den.

The white-tailed deer is now, and we hope always will be, the big game of the common man. The machine operator and the office worker, the small businessman and the farmer, share equal opportunity to return with the spoils of a deer hunt. Perhaps in no other way is this better exemplified than in the taking of outstanding whitetail trophies. Most often it is the man of comfortable wealth, the hunter with ample funds and time to spare, who hunts for and bags the largest trophies of other species — moose, elk, caribou, mountain sheep and bear. But most of the prize whitetail heads adorn the homes of the butcher, the baker, the candlestickmaker. Outstanding whitetail trophies are not isolated in faraway, inaccessible areas. They exist near farmlands, in your own favorite deer country or right by your home; in short, wherever you are lucky enough to find one. Every man who takes to the woods has an equal chance at a record buck. Many impressive heads are gathered under normal, almost casual, hunting conditions, and no doubt so were most of the best whitetail heads now on record.

Killing a record-head white-tailed buck can be a simple matter. Certainly there is no positive method by which the expenditure of time and money can produce a record or near-record whitetail trophy. We cannot say the same for most other species of large American game. A good hunter with unlimited means and much time at his disposal could undoubtedly hunt any other of our big game with a reasonable expectation of bringing back a head of near-record size in one or two season's attempts. But not so with the whitetail. Many, many expert deer hunters have spent the better part of their lives in hunting deer, and only a favored few have gathered unto themselves large whitetail trophies. Big racks on white-tailed bucks are a fortuitous combination of the right kind of food, a good growing year, proper minerals in the soil making up the buck's habitat, and a specimen of outstanding vitality, with the most active type of the correct hormone-producing glands. It is true that certain few areas throughout the country do favor the production of larger antlers, but big heads are spread throughout the land, each individual buck being a law unto himself.

There is no way a hunter can plan to kill such a record deer. In the first place, few white-tailed bucks are seen in any one season by the hunter. And the big-racked bucks seldom wait for the hunter to count points and estimate size before bounding for the brush. Few men have a chance to pass up a smaller buck to wait for a larger one. As a rule, the first legal rack to come before their sights is taken; and they are through for that season. The white-tailed deer offers the greatest challenge to the trophy hunter, and most of these head-hunters will pass to the happy hunting ground before laying sights on that near-record buck, unless Lady Luck guides a favored son to just the right place to meet his trophy of a lifetime.

Any man who hangs on the wall a prize whitetail can thank his lucky stars and not a superior grade of hunting skill. In the past 15 years, the author has taken two bucks with beam-lengths greater than 24 inches and with maximum outside spreads of over 22 inches, but believe it, this was plain, simple fool luck. I knew that both deer were large in body before getting a chance at either one. And reputation had given each a record head; but it was not until I had brought both to earth that I suspected they were this large in antlers. Neither, of course, is a record in any sense, but both are outstanding specimens of white-tailed deer in any part of the country.

Age Indications in the Whitetail

Angle of antler beam often changes proportionally with increasing age.

Antler Growth and Development

The antler growth and development of the white-tailed buck is an absorbing study, but in spite of much-published information on the subject, many hunters are ignorant of the facts about this intricate device of nature. Everyone knows, of course, that antlers are produced as an integral part of the male deer's mating processes. They develop concurrently with the increasing size of the testes, and are carried throughout the mating period to be used in warding off rival bucks from the desired does. When the rutting period is at an end, the useful life of the antlers has gone, so they drop off at varying periods throughout the winter.

Robert W. Darrow, a supervisor of game research for the New York Conservation Department, describes antler development as follows:

"The antlers of the whitetail consist normally of one main beam on each side that extends upward from the skull and curves forward with branches (tines) coming off at intervals on the upper side. Typically, these tines are not forked as in the mule deer. Except for an occasional "horned doe," antlers are a distinctive adornment of the buck. They first develop during the second summer of the buck's life and the following fall usually consist of slender twin spikes or forks, each several inches long. More mature deer grow heavier heads with longer beams, each having several points. A new set of antlers is grown every year, the previous set being shed during the winter after the end of the breeding season. The new antlers begin to "bud" in late April or early May and continue to grow during the summer. Throughout this period, when they are spongy and filled with blood vessels, they bear a protective covering called 'velvet.' Nevertheless, they are easily injured, which accounts for most of the deformities encountered. As fall approaches the antlers harden and the velvet is rubbed off."

Although their first set usually consists of spikes or forks, the number of points on a buck's antlers is not a reliable index to his age. Some yearlings have no more than "sub-legal" spikes, while others might grow several points, as was demonstrated by a known-age buck at the New York's Delmar Wildlife Research Center, whose first rack was a 9-pointer. Then, too, spikes are sometimes carried by old bucks past their prime but, in such cases, they tend to be rather long and unsymmetrical and are of comparatively large diameter at the base. Aside from spikes and forks, by far the most frequent number of points on the bucks killed each fall is eight. However, while there is no steady progression, as a buck advances in age and at the same time remains a vigorous animal, racks of 10, 12 or more points are grown more often. Also, the antlers of older deer are usually of larger diameter at the base than those of younger deer from range of the same quality.

The author would add to this that, in so far as the ratio of points-to-age theory is concerned, I had the opportunity to observe the successive antler growth of a game-farm buck over a period of several years. This buck developed very short, slender spikes in his first season, not more than 2 inches long. The next year he again grew spikes, this time about 8 inches long, somewhat heavier than the first set and with a slight outside curve. In the next year he jumped quickly to eight points, and from this year until the time of his death he grew three more 8-point racks in succeeding seasons, never exceeding the 8-point development although the antlers became larger in diameter, longer in beam and spread, and at a lower angle to the skull each year. This lowering of the angle of beam to skull is another characteristic of the whitetail's advancing age, and is a much more certain indication than the number of points borne on the antlers. As an interesting sidelight in whitetail antler development, the New York State Delmar Laboratories experimented for some time with hormones as antler producers. These bucks sometimes attained tremendous antler growths when fed the proper hormones, and antlers were readily grown on female deer by the forced action of such hormones. One summer I observed three of these antlered does at the Delmar Farm, but one had already dropped an antler and another had badly mutilated one of its branches. It seems likely that the females, unaccustomed to such headgear, have difficulty preserving them in the final form. Another interesting fact is that of the number of antlered does killed each year, all show most of the velvet still remaining, indicating that the female has none of the male's interest or ability to remove the velvet before the mating season.

The Races of the Deer

The whitetail's headgear is distinctive in that it definitely sets apart this species from the other native American deer — the mule deer and the Pacific Coast blacktail. Only the whitetail shows the characteristic forward sweep of antlers from a single main beam on both sides. Both of the latter species show a bifurcated antler, that is, the main beam separates into a Y-shaped fork and from each of these subsidiary tines other Y branches develop. Of course the whitetail's flag is highly distinguishing. Broad and long, with brown above and pure white below, it is distinctively different from the ropy, short, black-tipped tails of the mule deer and blacktail.

As a matter of fact, although whitetails throughout the country are of the same genus, there are several subspecies, all closely related and differing only in size, antler development and variations in body color. And so far as the author has been able to discover, there has never been a recorded instance of whitetails "crossing" with the other species, even on the same range.[1] Scientifically, the whitetail is called *Odocoileus virginianus*, which covers the entire range of subspecies, although there are variations and additions to this designation.

In its original distribution, the whitetail of the north-central and northeastern parts of its range (Minnesota, Wisconsin, Michigan, New York, New England and Canada) is a larger race than those found farther south. Broadly speaking, this is still true today, with whitetails of the southern Appalachians being distinctly smaller than those to the north, while those of Florida are smaller yet. But in the territory largely occupied by Pennsylvania, Ohio, New Jersey and southern New York, a good deal of intermixing has taken place between the typical race (*Odocoileus virginianus*) and the northern race (*Odocoileus virginianus borealis*). This has come about through introduction of imported stock from other districts. Thus, it's the author's belief that mid-1900s deer in southern New York and Pennsylvania tend much more strongly toward the northern type than in years before.

The whitetail is most at home in the temperate forest of the central and eastern United States and southern Canada. It thrives best in well-watered habitats characterized by dense undergrowth and thickets, interspersed with open glades, and subject to light or moderate snowfall.

Early History of the Whitetail

In colonial days, these deer were perhaps in greatest numbers in the river valleys and prairie-border country of Kentucky, Ohio, Indiana, Illinois and Missouri. But these areas were also best adapted for agriculture and soon became largely unavailable as deer range. The Northern Forests, as well as the higher elevations southward, were relatively less-productive deer territory under primitive conditions. Originally deer were found but little north of the St. Lawrence River, and were not recorded north of Lake Superior. In Nova Scotia and east of the Saint John River, in New Brunswick, they were unknown until after 1800.

Contrary to popular belief, the whitetail was not as abundant in Indian times throughout much of New York state as is generally supposed. During this period, before the white man spread out from the Hudson River Valley, deer were most numerous in the lowlands. Along the valleys of the Delaware, Susquehanna, Allegheny, Mohawk and Hudson, and in the Ontario-St. Lawrence plain, deer were fairly abundant, but elsewhere, in the extensive stands of big timber, they were less plentiful. This was particularly true of the whole Adirondack region, which at that time supported as many moose as deer.

As civilization entered, however, the entire picture underwent radical change. The deer, entrenched in the lowlands, was soon forced out by the tillers of the soil. These same early settlers depended principally on the deer for their fresh meat, and heavy hunting throughout each year soon

[1] *Although hybrids resulting from mating between whitetails and mule deer are uncommon, they do occur at times in Western states and provinces. Typically, hybrids are the result of a white-tailed buck breeding a mule deer doe. (Mule deer bucks typically won't play the drawn-out chasing games of coy white-tailed does.) Also, researchers such as Dr. Valerius Geist believe the mule deer species descended from matings of white-tailed does with black-tailed bucks eons ago, and that eventually the mule deer species will die out as whitetails out-compete it on shared ranges.*

virtually exterminated the large valley herds. On the other hand, civilization brought extensive lumbering activities to the Adirondack and Catskill forests, clearing out much of the virgin timber and opening up these areas into good feeding grounds for the deer. Then too, wolves and mountain lions, the principal deer predators, were soon exterminated, and these areas more and more became the deer's most favored habitat. Then followed a period of heavy market hunting, which all but exterminated the Adirondack herd and completely decimated the Catskill deer.

Soon after, conservation measures and growing public sentiment put an end to the slaughter of deer throughout the state. In the Adirondacks, for example, the establishment of many hundreds of lumber camps made it necessary to depend on whitetails to supply fresh meat for loggers. Other meats were not available because of transportation and preservation difficulties. But the senseless and indiscriminate slaughter was at last brought under control, and the passage of the "buck law" in 1912 saw the beginning of the return of deer herds to New York state. This law has been in general force throughout the state with one exception: In 1919 the killing of both bucks and does was permitted and the results were disastrous. It is believed that more hunters were afield that year than there were deer in the state. The number of bucks killed exceeded the number taken in the "buck law" years, and the does taken exceeded the number of bucks. It was estimated that 20,000 deer were killed in that year and since then the state has adhered to the taking of bucks only, with some few exceptions. Today we have not only as many, but far more deer in the Adirondacks than ever before.[2]

[2]In 1998, 50 years after Koller wrote Shots at Whitetails, *New York state gun- and bow-hunters combined to kill 230,758 whitetails.*

Deer were restocked on the Catskill area in this early period of conservation with a small herd of 45 deer, which were maintained in an enclosed park. Each year the overflow was allowed to run free, and largely from this small beginning do we have the present Catskill herd. Other deer were imported from Michigan and Virginia to improve the strain, however, and even now we can find the influence of these somewhat different species in occasional individuals.

In the early 1920s, only a few counties in the state were permitted open seasons. The rest of the state was kept under strict control. As a result, the deer have increased in leaps and bounds throughout the southern tier farming area until in the 1940s they represent the largest proportion of deer within the entire state. This agreeable increase led to open seasons in almost every county, and the deer show no appreciable decrease in numbers despite the tremendous increase in hunters afield each season. The southern tier area, directly adjacent to Pennsylvania, shows a much larger number of deer taken in the 1940s than the Adirondacks or Catskill regions. From this southern tier area in 1946, 6,609 deer were reported taken. The Adirondack region was second with 4,897 head, and the Catskill region reported 4,361. Certainly this is a remarkable indication of the efficiency of modern conservation measures and the outstanding ability of the white-tailed deer to respond to such treatment.

The history of Michigan's deer herd closely parallels that of New York's except that the state is divided into two widely different areas, the

Upper Peninsula and the Lower Peninsula. Here, as in New York state, the early deer population was most numerous in the more open, swampy marsh lands of the Lower Peninsula. In the Upper Peninsula, the entire area was of virgin forest and harbored comparatively few deer. Then with the influx of logging operations, the slashings created new edge growth for deer feed and the whitetail became numerous. In the Lower Peninsula, new agricultural activity created much of this same edge with resultant increase in the deer herd. However, the huge toll taken by farmers and the reduction of wild territory brought about the almost complete extermination of the herd by 1870.

In the Upper Peninsula the story was different. Extensive logging began about 1850, which opened up the area for deer. By about 1880, deer were numerous throughout the Upper Peninsula. But the opening up of the forests was overdone, and by 1890 most of the big pine was gone and a reverse condition occurred. In the early days, deer were forced to yard during the winters under big timber, with little food and poor cover and little of the edge lands for feed. Now in 1890 we find little heavy timber and wide, open areas ravaged by forest fires that destroyed all small growth and seedlings. Soon the deer disappeared generally throughout the Upper Peninsula.

Also during this period of increase in the deer herd began the tremendous slaughter of deer for food in logging camps and for market. As railroads penetrated this territory, market hunters came in during autumn and shipped hundreds of tons of "saddles" to commission houses in the cities. During the summer, these same men turned to "hide hunting," killing many thousands of deer for hides and allowing the carcasses to rot.

Recent History

By 1882 sportsmen were aroused, and some slight measures were taken to preserve the deer herd. But by 1890 the herd was on the downgrade because of a combination of market hunting, excessive logging and forest fires. Subsequent laws, passed by frenzied legislators, placed additional restrictions on hunting through the turn of the century, limiting the take per man severely and outlawing all market hunting.

Between 1915 and 1920 the public became "fire-conscious," and a huge program of fire control was instituted. This, together with improved conservation measures, began to build up the herd so that now Michigan enjoys some of the best hunting in the United States. However, the Upper Peninsula probably has not more than one-half the deer population of the Lower, owing to its heavier snowfall — with the deer again yarding — and the increase in new large timbered areas discouraging the growth of small browse for deer food.

Michigan has done much to promote the excellence of its deer hunting. Extensive research in deer foods, winter crowding and overbrowsing of certain areas has produced an intelligent approach to their deer problem. Of course, in this age of increased hunting pressure, new problems constantly arise.

Almost every state in the Northern section of the whitetails' range shows some similar condition — alarming decrease in deer population near the turn of the century, then a gradual up-trend until the early 1930s and the return of good deer hunting for all. Wisconsin and Pennsylvania have each experienced this decline, fall and resurrection of the deer population, to the extent that each of these states now offers some of the best white-tailed deer territory in the nation. Pennsylvania has a tremendous herd, but Wisconsin's deer average quite a bit larger. At any rate, the problem now seems to be not lack of deer, but in many instances too many deer for the available feed growing on the available range.

Deer Food Research

Deer food has been the subject of colossal research by game commissions and conservation departments across the country. New York state, for example, conducted an extensive experiment at Willsboro to determine, under natural conditions, which foods were most attractive to deer and which of these best sustained life during winter. In this experiment, conducted through two winters, deer were held in pens simulating conditions of the wild, but were so held that accurate observations about food taken and physical condition were possible throughout the period. An accurate and elaborate system of weighing the deer was devised, so positive evidence of the nutritional value of the given foods was obtained.

The summary of the tests shows conclusively that the best natural foods for supporting deer in normal health and vigor are the various species of browse, notably white cedar, yellow birch and soft maple. Further it was shown that animals which had suffered serious weight losses on such unsatisfactory foods as marsh hay and balsam could be restored quickly to a satisfactory condition by being fed white cedar and yellow birch browse. Researchers also learned which foods deer preferred. The accompanying list should prove of interest to woodsmen and deer hunters.

Alfalfa was fed also in the tests and found satisfactory, but owing to its weight, bulk and relatively low food value compared with concentrated foods such as grains, it was found much less desirable than other types of food for artificial feeding in winter yard areas where food must be transported by well-intentioned conservation workers.

Marsh hay was proven worthless as a nutritious food and was eaten only in small quantities, even though the deer were offered no other food. Balsam also was proved worthless as a winter deer food and to a lesser extent hemlock was found to be lacking in desirable nutritive qualities.

Best Liked	Readily Eaten	Poorly Eaten
White Cedar	Apple Wood	Alder
Black Birch	Mountain Ash	Black Ash
Yellow Birch	Balsam	Aspen
Sumac Bobs	Basswood	Beech
Sweet Fern	White Birch	Butternut

Witchhopple	Buckbrush	Chokecherry
Ferns (many species)	Red Cedar	Ironwood
	Black Chokecherry	Blue Beech
	Elderberry	Leatherwood
	Ground Pine	Sugar Maple
	Hazelnut	Red Oak
	Juniper	White Pine
	Red Maple (soft)	Red Sprucepar
	Sumac Stems	Willow
	Hemlock [3]	

[3]Hemlock browse was eaten, when other well-liked browse was available, only at temperatures near or below zero.

Subsequent studies at Ithaca, in efforts to find a satisfactory food in concentrated form for winter feeding, resulted in developing the famous "deer cakes." These are a combination of soybeans and molasses, packed in a tin, and weighing about 50 pounds. Extensive field experiments with these cakes proved they were readily eaten by deer and one cake provided adequate nourishment for eight deer for two weeks. An interesting side-light of these supplemental foods was that deer consumed them rapidly so long as snow remained on the ground. The day bare ground appeared, deer didn't touch the cakes, preferring to forage for natural browse.

The list of preferred foods includes only browse. Whitetails also like acorns, beechnuts, many types of lichens and mosses, and other bare-ground foods. But in winter when starvation and deep snow begin, such ground foods are seldom available. As a rule, deer are not grazers, although they like a farmer's young corn or wheat, and in some areas raise havoc with winter wheat during cold weather.

The greatest mortality in deer herds occurs in areas subject to heavy snowfall. When snow is deeper than a foot, deer congregate in cedar swamps or other areas of good thermal cover, and mill around until the snow is packed to the ground, forming the yard. Several yards are often made in a single area, connected by narrow trails through deep snow. As winter progresses and snow deepens, the herd clings together within the yard, eating all available browse, even down to branches an inch in diameter. With feed gone, even to a point as high as they can reach by standing on their hind legs, deer face slow starvation. Nothing, not even the presence of people, will make them leave the yard, at least for long.

People carrying in food for deer will rout them out for a short distance, but after a few bounds into the belly-deep snow, they stand and wait for the intruders to leave, then bounce back into the safety of the yard. It becomes a questionable refuge, however, for as soon as the food supply disappears, the weaker deer slowly die of starvation. This is the controlling deer-supply factor in every area of heavy snowfall. It is the unquestionable answer to the static state of the deer herd in the Adirondack region, Michigan's Upper Peninsula and other similar areas. No matter how large the fawn crop might be each season, only a certain number will survive the decimating effect of starvation in the yards, dependent by year on the severity and length of the snowfalls, snow covering and sub-zero temperatures. Other limiting factors exist, of course, but this is the major control. It explains also why deer made such remarkable increases in the areas of lesser snowfall: Pennsylvania, New York state's southern tier, Michigan's Lower Peninsula and many other such regions.

It's strange that animals of such protective instincts should so trap themselves. This is probably a carry-over behavior from the early days when wolves and mountain lions made easy prey of deer caught in deep snow. Nevertheless, thousands of deer die annually in the confines of the foraged-off yards, with good food only a short distance away.

CHAPTER 3

The Whitetail's Vital Statistics

Throughout our broad expanse of deer country, one of the greatest variables in whitetail characteristics is body weight. In the Deep South, a 100-pound dressed weight is extremely heavy for bucks; in Maine and Northern Michigan, 200-pound dressed bucks are common. Arizona whitetails too are small; exceptionally heavy specimens weigh not more than 125 pounds after hog-dressing. It's apparent the farther north we go in search of white-tailed deer, the more likely are we to meet big ones. Yet the average white-tailed buck is a much smaller animal than is generally supposed.

Full-grown bucks seldom reach a height greater than 42 inches at the shoulder, and the average Northern deer of the species weighs from 150 to 180 pounds on the hoof. Such bucks dress out from 120 to 150 pounds. Any buck over this top weight can be classed as a large deer. Larger bucks are not uncommon, particularly where range conditions are highly favorable: 200-pounders are killed every year, and in Maine, Michigan, Wisconsin and the southern tier area of New York, numerous bucks are taken that weigh more than 250 pounds.

The heaviest authenticated white-tailed deer taken in New York state was killed in 1890 near Mud Lake in Warren County by Henry Ordway — who, at this writing, still lived in Glens Falls. Ordway's 12-point buck weighed 388 pounds about five hours after it was shot and before it was dressed out. Its head was in possession of the State Conservation Department, and ranks 10th in the state list of record heads (based on size and symmetry) as of Spring 1947.[1]

In contrast to these exceptionally large deer, we find a much lower weight as the average throughout the whitetail's range. Most states have accurate data on deer weights, carefully checked from thousands of specimens taken during hunting seasons. Maine, for example, lists the weights and heights of its deer by counties, with bucks averaging 145 pounds and standing about 38 inches high at the shoulder. Does average about 110 pounds, with a shoulder height of 36 inches. Somerset County shows the heaviest average deer: bucks scaling almost 200 pounds and does, 120 pounds.[2]

Pennsylvania's deer average considerably smaller than this. Bucks average 115 pounds; antlerless deer, many of which are not adult, average 80 pounds. Here is a marked indication of the lower weights of deer subjected to overcrowding and overbrowsing, as well as the tendency toward smaller body size in the more southern subspecies of whitetails.

[1]*Henry Ordway's buck, which scored 166⅛ B&C points, ranked 88th as of 1999 in the New York State Big Buck Club. Ordway's buck scored 175⅞ on the Fritz system because it allowed for up to five circumference measurements. B&C only allows four.*

[2] *The Maine DNR no longer compiles information for deer older than 1½ years. Records for fawns and yearlings are kept, but height statistics are no longer tracked.*

The natural tendency of a hunter is to exaggerate the size of his trophy. It's an understandable quirk in every man's makeup, but it leads to false impressions that become deep-rooted with repetition. Almost every hunter we meet will tell us about killing at least one 200-pound buck, yet inquiry reveals that none of these 200-pounders were weighed, just "guessed at." Seldom does a hunter encounter one of these big bucks in a lifetime of hunting, and when he does down a really big whitetail, the impartial verdict of the beam-scales will most often throw the damper on his enthusiasm. In five years of hunting with one of the most consistently successful Sullivan County deer clubs, the author never saw a deer taken by this group that weighed more than 164 pounds for an actual dressed weight. In fact, I have seen in my lifetime of deer hunting only four bucks whose actual weight exceeded the magic 200-pound mark.

Dressed weights and on-the-hoof weights of white-tailed bucks are far different. Many formulas for obtaining live weight from dressed weight have been advanced, but actually there is considerable variation. The amount of herbage in a deer's paunch at the time of death has a marked effect on the accurate value of any of these, to the extent that any one can be proved 50 percent wrong with individual deer. Perhaps as accurate a method as any is to take the deer's dressed weight, divide by four and add the result to the dressed-weight figure to obtain the live, or on-the-hoof, weight. A hunter seldom has an opportunity to check such formulas. When a man kills his buck, his major interest is to dress the deer quickly, bleeding it well and cooling the body cavity. Then with the "innards" removed, the deer becomes a lighter burden on the way out of the woods, but still a sufficiently heavy one. However, on one occasion the author had the opportunity to observe a large deer being weighed directly after taking. This buck weighed 246 pounds before dressing and 198 pounds after the hog-dressing.

For purposes of comparison, I've taken the measurements of a large, fat Adirondack buck that weighed 212 pounds dressed. From these figures any hunter can form an accurate estimate as to whether his buck will approach or surpass the 200-pound mark. This particular specimen was not a heavily framed deer, rather it was of normally large size, but the fattest buck I have ever encountered. All measurements were, of course, taken over the carcass with hide still on and with the tape pulled firmly taut. The head measurements that are required in mounting are listed also, for any hunter who might wish to compare them with his own trophy.

Body Measurements

Length, nose to tail root: 6 feet, 6½ inches
Height, hoof to withers: 41½ inches
Circumference, chest behind forelegs: 43 inches
Rump, largest diameter: 46½ inches
Overall length, nose to hind hoofs: 8 feet, 4½ inches

Head and Neck Measurements

Length, withers to antler butts: 23 inches
Right antler butt to nose: 10½ inches
Left antler butt to nose: 10½ inches

Eye corner to nose: 8 inches
Circumference, neck behind ears: 22 inches
Tip of right antler to nose: 18 inches
Tip of left antler to nose: 17½ inches

That buck was killed in Hamilton County in the Adirondacks on Oct. 20, 1946, and while it was not an unusually large buck, it represents a good model for a 200-pound animal. Any white-tailed buck that compares with these figures can be well considered as an entry for the hallowed ranks of the 200-weight class.

Research into Mating Habits

Of perhaps more interest to hunters in any discussion of deer habits and characteristics are the mating habits and occurrence of the rutting season. This period is always the most fruitful for deer hunting. It is then that bucks lose some of their natural caution. In fact, a rutting buck can at times be dangerous. Several instances have been recorded wherein a white-tailed buck in the heat of mating frenzy has attacked men without provocation. Of course, this is rare but it serves to point out that the reproductive urge in whitetails is so great it transcends partially the normally greater instincts of self-preservation. Many a wise old buck would forever escape the hunter were it not for the heavy rutting period during deer season. And, oddly enough, it is the doe herself that sets up this mating time, rather than the buck.

Generally speaking, the buck is ready and willing for mating any time during the period between early September and the beginning of the next year. At the beginning of this period, the velvet is dug off the antlers and the buck begins to prove his virility by rubbing bark from small saplings, and hooking brush. As October wears along, many of these rubs will appear in whitetail haunts, indicating some does are beginning to accept service. This continues in ever-increasing frequency until at some time during November the rut will be at its height. This period varies with the locality, however, and as far as is now known, is connected in some way with the gradual diminishing in strength of the sun's rays as winter approaches. Once the doe is mated, she will no longer accept the buck, which accounts for many of the does a hunter sees running through the woods with the buck in hot pursuit. Neither will the doe accept service except at the critical period of estrus, and this period, research indicates, lasts about 24 hours.

If the doe is not mated and the embryo implanted at this time, she will not allow service until the next estrus, which will be about four weeks later. In some areas, the does might enter estrus or "heat" period three or four times until pregnancy occurs, or the doe remains without fawn until the next season.

Much research has been done on this fascinating study of the whitetail's mating processes. Many former theories have been discarded, and much new information has been brought to light. At the same time, new hitherto unknown problems have evolved. Dr. E.L. Cheatum, senior game pathologist at New York's experimental game laboratory, reports on the differences in regional breeding habits of New York deer in the *Conservationist*, the department's bimonthly publication:

> The character of our wild and woolly Adirondack mountain country has long given the average sportsman sufficient reason to believe it should be the state's best deer range. But in late years, he has seen the almost spectacular increase in deer herds in the central and southern counties and has begun to ask: "Why doesn't the same thing happen up north?"
>
> The hunters hears a lot of answers to that question. Two most frequently given are: "There is a shortage of breeding-age bucks, hence more fawnless does." Or, "Too many deer starve in winter, and the annual fawn production hardly balances these losses and the kill by hunters."
>
> Both explanations are premised on the idea that annual replacement of young stock is inadequate. There is some truth in that, but it complicates the problem.
>
> During a Conservation Department study from Winter 1938 to Spring 1942, a large number of does from these two zones (the Adirondack area and the southern region of the Catskills and south border counties) were examined for the presence of unborn fawns. From the Adirondack region we examined 158 does and from the rest of the state 258. The study included first-year fawns because we had previously discovered that, in the southern counties, does were frequently bred successfully at 6 or 7 months of age.

Dr. Cheatum summarizes the results as follows:

1. Of the adult does from the southern zone, 92.3 percent had been successfully bred; of the Adirondack does, 77.9 percent were with fawn.

2. Of the doe fawns from the southern area, 36.3 percent were carrying embryos, while the figure for the Adirondacks was a mere 4.2 percent.

3. Among the 144 pregnant does from the southern area, 48 bore singletons, 86 bore twins, and 10 triplets. The 67 specimens from the Adirondacks carried 54 singletons, 12 twins and one set of triplets.

4. Among the 37 pregnant fawns from the southern zone, 35 carried singles, and two bore twins. The three Adirondack specimens carried singles alone.

5. The egg production rate of Southern does was higher than that of Northern deer, and the percentage of eggs fertilized and developed as embryos was much higher.

After gathering the facts, Dr. Cheatum turned to the "why" question: "The facts show no hereditary differences between deer in the two zones ... so it would appear that differences in living conditions are the controlling influences in fawn production. And there is every indication to believe that nutrition is a primary factor." Further study shows that not only do the long winter and deep snow contribute directly to the high number of starvation deaths, but reduce doe fertility during the next breeding season, because of malnutrition.

As to the actual height of the rutting season, research indicates the sexual season represents a brief conclusion of the gradual increase of activity in sexual organs, initiated by the increasing daylight of spring and summer. The rut ensues under conditions of diminishing light. Captive animals kept in dim light directly after the height of summer's solar activity had been reached showed a disposition to breed earlier than normal. Studies of Alaskan reindeer near the 64th parallel show the rut began in late August and continued through September into October. New York deer (42 to 44 degrees parallel) breed heaviest in November. Mule deer in the Yosemite Valley of California (38 degrees) breed in late December and through January. Farther south, the Arizona whitetail breeding season occurs most frequently between Jan. 10 and mid-February. Thus it would seem some relationship exists between the progressively earlier breeding of the deer and increasing latitude.

Study of New York state's deer indicates that in the Adirondack area the period of heaviest rut occurs Nov. 10 to 16; in the southern region from Nov. 17 to 23. However, the actual period of the rut covers a wider span in the southern area than in the Adirondacks, indicating there is a greater recurrence of the estrous period in southern does than in the more northern regions.

In this study of New York's breeding periods, considerable research was done on male deer as well as female deer. Testicles obtained from bucks throughout the research period show a gradual increase in size concurrent with the development of antlers, ending with the greatest volume obtained at the end of November. It was learned also that, contrary to findings with doe fawns, bucks rarely attain sexual maturity in the first year of life in this latitude.)[3]

[3]*Michigan researcher John Ozoga reported similar conclusions during his research of deer in Michigan's Upper Peninsula during the 1960s, '70s and '80s.*

For many years it was thought that, because of the climatic differences in the Adirondacks and Catskill regions, the mating season in the Adirondacks would occur a full month before that in the Catskills. Accordingly, open seasons were so established. But the results of new research conclusively prove there is little actual difference in the mating periods in the two areas. If anything, the Catskill rut begins sooner and lasts longer than the corresponding period in the Adirondacks — the height of both periods is included between the dates of Nov. 10 and 23. It seems evident that in areas of better wintering conditions, the succeeding fawn crop each year is superior to fawn crops in areas of heavy snow, where deer are forced to the yards, thereby suffering the nutritional ravages of poor food. This, added to the number of yard deer that fail to survive winter, is evidence enough to account for the great increase in deer populations throughout most of the mild-winter zones.

Those Vexing Buck-to-Doe Ratios

Another deer problem that vexes the hunter is the apparent scarcity of bucks in proportion to the number of does seen each season. However, this sex ratio is not nearly as unbalanced as the unsuccessful hunter would have us believe. Actual figures on deer census reports, conducted with a high degree of accuracy, bear this out. New York state reports the ratio of bucks to does throughout the major deer-producing areas in the state is about 83 bucks to 100 does. However, in the Adirondack area, the ratio might be not greater than 38 bucks to 100 does. Even so, this is definitely a large enough ratio of bucks to does to assure full mating of all does in the area, provided contact is made at the proper point of estrus in the female. Any low fawn count among the does is much more likely to result from lack of egg production in females, because of various factors, rather than from a shortage of bucks.

An interesting variation in the buck-to-doe ratio is reported by Michigan. Extensive live-trapping operations show a ratio of 1 buck to 5.8 does, and observations throughout the year by competent conservation officials indicates a ratio of 1 buck to 5.38 does. But hunters' reports show a ratio of only 1 buck to 28 does — quite a substantial difference! In the Upper Peninsula, the ratio of bucks to does was somewhat higher — 1 buck to 4.26 does. During the period of the well-conducted Civilian Conservation Corporation Camp deer-census drives, the ratio of bucks to does was reported as follows:

	Bucks	Does	Fawns
Upper Peninsula	19	49	52
Lower Peninsula	16	52	32

The census reports of this same period show these interesting counts of deer per square mile:

Upper Peninsula	18.05
Lower Peninsula	45.60
State as a whole	32.59

Wisconsin, under much the same system of deer counting, shows a ratio of about 1 buck to 3 does over an area of roughly 60,000 acres. However, depending on the section of the state, some areas had a ratio of 1 to 5 while others graded all the way down to 1 to 1.5, all of this counting outside refuge areas. This includes records not only of the Conservation Commission but of the Federal Forest Service and the Federal Bureau of Agricultural Economics. At any rate, in no instance of accurate counting will the buck-to-doe ratio appear as unfavorable as in the reports of deer hunters. Every effort is made by conservation authorities to give accurate information to the deer hunting public, and there is no reason to doubt the overall accuracy of these figures. Undoubtedly, the scarcity of bucks reported by hunters indicates lack of competent observation and hunting skill. There is no doubt that under hunting conditions it is more difficult to detect the buck than the doe, as every hunter knows, and these figures bear this out.

In regard to the taking of does during a legal open season, each state works out this problem for itself. It is only since the inception of the "buck law" that we have seen the remarkable increase in the nationwide whitetail population. It is obviously true, though, that in areas where deer have increased to where the range's carrying capacity has deteriorated, and in regions where deer cause considerable crop damage, an open season on female deer will do far more good than harm. Pennsylvania was faced with this problem in the early 1930s. Deer had increased to a population far beyond the capacity of the forage crop of their range, and it became mandatory to thin the herd indiscriminately. Despite the howls of protest from nature lovers and sportsmen, Pennsylvania put into effect a program of systematic reduction of its overpopulated deer herd. The result through succeeding years amply bore out contentions of the Pennsylvania Game Commission that the state's deer herd was still ample to survive hunting pressure, and the overbrowsed condition of its forests is gradually adjusting itself. This is the same problem facing every state with an overabundance of deer in certain areas. These deer are a crop of the land and must be intelligently harvested as such.

There will forever be a certain amount of public sentiment against the killing of does or antlerless deer. It is agreed among all conservationists that reducing the number of fawn-bearing does has a marked effect on the ensuing deer population in every section of the country. In heavily hunted areas, a few years of indiscriminate killing of both sexes materially affects the deer herd in reducing its numbers to the danger point. Every hunter agrees the doe is an easy victim under all deer hunting conditions. Hunters who value the trophy above the collection of venison will never shoot the doe simply to fill a license. However, it is true the female makes the best eating and in those heavily overpopulated deer areas where available forage is being too rapidly reduced, good judgment indicates some thinning-out of the doe population is demanded. The argument has often been advanced that a buck will serve only a small number of does in one rutting season, therefore in heavily populated areas, the excess number of does should be killed. This, of course, is nonsense. Any virile, normal buck can and will serve as many does as come to his attention, provided the females are ready to accept service. The best research on the question tends to show the number of barren does is the result of several environmental factors, chief of which is the short period during which a doe will accept service, rather than the lack of willingness or ability on the part of the buck.

Buck Fights and Sparring Matches

Clashes between bucks during the mating season seldom result in injury to either contestant unless they are of equal size and antler development. As a rule, the bigger bucks ward off smaller rivals with a single shove, and the duel promptly ends with the little forkhorn or spike slinking off into the brush. A bitter, long-fought engagement is rare, although now and then two white-tailed bucks have been known to fight until the antlers locked, resulting in a lingering death for both deer. John Shufelt, of Northville, N.Y., tells of coming upon two fighting bucks that were so bitterly engaged that they noticed neither Shufelt nor his companion. The men thereupon quickly filled both of their licenses with a nice buck. But hunters are seldom privileged to witness one of these duels. Some years ago, I was still-hunting along the Shawangunk Mountain range when two bucks began to hit it off about a quarter-mile down the mountainside. After slipping down to the spot, I discovered the deer had finished the argument and had taken off, but it must have been a good scrap. The soft earth was torn up for a radius of 30 feet; small saplings were crushed to the ground, and scattered generously were big bunches of loose hair. No blood showed, so the only damage done was most likely a small loss of prestige for the vanquished. I would have enjoyed a look at this battle! I doubt either deer could have heard my approach above the crashing of brush, the grunting impacts and clash of antlers. It was just my misfortune to arrive too late either to referee the bout or to bag one of the gladiators.

There is little doubt, though, that smaller, less-mature bucks have a good deal of respect for the long-tined heavy racks carried by larger, more virile herd masters. This is just another method of nature to ensure the strongest specimens will sire future generations of fawns. With the end of the breeding season, bucks begin to lose their headgear, smaller individuals losing antlers sooner than the prime bucks.[4] Pennsylvania hunters, during the latter part of their December season, occasionally drop a small buck only to discover that the antlers fall free from the skull when the deer collapses. I have seen a few of these bucks coming out on cars during the season, completely bald, and with the dropped antlers tied to the deer's head as evidence of legality. During New York state's lone December season, in 1939, two cases came to the author's attention wherein bucks lost their antlers after being taken. In any case, this incidence of early-dropped antlers is rare and occurs only with the smaller, less-mature bucks, the spikes and small forkhorns. Many hunters complain that their failure to see bucks during the season's hunt is because the bucks have already dropped their antlers. So far as is now known, such a condition does not occur in any state during the regular open season with the late-season exceptions mentioned. We can justifiably add this to the already long string of deer hunting alibis.

An Evaluation of Whitetail Trophies

Comparison of trophies is another sore spot among the deer-hunting clan. Now and then, a lucky hunter kills a freak head, liberally studded with extra points, and immediately assumes such a head should be included in the record class. Unfortunately for the man who kills such a head, it will be classed as simply a freak. The tendency in establishing white-tailed deer head records has been to choose only those heads that accurately represent antler development peculiar to whitetails, discounting or penalizing the trophy for any extra points that detract from its character or symmetry. One of the author's friends, Joe Kelly of Pine Bush, N.Y., killed a many-pointed rack near Beaver Brook in the 1930s. This buck carried something over 40 points, but it was neither a large nor a handsome head.

The premium in whitetail trophies today is on size of antler development and symmetry of form, with a perfect balance between the points on each beam. So far there is no system in universal use, but for many years the Boone and Crockett Club's method has been generally accepted by most states throughout the country as a fair and representative means of establishing the merits of trophies. However, the Grancel Fitz system of point scoring is coming into use. New York state, for example, now lists its record heads under this latter system. Fitz apparently devised a system that placed greater emphasis on size and symmetry than even the Boone and Crockett Club's method.[5]

Scoring Methods

Briefly, both systems involve the total, scored as points, of the measurements in greatest spread, length of each beam, diameter of beams, diameter of burrs, number of normal points and length of each point from the main beam. The essential difference in the two methods lies in the fact that the Fitz

[4]*Most subsequent research indicates the contrary, that the herd's most sexually active bucks — usually the more dominant animals — will lose their antlers earlier.*

[5]*The Grancel Fritz scoring system was the first to recognize antler symmetry. After consulting with Fritz, the Boone and Crockett Club revised its scoring system to include the same methods. B&C copyrighted the revised scoring system in 1950.*

system calculates the greatest spread from inside the main beams and subtracts from the total score any point or points that mar the symmetry of the trophy by lacking a corresponding point on the opposite side. Under the Boone and Crockett Club method, it is conceivable that a "freak" head, having abnormal points jutting out at right angles from both sides of the main beam, could maintain a higher total score than other more representative heads that lacked such abnormalities. Then, too, in this system, abnormal, unmatched points are included, giving greater value as trophies to these more or less freak heads.

Of the five largest New York state record heads, published in the 1942 records, not one appears on the state's current list. In 1942, the Boone and Crockett Club method was official, but 1948 state records were obtained under the Grancel Fitz system. These are the statistics of both record lists:

New York State Record Nontypical Heads - 1942								
OUTSIDE CURVE		GREATEST SPREAD	DIAMETER OF BEAM		NO. OF POINTS		KILLED	YEAR
R.	L.		R.	L.	R.	L.		
28"	28"	23"	5"	5"	7	6	Adirondacks Taken by Detrich Wortman	1933
27⅛	27¾	26			11	10	Chenango Co. Owned by E.E. Risley	1933
27	27½	20¼	4⅜	4½	7	11	Adirondacks Taken by G.W. McEwan	1927
26¾	26¼	23½	5 1/16	5	4	6	Orange County Taken by E.J. DeLin	1933
26¼	24½	22¾	4¾	4¾	10	10	Adirondacks Taken by Russel Edick	1919
The World's Record Nontypical Whitetail (For Comparison)								
30¾	27½	33½	4¾	4¾	12	14	British Columbia Taken by J.G. Brewster ([6]245⅞B&C score)	1905
The Author's Two Best Whitetails (For Comparison)								
26¼	26	22½	4½	4½	5	5	Sullivan County	1939
23¾	24	21	4½	4½	5	5	Ulster County	1938

[6] *Wisconsin's Jim Jordan killed a buck in 1914 that scored 206⅛. The Jordan Buck eventually was listed as the world record in 1978. It held the top spot until Milo Hanson of Saskatchewan killed a buck scoring 213⅝ in November 1993. Brewster's buck remains the No. 1 nontypical for British Columbia and 57th of all time for B&C.*

All of these are scored according to the Boone and Crockett Club's system of measurement.

What follows is the record list of the 10 largest New York state heads in 1948 records, under the Grancel Fitz system of scoring.

Taken by	When	Where	Owner	Score
1. Robert L. Banks	189-	Hamilton Co.	Fort Orange Club, Albany	198.3
2. Denny Mitchell	1934	Essex Co.	L.P. Evans, Elizabethtown	189.4
3. Sidney Mawson	1938	Cortland Co.	Same, Manlius	187.1
4. R.I. Page	1938	Steuben Co.	Same, Greenwood	186.
5. Henry Van Avery	1921	Hamilton Co.	Same, Mayfield	185.7
6. Lillian Trombley	1942	Genesee Co	State Armory, Ticonderoga	183.1

7. Emilius Roberts	1906	Hamilton Co.	Same, Northville	181.2
8. John Galusha	1895	Essex Co.	North Woods Club, Minerva	178.5
9. Hans Oldag	1942	Erie Co.	Same, North Tonawanda	176.2
10. Henry Ordway	1890	Warren Co.	N.Y.S. Conservation Dept., Albany	175.7

(This 10th-place buck is the heaviest recorded taken in New York state.)

Original Boone and Crockett Scoring Method

Totals all points plus beam length, greatest spread, circumference of beam and burr to obtain final score.

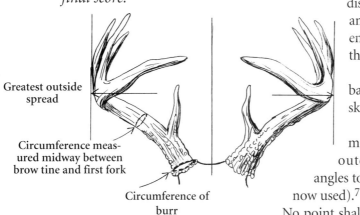

Doesn't Count

Beam length

Greatest outside spread

Circumference measured midway between brow tine and first fork

Circumference of burr

[7]*The inside spread between the main beams is now used in Boone & Crockett scoring.*

[8]*The Boone and Crockett Club is located at Old Milwaukee Depot, 250 Station Drive, Missoula, MT 59801-2753.*

Briefly, here is the procedure followed in obtaining the total scores with both methods:

First, the Boone and Crockett method:

Length of outside curve is measured as follows: Establish accurately the center line of the main beam by making a series of lead-pencil dots along the entire outside length of the antler. Then draw a ruled line through all these dots, beginning at the tip. Start by laying the tape flat along the line as far as it is straight, and mark a cross where the line curves away from the tape. Begin again at this cross and continue the process until the base of the burr is reached.

Circumference of main beam is measured at the narrowest point between the burr and the brow tine, or first point; then at the narrowest point between the first and second points. Many authorities discount the measurement between the burr and brow points, owing to the normal presence of irregularities or small protuberances that appear frequently in this section.

Circumference of burr is taken at the base of the antler where the antler joins the skull.

Greatest outside spread is the measurement between perpendiculars of the two outermost points of each antler, at right angles to the center line of the skull (inside spread now used).[7]

No point shall be counted unless it protrudes at least 1 inch from the main beam or tine. Total points include the number found on both antlers and those protruding from the burr, provided they accede to the 1-inch minimum.

Other pertinent information includes:

1. Description of characteristics that depart from the normal of the species.

2. Suitable photographs showing front and side views.

3. All measurements must be made with flexible steel tape and should be suitably witnessed if the trophy is to be recorded in Boone and Crockett Club records. Entry blanks for trophies can be had from this organization in care of the American Museum of Natural History, Central Park West at 79th St., New York City, N.Y.[8]

The Grancel Fitz system is somewhat more involved, but represents a more accurate picture of the trophies' excellence, with regard to size, thickness of beams, spread and general symmetry.

The spread is taken by measuring the maximum width between beams at a right angle to the skull. The beam length is taken in the same way as above, but normal points are measured from this same center line to the tips and abnormal points are measured to their intersection with the main beam or other point on antlers. To best exemplify the system and the scoring, a sample score sheet is filled in on the page opposite with the measurements of a large buck taken by Robert Banks, which once was the state's record buck.

The records of whitetail trophies, perhaps more than those of any other large game, are constantly in a fluid state. Records are recorded each season, and states revise their lists at the close of virtually every season. The state, national and world records are maintained by the Boone and Crockett Club.

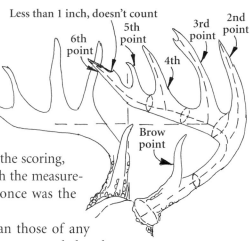

Grancel Fitz Scoring Method

Subtracts abnormal or unbalanced points from total score. Circumferences of main beams are taken as indicated above.

Points of Measurement	Right	Left	Penalty
Length of main beam	25.0"	25.1"	.1
brow point	6.0	5.7	.8
brow-point prong	2.5	2.1	.4
2nd normal point	7.0	7.6	.6
3rd normal point	7.7	7.8	.1
4th normal point	9.7	7.4	2.3
5th normal point	8.4	7.7	.7
6th normal point	3.9	3.5	.4
Circumference of burr	6.3	6.5	.2
Circumference between brow and 2nd pt.	3.9	4.0	.1
2nd and 3rd pt.	5.8	4.3	1.5
3rd and 4th pt.	4.7	4.3	4
4th and 5th pt.	4.3	4.1	.2
5th and 6th pt.	4.0	3.8	.2
Total length all abnormal points			4.1
Totals	99.7	93.9	12.1
Total for both antlers			193.6
Plus greatest inside spread			16.8
Total			210.4
Minus total of penalty column			-12.1
Final Score			198.3

Teeth as an Age Indicator

Every hunter who kills a fully mature buck has some degree of curiosity as to its probable age. We have pointed out that the number of points on the antlers is a poor indication, except in the early years of the buck's development — that is, until the typical 8-point rack is reached. But beyond this, the antler points themselves have little value in determining age. A buck might

Fawn

Few hunters have difficulty aging a white-tailed fawn, whose short snout and small body are usually obvious when viewed up close. If there is doubt, simply count the teeth in the deer's lower jaw. If the jaw has less than six teeth, the deer is a fawn.

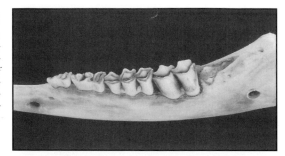

17-18 Months

The giveaway in deer of this age is the third premolar, which has three cusps. This is also the age where deer start to shed their "milk teeth." They'll either be loose or gone. In this photo, you can see the permanent premolars as they push up under the loosening milk teeth.

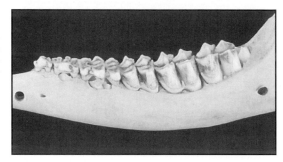

19 Months

At about 1 year, 7 months, most deer have all three permanent premolars. The new teeth are white in contrast to pigmentation on older teeth. They have a smooth, chalk-white appearance and show no wear. The third molar is partially erupted.

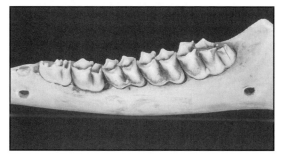

2½ Years

The lingual crests of the first molar are sharp, with the enamel rising well above the narrow dentine (the dark layer below the enamel) of the crest. Crests on the first molar are as sharp as those on the second and third molar. Wear on the posterior cusp of the third molar is slight .

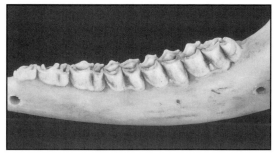

*Descriptions and photos from Deer & Deer Hunting *magazine.*

grow two additional points each year up to 12 (in his sixth season), but he is much more likely to stop at the 8- or 10-point mark. However, the antlers become heavier in beam thickness and greater in length with passing seasons, and at the same time assume a progressively lower angle to the skull-line, until the buck reaches his peak of greatest vitality and virility. After this period, the antlers show signs of increasing "senility." The points become less and less, shorter and stubbier, losing much of the graceful appearance of the long slender tines found on the best specimens. Finally, if the buck survives the winters and evades the hunters, he might carry only spikes in his last year of life, although such senile spikes will be heavy at the butts.

The only accurate method for estimating a deer's age is by examining the teeth, and this requires expert observation, much as it does with horses and sheep. Up until the fifth year, however, a hunter with little experience can determine the age of his quarry by inspecting the lower molars and premolars. The accompanying photos and explanations outline the tooth-wear-aging method, but there will be varying differences between regions, depending on soil types and browse composition. Experienced observers can accurately determine age by this method, but it must be based on many years of observation.

The Importance of Knowledge

All in all, the whitetail's life span and biological characteristics should be of ever-increasing interest to hunters. Shifts in deer populations, continued overbrowsing of range, and fawn production of favored areas all will affect your choice of a hunting ground. Paradoxical though it might seem, it has been proven that the best way to maintain a healthy, well-proportioned herd is to hunt them and kill off the excess numbers within sensible limits. In the wilderness areas, the influx of hunters tends to break up the large herds, so that there is less danger of overcrowding in yards with resultant decimation of the herds in far greater numbers than the hunter himself would legally harvest.

For the new hunter, the pursuit of deer can be discouraging. He might walk the woods day after day and seldom see more than an occasional doe, never a buck. But all of a sudden, one day he might encounter a sleek group of does, escorted by a majestic white-tailed buck, and his chance will have arrived. What happens from this point forward is up to the hunter's personal qualifications, but in order to see his buck he must first make at least a rudimentary study of its habits.

There is no magic in deer hunting. It is true that the element of luck is many times involved, but the young hunter who has yet to kill his first deer will fail to fill a license for many years if he must depend on luck alone. A good part of a deer hunter's share of woodslore must come from his study of the whitetail's home life, not alone his absorption of the limited knowledge in this field that he gains from his few days in the woods each season.

All conservation departments publish detailed reports each year on the condition of their deer herds. These reports can be had for the asking in most instances, and agencies that publish monthly or bimonthly conservation magazines will supply them to hunters at a nominal rate. These reports keep a hunter posted on almost every detail of deer conditions throughout his own state, and form the basis of many a successful and enjoyable hunting trip.

At present, the future of the white-tailed deer is apparently secure for coming generations. Heavy increases in hunting pressure will make a few

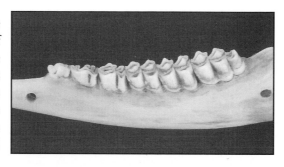

3½ Years

The lingual crests (inside, next to tongue) of the first molar are blunted, and the dentine of this tooth's crest is as wide or wider than the enamel. The dentine on the second molar is not wider than the enamel, which means this deer is probably 3½ years old.

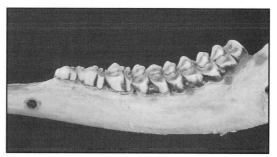

4½ to 5½ Years

At this point, it's often hard to distinguish between the two age classes. The lingual crests of the first molar are almost worn away. The posterior cusp of the third molar is worn at the cusp's edge so the biting surface slopes downward. Wear has spread to the second molars.

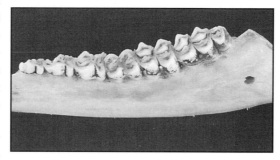

6½ to 8½ Years

By 6½, wear is moderate on the first premolar, and heavy on the second and third. Little or no enamel remains on the first premolar. At 7½ or 8½, the first molar might be worn within 2 or 3 mm of the gum line on the outside and 4 or 5 mm on lingual side.

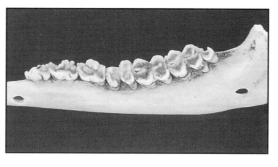

9½ and Older

Wear is more extreme than in previous photo. Pulp cavity might be exposed in some teeth. Some teeth worn to the gum line.

changes in local conditions, but the deer hunter's prospects look far brighter than those for many of the small-game hunting fraternity. The natural, God-given adaptability of the whitetail to fend for itself under all but the most adverse conditions, plus the more intelligent approach to conservation problems by our capable state organizations, has guaranteed solidly, for ourselves and our children, the heartwarming thrills of many seasons to come.

CHAPTER 4

Woodcraft and Whitetails

Of the many tales written around the drama of hunting whitetails, each one tends to stress the importance of woodcraft to the hunt's success and enjoyment. Aside from deer taken each season by pure luck — and believe it, that number is substantial — a knowledge of woodcraft plays a critical part with every sportsman. The still-hunter draws heavily on his knowledge of the woods during every moment on the hunt, for on this knowledge hinges the entire outcome of his trip. Even deer hunters who gang up on drives, following the accepted practice of most club-hunting, must possess the fundamentals of deer tactics and behavior to qualify on the score sheet.

Perhaps the original interpretation of our word "woodcraft" goes back to pioneer days, when its literal translation — craft of the woods — stemmed from its place in the era's economic picture. During those times, familiarity with the woods and its wild people had a direct bearing on the survival of early civilization. Food in abundance, clothing and shelter were provided for the woodsman with enough knowledge and skill to avail himself and his family of Mother Nature's benevolent gifts. All were there for the taking. Today's thoughts of woodcraft still swing back unconsciously to the early days, even though today's woodsman applies his knowledge only to increase his recreational pleasure and further appreciation of Nature's gifts, still here abundantly.

A New Generation of Whitetails

Much of the thrill and charm of deer hunting is influenced by our conscious knowledge of the whitetail's role in the romantic days of the Indian and buckskin-clad woodsman. Any glimpse of these splendid creatures along our wooded highways and parks will stop even the most blasé individual — sportsman or not — with a quickening of the pulse and a thrill of secret pleasure, as though he had been favored by an infinite glance into the pages of nature's book. Much of this same effect is captured by the deer hunter. Of all our outdoor pursuits, none except deer hunting is so wreathed by the aura of romance, none so connotative of our hidden pride in our American ancestry during its uphill climb for world recognition. The whitetail possesses every quality of a top-notch game animal — a position it undoubtedly commands — sufficiently to place it on the top shelf in every hunter's library of game birds and animals. No other game is so well able to adapt itself to changing conditions and the increasing spread of mankind's so-called civic improvements. The automobile and good highways, accused of ravaging the country of its small game and fish, seem to have simply awakened the competitive spirit in the whitetail. He flourishes now in many regions where he was unknown before the days of the machine age.

Our point is that the whitetail is so skilled in self-concealment and self-reliance that it requires the best of woods skill to beat him at his own game. In addition, most hunters of long experience agree the deer of today is infinitely wiser than his ancestors of 50 or even 25 years ago. Just as the hunter has increased his knowledge of the hunt, successive generations have planted new, or newly sharpened, instincts in our current deer herd. Thus, we must indeed know our deer if we would eat venison.

The study of woodcraft in its general sense offers an enormously widespread field, of such scope that a lifetime of effort would scarcely scrape off the top surface of possibilities. Still, the richer we are in this knowledge, the richer we become. Each action and habit of wild creatures dovetails inescapably into the lives of its brethren, so that each new bit of information gleaned in trips afield adds immeasurably to what we have seen before. Unfortunately most of us are so situated that we can devote but little time to days in the woods and fields, spent simply in studying wildlife, however desirable this may be.

Our actual hunting trips, then, must be the sole means of enriching our knowledge of woodcraft; and fittingly enough it is this absorption of woodslore on our hunting trips that forms the major part of our deer-hunting pleasure. Action in deer hunting, unlike other sports, occurs quickly, exists for only a few seconds — thrill-packed though they may be — then it's all over, ending in a successful bag or a heart-breaking missed opportunity. These few seconds of action may have been days or weeks in preparation, for bucks aren't seen every day in the woods by even the best hunters. These days, though, should have been made profitable by observation of deer signs, tracks, runways, antler rubs and bed-downs, giving the hunter further information for subsequent days in the woods.

In this chapter we will confine our discussion to that branch of woodcraft which deals directly with deer and deer hunting. We shall attempt to interpret the signs and existing knowledge of whitetails to the hunter's advantage. We must qualify these observations by stating the whitetail is often a most paradoxical animal. The one statement of fact that can be definitely and unequivocally made is that no one knows exactly what any one deer will do under any given set of conditions, not even the deer itself. The best we can hope to do is anticipate probable reactions with knowledge gleaned from previous experiences.

Finding Deer in New Areas

In strange deer country, both novice and expert hunter are faced with the problem of finding the deer. The novice usually elects to find a high spot overlooking as broad an expanse of territory as possible, in the hope a deer will walk out within his line of vision if he waits long enough. If by lucky accident he happens on a spot near feeding grounds or a well-defined crossing, he might get his shot — if he waits long enough. But as a rule this hit-or-miss method of deer hunting produces little results other than cold feet and discouraged impatience.

The experienced deer hunter wastes no time watching barren ground. His first move in new territory is to locate feeding grounds, bed-downs, runways and crossings to the best of his ability. He understands that movements and behavior of whitetails under normal conditions are influenced by only three factors: food and water, suitable cover for daytime hideouts, and the process of moving from bedding grounds to food and back again. The logical tactic is to locate these runways and feeding grounds and wait from some vantage point at times when deer are most likely to be feeding. All this, of course, is under normal conditions. But two factors that exist during hunting seasons might induce wide changes in deer behavior. These are the rutting season and heavy concentrations of hunters.

With hunters tramping through almost all available cover and feeding grounds all day, deer constantly move from one hideout to another, sufficiently breaking their normal routine so that no rules of conduct apply. Then, during the rut's height, all deer, bucks in particular, constantly move, spending little time feeding or resting. Any hunter who has killed a buck just after the rut can appreciate the tremendous amount of energy a buck expends during this period, taking little food in the process. Almost without exception, bucks taken after this period are exceedingly thin, almost to the point of emaciation, young bucks being affected to a greater degree than older individuals.

Whitetail hunters must bear those two facts in mind, for they control hunting conditions to a great extent. However, there are many times when neither influence is present, and a hunter must employ straight woodcraft to find deer.

First, the matter of feed. It's a recognized fact that deer feed little in heavily timbered areas, for the heavy top foliage discourages the production of undergrowth. Deer are browsers almost exclusively, feeding on the tender tips of second-growth timber and underbrush, although they're not averse to grazing off a farmer's young wheat or rye. Whitetails don't favor any one type of food to the exclusion of any other. Rather they select a varied diet from among the existing hardwoods and evergreens; among these are white cedar, hard or rock maple, black ash and black birch, white birch, scrub oak, ground hemlock, beech, poplar or aspen, yellow birch, dogwood and many others. The small pyramid-shaped nuts of the beech and acorns of all species of oaks are especially favored by deer during early fall, perhaps to the partial exclusion of other available food at this time. The important point to bear in mind is that deer can only obtain good browsing on low second-growth stuff, regardless of its species. It's useless to look for feeding grounds in heavy timber, unless large numbers of acorns or beechnuts are dropping in these areas.

In looking for feeding grounds, the deer hunter goes through all the heavy second-growth bordering heavy timber or in locations near good deer cover. He examines the tips of low-growing branches at about waist level, which is the preferred browsing height, looking for freshly nipped-off ends, evidence of recent feeding. He goes through heavy timber looking for beech trees bearing nuts or oaks laden with acorns. If there is evidence to indicate nuts and acorns are dropping yet none can be found on the ground, this also indicates deer feeding but it's not conclusive. If these areas are well populated with squirrels, it might be squirrels and not deer reaping the harvest. As a rule, though, hunters can detect squirrel workings quickly by the breaking of the acorn shells and the pulverized results of nibbling. Feeding deer make a thorough cleanup of acorns, shells and all.

These observations, plus fresh deer tracks on feeding grounds, are certain proof of recent deer activity, but the novice might have trouble determining the track's freshness. If leaves are falling it's simple, for some of the older tracks will be covered. If the ground is mossy, none but very fresh tracks will show. In firm, moist ground, a fresh track appears glazed at the bottom and old tracks appear dull. Almost the same holds true for deer droppings. These little, dark, elongated pills are dropped in bunches, and their freshness can be determined by their shiny surface coating. Old droppings are invariably dull on the surface and are firm and hard. It's good practice to pick up these little pills and squeeze them. If they're soft you can bet they haven't laid long.

Locating bed-downs is a somewhat tougher problem, for in most cases the terrain influences the deer's choice of a resting place as well as the weather. The whitetail inhabiting an area of good feed and cover usually leads a well-ordered life. He feeds in much the same areas every day; valley slopes, low ground between ridges, and along the edges of heavy timber. The best year-round deer feed is found in low places, with the exception of scrub oak and acorns. Most whitetails prefer high ground for bed-downs: ridges, hillsides and knolls, where they can be sure of detecting danger well in advance of its arrival.

The procedure of traveling down to feeding grounds and back up to higher ground for bedding is the most common of whitetail characteristics. It usually results in some well-defined runways connecting in some measure the two areas, for deer are creatures of habit. Although they seldom use the same spot twice running for a bed, they frequently use the same general area, perhaps the same slope or ridge. These spots can only be found by the most thorough search of likely ground, and even then only the freshest beds remain as evidence.

Fresh beds are well defined. Leaves will be pressed flat in an oval-shaped area about 3 feet long and 2 feet wide. Fresh droppings are almost always found near the beds, as are fresh tracks. But after a day or two, the leaves once again fluff up to their original shape, aided by wind and moisture, destroying all evidence. Of course the easiest way to locate a bed is to jump a deer, but this requires some skill in still-hunting and approach, or else the deer sneak off without being seen.

With bedding grounds and feeding areas located, it's simple to find well-defined runways somewhere between the two. This might be a good time to explain the difference between deer "runways" and "crossings." Deer hunters constantly use these terms interchangeably, yet they are not the same. A runway is a well-defined path followed by deer, whereas a crossing is a more general area where deer are likely to pass through.

Whitetails, with customary caution, dislike traveling the same beaten path day after day unless it is most convenient for them. We find runways, then, through thick cover — scrub oak, laurel, rhododendron, and other tough going where travel is almost impossible except on worn paths. Runways often follow brooks hemmed in by deep gullies, or go under rocky ledges and through swamps where deer have little choice except to follow a single path. On the other hand, when more open timber or cover is reached, they wander off a few yards on both sides of the line of travel, still keeping within the limits of a crossing, but not following a definite line. These crossings are often found in ridge "saddles," below knolls, through narrow strips of timber between open fields or meadows, or between heavy swamps or dense thickets. At few times will a whitetail reveal himself completely in open fields willingly, unless it's after dark, near sundown or sunrise, or when afflicted with rutting fever. When he approaches these clearings he usually skirts the edges, taking as much protection as the cover affords.

Runways are easily found simply because they are more or less beaten paths. In heavy scrub oak or laurel they show up at once, in less dense cover they can best be located by watching for fresh tracks following definite lines. In soft ground along brooks or through swamps they are at once apparent, but on mossy ground or hard-packed soil it requires closer scrutiny to pick them out. As a rule, though, deer keep their runways clear of growing twigs and branches by browsing as they travel, and this browse line is a dead giveaway.

Crossings aren't quite so easy. Perhaps the best plan for their location is to study the territory for spots previously mentioned — "saddles" over or between ridges, and such. Then minute examination of the ground should reveal clues: fresh tracks and old tracks in profusion, droppings, indications of feeding and, during the rutting season, antler rubs on saplings. These rubs are perhaps the most obvious hint of deer travel in any location, and usually they are numerous during deer season.

The general opinion on antler rubs is that bucks use this method to remove their velvet after the antler has hardened, thus polishing and staining the antlers in the process. I cannot subscribe to this theory. I believe rubbing occurs mainly when the rutting season is about to begin or has already started. The buck's antlers start to harden in late summer and early fall, and by mid-September are usually free of any signs of velvet. Yet rutting might not begin until late October or November, and if the observant hunter scouts the woods before the period begins he will find few, if any, rubs on saplings and brush.

Later, however, during the hunting season and after the rutting season, rubs will be noted in profusion through the same areas. I believe rubbing is performed by bucks while leading up to the mating process, merely to show off their various good points to the courted doe. In much the same manner, deer hunters will often see shallow holes about 2 feet across dug through the leaves down into the soil, with leaves and soil thrown to one side and scattered for several yards. This the buck performs with his front hoofs, pawing at the ground like an angry bull, again to give himself a good build-up with susceptible females.

Observations made at game farms throughout the country indicate the velvet is removed by the buck's digging it off with his hind hoofs. This velvet is attached to a thin skin, and once this is broken through with a sharp hind hoof it peels readily. In my years in the deer woods I have examined thousands of rubbed saplings, and I have yet to find a trace of velvet or skin on the ground below, although plenty of rubbed-off bark is often present. As an additional point, every experienced hunter has noted flat spots rubbed on the antlers just forward of the burrs, indicating still further that all, or nearly all, of the rubbing is done with the bases of the antlers at or near the burrs. If removal of the velvet were the primary objective, the antler would show no concentration of rubbing at one point.

Now, if many of these rubs are noted throughout deer country it is almost conclusive evidence the rut is on or has already passed. This can only be determined by close observation of the peeled area and the condition of peeled bark on the ground. I usually peel some bark off the first rubbed sapling I see at the beginning of the season's hunt and leave it on the ground with bark already rubbed off. I come back in a day or two and compare its condition with the rub, and from this I can form a fairly accurate idea about the rub's age.

All this might seem like unimportant detail in a small matter, but the success of a hunt often is made or broken by the rutting season. While the rut is on, deer constantly move. Bucks chase does over a wide area, and does that have already bred are running and hiding from the bucks. Likewise, the white-tailed buck loses a great deal of his natural caution during this period, and will blunder along runways and through crossings in pursuit of the doe with much less than usual caution. A high percentage of the odd deer stories that come out of the woods each season can be attributed to the height of rutting fever.

With light snow on the ground, all the problem of locating feeding grounds, runways and so on is at once simplified. It resolves itself into the single operation of finding tracks and following them, watching surrounding cover for evidence of feeding; and of course runways and crossings are at once evident. However, when snow covers the ground, deer are much more on the alert; they realize they can be seen more easily, so they stay close to good cover during all daylight movements.

In all our heavily hunted areas — which include most of our best deer-hunting territory — larger bucks stay off by themselves. They find a safe hiding place for their daylight bed, usually on a ridgetop covered with scrub oak or laurel, moving off the bed only after dark or at dusk. They travel down to low ground for nocturnal feeding, then return again to the ridge for rest. These big fellows are lazy and unsociable throughout the year, with the single exception of the rutting season. At that time they single out one or two older does and stay with them for the greater part of the season, protecting them from the attentions of the younger bucks until their job is done. Then they retire to their old stamping grounds until the next season. Most of their travels are made after dark, regardless of moonlight or pitch-blackness, and as the restless urge of early fall seeps in they become more and more furtive until the mating season begins.

Throughout the year they permit no intrusions by young bucks into their chosen bailiwick, and they demand no company of the opposite sex. All of these old bucks seem to realize the often-careless female brings bad luck, and they fight any of the association except for the few weeks of the actual mating season. Needless to point out, these bucks carry the heaviest heads and often the fattest venison and are highly prized by hunters. But it requires the best of skill and utmost patience to take these trophies by fair means. A "lone wolf" buck knows all the answers to a hunter's bag of tricks, but with a little luck on his side a good hunter can bring him to earth.

If a big buck is located in a given area, much missionary work must be done before the season in attempts to locate his habitat and feeding grounds. All runways and crossings must be examined for the imprint of heavy hoofs. If the buck is large, he will have a much longer stride than the average deer as well as leaving a deeper impression of hoofs. This can only be determined by comparison with other tracks, but it's a good rule. When a definite runway is located near his bedding ground, a black silk thread can be tied across it at waist level. If it can be conveniently done, the thread should be examined every night and morning to determine whether he leaves his bed by that route or approaches by it, for often separate runways are used for coming and going. Of course, if the ground is soft enough, a preponderance of tracks in one direction will give this information.

From then on, killing one of these big bucks is a matter of watchful waiting, taking a stand at daylight or moving in late in the afternoon, in the hope he will leave his bed before dark or delay his return until after dawn. It might require much patient waiting, but these big fellows aren't taken every season and the time is well spent.

The Whitetail's Eyes and Nose

Discussing woodcraft and deer hunting at once brings up the subject of the whitetail's powers of sight, scent and hearing. There is little doubt their hearing and sight are better than our own, and their powers of scent very keen. The most careful observers agree, though, that the whitetail's sight power is overrated. Deer always seem to have trouble establishing the identity of visible foreign objects unless these objects make a slight move. In the case of a hunter on a stand, if a deer is within only a few yards, even the winking of an eye is enough to start him off in a hurry. On the other hand, I have had deer approach within 25 yards and pass by with hardly more than a glance, even though I was in full view, when I was virtually motionless.

The whitetail places little faith in any one of his several senses unless alarmed. That is, if he hears a strange noise he usually waits to see just what has caused it. If the wind brings him man-scent, he sometimes bides his time until sight or sound confirms his suspicion. This natural curiosity has contributed directly to the untimely demise of more than one big buck. Perhaps in strictly wilderness areas or regions remote from human activities the whitetail is much more conscious of man's intrusion and alarmed more easily. But in areas where deer are taken in cover near farmlands or in any populated section, human scent is so often in a deer's nostrils that he pays little attention unless the scent is accompanied by more tangible evidence of danger. In most cases, this is a matter of near proximity or of an individual deer's experiences.

Any whitetail that has had a few close brushes with unfriendly Nimrods possesses a much higher IQ rating than his less sophisticated relatives. Such deer learn rapidly with little teaching. Their senses become more acute or they develop a keener recognition of facts established by the life processes of seeing, hearing and smelling.

In the early 1940s, I located a big buck through a little preseason scouting. I found he bedded atop a densely thatched scrub-oak ridge. In that refuge he was safe from any still-hunter, for the most careful stalking couldn't bring an approach within a hundred years without alarming the deer. By a bit of luck, I found a well-defined runway approaching the bedding grounds through a tiny uphill ravine, and it was there I elected to head him off, if possible.

I picked a good stand at the base of an uprooted red oak, giving me a view down the little ravine of about 50 yards and far enough away from its edge for deer using the run to pass by with little possibility of spotting me. With a definite project in mind, I eagerly awaited opening day, almost sure of a good shot. But my luck didn't hold out. Just the day before the season opened, our deer-hunting territory was blanketed in a nice snowfall of several inches, followed by a cold rain that quickly formed a most unsatisfactory crust. This made still-hunting in any form out of the picture, and tramping through the woods a hardship.

Nevertheless, at dawn that first day I crunched up the hillside for a noisy half-mile to my site. The dead air hung heavily over the hillside, sharply cold and pleasantly tingling on my cheeks. Hoarfrost formed lacy fringes on tree trunks and branches soon to sparkle with the first rays of the sun. Away off across the valley a blue jay sounded an early alarm as he policed his beat, his coarse, excited shrieking cutting crisply through the heavy silence and echoing among the white-bearded hemlocks along the slope. A beautiful morning to park quietly on a stand to listen and watch, I reflected, but that would be all.

On my stand, or seat — for I had snuggled down against the huge oak roots, well concealed — I amused myself by watching big clouds of vapor streaming out from my nostrils and lips. Trees were cracking and popping gently in the cold and a red squirrel chattered peevishly across my ravine. Soon the sun rose, spreading a deep pink over the white-blanketed forest floor, magically electrifying the frost-covered tree trunks and branches.

About a half-hour after sunup I heard faint crunchings down in my ravine. As I listened the sound increased in volume and came nearer. Just a steady mixed crunch, crunch — sounding like a herd of deer in the quiet air. Then quickly the sound materialized into deer; first a sleek doe, head bobbing, ears waving an out-of-step beat as she daintily lifted a slim hoof for each quick stride. At her tail was another doe, somewhat smaller, just as sleek, just as dainty but with erect head and ears laid back. Steadily the procession grew until five tawny-coated does drifted by, closely followed by a tiny spike buck. Directly in front of my tree the leading lady stopped, halting the line momentarily. She swept me with a quick glance, then lifted a slim hind leg and scratched her right ear. The red disc of the morning sun behind them made a striking tableau, for each one had suddenly stopped all movement.

As I held my breath momentarily they all swung their heads over their shoulders and looked back down the ravine. Ah! I thought, here follows the object of my main interest. Then without another glance in my direction they moved by on up to the ridge. I waited with pounding pulse for my buck to make some sound to indicate his approach, but after 10 minutes had gone by, I gave up hope. Then I again heard the confident crunching step as my buck came up the ravine, but when he was almost within sight his hoofstep faltered, then stopped. I knew he couldn't wind me in that dead air, and I was sure he couldn't see me. I tucked my chin still farther into the collar of my coat to keep the telltale breath vapors from fanning out before me. Hesitantly now his crunching hoofs came on until I could just see a faint movement through the saplings, then he stopped. There he stood, stamping his hoofs, suspicious now but not quite sure just what to do.

My view offered no possibilities for a shot until he emerged from those saplings, so I resigned myself to rigid immobility, but it was of no use. He snorted twice, stamped his hoofs again, then turned and jumped down the runway.

I never saw that deer again, alive. But as a matter of record, one of my hunting pals killed him two days later from this same stand. That morning had brought a gentle, warm rain and at about the same time the buck came up the little ravine without hesitation to meet his doom. He was a nice specimen, carrying 10 big points. To this day I am convinced he could see my breath through those saplings and so took alarm, but he was an old-timer, wise in the ways of hunters and cautious in the extreme. This incident is unusual and proves nothing beyond the fact that big bucks don't get that way by being careless.

It is possible this buck was well aware of the noisy progress of his travels through that deep, well-crusted snow. Perhaps this alone made him doubly cautious, so cautious that his senses were more than usually alert to possible danger. He might have picked up a tiny wisp of man-scent drifting from my stand, or seen some slight movement through the saplings caused by breath vapors. At any rate, he was sufficiently alarmed, giving me no opportunity to place a shot. But two days later, when a warm rain had softened the crust, melted the snow and beaten down any possibility of drifting man-scent, he walked unconcernedly past this same stand, giving my partner a perfect, deadly, broadside shot through the neck.

The matter of the whitetail's keen vision is more closely associated with hunting methods than with woodcraft, yet it is sufficiently important for discussion here. It is hardly possible that their sight powers are more acute than the normal human's. It is more logical to attribute their ability to pick out a hunter quickly to their intense familiarity with their daily haunts. Any foreign object in their home woods and covers must be as apparent to them as would be a frog on our living-room floor. Yet if the hunter remains still, their attention will wander and they forget about the strange object.

Many authorities on whitetails maintain deer are not color-conscious, and that it does no harm to wear red clothing in the woods. This theory I reject. It is incredible to me that the creative force that so lavishly spreads such vivid coloring throughout the land could at the same time create any creature without inherent ability to absorb it visually. I do subscribe to the opinion that the wearing of red in any form has little effect in alarming deer, but not for the same reason. During fall, the home covers of white-tailed deer are blotched in many ways with brilliant reds — the sumac, red oak and some maples — to name three. What is more natural than to assume that a deer glancing casually at a hunter on his stand should mistake his red cap and coat for a scrubby red oak or a low sumac?

Deer are much more sensitive to alarming sounds than to the sight of unmoving strange objects. Many times I have had does stand, quietly watching me from distances of only a few yards. But a single snap of my fingers would be enough to produce a quick, frightened reaction that would send them bounding and snorting to safety.

A decade or more ago, when old Abe Wykoff conducted the Buck Mountain Hunting Club in Sullivan County's Oakland Valley region, I was almost run to earth by two does. One morning Abe and I were hunting together, still-hunting the slopes on a long narrow hogback. Following our usual custom, I was covering the river side of the slope, Abe the back side that sloped over to the Hartwood Club. I had just discovered a well-defined runway coming down the slope in a long angle and was investigating the runway at a point where it passed between two husky oak trees only about a yard apart.

At this precise moment Abe's rifle cracked once, then again, and in a matter of seconds two deer came over the hill in full flight, pounding down the runway toward my somewhat untenable position between the big oaks. My first glance labeled both deer as does, both badly frightened and in bounding high gear. When the leading doe was three jumps away I waved an arm enthusiastically, thinking this would shy her off. Quickly then I jumped behind one of my oak trees, barely clearing the run for the two deer as they bounced by.

I suppose a good loud yell might have frightened them enough to swerve them off, but I didn't want to alarm any buck that might be following. Both these deer were blindly alarmed and might easily have knocked me down if I had stood in the run. Minutes later I found that Abe had neatly dispatched the 6-point buck that had been escorting these does, so my pains to keep quiet were unnecessary. Normally, of course, both these deer would have spotted me at once, but I am convinced that only a loud shout or a shot from my rifle would have swerved them from this runway. In like manner, many frightened deer, both bucks and does, have been known to run headlong into danger even though such danger was visually apparent.

Inversely, though deer are highly sensitive to strange sounds, the usual woods noises bother them not at all. This, too, is fortunate for the still-hunter, or else he would rarely get close enough to see a deer. Any deer must be hard put indeed to distinguish the step of the hunter's foot from the myriad rustlings of squirrels, the dropping of nuts and acorns, and the clamorings of crows and blue jays. Such sounds of the hunter's progress that he must make to move in the woods are not in themselves alarming unless the deer can confirm them by seeing or smelling the hunter. Snapping of heavy twigs underfoot, breaking branches and rolling rocks are, of course, all taboo. Such noises form little or no part of the usual woods complement, and deer quickly detect them as foreign.

Deciphering Buck Tracks

It is regrettable that of the hundreds of thousands of deer hunters spread throughout our white-tailed deer country only a few spend sufficient time in the woods for absorbing some knowledge of deer habits. Most hunters of my acquaintance seem content with their knowledge after they think they can establish the identity of the bucks' tracks from that of the does. And strangely enough, each hunter of some experience has decidedly definite ideas on this subject. For my part, although I have spent almost two decades in hunting the white-tailed deer in some of the best covers of the East, I am never positive of the buck's track unless I have seen the deer making it.

Perhaps I have heard as much discussion of the subject from the hunter's viewpoint as any other individual in the East. Over the gun counter, in hunting clubs, at sportsmen's meetings, in the deer woods, and in mountain taverns my ears have been bent with numerous positive rules for such identification. But still I remain unconvinced, for no two sets of rules seem the same.

It is my experience and steadfast opinion that no man can by examining the single track of a deer thereby determine the sex of the deer making it. The best we can hope to do is to make a reasonable deduction, considering all the factors involved, and then form an opinion. The shape of the hoof alone is not enough. Neither is a large hoof evidence of a buck. We have many does wandering our deer covers with hoofs as large as the biggest buck in the Catskills.

I have been told in perfect sincerity by some deer-hunting friends that the buck always has a long slender hoof. I have been told by an equal number of friends that the buck has a short broad hoof. Likewise, I have been informed on numerous occasions that the toes of a buck always spread. Perhaps they do, but I have tracked many does that displayed this not-too-unique characteristic. There exists also a group of hunters who believe the buck always leaves the imprint of dew claws directly behind the hoof. Perhaps no other item of deer lore carries more misinformation than this question of buck and doe tracks.

The best any of us can hope to do to settle this problem of sex differential in the hoofprint is to observe all the visible evidence, then make logical deductions. Snow or soft earth is the ideal and perhaps only medium in which this can be done. It is absolutely necessary for the observer to find enough tracks in continual line to be able to establish a trend toward the identity of the animal making them.

First, the size of the track is no criterion. Larger females will most certainly have hoofs of greater length and width than the hoofs of small bucks. Another factor is the type of terrain the animal uses. Deer living in soft, swampy ground or an area of heavy coniferous timber will develop a larger hoof. Deer that climb rocky ridges and rock-studded slopes will have smaller, sharper hoofs. I have killed several large bucks on the Shawangunk Mountain range in Lower Sullivan and Ulster counties, all of which had comparatively small hoofs. This mountain range is of heavy limestone with many jagged outcroppings and generally rock-covered. Deer living and feeding on this range keep their hoofs in a well-trimmed condition. In the swampy Wolf Pond area of Sullivan County, only a few miles north of the Shawangunk Range, the deer have somewhat larger hoofs.

During the latter part of December 1946, one of my hunting friends and

I skinned out our two bucks at the same time. One of these deer was unusually large, carrying a dressed weight of 212 pounds. The other was a normal 8-pointer that dressed out at 131 pounds. In the normal process of skinning and butchering we had disjointed the legs and thrown them into a single pile. Later, when we came to sorting out the respective hoofs, we would have been forced to pick at random were it not for the slightly longer and heavier leg of the larger deer. Certainly there was no apparent difference in the hoof sizes. In addition I have had ample opportunity during the past two decades to examine the carcasses of thousands of white-tailed bucks. I am still unconvinced the larger bucks carry the largest hoofs.

Depth of hoofprint is the more obvious indication of a buck's weight, plus the length of stride, both of which must be compared with other tracks made in the same vicinity by other deer. This gives an initial foundation for the hunter's deductions. Next, if the deer has been walking quietly, and a line of prints can be found, we must try to determine how closely each print will come to a center line, drawn lengthwise and between the tracks. The doe and young buck walk with hoofs placed close to this common center line, and are usually precise in placing the hind hoof directly within the print of the front hoof. Mature bucks are careless in this respect. The hind hoof is often placed closer to the center line than the front hoofprint or fails to come quite as far forward as the front print.

The fat, heavy buck shows a marked tendency to walk with front hoofs wider apart than the doe or small buck. Also these bucks usually show an inclination to toe-out with the front hoofs.

In following a group of tracks (in snow) there are some distinguishing characteristics that will help hunters pick out the buck's track — if there be one in the herd. The does have a tendency to wander aimlessly when the herd is moving; the buck is more purposeful and direct in his movements. The doe track will wander off the runway, then weave back. Often she'll playfully jump over a small bush or log, seemingly just for the fun of it. Her whole attitude as evidenced by the dainty hoofprints is much less concerned with a direct objective than is the buck. The buck seldom engages in the female frivolities. His walking stride is calm and purposeful. He seldom turns abruptly in his directional line to feed on a shrub just off the run. Rather he walks directly to the feeding spot. He engages in no playful antics such as the doe tracks indicate. There is little bush- or log-jumping to be found in the evidence of a buck's hoofprints.

Often the herd's entire group of does will fan out through crossings, covering an area 15 or 20 yards wide, as they precede the buck. The buck's track will usually be found, firm and purposeful, following up through the center of this welter of trails. Then again, the more wary old-timers will follow the doe herd but at a distinct distance apart. If the hunter discovers one of these lone trails showing a marked tendency to stray off a bit from the rest of the herd, he can bet his stack there is a buck ahead.

In snow less than 4 inches deep, the buck consistently gives away his sex by dragging his front hoofs. The doe lifts each hoof daintily, then places it carefully down. A buck carrying heavy neck and shoulders will not trouble to lift his hoofs clear of the snow. His dragging forehoofs leave a distinctive line behind each print. Of course, in heavy snow any deer will drag its hoofs, so the hunter must use judgment in making a decision of this kind.

Much has been said about the spreading of a buck's toes as a distinguishing characteristic. To me a spread-toe print means only a heavy deer, whether it be buck or doe. Any running or loping deer will leave a spread-toe print, particularly in firm soil. Neither does the shape of the hoof itself have a definite bearing on the deer's sex. Short, broad hoofs and long narrow hoofs will be found at random on bucks and does. The nature of the terrain under hoof has much to do with slight differences in shape of hoofs. Hard, rocky ground and generally rocky deer areas contribute to wearing off the front of the toes. The swamp areas and coniferous timberland allow the hoof to grow a much more pointed toe.

The woodsman who has opportunity to observe all the points we have mentioned will add up all of them before drawing a conclusion. In fact, the whole thing is not too important, because we must find the buck himself. Many times, though, we are forced to decide whether to follow a set of fresh tracks and we might be able to save a day's wasted hunt if we can make a logical and accurate interpretation. At any rate, the study of deer prints never loses its charm for a deer hunter. Rather it adds to the fun of a day in the woods.

Track Peculiarities

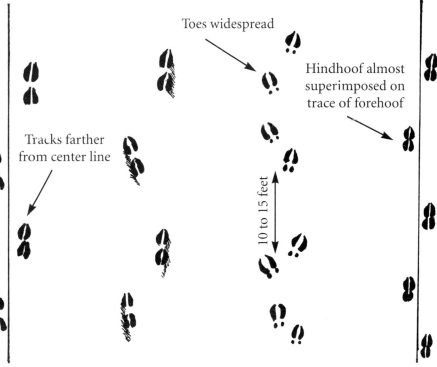

Buck walking, tracks toe out

Buck toe-drag in soft snow

Bounding track, dew claws seen

Doe walking, tracks point forward or slightly inward

Misconceptions About the Snort

There exists still another item of sex differential in deer that has caused many a clubhouse argument: the "snort" of the whitetail. Almost every hunter who spends much time in deer country has heard a deer snort. The sound is simply a whistling blast from a deer's nostrils, and can be caused by the deer's alarm or anger. Of greater importance, it is often caused by the deer's effort to rid the nostrils of the nose-bot. The deer bot is a worm-like parasite that afflicts deer in certain areas, but usually isn't fatal by itself.

Commonly, it is the deer's ability to rid itself of these bots by blasting them out through the nostrils that helps determine if the deer will survive the vitality ebb of a hard winter.

However, it is a prevalent belief among hunters that only the buck snorts. This idea is so widespread that any snorting deer faces immediate danger during the hunting season.

During one of my still-hunting trips in the lower Catskills I was working a big beech ridge. I had been in the woods about an hour and had not yet heard or seen any other hunters, so I was unprepared for a sudden burst of rifle shots that crashed out directly ahead of me on the ridge. Seconds later, two does crashed by just below me, unaware of my presence. Just beyond me they stopped, looked over their backs in the direction they had left, then, shaking their respective tails, they quietly trotted off down the slope to the valley below.

A light powdering of snow covered the ground, so soon I could see two red-capped hunters following the trail made by the two does. They were so occupied that neither hunter saw me and would have passed by if I hadn't whistled. I dropped down the hill then to talk with them.

"How long have you been standing there?" they both asked. "Didn't you see those two bucks go by?"

"Well," I said, "I certainly saw two deer go by, but if there had been any bucks you'd have heard some shootin'. Just what made you fellows think they were bucks?"

Both shifted their feet a bit and looked at each other before the older man spoke up.

"Well, we had just come up on this ridge and these deer were bedded down in some brush. When they heard us they both snorted and jumped on up the ridge. We could see their flags for quite a ways, so we started to pump it at 'em. We're glad we didn't connect, but that's the first time either of us heard of a doe snorting."

And so it goes. I have heard numerous incidents parallel to this one, and from widely separated whitetail regions, so the idea is by no means peculiar to a few deer hunters.

In this same connection, "way back in the early '30s" I had joined an Oakland Valley deer-hunting outfit called "The Beaverdam Club." On my first day's hunt, just after daybreak, I had found a tiny scooped-out gravel bank up on the mountainside, near the camp. The boys had been taking gravel out to repair the winding wood road over the mountain to Beaverdam Pond. The bank was just so deep that I could barely look over the rim from a spot within the scooped hole.

I had a good view from this spot. With only my head exposed above ground level, I could cover the little ravine running down the steep slope to my left. The whole white-birch slope to my right and the valley below was in easy view for just a shift of the eye. This I decided would be a good spot to spend an hour while the deer still would be on the early-morning feed.

Hardly had I settled down to wait when two deer came into view, gently picking their way down the ravine edge toward the valley below. They were not alarmed, and would wander a bit from the ravine to the low second growth to nip off a tender bud now and then as they progressed, ever coming closer to my stand in the gravel pit. Finally, they were only a few yards from my head, when the lead doe discovered me. At once her head was thrown erect, sensitive ears cocked in my direction. Then she lowered her head slowly and, at the close range, I could see her nostrils quivering as they sucked in air, filtering it for a taint of danger.

But the wind was right and she could find nothing for fear. Still, she was mighty curious, so she raised a slim foreleg and stamped it to the ground with an audible thump. Finding that I could not yet be frightened into moving, she again stamped. Meanwhile her companion doe had inched forward cautiously until they were nose to flank. Then, incredible though it might seem, they each stamped and thudded their dainty forehoofs into the hard ground, no doubt still expecting to frighten a move out of me.

At last, satisfied no buck was tagging along behind, I broke the tableau quickly by yanking off my cap and waving it. The response was electric. Both does jumped into the air with loud snorts, reversing their field as they headed back up the slope, bounding as though they were on springs — tails flying erect — and snorting at every jump. At the top of the ridge they stopped, shook their heads, snorted a final blast and walked off into the white birches, snapping their flags in evident disgust.

Other Deer Vocalizations

Deer of either sex seldom make any vocal noises other than this common snort, yet there have been many instances of bleating deer recorded. Bert Sauer, old-time deer hunter and once charter member of the Iroquois Hunting Club in mid-Sullivan County, has reported to me that many times he has heard female deer bleating, particularly when wounded. I have no firsthand knowledge of this, but I have heard the doe make tiny bleating noises to the fawns as they nestled against her flank. I doubt if the noise could be heard, in this instance, at a distance of more than 25 yards.

I remember a tender scene up in the Beaver River section of the Adirondacks. I had taken a stand at daybreak near the foot of a low spruce ridge. The morning was crackly cold; all was dead-still but for the chatter of chickadees and a red squirrel. After a while I became aware of slight rustlings that materialized first into a small fawn, just out of the spotted coat, then another fawn and the mother doe. The three stood at the edge of the birches, tiny wisps of steam fanning out from their shining black noses. The old doe then took the lead until she stood directly before my big spruce-tree stand, but the fawns hesitated. She turned her head and gave a little grunting bleat — almost a purring sound. I could see her flanks heave slightly and the vapor come from her mouth as she made this sound, so I could be certain it was not a low snort. Then the fawns hopped over to her, and one touched noses with the mother while the other nibbled playfully at her ear.

Again the mother gave this little purring bleat and the fawns moved off into the spruces, followed closely by their fond parent. Even after the little group had passed from my view I could hear the doe bleat gently now and then until at last all was still again.

Becoming at Home in the Woods

In bringing out some of these more intimate details of deer behavior, I have a definite purpose. There is a growing tendency among the great bulk of the deer-hunting clan to pursue the white-tailed deer in a hit-or-miss manner. For any man to gain the fullest success and enjoyment from his hunting each year, the whitetail must be made a hobby — a hobby of study that is as gratifying as the killing of the deer itself.

True, many men are fortunate enough to kill a deer the first time they set foot in deer country. This is not exceptional. Purely by the law of averages alone some small percentage of greenhorns will kill their buck, because with thousands of hunters in the woods each season some are bound to run across a deer. But the man who can kill his buck year after year is he who has a keen knowledge of woodcraft and deer behavior. No detail of deer lore is too insignificant to be overlooked. With the passage of years and the successive seasons, no one more than the deer hunter will appreciate this fact.

There is much more to killing a buck than finding good deer country and spending a few days hunting therein. Any woodsman worthy of the name covers his deer-hunting grounds with hawk eyes. He studies his topographical maps and from these alone — virtually without seeing the land itself — he can often locate the sections where deer cross from valley feeding grounds to hiding places in swamps and bedding grounds on ridges. These maps are invaluable to the deer hunter in familiarizing himself with areas to be hunted. Such maps may be had from the United States Geological Survey, covering in quadrangle sections almost any area in the country. The maps show elevations as contour lines, and all roads, trails and streams in any given area.

It is a far cry from covering alder thickets with a good English setter or crouching in a duck blind on the Sound to the successful hunting of white-tailed deer. The writer does not wish to disparage small-game hunting, for no one else enjoys that sport to a greater degree. However, I have always felt that such hunting calls more for good shooting ability and good dogs than for an abundance of woodslore. Successful deer hunting is the true test not only of a sportsman's shooting skill but of his specific knowledge of woodcraft and of his intelligent application of this knowledge.

A knowledge of woodcraft in deer hunting includes much more than a thorough understanding of deer habits and movements. The hunter himself must be at home in the woods, be able to detect good cover and feeding grounds at a glance, know his territory well enough to account for the movements of his pals, and above all be sure of his own position through every minute of the day. In small covers near farmlands and settled communities this is no problem. In the "back-country" and semi-wilderness areas, it is not so easy. Individuals vary much in this quality of directional sense, but every hunter can acquire enough of it to give him perfect freedom of movement in any territory he might like to explore.

CHAPTER 5

Still-Hunting the Whitetail

Sunup was moments away as I stood on the roadbank near the little old schoolhouse. Earl and Eddy had just dropped me off and had gone up the winding dirt road to the next farmhouse. They would park the car there and hunt up on the big hardwood ridge that parallels the course of the majestic Delaware River. I was to hunt on up this ridge and meet them a mile or so beyond.

Tale of a Still-Hunt

How quiet and lifeless were the slopes and valley below me! The quiet gray beeches stood like guardians among the little white birch and sumac by the roadside, gleaming damply in the early daylight. Now and then a heavy water drop would fall with a thunk on the dead-leaf carpet below. It had rained the night before — a soft, warm fall rain, bringing off the last reluctant leaves and opening the door to the hunter.

It was opening day some 10-odd years ago. We had decided to hunt here, in the Cahoonzie area of southwestern Sullivan County, purely on my say-so that it was good deer country. Of course, all of us knew there were deer in this area, but we had not yet hunted here for deer. I had, however, been over the section we were to hunt a few weeks before with the setter. I had combined grouse-hunting with a little exploration, and had decided the country offered good possibilities.

At that time I had been more or less driven out of my old stamping grounds near Wolf Pond by the heavy infiltration of new and reckless deer hunters. I had decided this year I would seek new hunting fields, where still-hunting would once again be practical and enjoyable.

Perhaps no one can say just why he picks a definite spot for a new hunting ground. On my grouse-hunting trip I had found many tracks, some well-defined runs, and evidence of deer feeding on acorns and beechnuts up on the big ridge, now above me. But I knew many other places where deer sign was just as abundant. Perhaps on the day I had been here before, the beauty of the country impressed me and now had lured me there again.

It had been a glorious, golden fall day. Riotous color had filled the woods — the warm reds of the young oaks, the pastel yellows of the beeches. Waxy-orange bittersweet berries clung to the tumbledown stone fences and clambered over dark green cat-briers like living drapes. Here I

had found grouse and the delicate heart-shaped prints of deer.

Topping the ridges were long lines of towering hemlocks, standing guard over their progeny in the struggle for sunlight among the heavy white birch. Ground-pine and creeping hemlock carpeted the white birch grounds, almost concealing great beds of wintergreen and partridge berries. And over all was the heavy rich glow of October sunlight. In the valley below, the Shinglekill gurgled and chattered on its journey to the Delaware. Both brook trout and the heavier browns were even now lying in the gravel-bottomed riffles, ready to spawn. To me, trout and white-tailed deer have always been closely associated. Perhaps it is because many of my deer have been killed near trout waters, or perhaps because in both there breathes the never-ending beauty of the wilds.

The first pink rays of sunrise bathing the top of the ridge above stirred me from my reverie. It was time now to get up on that ridge and look for my buck. Behind the little school ran a low ridge, gently sloping upward to meet the big ridge that I felt should be the resting place of at least a few deer. Slowly, reluctantly, fearful of making any sound that might break the spell of silence, I began the climb.

My shoe-pacs fell softly on the sodden leaves. I brushed through little hemlocks whose evergreen feathers dropped tiny showers at my intrusion. Every half-minute or so I stopped to look down each slope of the ridge, watching for deer sign as I progressed. Soon I headed into the base of my big ridge. Now the timber changed abruptly from small white birch and poplar to the heavy-trunked red oaks and big beeches. The beech is ever a lovely tree. Its smooth gray bark gives an impression of quiet, firm dignity, a strong contrast to the rough, black trunks of oak and hard maple.

The woods were indeed quiet that morning. The air had but a touch of chill; no breeze moved the last remaining leaves of the aspens — nothing but a "Put!" as an overburdened raindrop dripped from a high twig.

I struck a fresh track, and stopped to study it. The prints were deep in wet leaves, wide-spaced and toed-out; they were heading for the ridge. It was apparent this deer had spent the rainy night before down in the valley hemlocks, either feeding or in shelter from the rain, and was making for the ridge to bed down.

I took the trail to the top. It was easy to follow in the sodden leaves. But at the top of the ridge, the trail became fainter as it led through long stretches of moss and over rocky ledges. Finally, I gave it up altogether to concentrate on covering the long hogback before me.

For an hour I carefully walked the ridge-top, swinging first right, then left, that I might watch both sides of the slope. Much of the time I stood to listen and watch, but I heard nothing more than the scurry of a gray squirrel as he dashed for a den tree, or the distant "Pow! Pow!" of a rifle. Then I turned to step around a big stump, and a movement in a white birch stand to my left brought me to a halt. I could see moving bodies in the brush and now and then a slim foreleg, but no heads.

In a moment, two deer came out of the white birch and headed up the ridge. Both were does, or at any rate no antlers showed. I decided to wait for a bit and watch their back trail for any following buck. But for 15 minutes no other deer showed, so I took off again following the ridge and, in a sense, following the two does.

My route crossed many deer signs; fresh tracks coming up from the valley below and crossing over the ridge; many droppings sprinkled in the runs through laurel and rhododendron. Almost every visible track must necessarily be fresh, for the rain would have successfully obliterated all those before its coming. Here on a small poplar near a rocky ledge a buck had rubbed the bark — long shreds lay on the ground at the butt. No tracks were visible here; it must have been rubbed some days before. All these signs were heartening. Perhaps this ridge would develop into a deer hunter's Utopia.

At last I reached the crest of the hogback. Beyond, the ridge sloped gently down to the valley of the little farm near where my pals were to be hunting. Quietly and slowly I worked down the slope, aware now of a gentle breeze fanning my left cheek and murmuring in the topmost hemlock boughs. The sun was much higher now. The early rose glow had changed to a pale yellow, penetrating to the forest floor in the beech and white birch stands, but failing to dispel the moist and morose shadows of hemlock and buck-laurel. Deer should be bedding now, I thought. Not much chance to find any yet on the move.

In my musing way, I had passed a big windfall of white oaks, lying off the shoulder of the ridge, heavily leaved tops pointing down the slope. The uprooted trunks lay crisscrossed upon each other with the thick, brown dead leaves clinging to the branches in a high mound. I had stopped then for a moment, to wonder at the perversity of a flighty wind in singling out for destruction this particular clump of white oaks. And as I stood here my eye dropped to fresh deer tracks, tracks that headed toward this windfall.

Obeying the normal urge, my feet turned toward the fallen trees. No more than two steps did I make, when, with a bursting crash, a fine buck bounded out from behind the screen of leaves, hightailing it for the crest of the hogback. As he jumped, his antlers had flashed in the sunlight, and even as my rifle came up, both antlers and long white flag were bobbing over the low brush.

My first fright over, I settled down to stopping him short of the ridge-top. Swinging with him, my front sight touched his knees as I tightened off the trigger. With the crash of the .250 his forelegs crumpled on that last bound, his nose slid to the leaves and his chunky body swept over in a high arching somersault. He made one game effort to regain his hoofs, but the second bullet threw a tuft of hair from the far side of his neck and he thumped to the ground again, stretched out in death.

As he lay on the damp forest floor, I marveled, as I do over every deer I have killed, at the dead-whiteness of his white hair and the tawny gray of his body coat, so like in color to the leaves in which he lay. His antlers shone dully, hinting of many rubbings on the soft-barked saplings on his ridge. The main beams swept forward and upward, topped with 10-inch-long tines. His was not a magnificent head of wide spreading beams and many points, but simply the grand, sturdy crown of an adult 8-point buck.

And now, I reflected, as I dropped down on a log to steady my quaking knees, my hunting was over and the hard work — yet a labor of love — must begin. I had to get him out.

The Right Territory and Conditions

An experience such as this is the deer hunter's dream. On the day that I have related, still-hunting conditions were ideal. Each circumstance had been in my favor: quiet, damp woods, a gentle breeze favoring my direction of hunting and the common, natural tendency of the white-tailed buck to remain hidden even at the close approach of the hunter. It was mere chance that I discovered the fresh tracks, turning me toward the deer's hiding place; and at once he knew the jig was up — therefore his mad dash for safety.

It is in such a fortuitous hunt, when Lady Luck smiles, that the deer hunter reaches the greatest heights of hunting thrills and pleasure. True still-hunting will ever be a solitary effort, one in which the successful hunter can take the greatest pride of accomplishment. He has outwitted our most cautious and instinctively clever species of wildlife at its own game. The satisfaction of taking a white-tailed buck by still-hunting methods alone can never be approached by killing a buck that has been driven to the stander to be killed.

Of course, still-hunting poses myriad problems. Much of our good deer-hunting territory is not well suited for still-hunting. For example, the heavy scrub-oak territory of many Pennsylvania counties makes a close approach to deer almost impossible. A large portion of New York's Sullivan County is heavily thatched with scrub oak, laurel and rhododendron, so the hunter can never approach deer without driving them ahead, far out of seeing or shooting range. Many sections of representative deer country abound in similar obstacles to the still-hunter.

The ideal type of cover for still-hunting is the rolling, many-ridged hardwood lands, where timber is heavy enough to discourage dense undergrowth. This is not to say that virgin-forest growth is good deer country, for generally it is not. Rather the best still-hunting country is a combination of big hardwood ridges and small valleys covered with good, low undergrowth for deer feeding grounds. An example of such country can be found in the Northville area of New York state. Here, in the southern foothills of the Adirondacks, at the northern extremities of Sacandaga Reservoir lies just this type of rolling hardwood country. The tiny valleys lying within these hills are well thatched with small white birch, cedar, poplar and alder, as well as many other types of good deer feed.

The Catskill area offers many good still-hunting sections: Slide Mountain near Phoenicia, the Red Hill section farther south near Claryville, the whole Upper Neversink River Valley — just to name a few.

Heavy spruce areas such as we find in the western Adirondacks are difficult to hunt. Vision is limited to the extreme in such areas by the constant walls of evergreens. Under these conditions deer can gain a safe hiding place in a few bounds, in almost any direction, giving little opportunity for a shot.

But good still-hunting areas can be found in any state where the whitetail is numerous — Vermont, New Hampshire, Michigan, Wisconsin or Maine, or whatever state happens to be the hunter's choice. Most of my deer country is discovered on my fishing trips, for actually a deer hunter never stops hunting, even on his summer jaunts. Many of my best hunting experiences have been enjoyed in areas I scouted during summer. After arming myself with topographical maps of my chosen area, I would be ready to hunt when opening day came around.

Another and perhaps more important problem for the still-hunter is the abundance of other hunters in his area. Still-hunting is hardly practical when many hunters are tramping the woods in groups of two, three or even more. The deer become highly alarmed in any section where hunters are on the move all day; so much so that the slightest noise will tend to send them off at top speed. Deer under these conditions of heavy hunting have had their routine of natural habits broken. They feed little, if at all, during daylight and bed down in the heaviest thickets they can find.

There is a personal element, too, under such a setup. It is hardly advisable for any hunter to go pussyfooting through deer country if there are many hunters strewn throughout the area. There is ever the thousand-to-one chance that a slowly moving hunter can be mistaken for a deer by one of his brethren. It is highly important, then, to pick your still-hunting grounds with a view to hunting pressure as well as abundance of deer and favorable terrain.

However, we do have many sections of good deer country where straight still-hunting methods are the only practical means to kill your buck. We speak now of the great wilderness areas of Michigan's Upper Peninsula, the North Woods of Maine, a great portion of the Adirondacks, or any true wilderness area accessible to hunters only by trails or waterways. Here the deer are continually in a wild state, unfamiliar with the sight or scent of man. Perhaps many deer are born, live a normal span of existence and die without having seen a man. Hunting these deer successfully requires the best of woods craftsmanship.

It is just this type of hunting the writer prefers, but unfortunately, few of us have the time to devote to such a trip. Wilderness hunting involves considerable preparation, complete camping gear, and a knowledge of woodlore in sufficient quantity to make an extended stay outdoors a pleasure rather than a hardship. Its great compensation rests in the hunter's opportunity to disassociate himself from the humdrum existence and the platitudes of normal living. Here the hunter must be virtually self-sufficient. He must walk many miles over dim trails carrying his camping and hunting gear on his back. He must depend on his wits and ability to provide a good bed, good food and reasonable living comfort in camp. But most of all, he must lean heavily on his still-hunting knowledge and ability to bag his buck. Any white-tailed buck killed under these conditions will ever be the most highly prized trophy in a sportsman's collection.

And in wilderness areas there is no other way to kill deer. No methods of deer hunting other than still-hunting are practical. The terrain is of great scope. There may be many deer, but they are scattered over thousands of acres of timbered woodland. The still-hunter must seek until he locates his deer.

Many times I have thought deer hunters are becoming soft. Most of us can find deer within a few hours' drive of our homes. We drive into deer country, park our cars and in five minutes are hunting in productive country. I must admit this is good. In many cases it means a man is able to hunt deer where otherwise he would never be able to enjoy this sport.

But in another sense, much of the true hunting spirit is lost if we hunt deer only under these conditions. The man who has the initiative to seek deer in the wilderness areas is the hunter who gains the most from his deer hunting. Still-hunting is becoming a lost art in many sections, primarily because of unfavorable local conditions, but often because of general inertia on the part of the hunter. To those who say there are too many hunters coming into their favorite haunts, or that the deer are being killed off, we can advise turning to wilderness areas. There still are many thousands of acres of wonderfully scenic forests, abundant with deer, that have scarcely felt the tread of a deer hunter's feet. Let these men get maps of the areas they would like to hunt, study them well, prepare the necessary camping gear, and when the season is at hand "go back in" for a week or two where there are still many wild deer for the taking if the hunter possesses the skill and intestinal fortitude to make the grade.

Defining the Term

"Still-hunting" is, as a term, slightly ambiguous. It is not to be confused with the common practice of sitting on a deer run all day — day after day — hoping a buck will come along sooner or later. This method can be highly successful, but it should never masquerade as still-hunting. Rather it might be more aptly named "ambushing."

This difference in terminology was driven home to me quite a number of years ago, during my early days of deer hunting. I had driven up to Wolf Pond, right in the heart of Sullivan County's best deer hunting, one morning in the early part of the open season. When I reached the old hand-laid stone dam, there was a large party of hunters gathered atop the dam, waiting for good daylight before taking to the woods.

Sitting apart from this group was another hunter — advanced in years and no doubt, I thought, well learned in the art of deer hunting. I struck up a conversation by asking him if he was hunting with the gang.

"No," he said. "This bunch are going up in the scrub oaks and drive the hell out of 'em. They've been doin' it all week. Guess they killed one buck so far. But I'm going to take it easy and do a little still-huntin'."

I looked him over pretty carefully after that remark. He was bundled up in a heavy sheepskin coat, covering layers of wool shirts and sweaters. His feet were well covered with a pair of huge felt boots into the tops of which were stuffed at least two pairs of trousers. He carried a huge lunch basket in one hand with a giant-size "Thermos" bottle resting upright in one corner. In the other hand hung a double hammer-gun of ancient vintage. Quite an outfit, I decided, for a still-hunter. Then I made off up the trail to do a bit of hunting myself.

Later that day I happened on this same character, sitting a few yards off the trail, but not more than a hundred yards from the Wolf Pond Dam. I stopped to ask him if he'd seen anything yet and he told me, "Only a couple of does."

"Thought you were going to do some still-hunting today," I remarked casually.

"Well, by God," he replied, "don't you think for a minute that I ain't been. I been here all day — haven't moved a bit since sunup. This here's a mighty good run and I know I'll get a shot if I sit here long enough." So much for that brand of still-hunting.

I do not intend to ridicule those who prefer to hunt deer by careful watching and waiting near runways and feeding grounds. Many times it is the only way to kill a wary old buck that has been outwitting still-hunters and deer drives for season after season. The true still-hunter, as a matter of fact, does a great deal of watchful waiting as he moves over deer territory. Looking, stopping and watching with patience and care has many times filled a deer license, more often indeed than has barging through deer country without regard or respect for a deer's keenness of vision, hearing and olfactory senses.

The principal drawback in this ambush style of modified still-hunting is that the hunter sees but little deer country. More valuable in deer hunting than patient waiting is a true, firsthand knowledge of the movements of deer in the area. This can only be gained by moving quietly through the woods and swamps, studying tracks, runs, bedding grounds and all the many signs that the experienced woodsman can interpret in terms of deer lore. This is still-hunting's greatest boon.

Add to this that in cold weather only the most Spartan courage can keep a hunter on a stand hour after hour throughout even the shortest fall or winter day. Such hunting limits the scope of a sportsman's knowledge. I know a goodly number of men who hunt deer year after year, and of this group none have yet seen for themselves the telltale rub of a buck on a green sapling. These hunters lose most of the charm of still-hunting. Deer hunting for them becomes a battle with the elements, often antagonistic during the open season in any of the Northern deer hunting zones.

Frankly, I lack the infinite patience and courage to face a bitterly cold day on a runway stand. Feet become painfully inanimate lumps of frozen flesh, fingers almost crackle with frost, and the entire human frame soon vibrates like a strummed harp. The entire picture is out of tune with the normal theme of deer hunting thrills and pleasure.

Overlooking Hidden Deer

The hunter who follows the still-hunting game alone adheres to a typical ritual. He works the lower feeding grounds during the early morning and late afternoon hours. When the sun climbs above the treetops he begins to look for bedded deer on ridgetops or along the edges of heavy swamp or thickets of evergreens. In any case he covers ground slowly, traveling the route that will permit motion through the woods with a minimum of noise. Feet are placed carefully on moss or rock at every opportunity, keeping away from the noisy rustlings of dead leaves. He travels wood roads wherever possible to keep clothing from brushing noisily through the small branches. Many times a hunter will give up still-hunting entirely when the woods are dry and noisy. This can be a serious mistake. Deer are not instantly alarmed at the noise of a hunter's footfalls in dry leaves. Logically such a noise could be made by other deer, squirrels, partridge, wood mice or myriad other wood creatures. It is to be expected that deer will usually take off if they see the hunter after their attention is aroused by such noises. On the credit side of the ledger, we can say a smart still-hunter will often spot his deer before its alarm sends it crashing away. Again, white-tailed deer have a habit of standing still at the hunter's approach if they think they are well-concealed, or that the hunter will pass them by.

I recall an incident that illustrates this tendency to remain quiet in attempts to go undetected. I was not hunting deer at the time, for the season was a few days away. Following one of my customs, I was hunting partridge in a favorite deer cover up on the Shawangunk Mountain range. It was a windy day with a decided fall bite in the air. The birds were wild, and my setter was ranging out a bit more than he would have been normally. Now and then he would pass out of sight and I would whistle him in. The air was filled with falling leaves, setting the whole mountain slope in motion. There were many deer signs, but so far I had not jumped a deer. Nor did I expect to, for I had taken no pains to conceal my movements or the dog's.

At last there was a time I failed to see Pep for several minutes. I found myself near a high ledge that dropped away below me for 15 or 20 feet. I was not yet near enough to the cliff's rim to see beyond, so whistling and calling as I went I came to the edge for a look below it. I searched the long slope stretching down through the big timber below for several minutes, still whistling and calling for the dog. Suddenly he appeared by my side and at once he stiffened and looked down over the cliff.

Following his lead, I too looked down, directly below the ledge. Right at the base of the rock lay two deer, a forkhorn buck and a doe, both flattened out on the leaf-strewn ground as though they would like to sink still farther into concealment. For a space of several seconds they lay still, then in a single motion they leaped from their beds and disappeared along the ledge. The appearance of the dog was the factor that routed them out. I had stood quite a bit just above them, shouting and whistling like a maniac, and I have no doubt they would have remained there in frozen immovability had not the dog appeared. I am also certain I would not have been aware of them if they had remained quietly huddled at the ledge base and had not the setter come at that moment. At no time was I more than 30 feet from these deer, but they managed to fight off any wave of nervous timidity with the knowledge they were well hidden.

Deer continually follow this practice of allowing the hunter to pass and then making off quietly in the opposite direction. It is fully as important for a lone still-hunter to watch his back trail occasionally as it is for him to be alert for deer ahead. Every time the hunter passes a heavy thicket or clump of evergreens or rhododendron he should stop and watch behind for a glimpse of brown, sliding and shifting away through cover. And it's amazing to observe the ability of a sneaking deer to move with little noise, whether it be through scrub oak, tangled cat-briers or over crusted snow.

Weather has a bearing on a still-hunter's success. Ideal conditions are damp weather or the period immediately after rain or light snow. Dampness softens all woods noises and at the same time makes fresh deer sign more apparent. Connected also is the tendency of deer to hide during a storm and move about for feed directly after the storm clears.

A quietly damp day with little wind and with all dead leaves fallen clear of trees and brush makes an ideal day for still-hunting. I personally dislike still-hunting in windy weather. The thrashing of wind-whipped branches, the heavy sighing of evergreens, and the constant motion and rustling of dead leaves fills the ears to the exclusion of all other noises.

Yet I have several successful still-hunting friends who much prefer still-hunting on windy days. They maintain the noise of wind-swept forests effectively covers smaller noises made by their movements. Add to this the fact that with trees and brush constantly in motion, the hunter's movements are more or less concealed or made less apparent. I see the logic, but so far it has not worked out for me. I find that deer behavior on a windy day is skittish in the extreme, and that they often dash off at any slight alarm.

In my mind, the hunter who is most benefited by windy weather is one with defective hearing. Under normally quiet conditions, such a man is at a disadvantage. The deer can hear him long before he can detect their movements by sound alone. But on a windy day every hunter must depend virtually on his eyes alone, and this factor places the sportsman with poor auditory senses on an equal footing with those of us who are more fortunately equipped.

Old George Drake, well-known to fishermen and hunters alike in the Lower Catskill region, had poor hearing during his last few years in the woods. But he continued to kill his buck with astonishing regularity. George was a woodsman of outstanding skill carried over from his market-hunting days with the old muzzleloader. Several times he confided to me that the wind had helped him get close enough to a buck to be able to get his shot. Until the time of his death a few years ago, his vision in the woods was of the best, even though he could barely read the local newspaper at a close range. Nature might have helped balance the scales by enabling his old eyes to see well enough to overcome his other loss.

All other things being equal, the quiet day offers the best possible opportunities for the still-hunter. It is then he can match wits with whitetails on a more equal footing. I say "more equal" advisedly, for none of us can hope to be as familiar with any deer country as are the deer.

Using Maps to Pick Hunting Areas

An intimate knowledge of the terrain to be hunted is mandatory if the still-hunter would kill his buck by not merely trusting to luck. In wilderness areas of wide scope, no hunter will have the time to spend on preseason trips to learn the layout. It is here that topographical maps come into their own.

If the sportsman has a definite idea as to where he intends to hunt, it is advisable to acquire topographical maps of the region. I remember an incident that proved to me the infinite value of these maps. A few years ago, a friend took me on a deer-hunting trip up into Warren County in the Adirondacks. We planned a week's stay back in the woods, so we prepared our camping gear and started off. After getting in to the end of the road we packed in and made camp. We had a grand hunt; each of us had his buck at the end of the fourth day. We packed them out after breaking camp and started for home after a week of glorious weather and ideal hunting in some of the best still-hunting territory I have ever visited.

The years passed, and my partner of this trip had moved out to the Midwest. Once again I wanted to make the trip back to this hunting spot, but I had no accurate idea how to reach it. The topographical map came to my rescue. I picked out two quadrangles covering the general area and, together with a state highway map, I was able to locate accurately not only the exact route by car, but even the trail we had taken to the camping spot. Many times since I have had occasion to seek new hunting and fishing grounds with these maps. Indeed I am never without a complete set, covering most of my hunting and fishing grounds.

Of course, many maps are not up to date as to trails and highways, but the country is the same as it was the day it was mapped. By intelligent study of the individual quadrangles, an accurate mental picture of the terrain can be visualized. Streams, lakes and swamps are accurately detailed; contour lines show every elevation. Valleys and ridges, steep hillsides and cliffs are graphically detailed. In a word, no area can be strange to the hunter who studies well a topographical map.

Any experienced still-hunter can pick out on these maps the areas to hunt. Crossings through ridge saddles can be determined, and swamp hiding places brought to light. Watering places and streams are, of course, at once evident, and if the still-hunter plans a camping trip, he is able to pick out the exact trail to carry him to good water. The maps are roughly 16½ by 20 inches, and if they are to be carried on a trip, as they should be, they can be pasted on cheesecloth or muslin, rolled up and carried in a mailing tube. Reposing on my den wall is a large map of the Catskills area, made up by joining quadrangles together, the whole mounted on muslin. I have it covered with various colors of map tacks pointing out deer areas, trout and bass waters, and any other facts of interest to my sportsmen visitors. I consider it one of the most interesting additions to my equipment.

Still-Hunting the Wind

It has often been advised by authoritative writers that the still-hunter should always hunt upwind. The purpose, of course, is to prevent man-scent from reaching the deer in advance of the hunter. No doubt a deer can pick up scent for 200 yards if it's carried by a stiff breeze. Generally speaking, it is good advice to keep downwind of any game, particularly deer. I fear, however, that in some areas the hunter will be hunting uphill and down dale all day long if he sticks to the letter of the rule. If the ridge we propose to hunt runs north and south and the wind blows east to west, we have little choice but to follow the ridge. Certainly we will never hunt straight up the side of the slope and down over the other side merely to keep heading into the wind.

In every hunting problem, rules must be tempered with good judgment, and in this matter of hunting against the wind there can be no hard-and-fast rule. A hunter's strategy is dictated, for the most part, by the lay of the land. And in rolling, hardwood white-tailed deer country, the contours of the land are broken up in many ways by cliffs, ravines, pinnacles and knobs. Wind direction over such terrain is fitful and flighty. One moment we will feel a touch on the right cheek, and as we move past a rock ledge the breeze will come directly toward us. In mountainous areas the bright sunlight, beaming down on a southern slope, will create a heavy updraft, nullifying wind direction on this slope. Many times in a single hunt I have found the breeze shifting in every conceivable direction.

If the wind is fairly stiff, these modifying factors will be overcome, but in any case the hunter will abide by the influence of the terrain. He must keep a general upwind direction if possible, but it is not vitally important that he face forever into the wind. A good crosswind, either to right or left, is every bit as effective in keeping away man-scent from deer, at least until the still-hunter is abreast of the quarry.

In hunting a ridge, I prefer a cross-breeze, keeping on the downwind shoulder of the ridge as I move slowly along. Deer often keep constant watch along the top of the ridge in both directions. They seem vaguely to expect a higher incidence of danger along the crest of a ridge. It is wise then to keep just far enough away from the top of the ridge to yet be able to see any movement upon it. In no instance however, will a still-hunter move in a deliberate downwind direction — this simply advertises his presence to every whitetail in the area ahead.

The term "still-hunting" is in itself connotative of the hunter's actions while in the woods. Every effort must be made to move slowly, and with a minimum of noise underfoot. The cracking of dead branches, the rattling of loose rocks and other carelessly made noises are definitely foreign to the progress through the woods of any wild animal, except possibly a black bear or a frightened deer. Primarily, the still-hunter is most concerned with seeing or hearing his deer before the deer sees him. His every movement must be directed to this end.

Strive to Move Slowly

The thought that much territory should be covered in a day's hunt must be abandoned. This single factor has contributed many an unsuccessful day to a deer hunter's season. No one, even the best woodsman, can cover five or six miles of territory silently and with caution and see the movements of game within his travels. The watchword must ever be: Move slowly, watch carefully and listen closely. Each time the hunter comes to a strategic spot where deer might cross, let him stop, first picking a suitable background where his silhouette will not stand out in bold outline. Deer are highly conscious of any new object in their home covers. If the hunter is foolish enough to permit his body to be seen against an open skyline or atop a rock-ledge or big boulder he cannot, in all honesty, complain if he fails to get a fair shot at his buck. The best policy is to stand against a neutral background — a scrub-oak patch, a big tree trunk or a boulder, first being certain the background is large enough to cover his outline. Suitably placed, a passing deer might see him, but if he remains quiet and the wind favors him, there is every possibility the deer will not be alarmed.

There is still another important factor in watchful waiting. Often the most careful approach and intelligent observation will fail to give the hunter a look at his deer before it makes off. If the cover is good, and the buck has been making the area his regular hangout, the chance is great he will return shortly. Any prime, wise buck is reluctant to leave his home bailiwick unless he is badly frightened. The passage of an occasional hunter seldom routs a buck for long from his home coverts. The wise still-hunter who discovers fresh tracks leading away from an obviously good hideout will do well to spend a quiet hour waiting for the buck to come sneaking back home.

In any heavily hunted deer territory the older bucks have a habit of selecting a good high ridge, a heavy scrub-oak thicket or some other spot where a hunter cannot approach without the deer's being aware of the danger. When one of these bucks locates such a safe spot for his hideout, it requires plenty of hunting to keep him away from it. He might be scared off by a still-hunter or driven out by a drive, but 10-to-1 he will make every effort to get back again, provided the source of danger has apparently left the area.

I have had the opportunity to kill several bucks this way after locating their hideaways. One of these deer bedded down on a narrow scrub-oak ridge. Through the middle of the scrub oaks and lying along the crest of the ridge ran an old abandoned woods road. Many years of disuse had filled the road with tangled blow-downs and small brush, making quiet progress impossible. By the process of elimination, I discovered this buck would take to this scrub-oak patch as soon as the first rifles began to crack after the opening-day sunrise.

Twice in as many days I jumped him out of the scrub, but never caught a glimpse of him. Then I decided it might be good strategy to drive him out to a stand, giving someone a shot. I gathered together six of my hunting pals and mapped out a still-drive, thinking he would run atop the ridge, follow it to the end and give a shot to the standers I had posted at the top of the ridge where it sloped down to the creek bed. But he was too wise for us. Twice we jumped him but he failed to run the ridge. He went down the slopes to the nearest swamp, and there was never a stander near his route. He eluded our efforts that year, but I decided to try for him again next season if he still used that scrub-oak ridge.

Before the season came around the next year, I looked carefully for his tracks. They were sprinkled all over the ridge. I found two fresh beds in the scrub oak, and nearby a well-defined run where this buck had rubbed and gouged a small maple tree in pre-mating exuberance. There were many signs he had been active on the ridge, but no tracks of other deer were evident. Apparently the ridge was not used by any other deer, or else this buck had driven off outsiders.

I decided to wait for him on one of his runways after daylight on opening day. I waited and waited for two days but he never appeared. I believed then that he was leaving the ridge after dark each night, feeding in the lower valley areas, and returning before daylight each morning. His fresh tracks were much in evidence each morning so I could make no other deduction. Accordingly, at dark of the second day's hunt I tied my black thread across the runways in two places. Next morning both threads were hanging limply.

By this time I was a bit desperate, so I decided to jump him out of his bed just to make him "git." I swung up over the ridge, fighting my way down the wood road. I went through to the end of the cover, about a quarter-mile, then swung back through the scrub oak itself. I never heard the buck leave, but I found fresh tracks leading down toward the runway. The tracks indicated he was in a hurry.

Will He Return?

Satisfied that I had at least disturbed his siesta, I walked out to the edge of the scrub and dropped down on a mossy patch near his runway for a rest. Plowing scrub oak and brush for an hour had taken a little pep from my legs and shortened my breath to little pants. I soaked in a bit of November sunshine, listened to the red squirrels chattering and the little mountain brook gurgling below me. Suddenly a gang of blue jays set up a raucous chorus over on the next little ridge, and then just as suddenly flew off in silence. Disturbed by a hunter, I thought idly, wondering meanwhile if he had heard the buck come off the ridge.

I passed many minutes in this fashion, planning new stratagems to outwit this deer, for by this time he had become an obsession. In fact, I dreamed one night that I had killed him, but I had not dreamed in sufficient detail, so it wasn't of much help. I had not yet set eyes on this buck, but I could envision a great spread of antlers crowning a massive head and neck, an idea no doubt implanted by deep gouges in the trunk of the little maple he had rubbed.

Somewhat lost in this haze of thought, I gradually became aware of tiny noises, foreign to the normal sound pattern, filling my ears. I glanced across to the other ridge but saw nothing strange. Again I heard a mumbling footfall and rustling of twigs, but could not make out any movement in the low second-growth that separated me from the other hardwood ridge across the valley of the little brook. Without warning, I saw sunlight flash on antlers as a buck moved slowly through the underbrush toward the brook, moving ever in the direction of the runway. He paused now and raised his head in my direction, lifting it until I could see the full wide spread of his long-tined antlers and the tips of his ears.

I waited, then, until he began to move again; I shifted my position slightly until I could bring the short-barreled Krag into line with his path. He was in no hurry. He stopped many times, probably to test the wind and listen for noises up on his scrub-oak ridge. Now he was quartering toward me, only 50 yards off, and still I could see no part of his body through the underbrush. Approaching the brook, he stopped dead-still in a little alder clump on the far bank.

For many minutes he stood there, his antler tips shifting right and left as he cautiously looked over the area ahead. Then in a single leap he cleared the brook and walked into a big white-birch clump. At the edge of the white birch lay his runway. My front sight rested on the runway where he should emerge, held at knee level. My breath again was short, but for a different reason. My heart click-clicked in my throat. I thought he never would show himself. The suspense was frightful.

Slowly he poked a black nose out of the birches, head low now, as he sniffed at the runway. His front hoofs came into the opening and my front sight lifted to his neck as he quartered toward me. I squeezed off the shot. The muzzle blast blotted him out of my vision for just a fraction of an instant and then he lay across the runway, all four hoofs in the air, kicking out his last moments. He never regained his hoofs nor moved from the spot where he first came to earth. The open-point bullet had blasted a 2-inch section from his neck vertebrae.

Don't be Quick to Move

It was evident this buck never moved far from his hiding place in daylight. When alarmed, he simply moved off the ridge, crossed the brook and went up on another ridge, likely staying there until things quieted down, when he would again carefully pick his way back to safety. He was a fine animal with long wide beams and carried eight long points. His dressed weight was just over 180 pounds. A splendid buck added to my list of trophies, simply by watching and waiting in the luckily chosen proper spot.

A buck will often be aroused by a prowling hunter, and his natural caution will dictate moving. But until he has precisely located the hunter, he might remain hidden until he is certain in which direction the danger lies. On two occasions I have jumped white-tailed bucks while still-hunting, bucks that jumped only at the noise of my approach and who then stood quietly waiting to spot the danger. One of these moved into a heavy spruce thicket and stood there many minutes. When I alarmed this deer, I had been fighting my way through some of this same spruce and any progress I made was far from silent. However, when I heard the deer jump just ahead, I stood still and watched carefully all about me on the ridgetop. I was aware that after the deer had jumped I had heard only a few bounds, then silence. I suspected he might still be hiding in the heavy evergreens, so I waited for him to move out. The air was motionless, the day damp, giving any man-scent that might have carried from me a limited range.

As I stood there in the quiet of the spruces, I thought I could hear a faint sniffing noise. At first it puzzled me, but at last it dawned on me that my buck was a short way ahead, screened effectively and most likely wondering where I had gone. Perhaps 15 minutes passed before he decided it was safe, and he moved out at right angles to his original flight. I could hear him moving through the spruce off to my right and then I caught a glimpse as he crossed a small opening in the green curtain. He moved slowly, stopping often to listen and watch, but at last he came out of the spruce thicket, giving me a standing shot at its edge. This was another buck I did not have to trail after the shot.

Normally, of course, a buck fully aroused will move quietly away and never be seen, but every so often we'll run across one who pulls just such a trick as this. It pays then to play hunches when still-hunting.

CHAPTER 6

More Reflections on Still-Hunting

In rainy weather, many hunters are content to stay indoors and leave deer hunting to more hardy souls. But I remember several occasions when I've walked up on deer during a downpour.

Hunting the Rain

The day that comes most clearly to mind was in the Oakland Valley section of the Lower Catskills in the early 1930s. At that time I belonged to a little group of good old-time deer hunters who had a comfortable camp on the mountainside above the Neversink River Valley. In those days, perhaps even more than now, my deer hunting was secondary to making my living. I could hunt opening day, perhaps, and a couple of weekends. That made up my deer-hunting season. My fellow club members were more fortunate. Deer hunting to them was a two-week vacation — the entire season — and how I envied them! I had to hunt when I found time, and I had no choice about the weather.

Before daylight of this morning, I had driven up into the valley in a warm, steady autumn rain. I was prepared to hunt, though, for I had brought oilskin trousers, laced rubber knee boots and a light rubber rain-coat. When I reached camp, not a light showed. The gang members were still enbunked. I tried to rouse out a few, but I was turned down with profane emphasis. The entire gang was in accord on late sleeping. I gathered they planned a leisurely breakfast, then a session with cards and a 5-gallon demijohn of red Italian wine to keep up morale. They graciously consented to give me the freedom of the entire mountain for my hunting.

I was a bit downcast as I hit the long winding woods road leading to the top of the big hardwood ridge above camp. The gaunt black limbs of rock oak and hard maple dripped water steadily. The rain beat a steady tattoo on the flat dead-leaf woods floor. Tiny wisps of fog gathered in the tops of the big pines and beeches. Little rivulets slithered over the dead leaves, making their way down the mountainside. It was a dreary, dismal day, hardly one to fill a hunter's heart with joy of the outdoors.

I managed to make the top of the ridge, where I encountered heavy patches of fog. I was carrying a scope-sighted .250 Savage, but I had the leather lens-caps in place to keep out the rain. I had mounted the scope high enough so I could use iron sights if need be. I had those facts in mind when I picked this rifle for the day's hunt, rather than one of my other pets. I believed I might have need of the scope's definitive qualities on such a gloomy day, but if the rain held on, I could still use the iron sights.

As I reached the ridgetop, I swung toward the west and the big rhododendron clumps I knew were sprinkled along the ridge-crest. I suspected a deer or two might be hiding in the shelter of the big, flat, rubbery leaves, hoping to keep off some of the rain. I was not in the least concerned with walking quietly, for pelting raindrops covered any small noises I might have made.

I had covered only a few hundred yards when my eyes picked out a slight movement at the edge of a laurel clump. The fog had again come down and it was difficult to make out anything more than 30 yards away. But I stood quietly under a big, sheltering hemlock and waited for the concealing vapors to clear. Again I saw a flick of motion, which evolved suddenly into a deer's tail that twitched now and then. The deer was facing away from me in the heavy laurels with its head down, much as cows do in a pasture during a summer storm.

Carefully, I removed the lens caps from my scope and found the deer in its field. Now I could see the deer distinctly, but could not see anything but its hindquarters and that drooping tail, which still twitched every few seconds. At last when I saw the deer had no immediate intention of moving, I put the scope post on its back and whistled sharply. At the sound, the buck — for a buck it was — threw up a startled head, giving me a perfect opportunity for a shot through the neck.

Several times since then I have approached within close shooting range of deer during fairly heavy rains. The drumming of raindrops covers all movements of a hunter's approach, and at the same time dampens scents to a negligible factor. Deer hunting in the rain certainly is far from comfortable, but if hunters equip themselves with light waterproof clothing, it isn't unbearable. We must concede that it's often highly effective. In such wet weather, whitetails move around but little, and if they move, they skirt the heaviest covers, favoring the more open glades and bigger timber. Presumably, whitetails have no greater liking for traveling through the rain-sodden brush than do the hunters seeking them.

Still-Hunting with a Partner

Thus far we have been still-hunting alone, but some of the finest days a man can spend in the woods will be with a well-chosen hunting partner — a man as well-versed in whitetail lore as is he himself. Two men hunting the ridges and slopes together in the right coordination can develop into a deadly deer-killing combination. Old Abe Wykoff, of the Buck Mountain Club, and I had some fine hunting days up along the rugged slopes of the Neversink River Valley. Abe knew the haunts of most deer in that area, and soon I learned to match my pace to his, studying his movements and absorbing some of his skill. Together we jumped many a deer from the long slope above Kitchen Eddy, and not all of them got away to safety in the scrub oaks of the high ridges.

Before Old Abe and I would start our hunt, he invariably instructed me to take the high side or even the crest of a ridge. He would work the lower ground, knowing a jumped deer most often runs uphill. He would insist I keep about 100 yards ahead of him as we moved along, and to help me keep his location he carried a crow call. Every few hundred yards he would give out with a few short caws, and I never would be in much doubt as to his whereabouts. Each of us would follow the same hunting system, walk 50 yards or so, then stop to watch for several minutes. In this way I had a crack at any deer moving out ahead of Abe, as well as a jump-shot in my own territory ahead. Often it worked out beautifully.

One time we started a still-hunt just above Barber's Eddy. Abe went down the trail to the river's edge and he left me to follow the old woods road crossing the face of the valley slope. I waited in the road until I heard Abe's call down by the river, then I moved in, watching carefully. This slope of cover between the river and the woods road, which lay parallel to it along the mountain, is thatched heavily with laurel and small hemlock. It's a great hideout for deer in the morning, before they have worked up from the river to the mountaintops.

Not long after we had started, I heard Abe give a couple of short blasts on the call, quickly followed by two sharp reports from his little .32-20 Winchester. Then, with a great crashing of laurel and thumping of hoofs, a herd of deer — seven in all — bounced up and across in front of me. A big doe was leading, followed closely by a small buck, with the rest of the herd right behind. I riveted my attention on the forkhorn and threw three shots just ahead of him, piling him up a rod short of the woods road. The rest of the herd scattered into the heavy laurel without me being able to locate another buck in the bunch.

I soon learned Abe had connected with this buck as the deer first moved off. His bullet had ranged up after entering the back ribs, and no doubt would have dropped him shortly if I had not luckily broken his neck with my third shot. Abe stoutly maintained that another and larger buck had been with the herd, and that he had taken a crack at this one, too, not knowing he had hit the forkhorn. But we went back to the spot and looked it over thoroughly without finding evidence of a hit. I have no doubt I would have seen the second buck if I hadn't been so intent on stopping the first one. But such is deer hunting.

We both were pleased to have bagged this buck so easily, and within a few days I had killed mine, again with Old Abe's help. This time we were on the flats upriver, about a mile from Barber's Eddy. Here the river makes a wide sweep, leaving a flat several hundred yards wide between the foot of the steep slope and the roaring, boulder-strewn stream. The cover is good, mostly white birch and poplar. Again, Abe worked along the riverbank and I kept to the far side of the flat at the foot of the slope.

We had almost covered this flat strip — about a half-mile long — when I stopped under a big hemlock to watch for a bit. Glancing down through the white birch toward the river I saw two deer. They were sneaking through, stopping now and then to look back in Abe's direction. The cover was heavy and dark enough so that I failed to see antlers until the deer were within 40 yards. Then I could pick out the points on the second deer. As I raised my rifle, both deer spotted me, but it was too late for the buck. My bullet struck him low in the chest. He made two bounds and collapsed; he was dead when I reached him. Abe had started these deer but had not seen them. They had started for the safety of the mountainside, and it was my good luck to be in just the spot to intercept them.

In a like manner, I have had some wonderful still-hunting trips with a partner in Pennsylvania's Pike County, on the ridges along the Delaware River. This lad had a full quarter-share of Iroquois blood in his veins and his skill in the woods left little to be desired. His knowledge of deer behavior was uncanny. Many times he could call the spot where he would jump a buck and, even more remarkable, he would be able to tip me off to where the deer would run. If I followed his advice I soon would get a shot.

Strictly speaking, such two-man hunting is not pure still-hunting, but it produces results. It is made to order for a couple of good friends who like to camp in the wilderness, rough it for a week or two, and help each other kill their bucks. And when it's time to bring out that heavy old buck from behind a small mountain, four hands are far more efficient than two.

An additional point for still-hunters: Often in hunting over lowland country, where feeding deer might wander and browse, it's good policy to hunt over small ridges and knolls. By this I mean to hunt up to the top of these high spots, then look over the little valleys in between for feeding deer, then move across and up to the top of the next little ridge. Feeding deer spend much of their time in little valleys in low ground, and often it's easy to come up on them from over a slight rise. Under these circumstances, a hunter has every advantage. He can approach unseen and virtually unheard until his head clears the top of the rise. Then, with only his cap visible, he can scan the terrain beyond with little chance of being seen. Such "crossing" of the lay of the land produces excellent still-hunting results in lower deer areas.

In wilderness sections, the still-hunter covers not only the slopes and ridges looking for resting and bedded deer. The edges of slashings in heavy forest are always favored by feeding deer just after sunup and before sundown. In the heaviest of timber, many deer find all their available browse in these slashings. The big timber discourages the growth of small brush and offers little for hungry deer except acorns or beechnuts. Cedar swamps are regular feeding grounds, too, and in deer country where high ridges are lacking, any swamp ground may be the hideaway of a resting buck. It pays off to spend plenty of time looking over these spots during the normal daylight feeding hours.

Still-Hunting on Snow

Thus far, we have been hunting our white-tailed buck on bare ground. But in almost all of our great expanse of whitetail covers, the magic of snow-covered ground can reasonably be expected during some part of the open season. Snow in deer hunting changes many things. Many a fervent prayer has been offered by the deer-hunting fraternity that the all-revealing blanket of white may cover the ground next morning.

How strange it is that a deer hunter can become so snow-conscious that the first few flakes on the camp roof strike a hidden chord in his being! He will stir uneasily in his bunk or sleeping bag, get up and throw another stick in the fireplace. Then, prompted by some inner urge, he will throw open the door and find the first crystal flakes sifting to the ground. I can offer no explanation, but many times I have seen it happen. Its coming is unheralded. It drops softly and silently, yet seldom is a deer hunter surprised at dawn by the nocturnal visit.

The snow transforms the hunter's familiar slopes and ridges into a new world. Gone are the brown carpet of dead leaves, the gaunt nakedness of leaf-stripped hillsides, the crisp cracklings and rustlings of the fall woods. Instead, with the coming of the fresh, all-concealing blanket, a new brightness and a tender hush sweep deer country. The deep shadows and gloom of dense poplar and birch thickets are lightened by the new white base. The evergreen stands are limed to overloading with the contrasting spread of puffy snow on the outermost branches. The sweeping panoramic change wrought overnight is miraculous.

Now is the time for the still-hunter to venture into this revealing medium to read the pages of winter's new book. Every movement of animals and many birds is apparent to woodsmen who can read the signs. Here a squirrel has dropped from his den-tree, making a lacy four-point pattern in the snow as he searches for acorns hidden early last fall. A ruffed grouse has alighted from his hemlock tree roost, ready to try his new snow shoes along the hidden wintergreen beds. Now something has startled him — perhaps our approach. He bursts from the ground, leaving only a sweep of wing tips at either side of his trail's end to mark his flight.

Deer have been moving after the storm. Tracks fan out from the fringes of swamp and spruce thicket as the hunger urge prompts them to leave the shelters. The dainty heart-shaped prints move aimlessly here and there as deer feed on tender buds of poplar and black birch. We can see the freshly nipped ends. Here three deer have been feeding; two sets of prints are much smaller than the third. It may be a doe and two first-year fawns; perhaps it is a trio of two does and a buck. At any rate, we follow the prints for a while to detect indications of buck behavior in the larger prints. Thus we begin another interesting day in the deer woods, following and watching, anticipating the deer's movements, hoping to get a quick look at the game before it takes off in alarm.

A whitetail on snow becomes almost a different animal. His senses, if anything, become keener. He is alert at all times for any danger approaching on his back-trail. He stops frequently to scan the cover behind, and in snow-filled woods his vision is as much improved as the hunter's. Fortunately, snow covering the earth deadens the noise of the hunter's footsteps and with proper caution he has a good chance of coming within shooting distance of the deer before being heard. The game resolves itself into a chess match between hunter and hunted, anticipating each other's moves.

The problem, as always in still-hunting, is to see the buck in time for a shot. If a trailing hunter can keep always upwind of his deer he will in time get his chance. But as soon as a buck is aware of a following hunter, he picks a good location to circle, both to pick up a trace of man-scent and to throw the hunter off the track. A wise buck is full of tricks to fool the tracker. He will often head for a small brook, follow it downstream for several hundred yards, then come out again to the same bank and circle back to some higher ground to watch the hunter following the brook. He might even lay a straight trail for several rods, then reverse his field, stepping carefully in each hoofprint of his back-trail. Then with a tremendous leap he will leave the trail at right angles, often landing on a higher bit of ground. Many times the novice hunter will be fooled by the apparently abrupt end of such a trail.

Some years ago I followed a buck in a 6-inch snow-covering for several miles. He tried often to throw me off the track by heading into a herd of does, traveling with them for a while, then jumping off to the side, hoping I would keep on after the does. He tried backtracking, going through the heaviest swamps and scrub oak, but always I was able to pick up his track and keep up the chase. Finally he headed for a heavy clump of rhododendron. This patch was almost round, covering at least an acre of ground. His track led directly into it, past a big yellow pine standing at the edge of the cover. Of course, I kept on his track even through this thick stuff. I knew if I didn't overtake him soon, darkness would soon come to his rescue.

I reached the middle of this rhododendron thicket when I heard him moving ahead, perhaps 40 yards off. He would move when I moved, stop when I stopped, but always kept a safe distance ahead. When I reached the edge of the cover, his track swung around, circling the outer fringes, back to the big lone pine. He then had gone right in again over my tracks. This had me stumped. He could keep this up forever and I would never get a look at him.

I stood near the pine while I thought out a plan. Finally, I dug in the snow for rocks small enough for throwing. I quietly hung my rifle on a dead stub and began to heave rocks into the clump. I threw perhaps a dozen, then grabbed my rifle. With my back to the big pine I waited, watching his back track — and my own. Within two minutes I could see him picking his way around the fringe of the rhododendron, watching over into its center and looking behind him every few steps. Twice he stopped to listen, ears cocked toward the noise he last had heard. Thus it was that he never felt or suspected the shot that dropped him with a broken neck.

The major problem in tracking deer through snow is to anticipate when they're preparing to find a resting place after feeding. When deer tracks have been meandering through heavy second-growth in little valleys and ravines or in cedar swamps and open slashings, it's obvious they're feeding. When the tracks abruptly head for higher ground, it's equally clear they're looking for bedding grounds on a sloping sidehill or ridgetop. If the hunter has a reasonably accurate idea his game will choose a certain ridge for a bed, it's wise to leave the track and circle ahead and beyond the probable bedding spot. Deer often can be more easily approached by circling ahead rather than by following the trail directly. Again if a hunter knows his country well, he might be able to determine where his deer is heading and, by circling around behind a ridge or swamp, get into good position to head off his buck. If no deer appears after a reasonable wait, the hunter will again take to the track, planning new strategy. It requires much hunting to head off a white-tailed buck on the snow. For every buck killed there will be a dozen failures. This type of hunting demands the utmost in perseverance and patience.

Of all the advantages snow-covered ground has for the hunter, undoubtedly its greatest boon lies in the reading of deer movements. The still-hunter who is willing to expend a little energy can, within a period of two days' exploring, uncover all the major feeding grounds, resting places and connecting crossings and runways. Because these areas remain more or less unchanged from year to year in deer country, such information gained in one season will form the basis of the hunter's strategy for years to come.

The Roosa Gap Buck

In the late 1930s, word came to me of a big buck that had been seen for several seasons in the Roosa Gap section of Sullivan County's Shawangunk Range. For two years I failed to gain an inkling about where this buck fed and rested, even though I spent several days each season in the region hoping to jump him or find a bedding ground he used. He had been seen several times during summers in the valley, but so far as I knew, no one had ever had a shot at him during the hunting season. Legend had given him a huge body and heavy, wide-spreading antlers, but for all I could tell he was due to die of old age.

One day in early fall, two lads came into my shop and asked for a box of .38-40 cartridges. I had the shells but reluctantly I had to tell them they were too young to buy ammunition. It was evident neither of the two had seen more than 12 summers. I asked why two young lads would need a box of centerfire rifle cartridges of this caliber. So they told me a big buck had been coming down through their dad's meadow night after night just at dusk. They were going to be prepared for him when the season opened. After probing a bit more, I learned the boys lived close to the Roosa Gap road, and their glowing description of the buck seemed to fit stories I had heard before.

I told them I would be glad to drive up to their farm with the ammunition and deliver it to their father, provided they would show me where this buck came down off the mountain. It was a deal. The following Sunday I went up into the valley to the farm, and after I had delivered the shells, the boys guided me to the little ravine where a tiny mountain brook tumbled down the mountainside to the valley. In the soft earth at the roadside were deep tracks, widely spaced in stride, indicating a big buck. I thanked the boys and drove home, planning to make another visit a few days before opening day.

That year our New York state opening Catskill date had been advanced to Dec. 1. On Thanksgiving Day, we had a 10-inch snowfall, so on the intervening weekend I went up to the mountain for some investigating. At once I found the big tracks coming down the mountainside along the brook. They crossed the dirt road and went off down into the valley fields. I could find no returning tracks, so rather than cover the whole valley by following his feeding trail, I walked the road hoping to cut his track on the return trip up on the ridge.

Only a hundred yards beyond, a rocky gulch butted into the road. And again I found his tracks, an identical set heading up the slope through heavy alders and white birch. I took the track and followed it to the mountaintop about a mile off. At this spot the Shawangunk Range has a flat plateau for a crest; a plateau a half-mile wide, and every foot of this half-mile covered with the thickest sort of scrub oak, jack pine and laurel. Through all of this went the buck's track, heading for a swamp that lay in the middle of this plateau. The swamp was a forbidding place, filled with tangled cat-briers, piles of windfalls, thick, heavy swamp huckleberry and crowded stands of pin oak.

Just within the swamp edges I found beds — one for each day the snow had been on the ground. One bed fairly steamed. I had jumped the buck in my snooping! I took the fresh track and followed him throughout the length of the swamp. After he left the swamp he had circled and gone into the scrub-oak morass surrounding the whole place. But I was satisfied. I had located the buck's hangout. On the way down the mountainside I picked up his coming-down runway. It closely followed the brook outlet of the swamp, and continued all the way down the mountainside parallel to the stream.

On the way up the mountain, I had followed the buck's trail through the corner of a little clearing. Many years before there had been a house far up here on the mountainside, but all that now remained was a crumbling foundation and stumps of a few apple trees long since rotted away. This would be an ideal stand to kill this buck. I could crouch against the old foundation and pick off the deer the moment he came near the clearing on his way up the mountain.

But I had neglected to include Lady Luck in my plans. Long before all this I had invited Jim Deren, of the Angler's Roost, to hunt with me that fall. The night before the season opener, Jim hit the shop about 8 o'clock, loaded down with baggage and prepared for a week's stay. I outlined what I had learned about the buck, so we planned to hunt for this deer alone, to the exclusion of any other deer in the area.

The next morning dawned bitter cold, 6 degrees above zero, with a gale whipping through the treetops. Jim decided not to climb the mountain. He waited on a good stand at the foot of the ridge while I swung up over in a wide circle, following a woods road.

I took my stand just at good daylight. I huddled in the snow, trying to gather as much protection from the wind as the old foundation would give. For an hour I sat and watched — the roaring wind precluded any chance of hearing a deer approach, so I had to keep my eyes riveted on the runway.

After an hour my feet were tingling bitterly. I knew I must move or once again suffer frozen feet. I headed for the mountaintop a few hundred yards away. By the time I had plowed my way up to the top I was thoroughly warm. I turned around and dropped back to my stand at the old foundation. Once again settled, I began to look around.

About 30 feet away, I noticed a track that had not been there before. I rose and walked over. My buck had come up in my absence of a few minutes! He had stopped only 30 feet from my stand. From the nature of the tracks I could visualize him standing there, shifting his hoofs and testing the wind until he had located man-scent from my stand. Then with great leaps he had bounded down the slope and, making a wide circle, had gone up on the mountain to the safety of the swamp. I had missed my chance by a matter of minutes. There was no further use hunting for him that day, so I went down the mountain to where Jim was shivering on his stand.

Daylight the next morning found me on the same stand, but as soon as it was light enough to pick out tracks, I found my buck had already made a safe passage up the hill. Again I brushed out the tracks and resigned myself to coming up the next morning.

Overnight the thermometer rose slowly. The first rays of the morning sun softened the top layer of snow. I had again taken my stand after learning the deer had not yet come up the mountain, at least not on this runway. This time I waited with high hopes. It was Sunday, and an army of hunters roamed the mountaintop and valley below. From my stand I could hear talking and shouting above me and shots from widely scattered areas up and down the mountain slopes.

The sun rose high and still there was no sign of my buck coming up the hill. I decided to walk across the ravine and look over his other runway, which up until now he had only used for coming down from his swamp hideout. But no tracks were going up the mountain. I decided to swing down to the valley and try to cut his track. I had no doubt the noise of many hunters on the mountaintop had kept him in the lower ground where cover was good.

Halfway down the mountain, I cut his fresh track heading up the ravine. I stopped and watched above me, but could see no movement. Slowly I moved up, following the trail until I came over a ledge. From there the timber above was more open. As I glanced up the slope, I saw a movement as the buck sneaked up through the big oaks and beeches about 200 yards away. I knew I would never get a shot at him, for he had spotted me and would soon be within the safety of the scrub oaks.

Disappointedly, I stood for a while looking at the depth and span of those big hoofprints, wondering if ever I would get a crack at the buck making them. Even as the thought crossed my mind, a staccato flurry of shots erupted from just above me on the mountaintop. I took off like a sprinter at the starting gun. I raced across the ravine, jumped the brook and planted my feet in the runway coming down the mountain.

Hardly had I stopped for breath when, with a great clatter of rocks, my buck came crashing down the hillside toward me. The huge rack of antlers was flashing over the tops of the underbrush. His hoofs hit the opening through the brush at the foot of the slope 30 yards away, and my bullet met his chest as he emerged from the curtain of undergrowth.

Never did he falter. He made a mighty leap to my left, bounding over the brush. Fifty feet away stood a high stone wall; beyond, the ground sloped to the valley. Frantically, I threw the Krag bolt and as he left the ground in the last leap to clear the wall, my front sight swinging with him. As the report cracked out there was a heavy thump; then all was still. I ran to the wall and looked over. There in a mass of bloody snow lay my buck, on his back, all four hoofs kicking. His wide-spreading antler points were buried in the snow — preventing him from turning his head in the least. The white throat-patch gleamed in the morning sunlight, offering my favorite target, so I ended his struggles quickly with a shot through the neck.

This was the largest buck — not quite the heaviest — that it has been my good fortune to kill. His antlers were wide, covering a 2-foot spread. The main beams are over 26 inches in length. His body was huge, but he was in extremely poor flesh, with hardly a bit of fat visible on the skinned carcass. Even so, he weighed 202 pounds when field dressed. I doubt I would have killed this buck had there been no lucky snowfall to give away his habits.

For several years, Jim Deren had the mounted head of this buck hanging in the entry to the Angler's Roost. Of the many sportsmen who saw it and admired it, none would suspect such an innocent happening of nature as a snowfall contributed to its capture. But without snow there never would have been an opportunity to learn that this deer followed such a precise routine to get from feeding grounds to his hideout in the safety of the mountaintop swamp.

To the conservationist and sportsman, snow has a much more important value in hunting. Few badly wounded deer need ever escape to die a lingering death with snow covering the ground. Any hunter with even a slight degree of woods skill can follow and find his wounded deer on the snow. It would be a highly conserving factor if all deer seasons in Northern states would coincide with the first snowfall, but it would be a hopeless goal for legislators. I believe, too, that fewer hunting accidents would occur under such conditions. Game is much more visible in snow-filled woods.

Clothing for the Still-Hunter

Clothing has a direct bearing on the still-hunter's comfort and success. It is impossible to recommend the exact outfit for a still-hunter, because of the wide variation in weather throughout deer areas. Likewise, there is always considerable variance in seasonal temperatures in any section. I have hunted deer in the early part of the Adirondack season when the midday temperature was 80 degrees. However, early-morning hunting in the Adirondacks is always chilly, sometimes downright cold.

All garments worn in still-hunting should be wool. There should not be any heavy, bulky overgarment to hamper movement or load down a hunter who climbs mountainous terrain. Two suits of wool underwear or a good Duofold garment are efficient, much more so than a shirt-and-shorts outfit covered with sweaters and a blanket-type coat. As much wool as can be comfortably worn should be next to the skin. In warm midday, perspiration will be effectively absorbed and the wearer will still be comfortable after the late afternoon chill sets in.

If a still-hunter were constantly moving all day, proper clothing would be no problem. But a good still-hunter moves but little during early morning when the air is cold. Then throughout the day he pauses many times to watch, wait and listen. During these periods of inactivity, he must have sufficient wool clothing near the skin to retain body heat. So over the woolen underwear should go a pair of dark woolen trousers or roomy hunting breeches. Trousers, however, are much preferred, for they give greater freedom of leg action. A still-hunter does a lot of climbing — up steep slopes and over windfalls and rocky ledges. Any confinement of leg muscles brings quick fatigue. Trousers are much more comfortable in this respect, although if a pair of breeches are selected with wide, roomy knees and worsted cuffs, they will be satisfactory. Dark-red plaid makes a good color for hunting pants, but I prefer Oxford gray. Woolrich makes a "felted" line of trousers and breeches in Oxford gray. Both are durable, warm and comfortable. By all means, use a wide pair of suspenders to support trousers. If a belt is required to carry a knife, belt-ax or cartridge holder, wear both. A day's walk in the woods with only a belt holding up sagging trousers has left many a still-hunter with painfully sore hips.

A good solid wool plaid shirt is standard equipment. It should be a hard weave and all wool as heavy as can be found. Flannel shirts are much too light for woods wear, unless a hunter prefers to wear a heavy jacket over them. If the weather can reasonably be expected to be cold all day, a heavy sleeveless sweater should be worn over the underwear and under the wool shirt. Sheepskin vests under the shirt, too, are entirely practical. For normal temperatures — which, in most deer-hunting areas means somewhere between freezing and 40 above — the above outfit is sufficient for still-hunting comfort. In weather colder than this, add a light, short Mackinaw. It is of prime importance to have no more clothing than is required to keep comfortably warm. Too much causes excessive perspiration, so that as soon as a hunter stops to watch a crossing he begins to freeze.

Another garment I like for still-hunting is a light, water-resistant parka. For rainy or windy weather, the parka over proper underwear and wool shirt is extremely practical. Of course, it will not keep the wearer dry in a steady rain, but for foggy, drizzly weather or during a light snowstorm it's an effective garment. The close, water-repellent weave turns a good deal of moisture and gives comfort against a chilling wind. Another advantage: For cold, early-morning stands, the parka can be slipped on to take advantage of its heat-retaining close weave. Then, when the hunter takes to the ridges and hills, he rolls up the parka and slips it under his suspenders behind his back. If he makes another lengthy stand, he unrolls the parka, slips it on and is prepared to wait and watch, with some degree of comfort.

Footwear for the Still-Hunter

The most important item in the still-hunter's duffel is footwear. Foot comfort is of the utmost necessity in still-hunting. Much walking over all types of terrain must be done through swamps and slashings, over rocky ledges and steep slopes, crashing through scrub oak and laurel — and through it all the hunter must have good foot protection and comfort. The soles must be sensitive, so he can feel a dead branch underfoot soon enough to prevent cracking it. The uppers must be tough to withstand the ripping, tearing action of briers and scrub. The entire shoe must be reasonably water-repellent, so the normal amount of moisture encountered in a day's hunt will not reach the feet.

Many hunters prefer the rubber-bottom, leather-top shoe-pac, the so-called "Maine hunting shoe." In most respects these are good. They are light, waterproof and fairly comfortable, but they have two objectionable defects. One, they do not offer good foot support to those accustomed to street shoes 50 weeks of the year. They lack support to the arch, and are so soft in the foot that the foot lacks confining control. For hunters walking in rough country, they're not as desirable as an all-leather shoe. Two, the full rubber foot in this style of shoe-pac causes excessive perspiration. For many hunters, this contributes to extreme foot discomfort.

I searched several years before finding the ideal type of dry-weather hunting shoe for still-hunting. My requirements were rigid. I needed an all-leather shoe to overcome any excessive sweating caused by rubber. I wanted a shoe-pac type for comfortable and quiet walking, with a sensitive sole yet one that gave good protection against sharp rocks. I wanted reasonably light weight so I could cover plenty of ground without undue leg fatigue. It was desirable, too, to use a boot sufficiently water-repellent for wading a small brook or hunting through swampy areas without soaking the feet. The entire boot should be tough, to withstand enough hard usage for the investment not to be lost in two or three hunting seasons.

The first shoe I found to meet these requirements was Russell's "Ike Walton." These have been so highly satisfactory during my hunts throughout the 1940s that I had no occasion to look further. Other shoe-pacs might meet my requirements, but so long as I can buy Ike Waltons, I'll be content.

For hunting in rain or melting snow, there is only one type of footwear that keeps feet dry: all rubber. Of the many types available, the 12-inch snug-leg or ankle-fit with short lacing at the top is the most desirable. They should be purchased large enough, at least a full shoe-size larger than your size, to hold a light woolen sock and a heavy woolen sock easily. These boots are light and comfortable, but are not well adapted to long hikes over rough country. Neither do they give good foot support or adequate foot protection over rough, rocky ground. But they are the only medium for keeping feet dry under wet conditions. In wet weather, the still-hunter does not cover much territory as a rule, so these boots are practical for this type of hunting. I always throw a pair in the duffel bag when I plan a hunting trip of several days.

To further assure foot protection, the still-hunter must obtain boots sufficiently large enough to accommodate a light wool ankle-sock and a heavyweight pair of full-length socks. Warmth is a reason for providing plenty of socks, but equally important is the cushioning effect heavy socks give the foot.

Gloves and Caps for Still-Hunting

In cold weather, gloves are a problem. The all-leather, lined glove is too bulky to permit easy rifle handling. The unlined leather glove is hardly warmer than no glove at all. I have solved the problem — to my satisfaction at least — by using a light wool glove with full leather palm and finger facing. All-wool gloves are warm but are so slippery that handling the rifle and operating the action can be uncertain. Leather-faced wool gloves are warm and sufficiently high in friction coefficient for shooting with them not to be much different from shooting with bare hands.

The still-hunter's headgear can be left to personal choice. By all means let it be red in color. Likewise, the still-hunter should avoid any white in his clothing, even a white handkerchief. It's surprising how many hunters are ready and willing to blast a shot at a white flash in the deer woods. Better stick to somber grays and plaids for a general color scheme, and top it off with a red cap.

Add to the above outfit a small-bladed, sharp knife and a pair of rawhide shoelaces (for getting out your buck), and we are ready for a still-hunting trip. In wilderness areas we will need to add a small pocket ax, waterproof matchbox, and a floating dial compass (this we will deal with in a later chapter).

Final thoughts on Still-Hunting

It is with some reluctance that I close these chapters on still-hunting. No doubt a full book could be written about this one aspect of deer hunting, but space limits such expansion. I have endeavored to show some of the thrill and satisfaction that lives forever in the mind and heart of the still-hunter. Deer driving and club hunting, while highly productive, never reap the reward of glowing inner satisfaction gathered by still-hunting.

There will always be, in the still-hunter's memory, the song of a little mountain brook, discovered in his wandering; the heart-stopping clutch as a magnificent buck bounds from a windfall hideaway; the triumphant moment when, by wits and woodsmanship alone, he has tracked down his white-tailed buck and sent forth the well-placed shot that has brought his trophy to bag.

CHAPTER 7

Club and Group Hunting

A rifle shot cracked out sharply from the mountainside across the valley and below my stand. Echoes rocketed back and forth from the rugged hillsides in diminishing volume until their last whisper was lost in the river's dim roar. Expectantly, I waited for another but none came, so I fell to wondering whether another hunting brother had killed his buck. Perhaps, I mused, he had just taken a snap at a crashing, bounding deer in headlong flight up Old Baldy's gentle slopes, seeking security in the old mountain's scrub oak and laurel crown.

Then again, he might have risked frightening a feeding deer by potting at a red fox, which are numerous in these hills. These scattered shots that come to every deer hunter's ears during a hunting day are always the cause of such wonderment.

A Successful and Typical Drive

In fact, on a deer stand we wonder about many things. There is little to do but listen, watch and wonder. Wonder if the boys have begun the drive — and if they've started, wonder how far they have worked their way along the mountainside. We wonder, too, if deer will be started; if they will break for our stand or come out to another watcher. We wonder if deer are jumped, whether a big buck will be trailing the does or a lone buck will be sneaking through the heavy white birch, skulking along the heavy rock ledges, ready to break through the drivers' ranks.

This was a perfect morning for a perfect drive. The air was celery-crisp, with thick, crackly new-fallen leaves crunchy with lacy hoarfrost carpeting the forest floor. No steady breeze rustled the scrub-oak leaves or sighed in the hemlocks. Only a faint zephyr lifted and rattled a singleton leaf high in the tips of bare red oaks. The "crush, crush" of our own feet as we swung up the mountainside was the only disturbing and foreign sound.

Most of our little group of standers had dropped out one by one as we picked our way up and over ledges and washouts, following a woods road that carried on over the mountaintop. At last I was left to make my way alone, to take the highest stand on "Annemier Hill," a favored crossing on this drive, but one that deer did not often use unless forced to the top of the mountain. After arriving at the little group of outsized anthills giving the stand its name, I picked a spot at the lower edge of a bluestone quarry, just a bit above the crossing. I buried my outline effectively in a huge pile of loose flagstone, facing downhill and across the direction of the coming drive.

On a deer stand only the mind is active. The enforced limitation of movement stimulates mental processes, heightening the expectancy of coming events. Nothing moves within the watcher's field of vision but a stray gliding leaf or a falling acorn, bouncing down among heavy branches to fall crisply into a leafy grave. A red squirrel, chattering peevishly, clings head down to the rough bark of a big hemlock, resenting this intrusion of ours into his normally quiet household. We wonder how he appeared so abruptly on the scene, and as we wonder, he whisks his pert tail and, turning, scratches his way up the hemlock to disappear into a tiny nest high up in a crotch.

By now, I thought, the boys on the drive must have spread out around the old Paradise Quarry to begin the long trek up and across the slope. As I waited, I shifted my position just a bit so I could bring my rifle to bear more readily on the crossing. I inched around to the right, facing now almost into the drive, so that the crossing below me lay fully at my left. This move placed a small branch into my line of vision, bringing it right across my rifle barrel when I mounted it to shoulder experimentally, so I reached up and snipped it off with my knife.

At this moment the thin, trailing whistle of the drive-starter came floating up from the valley below. The boys were on their way. In 20 minutes or so, deer might be moving past my stand. But the action began much sooner than this. Just a few minutes after the whistle piped out came a staccato flurry of seven rifleshots. From the differences in the reports, I judged the shots were fired from two different rifles. Well, I reflected, the boys must have jumped a herd in order to do all that shooting. For the next few minutes, with nerves on edge, heart thumping audibly, all senses sharpened by the stimulant of anticipation, I waited tensely. But nothing appeared. Then below me a shot rang out, then another and another as the first stander, far down at the foot of the valley slope, opened up on the deer. That does it, I thought, sinking back against my flagstone back rest. The deer had taken the lower crossing and George, away down at the foot of the slope, had the shot. No doubt the deer was hit by now, and would make for the lower valley to hide out in the heavy rhododendron bordering the Bushkill. At any rate, the action was too far below to get me any shooting.

But I was wrong; dead wrong. Within a few moments two shots sounded off just below me. The next man to me was shooting at deer! Time to look sharp and prepare for action! Quickly then I could hear bounding, flying hoofs; the crashing of brush and rattling of rocks that spoke of frightened deer headed up to my stand. Then they appeared: two scared does, flags flying and hoofs flashing in the morning sunlight as they dipped and darted through the white birch, passing up the slope directly broadside to me.

No dice for me, I grunted mentally. George must have killed the buck. But wait, what was that crackle below to my left? I shifted my eyes from the spot where the does had disappeared and looked directly at a buck, showing small antlers, slowly sneaking through the small stuff, head bobbing as he pushed his way through. Quietly and slowly I brought the front sight up to bear on the edge of the thick brush, waiting until he should come clear. This he did, head down, all four legs bent in a gliding, slithering gait. He showed no disposition to stop, even though I knew he hadn't heard or seen me yet. I knew, too, that he was frightened and thoroughly confused and wouldn't tarry for a second if he did discover me. I shifted the sights then to a little opening through the heavier timber, and as his head appeared I held for the neck and squeezed the shot off.

Magically, the whip-snap report of my rifle pulled the string that threw the buck into a frenzy of action. He reared high, toppling over backward to land heavily on his withers. He thrashed and scrambled in the leaves, all four hoofs kicking furiously in a struggle to regain his footing. Anxiously I waited, my rifle ready for a finishing shot, but his wild movements made it impossible. Then for a brief instant his head lifted and held the pose, and my bullet ended all movement save a last shudder.

Once again, I sat down among the flagstones, partly to regain my composure. My scalp still tingled, my hands were trembling, and my ticker pumped furiously in my heaving chest. But principally, I sat back down to abide by the rules of the drive: never leave the stand until the drive comes through. Within five minutes I could see a tall, lumbering figure spooking through the tall beeches — Big Lew, the end man on the drive, coming up to see what the shooting was about. He spotted the buck almost as soon as he had picked me up, and together we looked him over. He was a nice fat 4-pointer, chunky and round, with the thickened neck of a rutting buck. My first shot had pierced the neck low, tearing out the windpipe and large veins. The finishing bullet broke the neck vertebrae.

We set to work then to get our buck dressed out and ready to hit the downhill trail to camp. I wondered aloud about all the shooting, but Lew didn't know any more than I. He had been up the slope, above all the commotion, and hadn't seen a deer. We wondered collectively how this little buck had escaped unhit to reach the top of the ridge at my stand. As we talked a bit and rolled our buck over to shake out the entrails, came the anticlimax.

We had laid our rifles off a bit, away from the blood-soaked leaves. I was up to my elbows in blood and Lew had the buck's head over his powerful shoulders, holding the forequarters high. I had the buck by the tail, shaking out the lower abdominal cavity. Suddenly a whistling snort blasted out below us, and, with the snort, a craggy-antlered buck wheeled and bounced down the slope, swinging around us and then heading for the mountaintop. He had caught us flat-footed and made an easy getaway. We had no chance to reach a rifle, for within mere seconds he had flashed out of sight into the heavy laurel.

This big buck had hung back, sneaking broadside past the line of standers until he had made the last ledge, then he had cut over the ridge shoulder, following the old, familiar crossing through the anthill stand. No doubt he had stood watching us, concealed in the brush through which my buck had passed. Momentarily he must have felt he had stepped into a trap, with hunters below him and two more of the obnoxious creatures barring his way above. Then in anger and alarm, he snorted his disgust and swung around, heading up over the hill to his original destination.

Reluctantly, we scored the first round won for this big buck, and hoped the second round would not be so heavily in his favor. We dragged our little buck down the slope to the next stander, where we found three of the

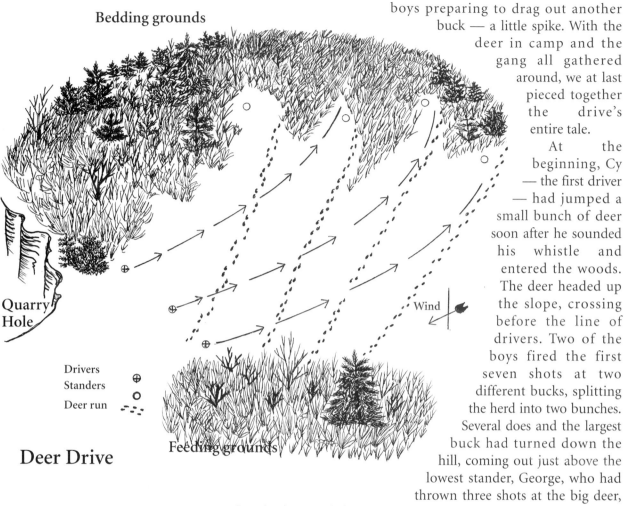

Bedding grounds

Quarry Hole

Drivers   ⊕
Standers   ○
Deer run   ‑‑‑

Deer Drive

Feeding grounds

Wind

boys preparing to drag out another buck — a little spike. With the deer in camp and the gang all gathered around, we at last pieced together the drive's entire tale.

At the beginning, Cy — the first driver — had jumped a small bunch of deer soon after he sounded his whistle and entered the woods. The deer headed up the slope, crossing before the line of drivers. Two of the boys fired the first seven shots at two different bucks, splitting the herd into two bunches. Several does and the largest buck had turned down the hill, coming out just above the lowest stander, George, who had thrown three shots at the big deer, turning him back toward the drive. The second bunch, two does, the spike and my 4-pointer, had swung up the hill heading for the mountaintop. The man on the next stand to mine killed the spike before he saw the 4-pointer, and that swung the herd toward my stand. But with all this shooting, and virtually surrounded by hunters, the herd's biggest buck managed to escape. Such is deer driving, but two bucks among a group of 10 men on the season's first drive isn't too hard to take.

This drive — the "Paradise Drive," the gang called it — was always made in the same way and at the same time of day, early morning. It was based on a certain knowledge of deer runs from the valley floor up and across the face of the mountainside to bedding grounds on the top. The standers year after year took the same stands, and the drivers began the drive in the same area — at the Paradise Quarry — and traveled the same route. The drive was useful only in the first hour after daylight when the deer were moving out of the valley feeding grounds and before they had bedded for the day. Many deer have been killed on this drive over the years. Many more will be killed in years to come. The group that hunts this mountain knows exactly, from experience, the runs and crossings deer favor on their way to the mountaintop. It is only necessary to post watchers on these crossings and start the deer moving up.

The success of any drive is predicated on two principal factors: exact knowledge of deer crossings and runs in a given territory, and the normal movements of deer in the area at any specified time. In general, deer drives can be classified into three wide categories: the morning drive, the late-afternoon drive, and drives between these two periods. Elementary, you say. That covers the entire hunting day. Indeed it does, but I wish to point out is the distinction between the three types. As a rule it's useless to make a morning drive in midday, or an afternoon drive in the morning. Of course, this does not apply to community drives, where 100 or more men are involved in a single operation. Such a gang can drive out deer in any area deer are known to be. But these affairs are not for groups of a dozen or so men, or for a small group of friends.

The Importance of a Well-Planned Drive

By and large, the most successful method of killing white-tailed deer is by driving. That is, it produces the most uniform results. Intelligent deer driving will kill more deer than any other method. In many sections it is the only practical way deer can be taken in any satisfactory number.

Let's suppose we take a group of 10 men, more or less experienced in woodcraft and deer hunting, and place them on any 1,000-acre tract of deer country. Let's suppose also that each man will be on his own. He will hunt when and where he likes, with no regard for the rest of the outfit. The result will be that no one knows where the rest of the outfit is throughout the day. The more energetic hunters will be out at daylight, watching the runs from the feeding grounds or still-hunting the ridge-tops. There is budding danger, however — for any 10 hunters to prowl any thousand acres of ground without knowledge of each other's whereabouts. Hunters might be sitting in another hunter's line of fire without realizing it, so it's not good practice.

After the first day or two, perhaps two or three bucks have been taken by hunters who have intelligently studied the signs and then intercepted their deer. When the rest of the gang learns of these good runs or crossings, they lump together around these select runways, hoping another deer will come along. Then, after the first few days of hunting, bucks seem to be scarce. They aren't moving in daylight. This setup leaves most of the group watching runways in a heavy concentration, with perhaps two or three hunters walking the woods in solo efforts to jump a buck from his bed. After a few days or a week of this kind of hunting, most of the outfit has a bad case of cabin fever. Jealousy and arguments break out as to who has the best spots on the runways. Altogether, this is not a desirable setup among a group of hunters, but it happens often every year.

The sensible approach to such a situation is to bring logic and cooperation into the picture. The still-hunting and runway-watching might, and usually does, prove fruitful the first day or two, but after this period the deer, bucks in particular, take to hiding, at least in heavily hunted areas. For this group to get a crack at deer, they must first locate the bedding grounds and hideaways, then try to move the deer out to where they can be intercepted by the standers. This isn't as tough as it sounds.

In any sizable area of deer country, we will find specific hideouts, feeding grounds and ridgetop or scrub-oak bedding areas. Using the methods of the still-hunter, two or three of the more experienced men will do the mission-ary work to find these spots and the runways deer use to enter and leave such spots. If it's apparent from fresh sign that deer are moving into a chosen spot before daylight, make an early-morning drive, posting watchers near the exit runways. Then have the drivers move into and through the area on incoming runways.

Deer are creatures of habits. They approach bedding grounds and hide-outs in much the same places, year after year. When a foreign element disturbs them, they leave quietly over well-ordained routes. If they are inter-cepted by a hunter, they usually try to go around, but will head for their orig-inal destination after bypassing the intruder. As the season advances and hunting pressure continues, deer feed more after dark, moving toward feed-ing grounds only near sunset, then returning to safety before daylight. Weather, of course, also has much to do with deer movements.

The three major factors controlling deer movements are food, shelter and mating habits. Weather changes the place of shelter and time of feeding. Heavy rains keep deer from feeding, and usually induce them to find better shelter than is normally used during dry weather. During storms, deer often bed in the deepest valleys, provided there is sheltering timber or evergreen scrub for cover. They wait for clear weather or a slacking in the storm before seeking their normal, higher-level resting places. Directly after a storm, large numbers of deer will be found moving to higher ground. Just before a storm, deer will move to lower ground.

There is no mystery in reading deer sign, which is found in most sections of deer country. Tracks, droppings, rubbed saplings and nipped-off branches are there for every hunter to see. The difference remains in proper interpreta-tion of signs. In this, the novice often fails. Deer tracks taken by themselves have little meaning. It is their relationship to surrounding cover where their value comes forth.

Suppose we are scouting an area to help plan a drive. We should know, first, the approximate age of tracks we find, and whether they lead to bedding or feeding grounds. At daylight, walk the bottom edge of a ridge that might hold bedded deer, and walk along the slope's foot where it joins the valley floor. We see a number of tracks concentrated in certain areas or "runs." Fresher prints have a crumbling edge of moist earth, and older tracks are rimmed with dried-out soil. If most of the fresh tracks lead up the slope toward the ridgetop, and we know the valley is a feeding ground at night, then logically, deer are heading for the ridge in early morning to bed for the day.

Next, scout the ridge, looking for beds and, more importantly, runways that lead off the ridge, which is determined by a preponderance of tracks going in that direction. It's logical, then, to drive this ridge, placing watch-ers near the runs leading off the ridge and driving runways that lead to bedding places.

If our group of 10 hunters locates these resting areas and hideouts, a drive should be organized this way: By mutual consent or vote, one hunter should be designated the drive-starter, or hunt captain. He will select perhaps three hunters for the drive, and then pick another hunter to place the standers. The standers will leave camp at daylight for the ridge, sweeping around it so as not to jump deer before the drive begins. The standers drop out at the best crossings and take up their watch facing the coming drive. The three drivers and starter give the watchers a 30-minute head start, and then move into their positions at the foot of the ridge. The starter whistles and the drive begins, with each hunter following a runway if possible, but never so far apart that any one driver will not be aware of his neighbor's progress.

The Still-Drive vs. The Noisy Drive

In a group like this, the best policy is the still-drive, in which drivers still-hunt through the woods to the standers. This system has a prime advantage over noisy drives — it keeps constantly guessing the exact whereabouts of each hunter. As a result, they tend to move slowly ahead of the drivers, and when they approach the stands the watchers get a better shot. If a driver advertises his location by shouting every few yards, a wary buck will often hide until the drivers pass, and then sneak off behind and never be seen. Also, noisy drives tend to send deer bouncing past standers, making a good shot almost impossible.

Proponents of a noisy drive maintain that it drives deer toward standers with more accuracy than does the silent method. I doubt it. I believe few, if any, deer can be driven to a specified spot. The best any drive can do is start deer moving and keep them moving until they find their way out, using favored escape routes. Through scouting and experience, standers will take up posts nearby.

With our group of 10 hunters putting in three short drives daily, many more deer will be seen than if each hunter spends the day idling on a runway, hoping a deer will come along. Contrary to what some hunters think, a drive requires hunters to study their ground and apply woodcraft logic to each drive. If the hunters do the requisite scouting, drives produce more venison for the group than any other method.

In fact, I estimate 60 percent of the Eastern deer-kill is taken on drives. It's the most logical method for the new deer hunter if he is to gain deer-hunting knowledge and possibly a shot during his first year or two in the deer woods. Much can be learned if he participates in several drives with seasoned men. After he kills a deer or two, if he prefers to go alone on the more sporting still-hunting trail, he will be better prepared for the challenge.

The Importance of Well-Chosen Stands

Deer stands have a magnetic attraction for deer hunters. They learn from their pals that many deer have been killed from Patterson's Rock or the Twin-Oak Stand or Skunk Gully. They swell mentally in anticipation as they approach any of these hallowed spots, knowing that when the drive comes through, their chances of killing a white-tailed buck are better than those who might be watching less favored areas. Every deer club has sacred spots. They have achieved reputations simply because deer favor these areas for moving from hideout to hideout.

I remember one such spot near a deer camp to which I belonged for a time. The stand was a huge boulder 10 feet high, which the Ice Age glaciers had stranded on an otherwise smooth, laurel-topped ridge. One year a new hunter climbed aboard this big rock and killed a buck and a big black bear.

The next year, again aboard this rock, he killed another fine buck. Forever afterward, this rock bore the hunter's name, "Brazington's Rock," and it will likely bear this name long after we who hunted with the man are gone. One year I stood with this big rock at my back during a drive, and had 17 deer pour past me in the largest mass movement of deer I have ever seen during a deer hunt. At least four bucks were in this herd. One of the bucks dropped at my second shot, and as the herd scattered, I saw the three others breaking into the laurel. This would be a tremendous thrill for any hunter. For several seconds I had been surrounded by deer large and small, does and half-grown fawns followed closely by bucks. Many of the deer looked at me, but were not alarmed. As they swerved to pass the rock, none gave me more than a glance. But when my rifle cracked, they scattered like scared rabbits, swinging around the rock in tremendous leaps. All headed at last for their original destination, the Hartwood Club and game preserve. For a full minute after they passed my stand, I could hear them crashing and rattling through the brush, snorting and blowing, the woods filled with bobbing, waving tails. It was truly an amazing experience and a never-to-be-forgotten sight.

The existence of established stands simplifies a hunter's post. Experience has proven these spots are located strategically for seeing deer for an advantageous shot, and preventing oncoming deer from picking out the hunter before it is too late. In crossings and runs that enjoy no such traditional distinction, a hunter must study the ground before choosing the right place for his stand.

It's too much to expect a deer, when approaching a crossing or "run," to follow an exact path. Rather, it will pass through the crossing area somewhere within certain limits, be it a width of 10 or 100 yards. That depends entirely on the crossing's geographic limitations. However, at no time should standers position themselves so that a buck approaches directly toward them. It's far better to be off a few yards to one side. Deer will have less opportunity to spot the stander, and the chances of a good shot are better. After all, a deer passing a stander broadside offers a better target than one approaching head-on. Head-on shots are critical in that the bullet must be placed precisely in the sticking place — neither too low nor too far right or left — to make a clean kill.

For a right-handed shooter, it's advantageous for hunters to select their stands so deer pass to their left. This makes it possible to take the shot across the chest without last-minute shifting of the body. That last shift has often alarmed wise bucks so that they never came out to the stander. Of course, there are other factors to consider in selecting stand sites. If a breeze is blowing, the stander should be positioned on the down-wind side of the crossing. If other conditions agree, the chosen spot should be on ground higher than the run. For some reason, deer seem to pay more attention to the area below their position than that above it.

It seems unnecessary to mention that hunters should pick stands to get as full a view of the crossing as possible. And this means a full view, right down to the ground itself. Many times a hunter has posted near a shallow ravine runway, forgetting to give himself visibility to the bottom of the depression. When a buck sneaks out on the drive, the hunter gets only a glimpse of an ear or antler tips, with no chance for a reasonable shot.

Many new hunters have only a hazy idea about how high above ground to look for a deer. Several times I've tried pointing out standing deer in laurel or scrub oak to new hunters, only to have them tell me they couldn't see it. Following their line of vision, it was easy to see they were looking too high above the cover, expecting to see an animal as tall as a horse. Even the biggest whitetail seldom scales higher than 42 inches above ground at the shoulders. To be able to see a deer, a hunter on level ground must look down into the cover, considerably below his eye level. Beginners constantly see deer too late because of their habit of looking at eye level over the top of cover. And if it's windy, the motion of leaves and branches covers up a deer's movements unless your eyes drop to the deer's level.

One day in the lower Catskills we were putting on a drive through heavy undergrowth. One of our watchers was a hunter spending his first day in the woods. We had dropped him at the first stand, and then gone on around the long strip of cover to begin the drive. During the last half of the drive, two deer broke out and headed toward the new man. We didn't hear any shooting, and so we concluded the deer were does. They well might have been, but we'll never know. After the drive came through, we wondered if any of the watchers had seen the deer. All declared no deer had come through. Then the new lad spoke up, saying that even though no deer had come out, two small dogs had sneaked past below him. He hadn't been able to see them clearly but he knew they weren't deer. They were too close to the ground! He wondered too, what dogs were doing "way up here in the deer country."

Conduct of Standers

During my early years of deer hunting it was considered taboo to smoke while on a stand. Even though I began to hunt deer before acquiring the smoking habit, it was always advised never to give away your presence by filling the woods with foreign odors of pipe or cigarette. Once having acquired the tobacco habit, it seemed impossible to get along without it, even for a day in the woods. As a result, I took up the gentle art of chewing, just for deer hunting. As I can determine now, some 20-odd years later, all this practice ever did for me in deer hunting was to inflict a daylong nausea and heartburn hangover. Finally, I gave it up. Now I smoke just as much as I please while standing or watching, and it has never had any apparent effect on my success or failure in taking deer. I doubt any deer, even catching the scent of tobacco smoke, can or will associate it with humans. It seems more likely that if a deer is alarmed by catching down-wind scent, it will be man-scent and not the smoke that provides the warning signal.

My original ideas in this connection changed abruptly some years ago. One late afternoon in autumn, while preseason scouting, I was walking a woods road that followed the crest of the Shawangunk Mountain range. I had spent the day looking over fresh tracks, droppings and crossings. On the return trip I swung along the woods road, making no attempt to move quietly. As I approached a sharp bend in the trail, a deer's hindquarters passed just off the trail beyond the bend and to my right. I dropped to the ground, expecting to see another deer or two following. After a few moments' wait no deer had showed, so I moved quietly up the road to a huge uprooted oak that lay at right angles to the path. I sneaked up behind the log and looked over it into a little clearing in the timber.

There stood seven deer — six does and a fine buck with slender, gleaming-white, wide-spreading antlers. He had not yet stained them by rubbing on juicy sapling bark. None of the deer showed any alarm. They moved quietly, nipping browse. It so happened I had lighted a fresh cigar just before sighting these deer, so this was a great time for an experiment. A slight movement of air was stirring from my hiding place toward the clearing, carrying my cigar smoke to the deer. I puffed furiously, laying a virtual smoke line toward the herd, but it had no apparent effect on any of them. The buck glanced casually in my direction once or twice. Perhaps he wondered about the trail of smoke rising from the log. At any rate, the deer all fed quietly, slowly moving toward a gap in the ridge on their way to the lower-valley feeding spots. I watched them until the last twitching tail disappeared into the white birches, fading now into the golden sunset. For several minutes more I could hear the whispered rustles and cracklings as the herd moved slowly along. Then I rose quietly from behind my log-blind and made my way homeward, satisfied none of these deer had suspected my presence.

To finish the story, I could say that when the season opened I returned to the log-blind and killed the buck, but nothing remotely like this happened. However, the experience went a long way toward dispelling any preformed theory I might have had about smoking in the woods. None of these individual deer were alarmed in the least, and I had laid down a screen sufficient to fill every nostril in the herd.

Of greater importance to deer standers is their ability to conceal their presence from not only the buck but the does. On a deer drive, if a buck is running with one or more does, the doe will usually take the lead. If the leading does detect a stander on his post and become alarmed, instantly, by some animal telegraph, the buck will be alerted. If his instincts are the same as any normal white-tailed buck's, the stander will never glimpse him. When does approach a stand, the hunter must make every effort to avoid alarming them. If his outline is well blended into a suitable background, this simply means he must keep dead still until they've passed. Any trailing buck, knowing the does have gone quietly ahead, will not hesitate to continue through the crossing. He might hang back 50 or 100 yards, or even farther, but if he is satisfied no danger lies ahead he will eventually come on.

There is yet another angle in a stander's reactions to does during a drive. As the drive progresses, he hears the rustlings and snappings of approaching deer. He tenses expectantly, facing the sound. He lifts his rifle, checking his sights' visibility. Then the gray-brown forms approach, bobbing and gliding through the trees. He searches the bobbing heads for antlers, but none appear. Now the deer are close. Still the heads are bare, and as they pass the stand he relaxes physically and mentally, disappointed no buck has shown. To relieve the tension, he rises, shifts his feet, and perhaps coughs nervously. Meanwhile, a buck might have been following the does at a respectably safe distance. If he sees odd movements, coupled with a strange sound, he will stop quietly, screened by brush or timber. Then, if the buck suspects the strange new moving object offers a threat, the hunter will never catch more than a glimpse of him. The buck will sneak away, circling the stand, quietly keeping enough cover between his body and the hunter.

For similar reasons, when standers pick their spots, they must avoid openings in the natural cover. Stay away from fields, clearings or woods roads. Any buck approaching such openings will pause, look over the open ground ahead, then flash across, especially during hunting season. It's far better for standers to take up posts a bit within the natural cover, away from open areas certain to be looked over by any buck before he crosses. A buck might approach such areas on a trot, but invariably he will stop before reaching the opening to be certain the coast is clear. Driven deer in heavily hunted areas are much more suspicious of openings than are deer moving normally toward feeding or bedding grounds.

Conduct of the Drivers

Although a stander's conduct is mostly fixed, the drivers' actions are somewhat more fluid. The best hunters I know make a drive in much the same manner as a still-hunt, except they might often walk through areas that would hardly be called still-hunting territory. If four or more hunters are making a drive, some effort should be made by at least the outside drivers to maintain an even line throughout the drive. This prevents in some measure a buck's sneaking around a driver who might have traveled too far ahead of the rest. One member of our deer-driving gang used crow calls for signaling. Two short caws started the drive after the hunters lined up. From then on, the two end men sounded a single caw every 100 yards or so, keeping hunters in between pretty much in line. At the end of the drive, the starter blew three caws, repeated twice, to bring drivers and standers together for the next drive. This method always worked well to keep drivers certain of their respective positions. And as the drive came through, the standers were warned to be alert. The simulated calling of crows should never alarm deer unduly.

On a still-drive, the drivers have almost as good of a chance to kill a deer as do the standers. When deer are moving away from one driver, they often cross before the next driver on either side, providing a good shot. Likewise, it's never necessary for drivers to yell and howl to make their presence known to deer. Once deer are started, the best policy is not to let them know each driver's location. A crafty buck, once he learns the positions of each driver, will find a spot to hide, allowing the drive to pass. A buck will occasionally do that on a still-drive, but experience indicates the latter method more effectively keeps deer moving.

Big outfits using 30 or more hunters on a drive might be more effective with a noisy drive, but it's my experience that even these big drives fail to move larger bucks past the stands. One of my hunting club's grounds were joined by a large tract belonging to a 50-member club. Each morning, 25 or more hunters took stands on a right angle line to our boundary. At the beginning of their drives, 20 or more paid drivers would enter the woods fully two miles from the standers. They then set up a tremendous racket by howling, baying, blowing horns, banging on tins and ringing cowbells. They carried on throughout the drive, until the drivers reached the standers.

The odd thing about this deal was that our small group killed more deer off their drives than they did. Time and again, deer cut out the side of the drive and headed for our grounds. I recall distinctly one season when this big group killed only three deer during all these long, noisy drives. During the same period, our own hunters killed seven bucks as a direct result of the ill-directed commotion.

Big drives are likely useful in areas where cover is thick and terrain more or less flat. New Jersey hunters kill hundreds of deer this way, but it requires many hunters, standing almost within view of each other, covering almost every avenue of escape. Even so, for the number of hunters involved, short still-drives, planned to take advantage of feeding habits at the right time of day, with proper runways picked for standers, produce many more deer per man than any other method.

Two Main Variables Affecting Drives

Many odd experiences occur on drives. Two variable factors are individual differences among white-tailed deer, and the element of chance — old Lady Luck. Those factors always keep anybody guessing about the drive's outcome. Perhaps the most outstanding of the buck's peculiar traits is his habit of breaking away from a drive's confusion and hiding near an open field, where nobody looks for a deer. Then, when the tumult passes, he sneaks back to his old hiding place. Another, and equally disconcerting trick, is for a buck to stay put until the drive is past or to sneak around the end of the drive, going back into cover around the end driver.

Quite by accident, I killed a small buck that had pulled the same trick on our gang for three successive days. This deer bedded on a laurel-topped ridge near an old abandoned apple orchard. Our drive would start at the orchard and carry through along the ridgetop to meet watchers posted at the end of the ridge. The drive was not over a third-mile long, and each morning we jumped this deer a minute or two after the drive began. Yet no one ever got a look at him after he jumped. We had covered every discernible runway leading off this little ridge but the ground was so dry and hard-packed it was impossible to pick up tracks to indicate which way he had sneaked out.

After circling the ridge and finding no fresh sign, I walked along the lip of a fairly high rock ledge that ran parallel to the ridge about 50 yards below the crest. Because this ledge averaged 10 to 15 feet high the full length of the drive, we didn't put a stander anywhere below it. We believed no deer would jump down from this height unless hard-pressed. While I walked the ledge, I saw no unusual new signs until I reached a cleft in the rocks. Running down through this cleft were the marks of sliding hoofs, and below, in softer earth, were deep, new tracks, three sets in all. Each of the clean, sharp hoofprints pointed back toward the orchard.

Next morning we started the drive, as before, but instead of taking my position as end man on the drive, I dropped down below the ledge. Soon the starting whistle sounded and the drive began. As I waited, my imagination almost made me believe I could hear the boys jump this deer again up in the laurel. Within a matter of minutes I heard bounding hoofs and the rattle of a loose rock. And there, headed toward me, was this foxy little buck who had given us the slip for three days running. We had him hanging from an old apple tree near camp before noon.

On another occasion, Jim Deren and I, along with another six hunters, had been fooled by an old buck when I was certain we had him trapped. This buck — and he was big, with a high, heavy rack — hung out just above the headwaters of a lake at R.H. Macy's summer camp in Burlingham. Each night he crossed the road about a quarter-mile below our camp, leaving a big set of widely spaced hoofprints in the sandy roadside. Jim and I waited near this crossing each evening for five straight days until darkness set in, but he never showed. Then, each night after dinner, we walked down to the crossing to find another fresh line of his prints. Evidently, he bedded at the head of a ravine, coming out only after dark, then returned by some other route. We never learned where.

In desperation, we tried to drive him to a stander. Geographically, we had a fair setup. I knew he favored the ravine's far side for his bedding ground, for I discovered him there one morning on a still-hunt. I had climbed the steep sides of the gully, rifle slung over my shoulder, pulling my way up with anything that came to hand — roots, saplings and rock outcroppings. As my head cleared the ravine's upper edge, I looked directly at a huge buck lying on a mound in a thick poplar stand. He looked me right in the face and, with the meeting of eyes, he was gone in a single leap. He had followed my noisy progress up the ravine wall, but laid low until I appeared. After I scouted the area, I found two more beds in the heavy growth, so I felt reasonably sure this was his favored bedding place. This ravine formed the base of a short triangle bounded on the other two sides by the dirt road he used for a crossing and another dirt road that intersected this one about 200 yards from the ravine. Within this triangle lay a heavy mass of cover: big hemlock and small jack pines, white birch, poplar and small hardwoods.

We planned to post all seven of our available hunters along the two sides of this triangle. I would try to jump the buck and move him toward his regular crossing. Accordingly, the boys took their places and I crossed the ravine far below to carry out our plan. I crept through carefully, stopping many times to look over the area ahead, but failed to see the buck in time for a shot. Yes, I jumped him near where I had first seen him. I took the track, following the deep prints easily in the damp leaves.

The deer crossed the head of the ravine, then sneaked back down the far side, heading for the crossing through the triangle. Hot on his tracks, I kept him moving directly toward the waiting standers, none of whom were more than 200 yards away. Once in the triangle, the going was heavier but I kept to his trail. Then, just as I saw the open area of the road ahead, the tracks veered sharply left, continued on for 50 yards, then swung back toward the ravine. The buck had sensed something wrong and had made a half-circle, going straight back to his old stamping grounds across the ravine. Every hunter watching had heard him coming through, but only one, the end man in the far corner of the triangle, caught a flash of antlers as he leaped down the ravine sides to safety. Never again were we able to drive this buck out. He had learned enough in that one lesson, even though not one shot had been fired at him. So far as I know, that buck died of old age. More power to him!

Three-Man Tactics for Snow-Tracking a Buck

On snow, driving deer is simplified. Once a track is taken, a hunter or two can keep the deer going until they pass the stands. If a buck slips out past or between standers, the hunters can take up a new watch farther along in an effort to head him off, leaving one hunter on the track. With snow covering the ground, any group of hunters can work out their own approach to the drive.

Yet another method of taking deer on snow is a modification of driving and still-hunting. It's not in general use, but it's one of the best ways to kill a buck. It requires three hunters: one to take and follow the track, and two others who keep just ahead of the tracker and as far to the right and left as they can be while still following his progress. Sooner or later, the buck will swing around and cross before one of the outside hunters. As soon as a deer is aware of being followed, it will concentrate on the tracker to the partial exclusion of other possible danger. If the other two hunters have the staying power of the tracker, they will eventually get a shot at the deer. It's not a game for greenhorns, however. But if three good woodsmen can get a buck ahead of them on such a setup, the deer's doom is almost a foregone conclusion.

Proper Clothing for Deer Drives

In cold weather, the big problem is to keep warm on the stand. On short still-drives, the watchers rarely remain long enough to become uncomfortably cold. If they begin to shiver by the time the drive ends, the usual practice of switching places with drivers for the next push will warm them up. For this type of driving, the regular still-hunting garments are satisfactory. Too much clothing builds up perspiration-soaked garments on the drive. Then when the drivers change to standing, they chill through quickly in the damp clothes. This is when a waterproof parka proves its greatest value. It can be worn on the stand and then rolled up and carried behind suspender straps or inside a game pocket while driving.

For long watches, and if snow lies heavily on the ground, keeping feet warm is a major factor. If your feet are comfortable, most hunters can endure a little discomfort. But when feet begin to tingle, the entire frame soon takes up the tune. I find that a short sheepskin boot worn under a large pair of rubber-bottom leather-top shoes solves most of this problem. The outfit is light enough to be comfortable during a drive, yet warm enough for a watch of an hour or two.

During bitter weather in late fall in Northern regions, the best medicine for warm feet is the 12- or 14-inch laced felt shoe with stiff sole and heel. Over this pull on a pair of light four-buckle arctics or overshoes. In dry, cold weather, the arctic should be the cloth type for lighter weight. When soggy snow lies underfoot, it's best to wear the all-rubber arctic over the felt shoe.

Generally speaking, any clothing for deer hunting should not be so bulky as to impede quick movement. (One friend of mine piled on so many sweaters and jackets he couldn't get the rifle to his shoulder. It was his misfortune not to discover this important detail until a buck came to his stand. In the resulting confusion, he managed to get off a shot, but this bullet whistled harmlessly over the buck's head.) Wool garments are the best. Duofold underwear or two suits of undergarments, one of cotton next to the skin and heavy wool over this, will do more to keep a watcher warm than a heavy Mackinaw over shirts and shorts. Many of the alpaca-lined, water-repellent outer jackets and pants, which occasionally have been offered as armed forces surplus, are the ticket for deer drives. They're lightweight but

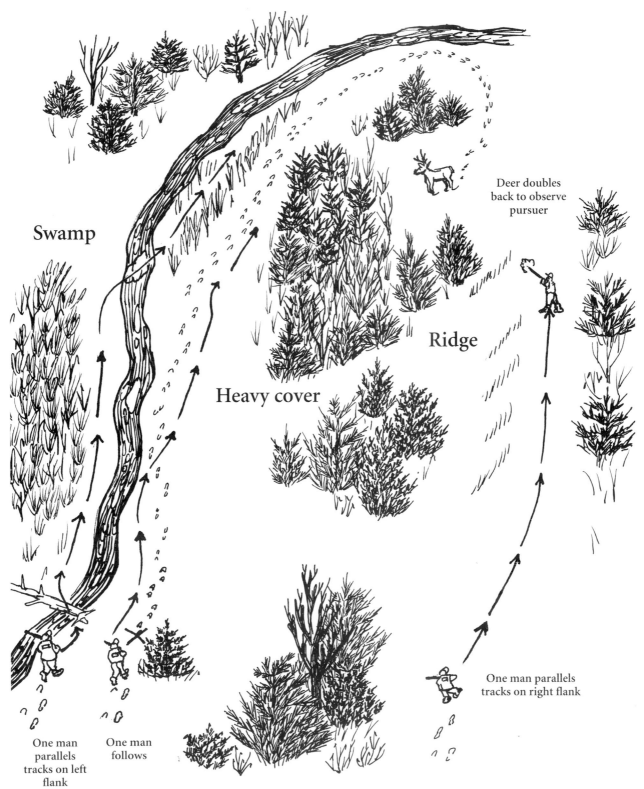

Swamp

Deer doubles
back to observe
pursuer

Ridge

Heavy cover

One man parallels
tracks on right flank

One man
parallels
tracks on left
flank

One man
follows

Three-Man Tracking on Snow

not bulky. They're as warm as any garments of equal weight can be.

If a stander has tender ears and must wear ear-muffs to ward off frostbite, he should punch holes through each one so as not to impede hearing. Many a bundled-up, ear-muffed stander has had a buck sneak up from behind, and crash away unharmed after he all but walked over the watcher. In this connection, the author believes that of all the normal senses with which we're equipped, hearing is of the greatest value on a stand. Most often a deer will be heard long before it can be seen. If the hunter has trained ears, he will be able to locate the deer's position almost as well as though he could see him. Good judgment in this sense of hearing enables a hunter to prepare for the shot. Best of all, exercising the sense of hearing requires no conscious effort. Even so, intense watching through heavy cover surrounding the stand, with the inevitable shifting of head and eyes in all directions, can be tiring. Trained hunters can learn to differentiate between the sound made by walking deer and the step of a hunter, or the amblings of partridge and gray squirrels. A hunter can drive himself into a funk of excitement by listening to the rustlings of the forest creatures, until he learns to pick out the more distinctive noises made by moving deer. In any case, though, a full command of all senses is vitally important to the stand-hunter.

Some Final Thoughts on Drives

While driving deer might not appeal to every hunter, the fact remains that this is the most effective method of taking Eastern whitetails. Obviously, no hunter will achieve the same measure of satisfaction in killing a deer driven to him as will the still-hunter who outwits a buck by skill and woodcraft alone. The glory of killing a driven buck will always be tempered in the hunter's mind by the fact that someone else had a large part in helping him get a shot. Nevertheless, it's fun. In no other phase of deer hunting do we encounter the same wealth of odd situations and humorous anecdotes than we do from the deer-driving fraternity. And success in this method requires a wealth of woodcraft, which helps us lay out the drive. It also requires a high degree of patience and intestinal fortitude to spend tense hours on a cold watch. And finally, it requires thorough knowledge of firearms-handling to kill a buck driven to a stand.

CHAPTER 8

Hitting Your Buck

After all, the primary consideration in deer hunting is to hit your buck. Weeks of anticipation, days of deliberation in choosing rifle, load and sights, plus plenty of shooting practice, all total zero if you fail to connect. Added to this is that sinking sensation in the pit of your stomach when your trophy vanishes in the timber, well under its own power.

Hitting your deer means not only planting a bullet somewhere between nose and tail; the shot must hit one of the vital areas, delivering such an explosive shock to nerves and muscle tissue that your buck will crash to the ground, staying down for keeps or providing an opportunity for a quick, final shot.

Of course, not all shots into the vitals will instantly ground a deer. Heart-shot bucks often run 50, 60 or even 100 yards before calling quits, but recovering these deer is comparatively simple. They leave a heavy blood trail and in almost every instance are dead when found.

Too many hunters simply shoot "at" the deer. They don't make a conscious effort to drop their game with the first shot. Under some circumstances, a snap shot at a rapidly moving deer is all the hunter gets. If his mixture of luck and skill is in correct proportions, he'll bag his buck. We can't forget, though, that most shots like this are graceful misses or the beginning of a long, hard job that ends too often with the unlucky hunter deep in a swamp or thicket several miles from his pals — and no deer.

The Necessity of Knowing Deer Anatomy

To ensure quick death, your bullet must hit one of only three portions of a deer's body: the neck, the chest or the spine. The head might also be included in these vulnerable areas, but no hunter wants to risk inflicting a grisly wound or ruining his trophy with a head shot.

The neck offers two good possibilities for quick, humane kills. Any shot into the top third of the deer's neck with a high-powered bullet of any expanding type is certain to break vertebrae and spinal cord, producing instant death. This is the most effective shot that can be fired at a deer, and is so decisive that I have yet to hear of a deer moving from its tracks after being hit in this area.

A shot in the neck's lower half will sever the deer's windpipe or jugular vein, or both. Such shots usually knock down a deer instantly and keep him down, because of the high levels of shock inflicted in this sensitive region. Lower-neck shots have much the same effect on deer as does an ax on the neck of a Thanksgiving turkey.

Some years ago I took a quick shot at a running deer, having time only to throw into an opening ahead of him, and snap off the shot as his head appeared. He dropped at once, but almost as soon as he hit the ground he staggered up to his footing. He wobbled crazily in small circles, finally dropping for good, all four hoofs kicking and head thrashing side to side.

After a quick finishing shot through the neck, I examined him for the first bullet wound. I found it behind the jaw, where it had passed through low, cutting off the windpipe and large neck veins. This buck never moved more than 25 feet from where he first hit the ground, and completely bled out in a minute, more or less. That is the usual story with neck-shot deer: instant death, or death within minutes.

Shots into or near the spinal column also have a quick, stunning effect. And while not immediately fatal, they keep the deer grounded, permitting an easy finishing shot. Guard against hitting the spine far back near the hindquarters. Any deer so hit will drop at once, but if you don't finish it quickly with a second shot, the deer might drag itself away with its fore-hoofs. That could give you some anxiety before you can follow and finish him off. Because such shots to the rear spine are far from humane, I never encourage them.

Ask deer-hunting friends where they try to hit a deer. Many who indicate a definite point of aim often say "through the shoulders." This is good, generally speaking, because it indicates the shooter wants his bullet to hit the chest cavity. Actually, if you shot a deer broadside through the shoulders you wouldn't kill it instantly, unless the bullet went high enough to shatter the spine and/or shoulder blades. The chest's vital organs, the heart and lungs, lie lower than the shoulder blades. They lie inside the ribs, directly between the points formed by the junction of the shoulder blades and the upper foreleg. Therefore, if you shoot directly at a broadside buck, your shot should land low enough to almost strike this joint, not more than 6 or 7 inches above the buck's chest line.

A bullet striking the shoulder area halfway between the back line and chest line will pass through the upper chest cavity, missing the heart and perhaps the lungs, unless it's a lightweight, high-velocity bullet that expands rapidly on impact. A buck so hit with rifles firing medium-velocity heavy-bullet types can travel up to three miles before dropping from loss of blood, unless by luck the shoulder blades are broken.

Standing deer offer no problem to an experienced hunter. In his own words, "they're duck soup," yet many, many standing deer have escaped the fire of the red-capped Nimrod. It seems odd that any buck standing for a shot within 30 yards of a hunter would escape being eaten, but it happens every year. Many factors contribute to such sad episodes, chief among them a hunter's ignorance of where to direct his shot. As a matter of record, standing broadside shots aren't common, and some hunters say they never get a standing shot, period. Of that group, I can only conclude they're poor woodsmen and, more than anything, they should absorb enough woodslore to enable them to see and hear a deer before it spots them.

A broadside shot gives hunters their choice of several marks: breaking the neck, cutting the jugular and windpipe, wrecking the heart and lungs, or breaking the spine at a high point through the shoulders. Any of these are easy kills on a broadside shot, because a bullet only must penetrate three or four inches of flesh to reach its mark. Hunters often rob themselves of a good broadside shot by shooting too quickly, before the deer reaches the proper angle in his travel to and past the stander. By plotting a buck's direction of travel, a stander can pick his opening ahead of the buck, and at just the right angle, to get the best shot.

I realize that formula is easier to talk about than to put into practice under the excitement of your first glimpse of an oncoming deer. But if your various plans are worked out beforehand, it's much easier to put them into action during the critical moments when game is first sighted.

Many bucks are killed as they approach a stander, giving a front-quartering shot, which is sometimes tricky to make. Assuming the deer has stopped and is looking your way, you have two choices for a fatal hit. Again, if the range is short, your first choice will be the neck, deadly from this head-on angle. The spot to pick is the near edge of the white throat patch, and in a line directly under the eye, at once severing the neck veins and windpipe. If the buck's head is erect, this shot will break his neck. Second choice is low in the chest, exactly on the line where the neck and shoulder meet, an almost certain heart shot. If the bullet should miss the heart it will clean house in the lungs. If your buck's head is held low, this neck-shoulder shot is your only opportunity. This same shot should be taken if you think your holding might not be close enough to make the neck shot.

The rear-quartering shot is common with the still-hunter as he approaches feeding deer, upwind and undetected. It's also common with standers who discover their deer has already sneaked past them. This shot is easy to make. All that's necessary to drop a quartering-away deer is to picture the position of the buck's far shoulder, and direct the shot to pass through or just beyond it to take out the heart/lung cavity. Stated definitely, on a quartering-away shot, the point of aim will be halfway between the last rib and the point of the shoulder. Neck shots from this angle are difficult to make, so they should be passed up in favor of this shot through the back ribs.

Any shot directly from the rear, affording no view of the deer other than the hind quarters, is not feasible except with a rifle of high penetrating qualities firing a heavy bullet. A well-constructed bullet from such a rifle is capable of penetrating completely through the paunch and into the chest cavity. Such shots cannot be recommended, but they've occasionally been made successfully. However, the chances of inflicting a painful, but not necessarily fatal, wound from this angle are so high that no sportsman will attempt it. A deer standing at this angle will often turn his head and look back over his shoulder, offering a fine shot at the neck, which promptly dumps the deer.

If a shooter insists on shooting at a deer's hind quarters from this rear angle, aim low between the hind legs on the chance the bullet will travel through the paunch and diaphragm, and still retain enough punch to blow up the chest cavity.

Deer hunting eventually affords shots at all angles from front to rear. The main point to remember for all these angle shots is to picture the bullet's path as it travels through the deer, adjusting its entry so it will emerge or stop near the opposite shoulder.

One of the trickiest shots is the direct head-on shot, with the buck facing directly toward the line of fire. If the range is close enough and the deer holds its head erect and looking at the hunter, my favorite shot is through the white throat patch or just below it, breaking the neck and causing instant death. But there is one factor to consider in this head-on, head-erect shot for the throat. During the firearms season in most states, the necks of larger, more mature bucks are often heavily swollen and enlarged, a characteristic of the rut. A buck in this condition is unable to raise his head fully erect because of this swollen neck. As a result, the shooter will see little of the neck, directly from the front, at least.

The only alternative shot from this angle is the middle of the chest, just above the brisket. A bullet aimed there will hit the junction of neck and shoulders, just between the points of the shoulders, which are clearly visible from the front. This shot is tricky, because a deviation of two inches to the right, left or below this point will cause a fluke hit. Here's why: the forward point of the deer's chest cavity is well protected with closely spaced ribs, well knit together at their lower points with tough cartilage. If the bullet strikes too low, it will glance down and off this cartilage or the rib tips, never entering the chest, but merely creasing it.

On the other hand, if the bullet strikes high but is not centered in the chest, it could glance off the same ribs to the right or left, and slide between the ribs and shoulder blades. This will cause no more damage than breaking the shoulder. Don't forget, a deer can travel almost as fast on three legs as it can on four. This shot, to be fatal, must be closely held, entering above the point of the brisket, where it tears through and expands in the middle of the heart and lungs, doing a quick, thorough execution.

Preparing for Other Angles

In all the foregoing explanations, we're assuming the shooter is on the same ground level as the deer. Obviously, there are other shooting angles a deer hunter will encounter, so let's be prepared.

For instance, a buck might walk out on a high cliff of rocks or the upper edge of a steep ravine well above the shooter. A shot might also need to be taken in the reverse position, with the point of fire well above the game. This is particularly true of hunters who like to watch runways from a seat high up in a tree. Occasionally, the angle of fire is directly down, as will happen when a deer walks right under your tree seat.

Everything we have discussed so far about shooting angles and vital areas still goes for shots taken from above or below a deer. The difference is that the hunter's view of the deer is somewhat compressed, depending on how steep the angle. Broadside shots from below must be held lower than before, with the bullet aimed to enter atop the foreleg, where it will range up into the vital organs. The above-angle is handled in much the same way, except the bullet should strike about halfway up the deer's side so it can destroy as much heart/lung tissue as possible before exiting.

One other point on above-angle shots: the tree-stand hunter or a hunter on a high ledge above the deer should never try a shoulder shot if the shooting angle is steeper than 60 degrees to the horizontal. Why? When the bullet strikes the wide, tough shoulder blade at a steep angle, it will glance to the right, left or low, making a messy flesh wound that won't slow down a deer. The best rifle-shot from steep angles is the spine, just between the upper shoulder blades, not forgetting the neck shot will be the best of all from above.

Head-on shots from below should be aimed directly at the center of the brisket or the throat patch. From above, drive your bullet directly between the withers (top of the shoulder blades), breaking the spine. Direct rear shots from above should also be aimed to strike between the shoulders. From below, the direct rear shot should strike the sternum, the junction of the last ribs, by firing between the hind legs. This shot will range forward and up into the chest.

Slight changes in shooting angles will necessitate slightly different holds on the body, but the single thought remains: Direct your shot to pass through the deer, to emerge somewhere in the area of the far, or opposite shoulder. Angling shots from the rear should emerge ahead of the shoulder; from the front, behind the shoulder.

The White Throat Patch: An Ideal Target

It is almost impossible for me to overemphasize the importance of the throat patch as a target. It stands out clearly against the deer's gray-brown body, and is large enough to make a good target if the hunter can hold his shots within a 6-inch circle at 50 yards.

My first buck dropped to a shot through the throat patch, and since that day this white target has added a goodly number of clean kills to my records. A year or two after my first deer kill, a fishing partner coaxed me to take him on a deer hunt, and start him off right on big-game hunting.

This chap was a fine wing-shot and handy with a rifle, but he had never hunted deer. He wanted complete information on where to hit a buck, no matter which angle the chance might present. Frankly, my experience at that time was limited to neck shots, so I advised the throat-patch shot, never considering that such a shot might not be offered.

We still-hunted until late afternoon without seeing a deer, so just before sundown I suggested a stand for him near the junction of two runways leading from a peat swamp. Not more than 15 minutes later, his rifle cracked one time. Then, a moment later, steady rifle fire roared from the same spot. I waited a bit, then rushed over to see what was going on.

I found him standing in a birch grove, pale, shaking, incoherent, and pointing to the ground nearby where a 6-pointer lay stretched out. Not much use talking to him now, I thought, so I went to look at his buck. Sure enough, his first shot had slid through the throat patch, breaking the neck. But he had dumped the rest of the gunload into the deer's belly as it lay dead in the ferns. He said the buck made one kick after it dropped, so he thought it wise to make sure it was down for good. I was tickled he dropped this deer so neatly, but the unpleasant task was left to me: dressing out a buck after five .303 Savage bullets had riddled its paunch.

The point to emphasize is that this chap, though a greenhorn in the deer woods, had the shooting skills and presence of mind to follow instructions to the letter, killing his first buck with his first shot. I don't know what would have happened had the buck presented a different shot, but the event illustrates the effectiveness of this throat target.

Many experienced hunters will say that, as a rule in deer hunting, there isn't much choice in shots. I agree. All deer, bucks in particular, take every possible advantage of cover and seldom offer a full view of themselves. During daylight, they usually avoid open places, and when they're moving to or from feeding grounds, they sneak through second-growth saplings, thickets and heavy timber. They invariably skirt the edges of clearings and glades. Driven deer often dash across these clearings and woods roads, but usually at such speed that even a fair shot is nearly impossible.

Briefly, then, white-tailed deer hunters can't expect to get a full view of their game, much less a wide-open shot. We must take our shots as they come, whether it's a head peeking out atop a neck from a clump of laurel or a few patches of chest hair showing through a screen of scrub oak or birch. We must study deer anatomy so thoroughly that we can estimate accurately where vital spots lie, even if we see only a head or a hindquarter. Deer are adept at sneaking past standers or still-hunters. One moment we'll see head, neck and shoulder through the trees and brush, and with the deer's next step the shot is gone. But we need to be able to judge from one glance the direction the deer's next move will take it. We must then align our sights at the right elevation, exactly where the deer will next offer a shot, and be ready to touch the trigger. A slowly moving deer offers a constantly changing target. First the head and neck will be seen, then this area moves out of sight and the shoulder comes through. Decisions to shoot must be made quickly, or the chance is gone. But if you know what spot to hit, most of the battle is won.

Reliable Sighting Methods

Driven deer often spot or scent a stander ahead of them, long before the hunter sees or hears them. Deer are cautious and suspicious by nature — more so when the woods are full of man-smell — and they watch a wide area ahead as they move before drivers, testing the wind carefully. If they scent or sight a stander ahead, they're caught between two fires. Usually, they try to sneak around the stander, skulking quietly and taking advantage of all cover.

On a drive one day in the Oakland Valley region, my stand lay on the edge of a wide area of scrubby laurel, none of it higher than 3 feet. As the drive approached me, I thought I heard a deer walking through the big timber to my right, skirting the edge of the laurel. A few minutes passed without any perceptible action, until I chanced to notice a slight movement about 30 yards ahead of me in the laurel.

I couldn't make it out for a few seconds, but it finally dawned in my mind that it was a deer's back just over the tops of the laurel scrub. This deer was so low to the ground that he must have been crawling. I couldn't see the head at all and could only catch occasional glimpses of the back. A sixth sense told me it was a buck.

I jumped to the top of my rock stand. I could now see movement in the laurel, but no deer. If it were a buck, I would have only a quick shot as it broke from the laurel and into the timber again. I lined my sights on the far edge of the laurel in the general direction of the deer's travel. My first view of him was a small head, neatly crowned with slender antlers, poking around the edge of the laurel, looking back at me. I shifted my sights to the throat patch and squeezed off the shot. Then there was heavy silence.

After the drive came through, I walked to the edge of the scrub to look him over. He was a fat 6-pointer, victim of his own "last-look" curiosity. It was only by the merest chance I discovered this deer, for he was almost past me before I had even a glimpse of him. Had he kept on going to the edge of the timber without pausing to look at me, he would still be safe.

Hitting this deer meant being ready for his first appearance. Sights were aligned, all but the last few ounces of pressure were on the trigger, and getting off the shot meant only a slight shift in my hold and squeeze.

[1]*Although some hunters and sight manufacturers painted the post and spots on the rear sight to improve sighting capabilities of their shotguns, muzzleloaders and rifles, paint is nowhere near as effective as fiber-optic sights, which were developed in the 1990s.*

Open sights have a nasty habit of blending into shadows surrounding the target. Flickering shadows and changing backgrounds make the front sight difficult to see.[1] The tendency is to hold the front sight above the rear notch for easier visibility, but this causes a high shot over the target. To overcome this, the front sight should be aligned in the rear notch against a good background, perhaps a tree trunk, rock or snow. Hold this elevation by pressing the cheek firmly against the stock comb. The sights can then be swung on the target rapidly and smoothly, and the shot released as soon as the front sight rests on your buck.

Of greatest value to hunters, whether shooting at moving or standing deer, is the well-fixed habit of shooting with both eyes open. Rifle shooters using iron sights at once lose two vital essentials of good hunting marksmanship if they close the "off eye" in sighting. First, you can see only half as well with one eye as with two. Closing one eye promptly robs us of our binocular vision. As everyone knows, a one-eyed man has trouble with perspective. Precise distance judging is based entirely on using two eyes. The brain then, by rapid triangulation coupled with experience, calculates the distance from the eye to the object. This point is not always of vital importance in deer hunting, but it helps explain why two-eye shooters are faster, more accurate marksmen afield.

More important to deer hunters, particularly those using the open rear sight, is that with the nonsighting eye closed, all vision of target and terrain is blotted out by the outlines of the gun and rear sight. The view is confined to the area above the sights, but the one-eyed shooter sees nothing behind them. And the man using the buck-horn or deep-notch sight will find a large part of a deer obscured by the sight's high side ears. With a deer moving in heavy cover, a hunter needs both eyes to follow the movement and find an opening to fire his bullet through. The use of two eyes permits a hunter to cheek his rifle stock, align the sights with his shooting eye, and still retain a clear view of target and terrain up to the moment his shooting chance appears.

One-eyed hunters must repeatedly raise and lower their rifles when a buck is passing through thick stuff. The shooting eye is overworked. It must pick an opening for the shot first, then align the sights for the trigger squeeze. This takes time, perhaps only an instant, but many opportunities are lost in tiny instants. I suspect also that many bullets which slam into tree trunks every season would find a better target if the hunter had been using two eyes to shoot.

Hitting Running Deer

On deer drives, most shots involve walking, trotting or running deer. It's always to a hunter's advantage, of course, to have a standing shot, but too few hunters try to make a moving deer stop for a second or two. By remaining silent, they miss a better chance to plant a bullet where it will do the best job. Granted, there isn't much chance of stopping a frightened buck or one that has seen a stander. But if a buck doesn't seem alarmed and hasn't located the hunter, it can usually be stopped by a low whistle.

With most of us, though, the heart pounds too loudly and the mouth is too dry to produce even a faint whistle when a buck is nearing. Often a slight movement, such as shifting a foot in the dry leaves, will stop a deer long enough for a quick standing shot. In any case, the hunter must be set and ready to shoot before he tries to stop a deer. Finally, of course, the best way to stop a buck is with a well-directed shot.

Hunters who shoot at hard-running deer should be thoroughly familiar with their rifle before even attempting it. This kind of shooting in deer cover is pointing rather than aiming, for the sights are never seen clearly, if at all, by the shooter. Any hunter who can be called a consistent shooter on running deer has developed a smooth technique of so cheeking his rifle stock that he knows instinctively his sights are properly lined up without hesitating to check. For in shooting at running deer, more than any one other field of sport, "he who hesitates is lost."

If there is any regular procedure of shooting at a running deer, this is it: Swing the rifle with the deer's directional flight, finding an opening, if possible, ahead of the deer. When he appears there, let him have it. The swing must be just like swinging a shotgun, smooth and steady, with the eyes watching the deer rather than the sights.

Such shooting is tricky to the nth degree and requires practiced skill with the rifle, produced by repeated handling of that particular gun. At close range, consciously leading a deer with the rifle, much as a bird shooter leads a grouse, is not necessary. The swing's follow-through is enough, if the shot is fired when the eye signals the sights are on target.

Vital hits are hard to make on running deer, but it helps if the sights are kept low on the target and well ahead. I like to swing the rifle under the deer's forelegs, forward then to under the neck, and fire at this instant. This always places the bullet in the neck or shoulder region and often grounds the deer at once.

Bounding or jumping bucks are something else again. To connect with these acrobats, everything we have said in regard to running deer applies, except that effort must be made to time the jumps, and the shot should be released when the deer's hoofs hit the ground. The hunter must estimate instantly just about where the deer will land on its next jump or two, throw his sights to this spot, and hold well down toward ground level. Then, as soon as those flying hoofs touch earth, the bullet must be on its way. This low holding of sights is essential in this kind of shooting, for the deer's body is low to the ground in the middle of his spring. Misses at bounding deer invariably are high shots, sometimes 12 or 14 feet above the ground. A high average on bounding deer is one hit for every three shots, proof that this type of work on deer requires the smoothest gun-handling, the best muscular coordination, and keenest judgment in making quick decisions.

Not too much can be said for a hunter who shoots at "flags." These straightaway shots at running deer rarely produce a fatal hit except by pure luck, and in most cases the shooter can't tell whether his target is a buck or doe, for the head is pretty well hidden from view. Flag shooting is excusable only if a hit has already been scored on a deer and it is trying to escape. Under other circumstances, flag shooting is never acceptable.

Finishing Off a Deer

After a deer has dropped to your shot, whether well-placed or not, it's the proper part of ethical hunting to finish him off as quickly as possible. A few of the old-time hunters would let a badly crippled deer linger in death, believing the deer would bleed out better. This is not only disgusting, but heartlessly and extremely criminal. It only serves to satisfy a sadistic urge that's planted in the black souls of a few gunners. Finish your buck — from a safe distance, bear in mind — with a single shot through the middle of the neck at the halfway point between jaw and shoulder. Better work around your deer and make this shot from an angle above the neck as it lies stretched out. The bullet will then sever the jugular veins and arteries, bleeding the carcass well, and break the spinal cord, instantly terminating the animal's agonies. And don't worry about a bullet hole through the neck spoiling your trophy. The taxidermist can easily sew up such holes so they won't be noticed.

Strangely enough, many deer hunters seem to think the traditional coup de grace should be made with a knife. To this end, we find the less-experienced hunter carries a huge Bowie-type knife — presumably for the purpose of finishing off a deer. For my part, though I have killed many deer, I have yet to puncture a buckskin with my knife until I prepare to dress the deer.

Some tragedies and more near tragedies have occurred — not to mention loss of deer — through this urge to use the knife. Hunters who should know better have laid down their rifles, unsheathed their knives and approached a wounded or dying deer. The blade's first prick sometimes brings a buck to alarming life, either to battle with the foolish soul or to escape to the nearest thicket if the timid knife wielder didn't make a decisive cut.

My one experience in this connection occurred during the 1938 season. I had walked up on a huge buck as it fed on the far side of a little knoll. My first glimpse of him showed just antler tips above the scrubby white birch. Either he heard my footsteps or sensed me, right at that moment. Raising his heavy rack for a better look, he offered a clean, clear open shot at his throat. I was ready. At the shot he thumped heavily to the ground, as motionless as death itself. Confidently, for I knew my bullet had centered that white throat patch, I approached. His sturdy forelegs were stretched forward, cradling that massively crowned head. His eyelids were drooping in death, and blood welled slowly from his nostrils. Fascinated by the heavy body and the magnificence of his antlers (he was then my biggest buck), I found myself standing almost over him. Suddenly I was aware he wasn't yet dead. His flanks heaved gently and a wisp of steam flowed from the crimsoned muzzle. Hastily, I snicked back my bolt to reload for the finishing neck shot. Because I was certain he would never move again, I had failed to eject the fired case and load a new round into the chamber.

With the click of the bolt, the buck was instantly on his hoofs, sweeping those sharp hoofs and heavy tines around and almost under my rifle muzzle. There was no semblance of attack. Rather, he wheeled as he left the ground, vainly trying to reach shelter in the birch clump behind. At his second leap my bullet smashed through ribs and chest, crashing him to the ground, this time for keeps.

This buck had been hit neatly through the neck, but his head had been cocked around a bit on a quartering angle. The bullet had sneaked through without severing neck vertebrae. All of the neck veins had been cleanly cut, and he would undoubtedly have expired on the spot if I had not alarmed him by my too-close approach.

My imagination is sufficiently vivid to paint a grim picture of the scene had I attempted to "stick" this buck. He weighed, cleanly hog-dressed and on tested scales, 196 pounds. His antlers carried heavy beams, with a 23-inch spread and 10 perfect points. Tangle with such a buck with only a knife? No, thank you. I'll continue to finish my deer with the rifle.

Deer Responses to Bullet Impacts

Deer undergo a variety of reactions after being hit in a vital area. Spine and neck shots, of course, ground a deer at once, whether the buck is standing or running when hit. But many deer vitally hit continue their flight for varying distances up to 100 or more yards before dropping. There is a difference, too, in reaction to a shot through the heart or lungs, dependent on the deer's activity at the time of impact.

A standing deer that has not been alarmed, and is unsuspicious of possible danger, often goes down at once if hit anywhere in the body area. If the bullet finds the lungs or heart, the betting is 10-1 that the deer won't again regain his hoofs. The bullet's impact has been a surprise and terrific shock to a quiet nervous system, so much so that muscles won't react to the brain message.

Running deer, or alarmed deer, often keep right on going, though their hearts and lungs might be shot to pieces. They are frightened, and their nervous and muscular reactions are at such a pitch that the bullet's shock doesn't have such stunning effect. These deer, so hit, run until the chest cavity fills up with blood, stopping lung and heart action until, at last, they can stand no longer. They literally suffocate, rather than die from loss of blood or shock.

Modern science indicates an additional factor in this connection.

Among the higher mammals, the adrenal glands immediately send into the bloodstream their charge of adrenaline as soon as fright, anger or alarm stimulates them. This quick spurt of adrenaline often keeps a heart-shot buck on his hoofs until death overtakes him.

Only a couple of years ago, I made an incoming quartering shot at a small buck, hitting him at the junction of neck and shoulder with a bullet packing high amounts of striking energy. The buck was running before a drive at the time I fired, but he showed no ill effect. Rather, he increased his speed. Thinking I might have missed or made a fluke hit, I swung and fired again as he passed below, luckily breaking his neck.

When I opened up the chest cavity, the heart, intact, rolled onto the ground, completely cut off from veins and arteries, the result of my first shot. The bullet had not come out, proving this buck took the full blow of 2,500 foot-pounds of muzzle energy at 30 yards and had not even flinched! This deer, although not shot at before reaching me, had been scared by drivers and standers, and must have felt a high degree of tension.

Paunch-shot deer — that is, deer shot through the body anywhere behind the diaphragm — usually present a tracking problem. A great many of these deer are lost. Rifles using cartridges of medium power and medium velocity don't deliver enough shock to put down a deer with a paunch shot.

Although high-velocity cartridges often deliver the necessary shock to put a deer down for the count when struck far back, we can't depend on it. Try always to keep your bullet well ahead of the stomach region if you want to hang up some venison. Deer shot in this stomach area leave a thin blood trail. After a short time, the holes might close up, cutting off even that small amount of blood. If this happens on bare ground, there is little chance of recovering that buck.

When to Trail Wounded Deer

Trailing wounded deer brings up new problems under current hunting conditions. The advice of experienced hunters in the old days of deer hunting — still good advice — was to sit 30 minutes and smoke a few pipes of tobacco before taking up the trail, allowing the deer to lie down and stiffen up. In wilderness country or when bow-hunting, no better advice could be given.

But today, most deer are killed in areas heavily populated with hunters. Many of these hunters, unhappily, are ready and willing to claim wounded deer, and not much can be done about it. It's remarkable how many hunters will make a beeline for a spot where a shot or two has just been fired, on the off-chance a wounded deer will run into them. If they're really lucky, it will drop dead at their feet or offer an easy finishing shot.

Sportsmanship seems to have little effect in areas with heavy hunting, possession being 10 points of the law. Many unpleasant scenes have risen from this wounded-deer problem. Under such conditions, the best advice is to follow your deer at once, and finish it off as soon as possible. Better yet, make a clean hit, dropping your deer for good. The trailing worry will be over. If you're sure your bullet struck a vital spot, a quick follow-up is in order, for the deer won't go too far. Also, as long as your deer is in your sights, keep throwing lead at him. And when he goes down, keep him down, even if it means emptying your gun and reloading. No one hates to see a deer mutilated by expanding bullets more than I do, but it's better than allowing a wounded deer to escape.

When you're not sure where your shot struck, you can find good information in the blood trail left by your wounded deer. Look for blood stains on trees, brush and saplings along the deer's trail. From the height of these above the ground, you can estimate how high or low the deer is hit. Examine the blood for color and quantity. If it's bright red and plentiful, your bullet severed large arteries and quick death has likely come to your buck. Further indication of large artery hits is blood squirting out from the deer's path for several feet.

When these signs are abundant, follow the deer at once, because it will probably be dead by the time you overtake him. Small quantities of dark blood in the trail, with no evidence of arterial squirts, are almost certain evidence the deer is lightly hit, or paunched. It's the better part of discretion to sit an hour or more, then take up the trail in the hope another hunter is not ahead of you.

An additional point: Be most reluctant to believe you missed when a deer runs off after your shot. Deer often show little sign of being hit, particularly if they were running at the time. Old-timers state with conviction that a buck drops its tail when hit, but I'm not convinced. I've had many reports to the contrary in my years of deer hunting.

Deer normally begin to bleed within a dozen yards of where they were hit. However, a shot far back, even though the bullet might have ranged into the chest, might not cause heavy bleeding for 50 or 75 yards. If the buck runs, apparently unharmed, after you shoot, don't run after him. Strangely enough, this often happens when a new hunter shoots at his first buck.

It's far better to stand still and pick out the spot where the deer happened to be when your rifle cracked. Drop your cap or handkerchief on the ground where you were standing when you shot. You might want to know this later. Only after marking the two spots should you look for signs of a hit.

Perhaps the most tangible evidence of a hit, other than blood, is a tuft of deer-hair on the ground near the scene. I think it's virtually impossible to hit a deer anywhere on its body without cutting off a bit of hair. Invariably you'll find the hair before you find blood. Unless a rapidly expanding bullet rips through heavy arteries, a running deer will not bleed during its first few jumps. In any case, spend all the time you need to be thoroughly convinced you did, after all, miss.

Back in the early 1930s, I jumped a buck from atop a big beech ridge. I glimpsed antlers just as he cleared the ridge on his way down. In a few leaps he had reached the adjoining ridge and was nearly out of sight. I fired a quick snap-shot just as he quartered over and down, flag flying and hoofs pounding.

Not willing to believe I could have had such phenomenal luck as to hit him, I hunted on down the beech ridge as I had intended. I spent a quiet hour working the end of this ridge, then I worked back. I decided to wander over to the little ridge where the buck had disappeared and look over his tracks.

I found tracks to be sure — great leaps that had carried him down the ridge slope and over the next, digging up the soft humus and scattering ground-pine from his path. Just over the ridge where I had fired my lone shot, I found a last bunch of four deep hoofprints. Then, to my surprise, I saw an upheaval of crisp leaves and sweet fern changing quickly to a dragging path down the steep slope, and at its end, my buck. There he lay, head curled about his neck, his antlers tangled in a tiny hemlock.

The little .250 Savage bullet had caught him in the right flank as he quartered away. It passed through the diaphragm, blowing up within the chest. The shock must have been terrific, for he did not regain his hoofs. How fortunate that I had been curious enough about my shot to check on that buck, and then found him. Even though I shouldn't assume any shot was in vain, I was thoroughly convinced I had made an excusable miss!

By all means then, follow up each shot with intelligent observation. Not all misses told about each year are really misses. As a matter of record, deer too often have struggled off to die and rot in a nearby scrub-oak thicket or spruce swamp. For reasons of sportsmanship and good conservation, every effort should be made to follow every shot, never quitting until convinced the deer still freely roams his range.

Deer Hunting with Shotguns

So far, everything we've said applies to the rifle shooter, but many deer hunters are not riflemen, either by choice, economic necessity, or local or state legislation. Many deer are shot at and killed with buckshot each year, and almost as many are wounded and not killed. Buckshot is a deadly load when it's properly handled and will kill any animal in North America within the limits of its range. But that range is short, because of the pattern's scattering tendency. Therefore, the buckshot slinger should know not only when to shoot, but also when not to shoot.

I place the outside limit of buckshot effectiveness on deer, regardless of shot size, at 50 yards. Furthermore, clean kills cannot be expected past 30 yards. Double "O" buckshot is large in size, but scatters widely even at short range. The single "O" load is better balanced and holds a good killing pattern to a farther range, but even this range is not farther than 50 yards. Granted, a deer will occasionally be dropped with buckshot at ranges of 100 or more yards, but one buck doesn't make a habit. Buckshot shooters must make a series of pattern tests with their guns and load before going into the deer woods. Only then will they know how far to take the shot.

Whenever possible, buckshot should be directed at the deer's neck. Shoulder shots ground deer promptly at close range, but so will the neck shot. Under all circumstances, I unreservedly suggest only the neck shot when hunting with buckshot.

A better load for the shotgun toter is the rifled slug, not the round single ball, which is hopelessly inaccurate. Rifled slugs are fairly accurate at normal deer-hunting ranges. Because of slight inaccuracies in loads, as well as the coarse sights found on shotguns, the rifled-slug load will be most effective aimed to strike low in the chest cavity, rather than to try for neck or spine shots. The terrific shock of these heavy slugs with their high striking energy, does good work on whitetails if placed in the chest.

Peep Sights and Riflescopes

With all kinds of rifles and every type of sights, many misses are made because of hasty shooting. Speed is necessary, but not undue haste, because this causes many high shots from holding the front sight too high over the rear notch. Overshooting deer is well marked in hunters who use deep-notch rear sights. In their haste to shoot, they unconsciously throw their front sight well above the notch where it can clearly be seen. When the rifle cracks, the bullet passes over the deer's back.

The aperture rear sight eliminates that cause of overshooting, because the front sight can only be held in one position relative to the rear sight: through the middle of the peep. It makes no difference in the size of the aperture. A front sight can be seen only through the hole's center, and the centers of all circles are the same regardless of diameters.

Good telescopic sights are a big help in hitting deer in the vital spot. Their wide field of view and great light-gathering powers make it easy to pick out deer under poor light conditions. Let's also not forget antlers show up readily on a buck's head when viewed through a riflescope.

An experienced scope shooter who knows his rifle can do remarkable work snap-shooting at running deer at close range. The scope so magnifies the target at close range that the shooter needs only to catch the forequarters of the deer in the scope to make a hit. After some practice, a riflescope user can take running shots and score a high average of hits, merely by catching the moving deer near the center of the scope's field of view.

It also goes without saying that a hunter equipped with the right riflescope can not only pick the vital areas to hit, but can almost call his shot to a finger-breadth. Neck shots on standing deer are much simpler with riflescopes, and one of their best features is the user's ability to pick out openings through timber and brush to find the deer and deliver the shot. Trees, saplings and other possible obstructions are clearly defined through the scope. Therefore, the shooter has little excuse for hitting intervening trees with his bullet.

At least three out of 10 hunters who buy deer licenses each year know where to hit a deer to kill it quickly and humanely. Unfortunately, I estimate only one in three can hit that spot consistently. All hunters need practice with the rifle, and this practice eventually leads to bringing home the bacon instead of making the usual alibis.

Deer hunters don't need to be expert shots, judged by the standards of the target shooter, but they must be able to lift their weapon, align the sights and squeeze off the shot, smoothly and effortlessly. And they must be able to do those things in almost a single movement, without wasting time looking for sights or the deer after the rifle comes to the shoulder. They must also be able to hold all their shots within an 8-inch circle at 50 yards in the standing, or off-hand, position. And they must do it without regard to stance or the deer's position. They should also be able to get all of their shots into the 8-inch bull within three seconds for each shot. Any shooter who can do that will seldom leave the woods with a flock of excuses for his season's work.

This standard of excellence is not too difficult for hunters of normal vision and average abilities. If anything, it's somewhat under par for a good rifleman.

A Valued Teacher: The .22 Rifle

Perhaps no weapon plays a more important part in the shooting skill of a deer hunter than the .22-caliber rifle. It's highly accurate, inexpensive to shoot, safe to use near settled communities, light in report and recoil, and gives the best opportunity for off-season deer-hunting practice. No matter what type of high-power rifle action a deer hunter uses in the woods, he can get its counterpart in a smaller .22-rifle: autoloader, slide-action, lever-action or bolt-action. Equipped with the same kind of sights as on his high-powered rifle, and with a trigger-pull adjusted to equal weight and crispness, the .22 rifle can almost duplicate the performance of a pet deer rifle. It lacks the weight, certainly, but weight can be added to butt stock and forearm by the hunter or by a gunsmith. This rifle has all the features needed for intelligent rifle shooting except recoil. But for practice, deer hunters are better off without the recoil.

Recoil plays a vital part in a deer hunter's shooting, especially if the hunter spends little time in practice. Why? Recoil is a major contributor to the flinching habit. No rifleman can expect to kill deer if he's a flincher. The jerk that accompanies the flinch always throws the sights far off the mark before the shot is fired. A great deal can be done to prevent flinching if the shooter begins with a .22-caliber rifle, developing a good trigger squeeze. Then, after learning the importance a good trigger squeeze plays in accurate shooting and "calling the shot," the shooter can apply it to the high-powered rifle.

No rifle-shot is worthy of the name unless he can call his shots with a degree of accuracy. Otherwise, he will never know whether his sights are correctly adjusted. Calling the shot simply means retaining an image in the mind's eye of how the sights looked in reference to the target at the exact moment recoil blotted out the shooter's view of the target. From this retained picture, the shooter knows where the shot should have hit. If the bullet didn't hit there, the sights are not looking where the rifle shoots, and should be adjusted to better suit the line of fire.

Trigger pulls on many rifles as they leave the factory are atrocious. They often pull 8 to 10 pounds, and have creep, drag and rough places that can be felt distinctly as the trigger is squeezed. With such a trigger release, the shooter has no accurate idea about when his hammer or firing pin will fall. And if the pull is very hard, sights will be pulled off the mark, even though they might have been correctly aligned before the final squeeze.

All of these pulls can be greatly improved by proper stoning, and should be reduced in weight to pull off at about 5 pounds. A clean, crisp trigger of 5 pounds' weight is just about ideal in deer rifles. It's heavy enough to be safe against accidental discharge, yet light enough to permit quick, smooth, accurate shooting.

The Importance of Practice

Even in this modern age, there is no substitute for practice in developing shooting skill. A fine rifle, carefully selected sights or scope, and a good choice of ammunition will fail to fill a license if the hunter does not have good shooting mechanics and a good sense of gun handling. Under the excitement and strain of sighting your buck, all book lessons pass fleetingly from your mind. In their place remains only the burning urge to bring down that buck — a blinding urge that transcends reason. The hunter's entire being is concentrated on the deer. He has no brain power left for coherent thought. At this critical period of the hunt, only the mechanical training of body, hand and eye will support his desire to down his deer. The mechanics of shooting must be performed easily, smoothly, and without conscious thought.

To this end, every hunter who takes to the deer woods during autumn in our states must find time and energy to develop shooting skills. This he owes to himself for the success of his hunt, and to the game for the sake of good sportsmanship.

Perhaps the best and most easily available shooting practice for white-tailed deer hunting is pursuing gray squirrels — with a .22 rifle, of course. Squirrel hunting develops hunting technique and rifle handling. Secondly, and available to perhaps more hunters, is woodchuck hunting. Either type of shooting is valuable in that it engenders a gradual familiarity with handling the rifle while under nervous tension. This is a most desirable result, never to be achieved by shooting at inanimate targets.

Smooth rifle handling comes only with much practice. Keep your unloaded rifle handy at home and whenever you think of it, pick it up, ensure it's unloaded, find a target in the room that can be seen distinctly, and throw the sights on it as quickly as you can. This kind of home practice, together with field shooting with the .22 at informal targets — tin cans, bottles, wood blocks floating down a fast-running isolated stream — will do wonders for your gun handling. Almost before you know it, those sights line up wherever you look as soon as the rifle butt touches your shoulder.

Every group of deer hunters has its good shot; the instinctive type of shooter who never seems to take time to aim his rifle, but somehow always gets his buck with the least number of shots. Just remember that no man is born with this ability, and no matter how easily these instinctive shooters seem to hit their target, it's the result of years of steady practice and gun handling, not of favorable stars in their horoscope.

CHAPTER 9

Getting Out Your Buck

Last year, the third day of the Catskill deer season ushered in a cold drizzly rain. My hunting pals weren't enthusiastic about still-hunting or driving the heavily thatched ridges of the Shawangunk Mountain range, which had been our stamping grounds the first two days. In fact, the best offer to hunt that anyone suggested was to take a runway stand — not too far from the road — and spend an hour or two waiting for a deer to come along. Accordingly, the boys moved off to favored spots atop the ridges to stick it out, for the morning at least.

I suspected few, if any, deer would move in such weather, so on the chance one of the gang would get a shot, I swung out of the heavy cover and took to the clearings for a half-mile. Then I cut back into the heavy white-birch stands lining the lee side of the ridge to begin a one-man drive, or still-hunt. The woods were soggy, and every bush showered a deluge at my passage. All fresh signs had been erased by the night's rain. Nevertheless, I worked slowly toward the spot presumably occupied by the last watcher, hoping to move something out in my wide sweep through the birches.

A Greenhorn Gets His First Buck

Two-thirds of the way through, heavy crashings and waving tails signaled the rapid exit of three deer. They headed for a wire fence running diagonally toward our last stand. Moments later, four shots ripped through the drumming rain not more than 200 yards off. After waiting a bit, I moved to the spot to discover an unknown hunter, highly excited, looking for some sign of his departed deer. Somehow this lad had gotten into the middle of our party shortly after my gang had taken their stands, in just the right spot to intercept the deer. That, of course, was his good luck, but he said he had failed to kill or even scratch the buck. I asked which direction the buck had run, but he didn't know. Neither did he know for sure if he had shot at a buck. He had just shot at the biggest deer of the three.

I looked over the scene, knowing it would be tough to find any blood remaining in the downpour, but hoping to find some other indication of a hit. I asked him to take the same spot from which he had fired the shots, and I would come through on the runway along the fence. He was to signal at whatever point the deer had reached when he began the barrage, at least as closely as he could tell. We carried this out. Tracks showed the deer moving along at a stiff trot, then at a point some yards beyond where my hunter friend believed the shots were fired, I found a fistful of hair and two sliding hoofprints, certain evidence the deer was hit. He decided then that the bunch had scattered in three directions. One had leaped the fence and gone into a heavy slashing, and the other two he knew not where. Nor was he sure which deer had been hit. He was inclined to follow the deer that had crossed into the slashing, so off he went.

I continued along the fence, picking up the track in the scuffed-up leaves. Fifty yards beyond, the fence abruptly ended at a woods road. In the middle of the road was a thin bloodstain, with more faint blood leading to the ridgetop. I turned to look for my new acquaintance, but he was out of sight in the slashing. I carried on then, picking up the trail, which sloped up to heavy cover. I had moved perhaps 30 yards when, at a movement ahead, a small pair of antlers appeared, feebly hovering above the sodden leaves. Thirty yards ahead, the buck lay on his side, able to raise only its head.

Covering the deer, I yelled for brother-hunter over in the slashing. The buck made an effort to rise, then fell back feebly. Within a moment, the young hunter galloped over and, at my insistence, delivered the coup de grace through the neck.

"Gee," he puffed, "what am I gonna do now? I never killed a deer before. I've got a knife, but I don't know how to get his guts out. There's a certain way you're supposed to do it, isn't there?"

I assured him there was. He pulled out his knife and, surprisingly enough, it was a sensible-looking blade, about 4 inches long, with a curved skinning edge. But it was as dull as a stone tomahawk. I handed him my knife and outlined the process. Together, we had the deer dressed, skidded out on the wet leaves, and hung to drain and cool by his car within 20 minutes.

Approaching and Field Dressing Whitetails

This year, and for many years to come, new hunters will take to the woods. Many will kill their first deer, many more will not. As this is written, meat prices are the highest in history, making venison on the hoof a valuable piece of property for the hunter taking it. Many of venison's good qualities can be preserved by careful, intelligent handling of the carcass as soon as it comes into the hunter's possession. Venison care has three important phases in this first handling of the carcass: quick, thorough bleeding; prompt removal of entrails; and cooling the body cavity by exposure to the air.

The white-tailed deer has a thoroughly blood-filled body. The hunter's first obligation is to remove as much of the blood as possible with the kill itself. Nothing is more unpalatable than venison filled with settled blood. Sometimes it can't be avoided, but if the animal is reached within minutes of its death, there is no excuse for blood-settled meat. That is, unless the carcass is riddled with expanding bullets.

The most efficient way to bleed a deer is to cut its throat or pierce his heart or lungs with your first shot. Most often we won't have too much choice, but neck and chest-cavity shots always produce a neatly killed, well-drained deer.

When approaching a downed deer, stay out of reach until you can see its eyes. If they're glazed, your deer is now venison. If the eyes are still bright or other signs of life are evident, place your finishing shot to break the neck and sever its large veins. With modern quick-expanding bullets, this is no problem. You might have to work around your dying deer for the right position to make this shot. If you take your place directly behind the deer's back, you'll be able to place a bullet that blasts through the top of the neck, breaking the spinal column, and then passes through the windpipe and neck to exit on the lower side, leaving a large exit hole for bleeding. This shot instantly ends the buck's suffering while bleeding him out.

"Sticking" a deer with a knife is never recommended. First, it's a dangerous practice for anyone, especially a novice. The deer might not be quite dead, and the prick of the knife will bring it quickly to life. Hunters have been badly hurt by wounded deer. Second, thorough knowledge of deer anatomy is necessary to stick a whitetail effectively. I've seen numerous deer carcasses badly incised throughout the chest with little or no bleeding effect. The cape on many of these deer was so badly cut that a taxidermist would have been hard put to make a presentable mount. Besides, sticking a deer will do little good unless the large blood vessels connecting the heart are severed. To do this blindly, with the point of the knife buried deep inside a deer's chest, requires more butchering skill than most hunters possess.

In fact, the process of killing a deer normally produces the necessary bleeding. In addition, cleaning out the chest and abdominal cavity is much more effective than sticking, once a deer is dead. Dressing the deer quickly achieves blood drainage that's as effective as any other post-death method.

To begin field dressing, which some consider an unpleasant little task, the deer should be turned over on its back. Then, straddling the deer's chest and facing the rear, begin the cut by penetrating the point of the knife into the junction of the last ribs. As soon as the hide is pierced, turn the knife so the blade edge lies uppermost, then cut straight back along the genitals to the straddle. The knife-point should lie just under the hide and ahead of the cut, as it moves back, to prevent slicing the paunch or intestines. Now, cut a stick about 1 inch thick and 12 inches long. With this, wedge open the sides of the abdominal cut, giving access to the chest cavity. The paunch, liver and intestines can now be rolled back out of the way, exposing the diaphragm. This is a thin wall of tissue separating the chest and abdominal cavities, and joined fully around inside at the last ribs.

This should be cut through, close to the internal walls, all the way around to the backbone, on both sides. Now, roll up your sleeves, reach into the chest cavity, and grasp the neck veins and windpipe just above heart and lungs, with one hand. Pull back on this handful as far as it will come. With the other hand holding the knife, cut the whole works off. This frees all the internal organs with the exception of the rectum.

Now with the sharp point of the knife, cut entirely around the rectal opening, freeing the tube from the sides, until the rectum can be pulled out a few inches. Tie this tightly with a piece of string, rawhide or strip of narrow white-birch bark. (The rectal tube is tied before pulling it back into the abdominal cavity simply to prevent droppings from lodging within the straddle opening and contaminating the meat.) Once tied, pull the rectal intestine back through into the intestinal cavity. The whole set of "innards" can then be dumped out by turning the deer over and picking up first its head, and then its tail, and shaking them out. This procedure is all that's required to field dress a deer.

Hanging a Large Buck

If your deer is too much to handle alone, drag it to a sapling that is about 3 or 4 inches at the butt. A white birch does very well. Fasten a rope or rawhide to its head by looping it around the antler butts. Make the abdominal incision, and tie off the rectal tube as outlined, before lifting your buck off the ground. (It takes an expert to make the abdominal cut in a hanging deer without cutting through the paunch or intestines.) Now, climb the small tree and bend it down to a point near the deer's head. Straddle the branch and cut the top off, then trim off some of the smaller branches to clear your way. Bend the springy pole down to the deer's head and tie it fast with a couple of half-hitches. When you release the pole, if you've chosen a stiff one, the buck's head and forequarters will lift partially clear of the ground. Now cut two crotched poles, fairly sturdy and about 8 feet long. Place the crotches under the spring pole, right where the deer is hung, and jack up the carcass by shifting the butts, one at a time, toward the deer. As soon as the deer's hindquarters are off the ground, dress it out as previously described, cutting loose the diaphragm and severing the windpipe and neck vessels from inside the chest cavity.

Irrespective of the method used, try to keep the carcass away from blood or other drainage from the body cavity. Deer hair stains readily, and if you want to keep your trophy looking presentable, take pains to avoid soiling the carcass. If possible, when dressing a deer on the ground, lay it on a slope or bank so the insides can be shaken free to roll downhill.

Also take some care to avoid touching the tarsal glands while dressing the deer and handling the carcass. These glands are the tufty spots on the hind legs, surrounded by somewhat coarser and longer hair. Some hunters believe the glands should be removed before field dressing to ensure the venison is not contaminated with glandular secretions. Personally, I don't worry about the glands, other than avoiding contact with them.

With the deer dressed out, try to cool the body cavity's interior before starting for camp. If you hung your buck to dress him, simply prop open the abdomen with a stick, allowing body heat to escape. If your deer is on the ground, turn the carcass on its back and then insert the abdominal stick. The body can be propped against a log or supported by a couple of rocks, leaving the open cavity uppermost for better heat dissipation.

While waiting for the carcass to cool somewhat, you can remove the genitals from the skin. Most states require evidence of sex remains attached to the hide during transportation or possession. This does not necessarily mean the organs remain fast to the carcass, for these parts spoil readily in warm weather. The sensible solution is to remove the testicles by squeezing or pulling them out of the hide and leave the hide pockets attached to the carcass. No game-law official can dispute the sex of the deer, even with its head removed, if this is done.

Under no circumstances should a buck be hung by its hind legs for hog-dressing. In this "upside-down" position, all the work in cutting and removing the entrails takes place on the deer's top half, out of the hunter's reach. When the entrails are loosened, they drop into the chest cavity and must be lifted out by digging into them and hauling them out. In addition, all the remaining blood and juices from the abdominal cavity flow into the chest. Loose entrails always drop out over the deer's head and neck, making an unsightly, smelly mess. If you decide — in spite of all logic against it — to dress a deer in the head-down position, first lift it partially off the ground before making the first cuts. Then, start to pull out the entrails, stop to jack the deer up a bit more, tie the head up out of the way of descending intestines, and, in the process, get yourself and the deer thoroughly messed up. To remove the lungs and heart without diving for them, split the chest cartilage all the way to the brisket — no little stunt in itself, unless you have a saw or small ax. Next, try to drag the chest entrails through the cut's ragged edges, with the springy ribs always closing the opening like trap jaws. Even after removing the entrails in this manner, you must still hang the buck by the head for proper draining. Obviously, it's better to hang it this way in the beginning, if the deer is to be hung at all.

Despite all the foregoing descriptions, not more than once in a thousand times is it necessary to lift a deer from the ground to field dress it. Few deer attain so much weight that an average-sized hunter cannot effectively field dress the deer by himself. With a partner, the operation can be completed in five minutes or less.

With the deer cooling a bit, rescue the liver and heart from the steaming pile of "innards." If you planned thoroughly, you will have packed an empty salt sack or cloth square for wrapping these delicacies. Otherwise it makes a sorry mess in a coat pocket. If extra hunters are in the party, one can be pressed into carrying the liver on a forked stick.

With field dressing, hunters must have a plan before shooting the deer. Only then can we tackle the job quickly and complete it easily. All cuts must be made firmly and decisively. The belly cut can be made in one sweep with a small, sharp knife. The rectal tube can be freed in 10 seconds, just like coring an apple. Normal care must be used to avoid cutting internal organs. Puncturing the paunch or intestines makes it more difficult to perform a neat, clean operation. Don't fail to give the body cavity time to cool. Body heat spells the beginning of spoiled venison, so don't too hastily throw the deer onto a fender for a triumphant trip home. The ride home can wait, but cooling the carcass cannot.

Skidding Your Deer from the Woods

When the deer is neatly dressed and cooled a bit, and you wipe blood from your hands and forearms, decide how to get the deer to your camp or car. On snow, wet leaves or downhill slopes, dragging a deer will be the easiest method, unless you have a long ways to go and you value the condition of the deer's hide. Probably 95 of every 100 deer killed each year are dragged out of the woods. This is ideal under suitable conditions, but if you drag a deer over rocky ground too far, the hide and meat can be badly bruised. Then again, if you kill a deer in heavy laurel or scrub-oak country, it is much more difficult to drag than to carry the carcass. The nature of the terrain between your deer and your destination will be the deciding factor.

Although skidding out a deer is the widely accepted method, there are right and wrong ways to do it. Any deer will slide fairly well on the white-tail's coarse, heavy-hair body covering, but two factors can make the job more difficult. First, antlers seem to reach out and grab every passing bush. Second, all the weight of a deer's chunky body rests on the ground, building friction. We can reduce both factors this way: When the rope is made fast to the deer's head, tie and hitch it to keep the nose in line with the rest of its body, throwing the antlers back and more or less out of the way. Then, by using a short rope and tying it to the middle of a short heavy stick, part of the deer's weight can be lifted from the ground as it's dragged.

This is a simple way to make the head-hitch: Throw a loop around the deer's head, just behind the antler butts. Tighten the loop so the knot lies under the throat between the jawbones. Then, bring the rope forward under the chin and make a half-hitch around the nose. Now, when tension is put on the rope, the buck's nose, head and neck lie in a straight line, with the antlers well back on the neck, as much out of the way as possible.

Two men on a short haul need never touch a rope to the buck. Each can take an antler in hand and make the drag, but for any considerable distance this is tiring. For a long drag, a rope should be tied to the middle of a stout stick, about 3 feet long. Then, with a hunter on each side, the pole can be laid across the upper arms, giving maximum pulling efficiency.

How to Carry Out a Deer

Alone, and with rough country to cover, a hunter must carry out his deer. There are two good methods, both involving a little preparation before the deer can be swung up for the carry. One way is to make a "knapsack"' of your deer by connecting the forelegs and hind legs to form two "straps," into which the hunter thrusts his arms for carrying. Although I know two or three methods for making the "knapsack," I will describe only the simplest. First, slit the skin through each hind leg just above the hock and between the large tendon and leg bone. Through these slits insert the corresponding front leg, pulling it through up to the front knee joint. Make ready two short sticks a half-inch thick and 6 inches long. Sharpen one end of each. Punch a hole through each fore-leg directly below the knee and close to the bone. Insert the short stick through the hole, making a lock within the hind leg.

To get into the "knapsack," grasp the deer by the hind hoofs and pull him up on his rump into a sitting position. Steady him thus, spread the hind legs apart, and sit down between them. Lean back, grasp a foreleg in each hand and swing the deer up over your back. Now insert your arms through the loops formed by the joined legs. Next, roll over onto hands and knees, throwing as much of the deer's weight as possible above your shoulders. Leaning forward, bring up first one foot, then the other, and stand up. Now the deer's head will be rolling to the side, so reach out and hook your right arm into the near antler — assuming it's a buck. With the buck high up on your back, you can cover long distances without unhooking him for a rest. Every time you near a fair-sized log or rock, back up to it and rest the deer's weight thereon, while you have a quiet smoke and catch your breath.

Another good method is to "rump-pack" your deer. This involves more preparation, but under some conditions it makes a more comfortable burden. To do this, skin the deer's legs up to the first joint of each. With your knife, sever the tendons across the front of the joints and break off each leg. This leaves four straps of hide, which are tied together with square knots. Tie the two front legs together and the two hind legs likewise, making the knots as close as possible to the ends of the joints. Now, sit down with the deer at your back, slip into the shoulder straps and roll forward, then stand up. You now have a fairly comfortable pack, supported on your shoulders by the straps and with much of the deer's weight carried just above the hips. The deer's head will swing down to the side, so reach out and hook its neck with the crook of your arm and carry your rifle with the other hand.

When carrying out a deer in heavily hunted areas, hang your red cap or handkerchief on the deer's head or antlers to maintain your good health. I also recommend you make plenty of manlike noises as you make your way out. Whistle, shout or talk to yourself — anything to make it impossible for a shooter to mistake your trophy for a deer still on the loose. I know a hunter who was drawing a bead on a deer moving through scrub oaks when suddenly smoke began to emanate from about the buck's ears. The deer was moving under one-man power, and the man was lucky enough to be smoking a corncob pipe at the time.

The Two-Pole Carry

Today, getting out a deer is seldom a one-man effort. Most hunters have at least one partner with them in the woods. Often there are plenty in the party to get out a deer with minimal effort. One buck I shot back in the dense laurel and scrub-oak lands between Wolf Pond and Westbrookville, never touched the ground after he was first lifted, until we reached the road about two miles from the spot. I had made a two-pole carry of this buck and, with eight men in the bunch, a fresh pair were always at hand to relieve the two boys with the deer. In this type of country, Sullivan County's heaviest covers, it's almost impossible to drag a deer any distance. The ground is rocky, the trails narrow and twisting, with dense scrub oak and laurel clutching at your clothes and the buck's antlers every few steps.

The easiest way out is to get the deer above the ground, sharp rocks and tearing underbrush. A bad way to do this is to sling the deer on a single pole, where it sways and lurches at every step the two porters make. Our group prefers two poles that are heavy and stiff enough to not spring to the rhythm of the hunters' steps. Between the two poles we lash the buck belly up, with each leg lashed high up and as close to the poles as the body can be made fast. For further support, we pass the rope under the deer, one slung under the withers, the other under the rump. With the buck in this semi-rigid position between the poles, we have a more comfortable carry. There is no back-breaking sway to the carcass, and the head is supported between the poles by lashing an antler to both sides. The load is distributed equally on both shoulders, and both men can walk erect. Our group has rapidly carried out many bucks this way in rough, brushy cover.

Of course, there is no way to take a buck out of the woods in total comfort. At best, it's hard work. A dead deer, while not too heavy for a man of normal strength, can be a loose, slippery, almost liquid bundle. The hair is slippery, the antlers flop around on a loosely hanging neck, the hoofs stick out almost yards away, it seems. But we must get the deer out, and in good condition. No one worthy of the name "sportsman" will kill a deer and neglect to bring it out without expending every effort to protect both hide and meat.

Other Methods of Transport

Up in the Oakland Valley, one of my old deer-hunting outfits had a dandy setup for bringing out bucks. Through the club's grounds, right past our sleeping quarters, ran a single spur railway. It wound up through the valley from Valley Junction, following the Neversink River till it passed our place, then on up the Bushkill toward Hartwood and St. Joseph's. The double line of steel ran conveniently along the base of our mountain, making any point on our hunting grounds not more than a half-mile from the tracks. When any of the boys killed a buck near one of the firelines, we dragged it down the slope the shortest way to the rails. Then a runner would dig out Old Bert Ogden, our caretaker, and Bert would haul out the old "pumper" from the shed. He pumped the old handcar up the tracks to the deer. We would then load it on and away to camp, a mile below. Within minutes, our latest kill would hang from the camp deer rack to cool off before heading into town to the cooler. Several times Old Bert had two or three deer piled on the handy old car, pumping down the tracks for dear life, while two or three of the boys would tag along behind to hang the bucks at camp. Altogether a great way to "get out your buck."

My friend John Shufelt of Northville, in the Adirondacks, sometimes uses a novel method to bring out his buck. He deer hunts along the rugged slopes bordering Stony Creek up in Hope Valley. Quite often he downs a buck several miles up the creek, away from the nearest road. Rather than drag or carry his deer, John lashes it to a short pole and drags it into the creek's clear, fast-running waters. He then follows along the bank with a slender pole and pries the deer loose whenever it comes up against a boulder. John says he'll never carry out a buck if there is a fair-sized stream nearby, heading the same direction he's going.

In every situation, the hunter must "cut his garment to fit the cloth," in getting his buck to car or camp. In really open country, a lone hunter could rig the buck between two springy saplings, lashing him well up to the poles. Then he could get between the "shafts" and drag out his deer by the old Indian travois method. The poles' springy ends drag on the ground, supporting the deer and absorbing the shock of uneven ground.

Many hunters who kill their deer near farmlands can often obtain the use of a horse for taking out a buck. The deer can be thrown across the saddle and the legs cinched tightly to the saddle rings. Then the head should be pulled up and over the saddle's pommel and lashed fast. Under no circumstances should the head and antlers swing free. A horse carrying a freshly killed buck is often skittish, and jabs from sharp antlers are all that's needed to throw it into a bucking, kicking frenzy. For those remembering that advice and exercising such precaution, packing out a deer on a saddle is one of the easiest ways to bring out the venison.

The Lone Hunter's Dilemma

A lone hunter in a wilderness area might not care to carry his deer to camp, particularly if daylight is ebbing. Normally, it's safe to hang your deer overnight in wilderness areas, but in deer country with a normal complement of hunters — never! That's an easy way to lose a deer. But if circumstances make it impossible to bring out your deer alone, prepare to hide it overnight. Hang it with the bent sapling and crotch-pole system so it will cool and drain thoroughly. Stay with it until there is just enough daylight to make your way to camp safely, then lower the deer, cover it with brush and leaves, and blaze a trail to the nearest landmark. Do not blaze your trail too near the deer, thus giving away your hiding place to any possible prowling hunters. Strange as it might sound, in heavily hunted areas it pays to trust no one where a white-tailed buck is involved. Many hunters would cheerfully return to you a well-filled wallet, but just as cheerfully steal your buck.

I know a man who returned home after dark with his deer atop the car. He parked in his driveway and went in to rouse the family and give them the good news. Going out to the car en masse, they found each and every fender without deer. Some of his hunting brethren had decided that stealing his deer was easier than killing one themselves.

Although a wilderness hunter is safe in leaving his deer until the next morning, he should consider hanging it high enough to keep it away from night-prowling scavengers. In addition, he must be sure to mark well the spot for his return. Blaze several trees facing to the four compass points, and clearly mark the trail by blazing or breaking branches on the way out. As an added precaution, leave a cap, handkerchief or a shirt tied fast to the carcass. Wild creatures, with the possible exception of a black bear, seldom bother a deer contaminated by odors from the hated and feared man-animal.

Equipment to Get Your Deer Out

As to equipment for dressing and hauling out a deer, this needs to be nothing more than a pair of heavy rawhide, high-top laces and a small, narrow-bladed sheath knife. Rawhide laces have filled the bill for me for several years, but if a hunter believes his deer should be hung for dressing, let him carry 10 feet of light nylon cording. In a pinch, the laces will do this job, just as they're adequate for dragging out a deer or lashing it between two poles for a carry.

A deer hunter's knife never needs to be a fearsome weapon. There is no use on deer hunts for the 6- to 8-inch, wide-blade knives we see every year dangling in a sheath halfway to a neophyte's knees. Such blades are too cumbersome for dressing a buck, and are even unhandy for the final skinning-out. Conceivably, a heavy knife might be used for chopping down saplings, but if a hunter thinks this job is too much for a small knife, he is better suited with a pocket ax.

With the buck in camp or at home, the body cavity can be swabbed clean and dry. Many hunters have a phobia about touching a buck's carcass with water. This is all foolishness, provided the carcass and body cavity are dried after the washing. It has always seemed logical to clean the carcass and wash off excess blood outside and inside the body, if it seems required. Certainly there is no logic in allowing intestinal juices and matted blood to remain inside the body to harden and dry. Better to wash the mess off and then dry thoroughly with rags, paper towels, dry moss or whatever absorbent material is handy. Washing has never harmed a bit of my venison. I doubt it will harm any other hunter's deer.

Preserving Venison in Warm Weather

In warm weather, the hunter's big problem in saving venison is keeping meat away from blowflies. Unless the carcass has every body opening thoroughly screened, these flies will crawl inside and deposit eggs in every moist pocket of flesh. Within two days, the body cavity will teem with squirming maggots. At the same time, the carcass should not be so tightly covered to exclude air circulation. The best method to escape a ruined deer is to keep it inside a screened shed or, best of all, in a refrigerated cooler.

In camp, however, neither is usually possible. The camping hunter will bring several yards of cheesecloth or porous cloth tubing from a meat-packing house. A few yards of this tubing will cover a buck, screening out flies while allowing air circulation. Cheesecloth or tubing means only a little extra weight to a hunter-camper, and it might mean the difference between saving a fine chunk of venison and giving it up to maggots.

Normally cool weather in camp will keep a deer in its hide in good condition for days. Hang your buck in the shade, off the ground, and head up if it's not fully drained. Also, keep the body cavity well aerated, free from flies, and wiped dry until the drying action of air forms a hard shell over the inside. Then you'll have good venison to carry through winter.

Whether hunting the West, above, or picnicking, left, with the Eden Falls Hunting and Fishing Club in New York's Catskill Mountains, Larry Koller was known as an unselfish, highly skilled hunter and marksman. The photo above shows Koller, foreground, relaxing during a hunt in Montana in the 1960s. Pictured at the Catskills camp, from left, are Dorian St. George, Harry Wall, Bill Ziegler, Frank King, an unknown club member, Joe Colapietro, Koller and Fred Schwerd.

When he wasn't deer hunting or shooting his rifles and shotguns, Koller frequently pursued his other passion: trout fishing. He's seen here leaning against a '54 Ford with his friends Bill Ziegler, left, and Jerry Mason. Below, Koller on horseback glassing for elk during a hunt in Montana. Below right, Koller can be seen in this Eden Falls camp photo, second man from right, on a lunch break during a weekend of trout fishing.

Although it's not widely known outside of his friends and family, Larry Koller was an excellent cook. On this early '60s Montana hunt, Koller demonstrated his culinary skills for his companions.

These photos show the final days of the original Eden Falls Hunting and Fishing Club campsite. Right, Koller bunked near the cabin's far right window (next to the short ladder leaning on the tree). Below, Eden Falls camp members start tearing down the campsite in Winter 1994 after New York state acquired the land.

Photo courtesy of Chris Thiesing

Before and after: Above is one of the last photos taken of the original Eden Falls Hunting and Fishing Club's campsite. Note the tree on the right side of the photo. Right, the tree casts its shadow on the now-empty site, as Paul Koller and Chris Thiesing reminisce. Paul Koller is Larry's last surviving offspring. Thiesing was the club's historian and president when this photo was taken in March 2000.

Photo by Patrick Durkin

The top photo was likely taken in the late 1940s or early 1950s, when the camp was still known by its original name, The Eden Brook Club. From left, Frank King, Fred Schwerd, Bill Ziegler, Dorian St. George, Larry Koller, Joe Colapietro, an unknown hunter, and Dick Wolf. Left and above, Koller's biggest buck, a 16-pointer shot in the early 1950s. Koller shot the buck with his pet .30-40 Krag, which he customized from a standard-issue military rifle.

The photo below of Larry Koller is from the dust jacket on the original printing of Shots at Whitetails *in 1948. Notice he's holding his .30-40 Krag. In Spring 2000, Larry's youngest son, Paul, returned to the Neversink River Gorge, below right, and brought the Krag, one of his few keepsakes from his father. Right, Larry Koller helps the camp cook in the '60s Montana tent-camp.*

Photo courtesy of Gary Ziegler

Photo by Patrick Durkin

Photo courtesy of Gary Ziegler

Members of the Eden Falls camp often hunted on the other side of the Neversink. They built "Ziegler's Bridge" to make the crossing more convenient. Dana Thiesing, below left in Winter 1988, is seen in one of the last photos of the bridge. It was torn down when New York acquired the land. Below, camp members such as Mike Keiser and Chris Thiesing now use a boat to cross the river.

Photos courtesy of Chris Thiesing

The camp's namesake, Eden Falls, top, isn't far from the original campsite in the Neversink River Gorge. At left are Chris Thiesing and Paul Koller at the falls in March 2000. The scene above shows the Neversink River directly below Eden Falls.

Photos by Patrick Durkin

Larry Koller never tired of roaming, hunting and fishing the picturesque Catskill Mountains in eastern New York. He also deeply admired white-tailed deer, and was the unofficial "huntmaster" when the club organized deer drives. Because he also still-hunted the area so intensely, club members knew he understood local deer habits better than anyone. During the club's drives, Koller was almost always a driver, allowing other hunters to take stand sites he had scouted.

Photos by Charles Alsheimer

Larry Koller's Corner of New York

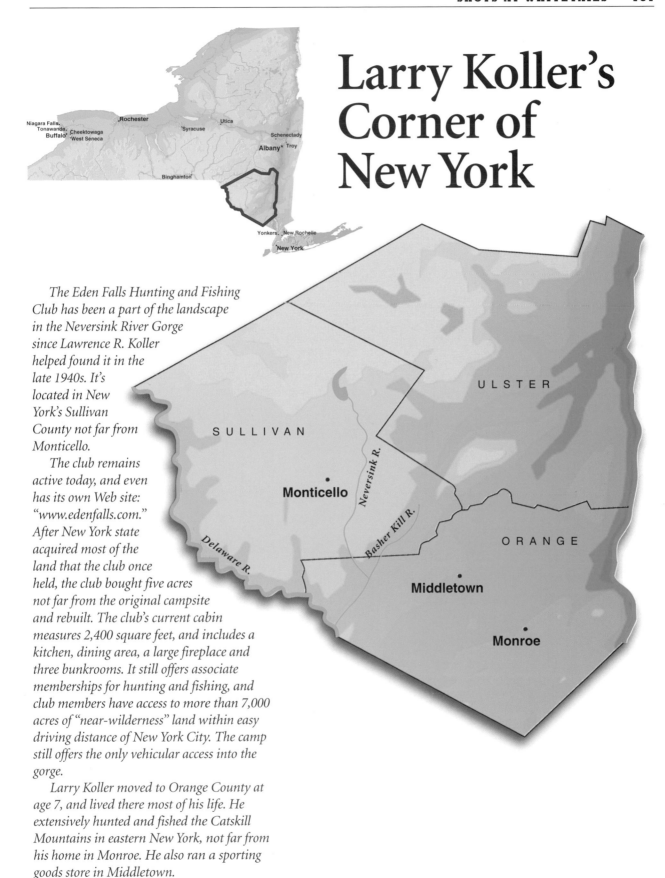

The Eden Falls Hunting and Fishing Club has been a part of the landscape in the Neversink River Gorge since Lawrence R. Koller helped found it in the late 1940s. It's located in New York's Sullivan County not far from Monticello.

The club remains active today, and even has its own Web site: "www.edenfalls.com." After New York state acquired most of the land that the club once held, the club bought five acres not far from the original campsite and rebuilt. The club's current cabin measures 2,400 square feet, and includes a kitchen, dining area, a large fireplace and three bunkrooms. It still offers associate memberships for hunting and fishing, and club members have access to more than 7,000 acres of "near-wilderness" land within easy driving distance of New York City. The camp still offers the only vehicular access into the gorge.

Larry Koller moved to Orange County at age 7, and lived there most of his life. He extensively hunted and fished the Catskill Mountains in eastern New York, not far from his home in Monroe. He also ran a sporting goods store in Middletown.

Photos by Patrick Durkin

A reunion of sorts occurred in March 2000 for some members of the Eden Falls Hunting and Fishing Club when Larry Koller's only surviving son, Paul, returned for the first time in nearly 40 years. Above, the group posed in front of a shed, the only building remaining from the original camp. Front row, from left: Victor Perruna, Paul Koller, Gary Ziegler and Pete Marchese. Back row, from left: Chris and Mary Anne Thiesing, and their father, Ernie Thiesing; and Frank Degrigrio. Left, Koller and Chris Thiesing admire the late author's .30-40 Krag. Above is a painting of the original camp, done by G. Don Ray in 1958.

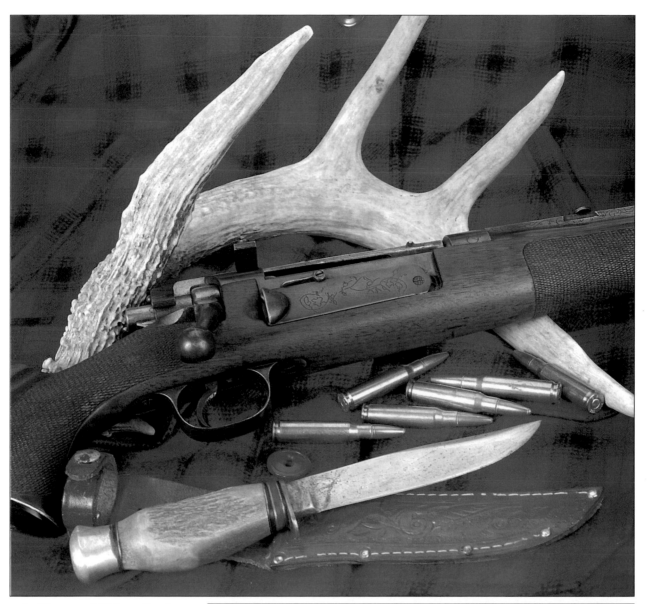

In Shots at Whitetails, *Larry Koller demonstrates not only his hard-earned insights into white-tailed deer, but also his deep love for deer hunting firearms. Shown on this page is the author's most famous deer rifle, his sporterized .30-40 Krag. Koller did all the work himself at age 19 in converting this rifle, and he includes nearly an entire chapter in* Shots at Whitetails *on sporterizing military rifles.*

Photos by Ross Hubbard

Photo by Ross Hubbard

The book you're holding is the third edition of Shots at Whitetails *since it was originally printed in 1948 by Little, Brown & Co., and then reprinted in 1952 and 1958. In 1970 and 1975, Alfred A. Knopf publishers reprinted* Shots at Whitetails *and offered it to many thousands of new Larry Koller fans, including those in the Outdoor Life Book Club. The first two editions featured the painting and drawings of Bob Kuhn. The cover of the 2000 edition by Krause Publications features the painting, "Play the Wind," by Michael Sieve. The inside drawings are by Ruth Pillath.*

Left, Paul Koller lines up the peep sights on his father's .30-40 Krag. Larry Koller much preferred peep sights to the more conventional open sights. Below are two views of Larry Koller's former home in Monroe, N.Y., as the house appeared in March 2000. Koller used to practice with his shotguns and rifles in the back yard, but the area is now too densely populated to allow safe shooting.

Photos by Patrick Durkin

Deer Anatomy Facts

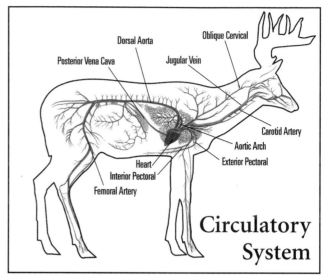

Circulatory System

➤ *Making quick, certain kills should be the main goal of every hunter, no matter if using a bow or gun.*

➤ *When shooting at deer with a bow and arrow, aim for the heart region. If the deer "jumps the string" by dropping sharply before bounding away, the arrow will still hit the lungs.*

➤ *The average white-tailed deer, weighing about 150 pounds, carries about 8 pints of blood in its circulatory system. Massive hemorrhage is necessary to bring a deer down quickly.*

➤ *A deer must lose at least 35 percent of its blood, or $2^3/4$ pints in a 150-pound animal, before falling. The better the hit, the quicker blood loss occurs.*

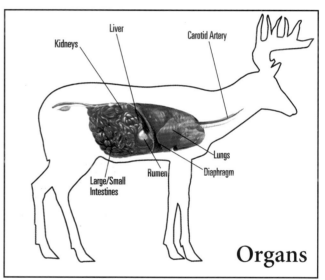

Organs

➤ *Deer blood carries high levels of Vitamin K1 and K2 in early autumn. Vitamin K is an antihemorrhagic agent, which greatly aids blood clotting.*

➤ *Frightened whitetails produce high levels of B-endorphin, which supports rapid wound healing. Endorphins consist of morphine-like chemicals from the pituitary gland, allowing the animal to control pain.*

➤ *Hunters must study white-tailed deer anatomy to learn to put their bullet or arrow where it can quickly destroy the deer's circulatory and/or respiratory system.*

➤ *Before shooting, always take into consideration the deer's body position. On angling shots, picture where the bullet or broadhead will exit on the animal's offside to determine where the shot should enter on the side you're facing.*

Illustrations by Wayne Trimm

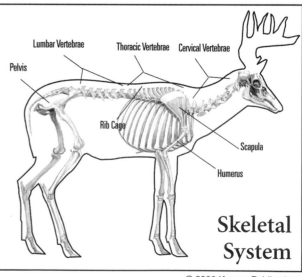

Skeletal System

CHAPTER 10

The Deer Hunter's Camp

Lucky is the man who can take his deer hunting in large doses, who can get off into the woods a full two weeks or a month in close association with his quarry and, in a sense, become part of the country he hunts. These hunters extract the keenest possible enjoyment from the sport, and in time prove to be the most adept woodsmen and deerslayers.

There is no substitute in hunting for a close association with the territory one hunts and game living therein. The hunter-camper who has the interest and courage to pack his duffel into the deer country, set up camp, and stay until he bags his buck is a most self-sufficient individual. He willingly divorces himself from the cloying taint of civilization, temporarily at least, and once in the woods unconsciously becomes an environmental part of the scene.

The Value of a Good Deer Camp

In true wilderness areas — the back country — a man must set up camp if he is to kill one of the wild whitetails found in such territory. And for the hunter who loves the wilds and will kill his buck by no method other than still-hunting, this is the only answer to urges that creep into his veins with the first frosts. Few who hunt deer have opportunity to make such a trip, but no man can know the fullest satisfaction to be gained from deer hunting until he kills a prime white-tailed buck under full wilderness hunting conditions.

It hardly seems necessary to compile lengthy information about equipment and camp procedure for the hunter who takes to the woods, making his home there until he kills his buck. These hunters must, of necessity, have a background of woodcraft and experience that precludes the necessity for advice. But a new generation of coming hunters might not be completely woods-wise in cold-weather camping, yet still crave a wilderness hunting trip. I direct the following hints to those hunters.

First, although a hunter might have wide experience in summer camping, his approach to a hunting and camping trip must be different. "Roughing it" in a camp might be a thrill for a day or two, but unless the camp has been carefully planned, it can be a dismal hunting trip. Such camps have created sad, unhappy hunters who bolt for home after sleepless, freezing nights in an uncomfortable bed, meals of greasy, unpleasant food and tramps through the woods in sodden clothes.

Selecting a Camp Site

To do the job right, choose your spot and make a pre-season visit, if possible. Pick a campsite that is well-sheltered from prevailing winds, with a good supply of water and firewood nearby. It's wise to cut your supply of firewood well in advance of the hunt, for this chore can take plenty of time from hunting. The site should be well-drained, not at the foot of a steep sidehill where the first rainfall will sweep your tent floor. Keep the location in good sunlight to eliminate a damp tent, and be sure no dead limbs will drop from a nearby tree in a heavy blow to crash through your tent roof.

Unless the hunter is a seasoned woodsman with much experience in building the right lean-to shelter, a good tent is a must. For a group of four to six hunters, a 14-by-16-foot wall tent is the answer. Two hunters can get along with a small miner's tent or an army surplus two-man tent. But small shelters cannot provide inside heating, and a warm tent is a great comfort after a long, cold day in the woods. It will pay for even a two-hunter party to pack in a 10-by-12-foot wall tent, unless the trip will last only a couple of days. It might be fun to recount your experiences in a makeshift shelter to friends after the trip, but for honest-to-goodness comfort during the trip, nothing compares with a roomy wall tent and a collapsible sheet-iron stove for heating. Cooking will be a pleasure in a warm place, rather than struggling over an outside open fire. Food can be kept warm, and the eating itself will be much more comfortable, taken within the cheery snug harbor of a heated tent. The novice never fails to express surprise at the warm comfort of a heated tent, even in bitter weather.

With the tent selected, plan well beforehand the room needed for sleeping, cooking and storing equipment, so the stove's position can be fixed and a hole cut for the pipe. Collapsible sheet-iron stoves with built-in ovens and telescoping pipe can be obtained, and are just the ticket for the deer hunter's camp. Of course, you can make a stove from sheet iron, but it hardly pays because they're already inexpensive. With the hole cut for the stovepipe, be sure to insulate the tent with fire-retardant material.

Always remember that a stove presents a certain amount of fire hazard, but if you take proper insulation precautions and keep the stovepipe opening away from flammable branches, there will be no trouble.

A deer hunter's tent needs no floor. In fact, a floor is a disadvantage because, with the inside stove, insulating material must be used to prevent burning it out, and it serves no useful purpose.

Of all the necessary equipment for a comfortable hunting-camping trip, a good bed is the most important. A sleeping bag is a must. Never depend on providing a bed from nature's materials found on the spot. No natural material found in the deer woods provides a warm, comfortable bed. A hunter might get by with a moss or balsam bed during summer, but not in fall. Nothing does the job as well as a good down-filled sleeping bag placed over an air mattress. With this outfit, a hunter can sleep in comfort on a stone wall. In addition, it's light to carry, and easy to clean and dry out. The Army turned loose many thousands of these as surplus material after World War II, so there is little excuse for a hunter-camper to be without one. In the absence of an air mattress, you can make a bed by rolling up two 6- or 8-inch-diameter logs, laying them parallel about three feet apart, and filling in the space, first with a covering of newspaper or tarpaulin next to the ground, then a thick pile of dried ferns, leaves, balsam tips or any other soft material found near the campsite. If you have a few gunnysacks, stuff them with the same material and use them for a mattress, rather than have the loose stuff strewn around the tent. Even so, none of this works as well as an air mattress and nothing else sleeps as comfortably. Makeshifts are feasible only for a temporary stay, but for a hunting trip of a week or two, an air mattress and sleeping bag answer the deer hunter's prayers.

Planning the Right Meals

With the tent, stove and sleeping equipment decided upon, the campers should get together and make a list of all other items of equipment, and plan meals for each day, providing enough food for each man. This might seem a childish procedure, but for campers short on experience, it pays off in full stomachs and good dispositions instead of tight belts and strained relations. It might also be smart to add 20 percent for the increase in appetites when the gang has spent a day in the woods.

I recall an incident that illustrates the tendency of a new hunter to consume huge portions of food after a day in the woods. One of my friends, a traveling man and bachelor to boot, decided to spend a week at our deer camp for his initiation in the gentle art of deer hunting. He had been overweight for years, on a rigid diet, and subject to stomach disorders if he overate. He had some misgivings about living on camp fare, but after I assured him we would provide and cook for him any of his special foods, he decided to take a chance.

On the way to camp we stopped and bought his special cereals, rusks and other assorted dainties. The first meal in camp that night found him eating a rugged bowl of milk toast. Next morning we prepared him a hot cereal, with which he ate a dried rusk or two. He passed the day in the woods without lunch, refusing our sandwiches because his diet forbade eating at midday. He was a willing hunter. He took part in every drive and never complained, even though he must have been leg-weary and foot-sore by the end of the day.

We came into camp that evening with a nice buck and, after hanging it on the camp rack, we set about preparing the evening meal. The night before I had skinned out six cottontail rabbits — part of the supply we brought in for camp food. The rabbits, together with 3 pounds of hot sausage and six pork chops, had been simmering in Italian spaghetti sauce on the big camp range since noon. To complete the meal, I had only to boil 4 pounds of spaghetti and put two big pots on the camp table; one of spaghetti, the other with meat and tasty tomato sauce. In the meantime, I had put out our friend's special meal of cereal and light cream.

Our gang of eight had a little trouble polishing off all the rabbits and spaghetti. If memory serves me, there remained in the pot about one whole rabbit, one pork chop, and a couple of sausage links, and the other pot held a fairly good-sized wad of spaghetti. Now and then our new friend glanced hungrily at this surplus food. Finally, his resistance broken, he asked somewhat timidly if we would mind him tasting the rabbit. Promptly the two big pots were pushed his way, and for 30 minutes this diet-ridden victim of general inertia fed his face in a way that would delight any chef's eye. In the end there was little, if anything, to donate to the skunks. For a week, this chap ate our food, enjoyed it tremendously, and went home, alas, minus deer, but feeling in fine shape physically and mentally. His special cereal, breads and other light fodder were cast aside that night of the first day's hunt and were never mentioned again. Beware, then, of a meager food supply for your deer hunting and camping trip!

Although the food supply will be dictated by the group's personal preferences, it should include staple items of flour, sugar, salt, eggs, bacon, baking powder, prepared pancake flour, dehydrated soups, cooking oil or fat (unless plenty of bacon is used), canned or dried milk, canned or fresh carrots, dried beans, and canned or dried fruit. If supplies must be packed in, canned goods must be kept to a minimum, and substituted with dried foods and dehydrated items wherever possible, to save weight. For an extended stay, don't try to get along on fried foods for every meal. It palls on the appetite and soon the gang will wish for a home-cooked meal. Add fruits and vegetables liberally to the diet if you want to keep the crowd healthy.

Bake fresh biscuits in a reflector oven or in a collapsible oven on the sheet-iron stove. Or, if you prefer, fill your frying pan with a prepared biscuit dough or flour-and-baking-powder dough and bake over a fire. Hot biscuits and pan-baked bread are always welcomed. Start your evening meals with a pot of hot soup made from prepared package mixes; follow it with a rugged hunter's stew of beef, venison, rabbits or any other available red meat; and smother it with carrots, potatoes and onions thickened with a little flour. Top it off with stewed prunes or canned pineapple, and you'll have a contented, sleepy bunch of hunters, ready to turn in early, sleep well and be on deck next morning ready to hunt. Next to a comfortable bed and warm, dry tent, nothing adds to the pleasure of a camping-hunting trip like a balanced diet. It's no more trouble to prepare sensible meals in a well-organized camp than it is to throw a gooey mess into a greasy frying pan and expect the boys to enjoy it.

Setting up the Camp

When the time for the trip arrives, give yourself plenty of time to get into camp early in the day, even if it means starting a day sooner. Have your grub list filled and equipment list checked by every member before leaving home. Don't depend on picking up food or duffel along the way. Something is certain to be forgotten. It's far better to lay out every item at home and check each off the list before packing it for transportation. When you arrive at the chosen spot, you'll need at least a half-day to get the tent properly set up, drainage ditches cut, a rough table and benches put together, and the stove up or reflector-fireplace built. In addition, you'll likely need to cut firewood and get ready the sleeping quarters.

As far as the tent is concerned, no poles need be carted along. Cut a ridgepole at the spot and make it long enough to project through both ends of the tent, even if holes must be cut to permit its passage. Cut two pairs of fairly long, stiff poles to be used as "shears" for supporting each end of the ridgepole, then wire them together near the top like the letter "A" and lay the ridgepole on the wire-crossed joint. Set stakes for the guy-ropes and tighten the whole tent by pulling tight the guys and ends of the shear poles together.

The use of shear poles rather than conventional end poles under the ridge allows easier passage into the tent, and at the same time makes a more stable job. If you like an open fire — and what camper doesn't? — build a rough stone fireplace six or eight feet from the tent flap and back it up with a reflector of green logs, which should be piled atop each other and wired fast to a pair of stakes driven into the ground. Complete the job by cutting two crotched stakes for both sides of the fireplace and laying across them a pole to support stew kettles or a roast. Such an open fireplace makes a good medium for starting the evening meal. In our camp, one of the boys would come in at noon and roll a couple of good red-oak logs onto the fireplace and hang a big kettle of stew or a roast to simmer until evening. Then when the hungry crew began to show up at camp after the day's hunt, dinner would be a matter of simply taking off the stew or roast, putting on the coffeepot, and sitting down to the meal.

The Value of Community Effort

I must re-emphasize the importance of setting up camp completely before even thinking about hunting. In setting up camp, there is no time like the present for taking care of all the little jobs that make camping a comfort. The member who grabs his rifle as the tent is unpacked "just to take a look up on the ridge" while the rest of the bunch makes camp will likely wait a long time for another invitation. A deer camp is a community effort, and each hunter should have a job to carry through to completion. For example, one of my camping parties would select an experienced man to cook, but he was not expected to gather wood, tend fires or wash dishes. Those chores were divided among the rest of the group. The stay in camp was always pleasant, with no bickering or arguing over who would do what.

Setting up camp is made much simpler by adding a bit of extra equipment. A hammer, handsaw, nails and a roll of soft iron or copper wire goes a long way in providing extra comforts in the form of stools, drying racks and extra benches. In a well-organized camp, nothing in food or equipment is left on the ground. Racks and benches provide for everything, and the firewood supply will be covered with a tarpaulin or placed under a lean-to before rain or snow gets to it. In such a camp, the hunting trip will be fun, and every hunter will be comfortable, healthy and happy — unless he misses a big buck.

Camp Rules

Few problems crop up in a well-established camp, other than forming rigid rules for the group's safety. In firearms handling, my Buck Mountain outfit enforced a strict, perhaps unconventional, rule: All firearms had to be loaded and kept loaded while in the camp building. It was agreeably surprising how this simple rule kept the hunters from picking up and fondling someone else's rifle at odd moments. The wall rack was always full of rifles, and at no time was a rifle passed around for casual inspection. Our reasoning was simple: Many times it is this odd-moment inspection of firearms that leads to accidents.

It's also a good policy for a large group in a permanent camp to hire a full-time cook, preferably a person who likes cooking but not hunting. If you can locate such an individual, pay him well and treat him with the respect due his position — that of filling the inner man. The hunters are still expected to provide firewood and wash dishes after the evening meals, but this is little enough to give in return for good meals served on time. It never works well in a large group to have one person cook for the rest of the gang. The cook usually wants to hunt as much as the rest of the party, and that's hardly possible if the bunch is to be well fed for at least two full meals a day.

As to utensils for camp cooking: Try to save as much room and weight as possible. Nested aluminum pots and pans are the only solution for the tent-camper, and these can be had with folding handles for carrying in a pack-sack or pack-basket. But for making griddlecakes, nothing works as well as the old-fashioned rectangular heavy iron griddle. These are worth every effort necessary to get them to camp, even if you must hang one around your neck with a rope.

For permanent camps, an unlimited number of utensils can be used. Generally, there is no transportation problem to the fixed camp building, so a camper can take just about what he likes. However, the most useful article in camp-kitchen hardware ever conceived is a large pressure cooker. These magic vessels turn out a big stew or heavy pot roast in one-third the regular time, and food so cooked seems tastier.

The Hunter's Attitude Toward His Pals

Fully as important in camp as good equipment and know-how is the attitude of each hunter toward his fellow camp member. Each man must keep his personal belongings in his allotted space, not strewn around the tent to mix with his comrades' gear. And besides doing his share of the work, if cooking chores are to be shared, each man must take his turn and give no thought to hunting until the work is done.

Beware also of handing out advice to fellow hunters. No one likes to be criticized for his firearms handling or hunting methods. If your system seems to work, the rest of the gang will follow suit quickly. Also, keep your hunting stories to a single telling. Don't bend your campmates' ears with the same tale over and over again.

The proof of a man's worth as a camp companion will not always be apparent on the trip itself. In retrospect, cooperative qualities, good common sense, and a willingness to equally share labors and discomfort will shine in the golden light of memory when the next autumn finds Jack Frost painting his landscapes.

CHAPTER 11

Sportsmanship and Safety in the Woods

Sportsmanship is an ethereal quality, an intangible characteristic existing in the minds of hunters and displayed by their conduct for all to see. It is the highest type of hunter who congratulates a fellow hunter for taking a fine buck, with a genuine warmth, not the dark looks of envy. He is the hunter who, although a stranger, helps trail your wounded deer, even finish it off, then helps you get it out of the woods. He is the hunter who offers you his last smoke or sandwich, who puts you on a better stand than his own, hoping to get you a shot. He also handles his firearm forever with caution, and when his rifle cracks, he knows his sights are on legal game.

The Good Sportsman and His Opposite

Sadly enough, we have with us in much greater numbers his opposite — the obnoxious character who rushes to the best stand, heading off the rest of the party. This character also shoots — or shoots at — any deer coming to his post, ever hopeful one might have legal antlers. This is the ever-alert opportunist who pounces like a hawk on another man's wounded or dead deer, frantically tying on a tag before the trailing hunter appears. He also sneaks into the woods at the beginning of another party's drive, then leeches his way into the best place to cut off oncoming deer. This is the same person who rocked your boat when you were bass fishing or who stood up in your canoe while making a fast-water run. And now, in the deer woods, he shoots at noises in the brush.

Perhaps I paint too dismal a picture of the unsportsmanlike hunter we find in the deer woods, but his clan increases in numbers every year. Deer hunting in many areas becomes highly competitive; the prime objective is to intercept a buck before the next fellow sees it, blast it down and tie on the ownership tags before another hunter reaches the downed deer and performs this task. Personally, I can't understand what measure of satisfaction a hunter can feel in taking home a trophy killed by someone else, yet it happens frequently. If a man is meat-hungry, we can understand some of this attitude, but we who hunt deer never hunt for meat alone. The venison is but a final complement to the thrill and satisfaction of a successful day or week in the woods.

A Deer-Stealing Attempt

One of our Oakland Valley club hunters had an amusing experience with a pair of deer thieves. Charlie was one of the older men in our group, and had been advised by his doctor to quit deer hunting. For years the doctor treated Charlie for a weak pump, and he believed the heavy exercise and excitement of deer hunting could easily finish him. But Charlie had spent too many deer seasons in the woods to give up easily. As he put it: "I'd just as soon they'd plant me if I have to give up huntin' deer. Not much use of livin' if a man can't hunt." (As it turned out, the doc was right. One year we carried Charlie out of the woods, never to return, but that doesn't concern this story.)

Our bunch came down off the mountain each midday for lunch and a hot cup of coffee. Charlie, with his bad ticker, couldn't take the climb twice a day, so he carried a lunch and ate while the rest of us went down to camp. One day, just as we hit the grub-shack, two shots cracked out near the top of our little mountain. It could be no one but Charlie, we thought, so we grabbed a quick bite and got up on the mountain to see if he needed help.

Perhaps an hour later we found Charlie, sitting by a nice 6-point buck. He was visibly agitated, much more so than he might have been from simply killing a deer.

"Well, sir, I never seen anything like it," he said. "Here this buck had just sneaked out from that laurel over the ridgetop, prob'ly gettin' out after you fellas left for camp and things had quieted down. Anyway, I knocked him over — hit him both times — and he dropped right here. I got over here and opened him up and dumped his guts out, 'cause I knew you boys wouldn't be back for a while to help. Then I figgered I'd find me a spot to set down and eat my lunch. I went up the hill there a bit and set down by a stump where I could watch the deer.

"Pretty soon," he went on, "I heard sumthin' over near the fireline and there was two guys sneaking up this runway, here, and lookin' all around, pretty cautious-like, so I got behind that big stump just to see what was goin' on." Charlie's eyes were twinkling now in anticipation as he unfolded the story. "These two birds must have heard the two shots and come over from the next club to see what was goin' on.

"Well, anyway, they come on up the runway a bit and then one spies the deer layin' on the ground. He puts his finger up to his mouth and grabs the other guy by the arm and points to the deer. Then they both look all around very careful to see if anyone was comin', but they don't spot me hidden behind that stump. They didn't look at the deer very carefully either or they'd 'a' seen his guts were out and the tag's on his legs. Guess they was excited a bit. They were havin' a conference now to figger out what to do. I could hear 'em mumbling to themselves and one of 'em was shakin' his head at what the other guy was sayin'. Finally, the little one went back a ways toward the fireline and stood there. Then the other one points his gun up in the air and fires a shot. Then he hollers as loud as he can for the other guy: 'Come on over, Bill. Here's the buck we was followin'!' So the other hollers back, as loud as he can, 'Hey, did ya find 'im?' Then they got together, about 30 feet from the deer, and looked all around again.

"'Bout this time," said Charlie, "I was gettin' a little mad. These birds was figgerin' on dragging that deer over across the fireline and claimin' it. So just as they was starting for the deer, I stuck my rifle over top o' that stump. Just as one of 'em was reaching down to grab the buck's horn I yell out: 'The first man touches that deer dies!' Brother, you never saw two scared guys get the hell out of there and back across the fireline in such a hurry!

"Here these birds figgered they had found a buck that somebody had wounded — they'd heard my two shots — and they just sneaked over here on the chance the deer was wounded and might come runnin' down on that crossin'."

Undoubtedly Charlie was right, and regrettably there have been, and will be, many more such instances. I once killed a large buck that had been missed several times in a flurry of shots by two other hunters. After I examined the buck and the tracks in the snow behind the deer, I was satisfied only my two bullets had scored. Accordingly, I tagged the buck and was about to dress him when two hunters came through on the buck's back trail.

Seeing I was alone, they argued they had hit the buck first, intimating the deer was dead, or nearly so, when I had come up to him. I stood off a bit with rifle ready, and invited them to look over the buck, and then examine the snow for evidence of a hit before my shooting. Neither of them wanted any part of that. They simply wanted to talk me out of the deer. One lad reached over and, lifting the buck's head, moved its lower jaw side to side. "Sure," he said, "this buck's jaw is broken. We must have hit him in the head." Of course, the buck's jaw wasn't broken any more than theirs or mine. Every deer's lower jaw swings loose in death.

Fortunately, and preventing any unpleasant scene, one of my friends, Miles Winner, happened to come along. He broke up the discussion by taking the men along the deer's back-trail through the snow to where they had shot, while I dressed the buck.

I had been tracking this buck, and had driven him to these two hunters as they sat on a big rock. The deer had walked to within 30 yards of them, whereupon they emptied their .30-30 carbine and autoloading shotgun without touching a hair. These men knew right well after following the deer's tracks in the snow for a quarter-mile that they hadn't touched him. But seeing I was alone, they hoped to scare me off. Such incidents are, at the least, unpleasant, and detract immeasurably from the joy and thrill in taking a white-tailed buck.

Settling Disputed Deer Claims

Sportsmanship involves many things in deer hunting. It is the ungrudging willingness, among other things, to share equally in deer drives with no grousing when a less-favored stand is drawn. Every hunter on a drive has almost an equal chance of killing a deer. The element of luck in deer drives is an all-important factor, and that can never be preordained. But besides it is also the willingness to give to its rightful owner any deer you might stumble on, or have stumble over you, badly wounded and dying. It's true that possession is 10 points of the law in deer hunting, but a sportsman yields his desires for a buck to the man who inflicted the fatal wound, brushing aside the legal aspects.

In most club and group hunting, the unwritten code of sportsmanship delivers the deer to the hunter making the first vital wound, even though another hunter might be called on to stop the deer. Hunting deer in open lands is another story. Here the hunter must get to his deer first if he would keep it. There will never be a satisfactory answer to the problem of a hunter who trails his wounded deer and finally comes upon a man or two dressing it out to carry off. The solution lies not in law but in the heart of every man who takes to the woods during deer hunting season.

We have with us now, and ever shall have, the "sob sister" who bewails the taking of deer by hunters as a cruel, bloodthirsty slaughter of innocent wildlife. Yet these hypocritical individuals never hesitate to sink a fang into a succulent lamb chop, veal cutlet or tender porterhouse steak. They refute such argument by stating blandly that such animals are raised for slaughter and are intended to be eaten by man. Obviously true, but so are the deer raised by nature (and the eternal vigilance of Conservation Commissions) for just such a purpose. In addition, hunting enables man, with the fundamental human impulse of the chase, to express his individuality in taking to the forests to kill a buck on more equal terms than provided for slaughterhouse animals.

White-tailed bucks have a much higher incidence of survival than all the millions of cattle, sheep and hogs raised for meat. No one can justly object to killing a deer, or any other of nature's creatures, for food and sport, provided it is merciful and cleanly done.

It has long since been proved that to have abundant deer, the taking of a normal number of deer each season is a prime necessity. The hunter forms the controlling factor, and an important one, in wildlife management. Deer that are permitted to propagate and exist unchecked year after year are their own worst evil. Disease, overbrowsing and starvation eventually combine to decimate herds to only a shadow of their peak abundance. The so-called nature lover who opposes deer hunting must decide whether it's more sportsmanlike to harvest a reasonable crop of deer each year by orthodox hunting methods, or permit them to die lingering deaths by starvation and disease. And there is no alternative, for deer must be controlled by sensible hunting or nature will step in and take a hand.

It is, however, up to hunters to make killing of game as sportsmanlike as possible. They must make sufficient study of deer anatomy to make clean, quick kills. They must spend such time as necessary to develop shooting skills of a kind to hit vital areas. Most importantly, when they at last see a buck, they must make doubly sure of their shots. There is ever an urge to take a chance on hitting a buck somewhere in a spot that downs him. But irrespective of the great power lying within the hunter's bullet, few if any kills result unless the shot is directed to a well-chosen spot. This is not only common sense, it is an all-encompassing obligation of every hunter who cares to wear the banner of true sportsmanship.

Deer hunters should use a firearm of the greatest power they can shoot well. Certainly nothing less than a rifle in the .30-30 class can be counted on for clean kills under average whitetail hunting ranges. A higher-power rifle is even better if the hunter can shoot it accurately, always knowing that heavier calibers induce more flinching.

The hunter who subconsciously fears recoil will seldom hit his deer and, even hitting it, will often fail to make a clean, merciful shot. Many of the more experienced hunters of the 1940s are going to the .300 Savage as a better deer killer. Possessing more shock than calibers of the .30-30 class, it's a better deer killer, but only in the hands of qualified users.

We can carry this excess of power too far, though, and select a caliber and bullet with too much power. The .270 Winchester, for example, when loaded with the lightest bullets, kills the deer but mangles too much meat and tissue. If the bullet strikes the neck or chest cavity, this is of little matter. But if the shot hits the back or hindquarters, much meat will be lost. Even so, it is far better to recover your deer by using such rifles of excessive power even though much meat is ruined rather than have the buck stagger off and die unrecovered. In this case, not only is a small portion of meat lost; all of it is lost.

Modern hunters try to strike a happy balance between their own shooting abilities and the killing effect of the caliber and bullet he will use. No one but each hunter can make this selection. But hunters owe to the laws of good sportsmanship and the future of their own hunting pleasure the making of wise choices.

Safety and sportsmanship in the woods are each to some degree dependent upon the other. A good sportsman is a careful shooter. Under no circumstances does he take a shot until certain of his target and equally certain no one is in the line of fire should he miss. Likewise, he reserves his shooting, in deference to other hunters, for deer only. It never assists any deer hunter's effort when others shoot at squirrels, partridge, foxes, coyotes or rabbits. Besides, any rifle bullet directed into a treetop at a squirrel could travel a couple of miles to a farmhouse or village. I would bet that most of the stray shots we read about during deer season come from this kind of foolish negligence.

Such carelessness and thoughtlessness has likely induced much of our legislation against the use of rifles in some areas. It's obvious that a bullet fired at deer level within the woods will not travel too far before spending itself in brush or timber. It's also obvious it won't require many high, stray shots in a settled area before sizzling letters from irate farmers and villagers fill a lawmaker's mailbox. As a result, deer hunters who prefer hunting deer with a rifle must use all discretion in shooting, and devote all their shooting in the deer woods to legal deer.

Trailing Wounded Deer

High on the list of sportsmen's qualifications rests the skill of trailing

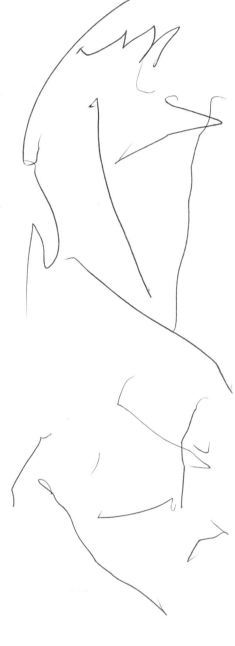

and recovering wounded deer. Not only does each wounded and unrecovered deer represent a loss in conservation figures, it represents an unfilled license that still gives its holder the right to kill more deer, to say nothing of the lingering torment to the animal involved. If a buck is mortally wounded, trailing is seldom a problem. A blood trail leads the hunter quickly to a dead or dying deer. But what of a deer hit through the flank or paunch, deer that bleed only a little and, after a short time, fail to bleed at all? And then there are seriously wounded deer that fail to bleed directly after the shot. Many of these are chalked up as a clean miss, even after a hunter examines the ground where the buck stood at the shot.

Deer often fail to bleed for easy trailing until running 50 yards or more. A solid hit will not always down a deer, nor will it show evidence of being hit. The old rule of a deer dropping its flag when hit has been proven wrong so often it can be disregarded as a rule. More positive evidence of a hit is hair on the ground at the point where the shot was made. It's almost impossible to hit a deer anywhere without clipping hair. It might be only a tiny bit, but observant hunters will find it if they spend time to look. Once a hit is confirmed, it's time to take up the trail to look for blood.

When blood is discovered, note its quantity and nature. If much blood is found on both sides of the trail, the deer was likely shot clean through and suffered a quickly fatal wound. It should be dead within 100 yards. If blood signs are small and dark, the possibility of a soon-fatal death is remote. This deer should be allowed to lie down at least an hour before you take his trail. If a follow-up is made too soon, the deer will get up and leave without giving a tracker time for a finishing shot. Worst of all, the wound could close, leaving no more blood to guide the hunter.

I have one safe rule for tracking wounded deer: If you follow the trail for 150 yards without finding it, give it an hour before taking the trail again. A solidly hit deer seldom moves far if it's not driven. It will often go downhill to heavy cover or head toward water to lie down and rest after taking a drink. To keep on the trail of such a wounded deer will only keep it moving farther away. Meanwhile, blood loss becomes less and less until it disappears and the hunter loses a deer. It's all right to follow a deer immediately only when the blood shows, in great quantity and bright color, that the deer will be dead within seconds or minutes.

Tracking a deer that shows no sign of heavy arterial hits could also drive it into the lap of another hunter. In heavily hunted areas this dilemma of trailing or not trailing your wounded deer will always be a problem. But good judgment indicates that only if the deer is solidly hit and bleeding profusely will it be wise to follow immediately. If the deer is lightly hit or paunch-shot, shown by the small dribbles of dark blood, the only possible procedure is to wait, giving the deer a chance to lie down and weaken. If the deer was wounded near the end of daylight, blaze some trees nearby and return at daylight before resuming the trail. Chances are, you'll find the deer not too far off, either dead or incapable of moving.

With snow on the ground, trailing wounded deer becomes much simpler. However, snow exaggerates blood quantities, and might tempt a hunter into following too soon. On snow, of course, a wounded deer tries a few tricks to making tracking difficult. It might head for the nearest brook, wade up or down the stream, and then leave it with a tremendous leap into a brushy spot to cover its tracks. Or it might join a herd of deer and cover its tracks by mixing in with the group. It often succeeds, particularly if the blood-flow clots and ceases.

It's tough for any hunter to control the urge to chase a wounded deer before giving it necessary time to lie down, particularly if other hunters are in the woods. But remember that nothing will be gained by driving the deer, except to give it up to someone else. Most often, impatiently chasing lightly though fatally wounded deer helps no one make a recovery.

In club and group hunting, good sportsmanship calls for some equalization in dividing the spoils at season's end. Arguments and hard feelings can be avoided if some rules are stipulated before hunting begins. In one of my clubs, our rule was fixed and essentially fair, so much so that almost every club in our area used it for years. The hunter who killed the buck received the head and hide, and the carcasses were equally distributed among all club members at season's end. If a guest was brought in for a few days' hunting at the stipulated daily fee, the same rule applied. In this way, each hunter saved his trophy and hide, yet each man was equally rewarded in meat for his part in driving and getting out the venison.

Safety on a Deer Drive

Safety in group-hunting involves proper procedure on drives. The drivers should carry a crow call or whistle, both to maintain proper distance from their pals in the drive and to make known to all that their movements are not of deer. Standers should be placed on definite posts, known to all hunters involved, and they must stay there until met by the drivers.

I heard of a case where a hunter accidentally killed one of his hunting partners simply because one of them failed to keep his stand. The accident was inexcusable, but it's easy to see how it could happen.

Both hunters were on watch and next to each other. Separating them was a thicket of laurel and white birch. During the drive, a buck came out to a point between the men and about 40 yards off. The hunter fired, dropping the deer, which fell into heavy ferns and other cover, screening it from view. Shortly after the deer dropped, the shooter noticed movement in the brush where the deer had fallen. He fired again, thinking the deer was getting up, even though he couldn't tell it was a deer making the movement. When the driver came through, the hunter left his stand and walked over to find a buck and his hunting partner, both dead. This was a tragedy that wouldn't have happened if the victim had stayed on his stand.

Old Abe Wycoff had a good system for locating stands for his hunters in the Buck Mountain Club. Abe armed himself with a box of metal house numbers and nailed them to a tree in the right location for each watch. On the wall of the club's shack hung a crude map showing each location with the stand's corresponding number. Each hunter knew precisely the location of each stander, greatly assisting safe drives —

provided, of course, that each hunter stayed where put. Obviously, every stander and driver held their fire if they could possibly expect someone to be somewhere in line.

The Prevalence of Deer Hunting Accidents

As a matter of cold fact and contrary to public opinion, deer hunting is one of the safest participant activities in the country. For example: During the 1946 season in New York state, more than 350,000 hunters took to the woods for deer season. Of that number, there were 26 shooting casualties, and only six were fatal. Furthermore, eight of the shootings were self-inflicted because of careless gun-handling.[1]

Carelessness is responsible for most hunting accidents. Not carelessness in mistaking hunters for deer, but negligence in handling firearms. During the mid-1940s, I spent the eve of the opening Adirondack date in Perc Flewellin's hotel in Northville. My buddy and I were in deep slumber when suddenly we were jolted awake by a blast in the next room. Because we were sleepy, we weren't too curious about the cause and fell back asleep. We learned the next day from the proprietor that one of his guests had accidentally discharged a revolver. Luckily, the bullet struck the hollow steel post at the foot of the bed and lodged within. Conceivably, the bullet could have missed and passed through the thin sheetrock walls to injure my partner or me as we slept, this in a place presumably safe from careless people. Had one of us been injured, another accident would have been charged to deer hunting!

Here is another incident involving foolish gun-handling. A friend of mine has long held the peculiar belief that the best stand for a drive is high up a big tree. This chap had the good luck one day to be in the right spot to intercept a buck driven out with a herd of does. He had picked a big oak tree for his stand, and climbed up to the first big limb, where he stood throughout the drive. By chance, this oak stood on the runway and, as the deer ran past below him, he began shooting at the buck. He shot and killed the buck well enough, but as he blazed away at the running buck, one of his shots blasted a ragged hole in his left foot. Instantly the leg crumpled beneath him and he spilled to the ground. By great luck he didn't break any more bones, but the bullet-torn foot kept him on crutches for weeks.

Hunting from a tree has all the earmarks of prime foolhardiness. For the bit of extended vision it grants, a hunter pays the price of limited movement, exposure to wind, tree swaying to deflect his aim, and, more importantly, the hazard of falling out when he shoots.[2] I met a hunter just entering the woods one day who was carrying a .348 Winchester. The rifle was a new model then, so I asked how he liked it. He said he hadn't shot it much, but he'd bet it would sure kill a deer. No doubt that Winchester kicked just as hard then as the .348s do now. At any rate, he passed me on his way out later that day, carrying the action in one hand and the stock in the other. I noticed his face and hands were badly scratched and bleeding, so I questioned him.

"Well sir," he replied, "to make it short and sweet, I was up a tree watching that run over by King Swamp. A little while ago a damned big

[1] *In 1999, New York had about 640,000 firearms deer hunters, an 82 percent increase from 1946. Even so, New York has experienced far safer seasons in recent years than during Koller's era. In 1999, those 640,000 deer hunters were involved in 25 shooting accidents, of which three were fatalities.*

[2] *By 1998, about 75 percent of the United States' estimated 10 million firearms deer hunters preferred using tree stands or other elevated platforms.*

buck walked out of the swamp and I took a shot at 'im. And that damned big cannon knocked me right to hell out of that tree. Skinned me all up and busted the gun right in half."

He was mad clean through, but he never stopped to think he could have broken a leg or arm, or fractured his skull in his fall. He was mostly concerned about missing the deer and wrecking his gun in the process.

One of my fishing pals also climbed trees to watch deer crossings, and carried a pair of linesman's spurs to facilitate the job. During an exceptionally warm, drowsy day, he fell asleep and dropped out of the tree like a ripe acorn. Not in the least disturbed, he returned to camp, gathered himself a piece of rope, climbed back up the tree, and tied himself fast. I believe he still carries the climbing spurs every season, but I hope he doesn't ever forget the rope.

Statistics tend to show that deer hunting is just as safe a place to be as in your home, in weekend traffic or visiting your mother-in-law. I have a good deal of pity for those who will not take up or who give up deer hunting simply because of "danger" perceptions. The New York state figures cited previously are borne out pretty well for deer hunting throughout the nation. I obtained the figures on hunting accidents for all major deer-producing states throughout the 1940s and can find no excuse for listing them all here. Suffice it to say that the dangers involving deer hunting are highly exaggerated.

Care in selecting proper clothing helps give a hunter some measure of self-protection, yet strangely enough, all the accident reports from various states indicate many injured hunters wore red garments or caps. Some hunters believe wearing red in any form makes too good a target for those who will shoot blindly without first determining their target is not a deer. These hunters prefer to take their chances with neutral colors in clothing, and depend on the law of averages to protect them. In any event, it seems foolish for a hunter to wear or carry anything white while deer hunting, even a handkerchief.

One of my younger friends was hunting in Delaware County several years ago, in a section where hills and valleys are high and deep. All morning he had watched the opposite hillside several hundred yards away, but saw no deer moving. About noon he was eating lunch atop a big stump near the top of his ridge. During his vigil, his toes had become a little frosty, so he swung his legs vigorously, banging his heels against the stump to restore circulation. In a moment there came a ripping thud into the stump at his feet, followed instantly by the crack of a rifle from the far slope. Scared and angry, he dropped behind the stump and fired a load into the hillside across the valley. He promptly scared out the would-be killer, but the shooter traveled much too fast for my friend to catch. He deduced later that his white-topped hunting socks, shining out over his boot tops, had been the innocent cause of a near accident.

My next-door neighbor once had his Remington autoloader knocked off his knees as he sat on a stand near Rio in lower Sullivan County. He had been sitting since daylight, and decided to light a cigarette. Sitting calmly and quietly in peaceful contemplation of the valley crossing below him, his rifle was suddenly and violently knocked from his knees. The bullet struck the side of the rifle's receiver, splashing him with bits of bullet and at once ruining the weapon. He had just pulled out his handkerchief — a white one — and was about to lift it to his nose when the blow fell.

Both of these men were in rather plain sight, but the flash of white was all that was required to touch off a hasty trigger finger. Perhaps the day will come when every person who hunts deer will be sure of his target before shooting, but at present, such a utopian situation doesn't exist. Thus, to gain full protection, no deer hunter should wear any white, and it seems wise to wear red, even if it is only a red cap. Even though accidents are rare in proportion to the number of hunters in the woods, it's best not to flout danger by wearing clothing that could be mistaken for deer.

Although red is traditionally the coat of arms for deer hunting, and several states compel hunters to wear it, I don't think it's the ideal color for maximum visibility in the woods. Every season red-garbed hunters are shot at by their brethren during deer season in spite of the obvious: No deer wears red, other than its reddish-brown summer coat. For some hunters, a more vividly contrasting color is necessary. In addition, on cloudy days or in early morning or late afternoon, red changes to more somber shades.

The Importance of Color Visibility

Scientific experiments in color visibility by highway commissions and the armed forces conclusively prove bright yellow is the most visible of all colors, at least to the human eye. With that in mind, I once managed to obtain a long-peaked, white sword-fishermen's cap from Jim Deren's Roost. After immersing it a specified time in Putnam's yellow dye, the cap was ready for a woodland trial.

I wore the yellow headgear first in the Adirondacks. On the season's first day, no less than 10 hunters, all strangers to me, commented on the cap's long-range visibility, even in heavy cover. While hunting down in the Catskills, I received the same comment, so much so that I began asking hunters how far off I could be seen. Distances varied, of course, depending on the cover, but the estimates indicated yellow provided at least a 50 percent greater advantage than the conventional red hat. This is food for thought for the future. I'm certain the first capmaker who offers hunting headgear in a bright chrome-yellow shade will have plenty of takers.[3]

Aside from the fact that someone who wounds a brother hunter will forever be an outcast among deer hunters, it's no longer possible to escape scot free from penalties for such carelessness. Courts no longer look upon hunting accidents as "acts of God." The wanton perpetrator of these bloody acts can be convicted of criminal negligence and forced by law to support the victim's family for years to come. Hunters who keep these penalties forever in mind will think twice before allowing an itchy trigger finger to send a bullet into an unknown target.

As anyone knows, mixing alcohol and hunting is not only incompatible but downright dangerous. A hungover hunter is far from a cheery,

[3]Until blaze, or fluorescent orange, technology became prevalent in the 1970s, the use of bright yellow clothing often was encouraged in state regulations and hunter education classes. By the mid-1990s, only nine of the 48 continental states did not have a law mandating the use of "hunter orange" safety garments for deer hunting. (New York state currently does not require hunter orange, but an estimated 85 percent of the state's deer hunters now wear it.)

alert companion. His head aches, his nerves are jumpy and jittery, and he is far more likely to do something foolhardy with his gun than someone who basks on his stand in sobriety. Liquor is a wonderfully heart-warming tonic, but must forever be used with discretion by the hunter, particularly the camper-hunter. Good sportsmanship decrees that each person in a deer-hunting group be willing and able to start at daylight with a clear head and steady hand, and to take part in each drive and be alert to kill a buck driven to him. After a tough "night-before," no normal person can do justice to his pal's expectations, nor to himself. No one enjoys the lift of a good shot of Old Granddad after a day's hunt more than I do, but not to the extent that rising at dawn for a day in the woods becomes a hardship.

Success and safety in the woods is greatly dictated by personal comfort. Hunters must be warmly and properly clothed head to foot, have a good morning meal under their belt and a long night's rest behind them. Roughing it in deer camp does not need to include uncomfortable beds and skimpy meals. No one can really enjoy the grand sport of deer hunting to the fullest unless they're physically and mentally in shape every day.

The Lost Deer Hunter

Most important to the safety of deer hunters is their ability to find their way around the woods in strange or wilderness territory without becoming lost. A confused, fear-crazed, panic-stricken hunter is a pitiable sight. With his sense of location gone and the fear of a long black night in the woods curdling the blood in his veins, a hunter can go completely crazy and blow his top. We picked up one such man late at night a few years ago in the scrub oak and laurel bush between Wolf Pond and Westbrookville. When we found him, he was a gibbering wreck, clothes ripped off to his waist, pants in shreds, rifle and ammunition gone — and lacking even rudimentary sanity. He had wandered from the rest of his party in country he didn't know. When darkness caught up with him, he was several miles from his group. But when we found him, he was no more than a half-mile from a well-traveled highway and fairly large river, each of which could have brought him to safety if he had studied a map of the area. Even without a compass, he should have been able to find the river or highway, for the weather was clear. Just a few minutes' walk into the setting sun would have brought him to the road, but this victim of ignorance and inexperience couldn't manage it.

In contrast to this experience, I remember the time Old George Drake, one of our outfit, lost himself in the woods. George was a man with a lifetime in the woods, but at his advanced age his hearing was far from acute and the old eyes were dimming. He had gone off by himself to sit on a runway until sundown, and had inadvertently fallen asleep. He roused himself at last, into pitch-blackness, and in the momentary confusion he forgot the lay of the trail. Meanwhile, our outfit was much alarmed, thinking, not that he was lost, but that he had passed out from a heart seizure and might be lying helpless and freezing to death. We scouted his known haunts without success, and were almost ready to give up when a shot sounded faintly behind a ridge about a mile from camp. We made a

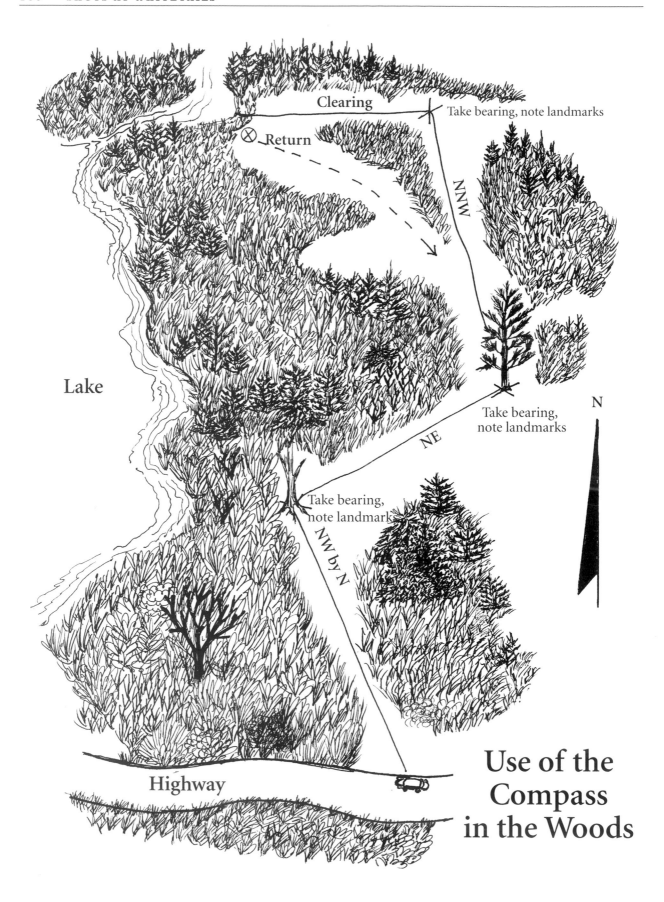

Clearing

Take bearing, note landmarks

⊗ Return

NNW

Lake

Take bearing,
note landmarks

NE

N

Take bearing,
note landmarks

NW by N

Highway

Use of the Compass in the Woods

beeline for the spot, and just before we arrived another shot rang out.

We found George sitting near a little fire, with a big pile of dry wood handy, calmly smoking his cracked briar. He was glad to see us, of course, and a little ashamed at pulling such a stunt, but he apologized for keeping us up so late. In fact, George had decided to spend the night there, but after thinking it over and knowing we would be looking for him, he fired shots to guide us. "Didn't like to do it, though; too damned much shootin' in the woods as it was," he said. Besides he didn't like to use up ammunition, not unless he was shooting at deer.

No man, regardless of experience, should enter large areas in strange territory unless he takes along a compass and a detailed map of the territory. The U.S. Geological maps are ideal. They show the land's physical characteristics — streams, swamp, lowlands, ridges, cliffs and mountains. With one of these maps and a compass to give a constant directional beam, even a rank greenhorn should have little trouble placing his location. He must, of course, have some rudimentary knowledge of using the compass with the map.

One of my early deer-hunting pals showed the typical tenderfoot's reaction to a compass. We had been still-hunting all morning and had covered a couple of miles through an area new to him. When we stopped for lunch at midday, we sat down on a log for a rest and to compare notes. As we chewed the rag about the morning's hunt, he suddenly discovered we were lost. At least he was. Then, struck with a thought, he reached into his shirt pocket and pulled out a beautiful floating dial compass. He carefully placed it on the log, waited for the dial to settle, and then said: "Well, there's the new compass. What do we do now?"

"Nothing, of course," I replied. "You haven't looked at the thing all day until just now, have you?"

"No. Didn't think it was necessary. I thought you could tell just by lookin' at it where you were s'posed to go."

After I stopped laughing, I explained that a compass is useful only if he refers to it frequently on his way through the woods, using landmarks to orient his position at each change in direction. Then, with this information logged mentally, a hunter can reverse his direction to find the way out.

Preparing to Hunt New Territory

Actually, this is all that's required for hunters making short forays into strange country. If he leaves his starting point and heads into the woods due west and maintains that course until ready to come out, then he needs only reverse his direction to return to the starting point. However, if he makes a wide sweep through new forests and ridges, such a simple system fails to help. In this event, he begins his hunt by taking a fixed direction to a visible landmark — a lone pine on a ridgetop, a rock outcropping, or something else distinctive. Then, when he changes direction, it will be at easily remembered points. He then strikes out in a new line, checking always with his compass for another landmark, continuing this procedure throughout the day. Then, when the sun begins to close the day, he retraces his steps, switching his directional travel at the landmarks.

Such a hunt requires a keen memory for cataloging the directions and landmarks in their proper order. If directional changes are too varied, it's wise to make notes as you travel. Best of all, if he has a topographical map, he can make the notes and line of movement on the map and never doubt his precise location. This procedure might seem to be a lot of trouble to a new hunter, but practice in compass and map-reading is invaluable to deer hunters for the rest of their days. Such training forms the basis of true woodsmanship, and can only be acquired through repeated practice. Few of us are born with a keen directional sense, but every hunter can acquire enough of it within a few years to carry him safely through any tight spot.

Experienced hunters and woodsmen somewhat familiar with their hunting areas never need a compass when the sun shines. A good man in the woods can tell time to within 15 minutes by glancing at the sun's position. From this, he can plot any point of the compass. In a pinch, a watch can be made to serve roughly as a compass if the sun shines. Simply hold the watch level, point the hour hand in a direct line with the sun. In this position, due south will lie between the hour hand and the 12. Knowing south, or any other compass point, woodsmen can plot a course in the required direction.

Carrying maps might not appeal to every hunter, and it is not vitally necessary for a map to be carried, provided the hunter has a good memory and can recall the area after studying the map before each hunt. Streams, lakes, ridges and roads can be memorized for direction and relation to each other. The map can then be left behind. But if a hunter is at all hazy on this point, it's wise to mount the map properly and carry it on the hunt. It's simple to mount a map for carrying. And once it's done, a hunter will hate to leave it behind, if for no other reason than it gives him comfort and security in a wilderness area.

A topographical map can be carried as it comes, folded like any other piece of paper. But in a short time, constant exposure and handling will ruin it. To work for the long haul, a map must be mounted firmly on cloth, leaving spaces to allow for folding. What follows is one way to do it:

Mounting a Map

Get a piece of muslin about two inches longer and wider than the trimmed map. Tack the muslin to a board or old tabletop, remembering it takes a day or two to dry the map. Be certain the muslin is stretched tightly both ways, using tacks every inch or so along the edges. Now, take the map, trim the edges and cut it in pieces, following the longitudinal and lateral lines that divide the map into nine parts.

Dampen the muslin thoroughly and work into it a thick paste of laundry starch, then scrape off the excess. Next, apply a heavy coat of wallpaper paste (flour and water) and work this in well, smoothing off the excess. With the muslin prepared, take your nine map parts, keeping them in their proper order, and soak them a minute or two in water, then drain them on blotting paper. Now lay them on the prepared muslin, in proper sequence, leaving a quarter-inch between each section for folding. Allow the map to dry for a day or two after smoothing out the sections. When thoroughly dry, remove the map from the board, trim the outside muslin edge, and fold flat along the section lines. These maps will serve faithfully for many years in the woods.

Using a Compass with a Map

With a map and good compass in his pocket, the hunter can fix his starting point and, as he moves along, compare the streams and elevations with the map outlines. He can note landmarks and, in time, calculate distances accurately. A little study adds much to a hunter's woodslore.

In spite of all readily available advice on this subject, some deer hunters will get lost every year, at least for a short time. If they use a little natural sense, such an incident — while uncomfortable — need not become a calamity. Unfortunately, some hunters have no orienting abilities, nor will they take the time and trouble to learn such rudimentary woodcraft. They should hire a guide and depend on his experience and woodsmanship to keep them in hand at all times.

What to Do When Lost

When a hunter becomes lost, he must follow a definite procedure to retain his health and sanity. First, sit down and take stock of the situation, fighting any feeling of panic. Try to assemble all moves before becoming lost. Console yourself by realizing you cannot be far from familiar ground. And perhaps by clear, straight thinking, you might figure your way out of the situation. Try to remember the general lay of the land. Main ridges tend to follow uniform lines. By thinking back, try to figure out if this new strange spot is merely parallel to the next ridge you followed on the way in. Try to locate the compass points from the sun and time of day. Lacking sun, it's tough to do this. The old cliche about moss growing on the north side of trees hardly works in heavy timber. It is not a reliable guide.

Next, if all your best thinking cannot find a solution, make a small foray to find a logging road, skidway or small stream. Following a stream will in time bring you to civilization, though it might be a long way. At any rate, there is no need to become so panic-stricken that you run crazily in circles, terrorized by the silent loneliness of big timber and the eerie blackness of night. It's far better to decide right away to spend the night in the woods and allow ample time for preparations.

The first step is to find a naturally sheltered spot, such as a rock ledge, an overhanging boulder, a big log or even a heavily thatched evergreen tree. If you have a small ax or heavy knife, erect a couple of sloping poles and quickly thatch them with evergreen branches, forming a tiny lean-to. Next, gather sufficient wood to start a fire and keep it going.

Virtually every deer woods contains plenty of burnable fuel, both for kindling a fire and keeping it going all night. Dead under-branches of most conifers, beech trees and white and yellow birch can be broken off and cracked up for starting the fire. In wet weather, a fire can be started by peeling loose bark from yellow, white or paper birch. Even when damp, these resin-filled scrapings ignite at once to start the fire. Likewise, the lower dead branches of evergreens make the best fire-starters in damp weather. However, the primary function of this small stuff is to get larger wood burning, and the real fire, once started, with proper tending can be maintained all night even in a steady rain — provided some sort of overhead shelter is selected beforehand.

In starting an overnight fire, build it against some sort of reflector — a big log, rock or bank. Lay the tinder and place on it a handful of small under-branches. When the flame catches, feed it more branches until the blaze is going. For heavier firewood, scout until you find several down-branches or windfalls. Never use wood that was flat on the ground. Capillary action makes this wood damp and dozy, and it can be kept burning only by constant addition of more kindling. In every forest, good firewood can be had for the picking, and there is no need to use an ax for chopping the wood into short lengths, even if one is at hand. When the blaze is going, the ends of the heavier branches can be laid on the flames. As the wood is consumed, the limb is moved up for a fresh bite. By shifting the logs and branches as they burn, a warm bright fire can be maintained without using an ax. The best woods for all-night emergency fires are maple, oak, beech and birch. These woods will burn green, particularly in autumn once the fire is well started, but a hunter without an ax will have trouble breaking limbs from living trees. It will be easier to look for dead timber than to wrestle with live stuff.

When you are certain you have enough fuel and a reasonably secure spot for the night, begin to fire signal shots to aid possible searchers. The standard signal is three shots, spaced 10 to 15 seconds apart, but here again, subdue the temptation to burn up all your ammunition in a hurry. Warning signals can be fired every half-hour or so, but not sooner. It requires at least this much time for searchers to move out of earshot of a rifle report, so more frequent firing is unnecessary, and a hunter's ammo supply is seldom extensive. The most important step is to remain in one place, giving the searchers an opportunity to find you.

If you're so unlucky to not have a supply of matches, don't be alarmed. Everyone who carries a firearm can readily start a fire. Prepare the birch bark tinder and small stuff for starting the fire, then take a cartridge and pry out the bullet between two stones. Pour most of the powder onto the tinder, then tear off a piece of a handkerchief or shirt tail and wad it into the mouth of the cartridge case. Fire the cartridge in the rifle, and when the cloth spurts out of the barrel smoking and smoldering, pick it up and blow on it until it glows, then drop it on the spilled powder in the tinder, and it will burst into flame.

A handy fire-starter to carry is an ordinary candle, household size. With one or two of them tucked in the recesses of your coat, you can start a fire quickly with little or no tinder, even in damp weather. For igniting damp wood or bark, the candle can be lighted and the drippings allowed to flow over the tinder. When the flame is touched to the tinder, a prompt fire results. Nothing in your fire-making gear will give such quick, positive results for the room it takes up in a pocket.

Any hunter with a small amount of woods sense will never get into real trouble in the woods. First, he will seldom get lost, and if he does, he will sit and take stock of the situation calmly before panicking. As the realization dawns, his hunting pals will be looking for him shortly. Meanwhile, he will prepare to stay on the spot until his signal shots bring help. Few hunters ever move so far in a day's hunting that they will be out of the hearing area of a rifle report, unless they drop into a deep ravine. In daylight, he can build a big campfire and throw up a smoke screen with evergreen branches. These smoke signals won't go unnoticed for long in the deer woods.

To be safe, wilderness deer hunters should carry a map, compass, knife, chocolate bars, matches in waterproof case, a small roll of twine and perhaps a pocket ax. With this equipment, a hunter can spend a night in the woods with little discomfort. He might lose some sleep and be mighty hungry when he gets out, but that's about all.

A woods compass need only be of a simple type. The floating dial and heavy-needle types are best, because they're not so sensitive to changes induced by outside influences. And in using a compass, never hold it near your rifle, knife or other magnetic metal. Set it on a rock or stump, back away until the dial settles, then check the readings. There is seldom need for a highly accurate compass in deer hunting, but there is a definite need for a simple instrument that furnishes constant bearings.

An Obligation to Self and the Fraternity

A good hunter will take all the time necessary to acquire such knowledge as he needs to follow the grand sport of whitetail hunting. Such knowledge increases his own satisfaction and generates the everlasting gratitude of friends and brother hunters. No man must be a blood brother to the Indian or a direct descendent of Daniel Boone to safely pursue white-tailed deer, but be must use the same good judgment that he would to drive his car on a crowded highway. He must forever be alert to his own mistakes, as well as to the other fellows, tempering every move with basic common sense.

For some obscure reason, many a man becomes a different personality in the woods. At home, he might be a good neighbor and fine friend, but this same man can become thoughtless, selfish, greedy and dangerous while deer hunting. To such a man, bringing home the trophy is of paramount importance, whether it involves sportsmanship or regard for the normal human rights of others. Fortunately, almost all of these men grow up mentally after a few years in the woods, to the eternal betterment of their own sport and the safety of the ever-growing fraternity of deer hunters.

CHAPTER 12

Buck Fever

Whitetail hunting embraces many variables in its numerous phases, but none is more mysterious than the strange malady known as "buck fever." The term has come to mean, through the broad usage of many years, any foolish thing a person might do under stress of high emotional and physical tension or excitement. Originating in the deer woods, it now is loosely applied throughout the entire field of sporting pursuits, both fishing and hunting. If a fisherman regales us with a long sad tale of the big trout that escaped his landing net at the critical moment, does he accuse himself of having had trout fever or fish fever? No. Always it is the admission, if any such explanation is offered, that the unlucky angler must have had a bad case of "buck fever."

Buck Fever and its Effects

Is there such an affliction that can be honestly termed "buck fever"? I believe not. "Buck ague," "buck fever," call it what you will, has a much greater implication of emotional instability than the simple term that sweepingly groups all hunting thrills and excitement into a malady of narrow limitations. Probably a more exact terminology would be possible only for a student of individual psychology. Certainly I would never try to give it a more precise name. Perhaps careful analysis of a hunter's probable reactions to the emotional drive of deer hunting will give a better insight to the problem. And in many cases it is a problem, one far more dangerous and pitiable than humorous.

There seems little doubt the buck fever victims are, at the moment of their travail, entirely different characters from the pals who share your camp roof and venison stew. All during the long weeks of waiting for opening day, through the nights of planning and preparation, right up to the moment of their actually seeing deer, they show normal enthusiasm. Perhaps they are inclined to ply the more experienced hunters with a greater-than-usual number of questions, but in all other respects they are just eager hunters, carrying high hopes and expectations, along with the rest of the party.

With the coming of opening day, they are given good posts to watch the drive. Halfway through, the drivers jump a fine buck and, as so often happens, it heads directly for a new hunter's stand. In a few moments there might be a hurried flurry of shots or perhaps only a single report or none at all. When the drivers come through, they find a shaking, palsied hunter, pale of countenance, sweat oozing from every pore; but no buck. The forthcoming explanations might differ in minor details, but they all follow a familiar pattern. The end result is the same: The buck gets away. This is the situation that is humorous for all the party, other than the unhappy victim. Fortunately, this is the usual result of a buck-fever attack, but now and then a victim will become so emotionally out of hand at missing or failing to shoot at a buck, that he might take a crack at the coming driver when movement shows through the cover. This is the tragic side of the buck-fever picture.

The Shooter's Reactions

Let's analyze the shooter's reactions, if we can, throughout the whole period, up until the time his buck vanishes from sight. It might give us a better understanding of the problem and help stave off possible future attacks. First, it is most likely the buck-fever victim has yet to kill his first buck. True, now and then a hunter will be gripped by the seizure with his second, third or fourth deer, but it is not so common as with the first deer.

Starting then with a virginal deerslayer, we follow his approach to the hunting trip. Undoubtedly, the urge to hunt deer has been implanted by the sight of his friends coming home with a buck or two on their cars. He reads of Tom, Dick and Harry bagging their bucks the first day of the season. He learns from his outdoor magazines that deer are on the increase throughout much of the whitetail's range. Young lads and old-timers alike bring home their buck each season. He visualizes also a wide-spreading trophy hanging over his fireplace or mantel. One of the boys in the office belongs to a hunting camp in the Catskills and, in a moment of largess, invites our hero to spend a weekend trip early in the season. Until now, the victim has been more or less content to spend autumn weekends with the scattergun and cotton-tailed rabbits. But with opportunity knocking, his heart leaps with enthusiasm into the spirit of deer hunting. He buys unlimited quantities of new equipment — extra-warm clothing, comfortable boots, heavy long underwear, knife, compass, etc. Then, after consulting his hunting friends and the oracle of the outdoor magazines, he buys, begs or, more often, borrows a "deer rifle."

But that which is most important to the hunt's success, and which he cannot obtain with mere cash, he neglects to obtain — familiarity with his rifle and the development of a certain degree of shooting skill. He might go so far as to spend an afternoon with his office friend to try out his newly acquired gun, but as for practice, he'll wait until he sees his deer. That'll be time enough, right?

The week before his trip to camp is a frenzy of activity. When the day of departure at last arrives, all of his friends and his patient mate are glad to see him off. But in fairness to the poor fellow, we must admit that such enthusiasm is a large part of any deer hunter's trip. Anticipation is often greater and more pleasing than realization. Arriving in camp, the new lad is introduced to the rest of the bunch. He sits in on the evening bull session with ears wide open, firmly endeavoring to glean such deer lore as he is able to extract within the next few hours. He learns deer are forthright creatures with minds of their own; that no one knows precisely what to expect of a white-tailed buck in the woods. He listens avidly to tales of bucks, large and small, that have outwitted the gang season after season.

Doubt Creeps In

A creeping doubt, dormant for weeks, but now fully aroused, fills his mind.

Next morning, with the new dawn gray in the east, the standers make their way to the posts. A last-minute huddle outside the camp has formed the quick decision to put the new lad on the watch nearest camp. Deer seldom hit for this run, but at least the boys won't be scouring the woods for a strayed stander instead of hunting.

On the watch, the new man is instructed as to where the deer will most likely appear. Then the party passes on, leaving him to his thoughts. For a time he enjoys himself. He sits on a smooth stone, back to a big beech, and snuggles down within his new warm clothes, shaking off the early-morning chill. The rising sun casts a pink glow through the bare treetops canopying his stand. Momentarily, he wonders at the dead stillness of a forest sunrise.

Suddenly, a lone acorn splats noisily onto the crisp, dead leaves. Nervously, he glances that way and then checks his rifle to make sure the cartridge is in the chamber and the action is cocked. He shifts the safety off and on experimentally, wondering why it now seems to click so stridently. For a time all is still until vague scratchings, followed by a rapid crush, crush, crush in the dry leaves, raise his back hair and start his pumper to thumping. Cautiously, he strains his head to peek behind the tree from whence this new disturbance arises. At first nothing is changed in the woodscape, but still the noise persists — quiet rustlings increasing in tempo, then subsiding to a faint murmur. At last, when his mental agitation is at the bursting point, a ghostlike gray tail appears from behind a big oak — only a gray squirrel. With a sigh almost of relief, the hunter once again leans back against his beech tree and attempts to regain his composure.

No sooner has his breathing slowed to normal and his heart pulsing away at its normal smooth rate then, with a quiet swish of wings, a blue jay swings into a nearby tree. With a great show of efficiency, the jay announces the hunter's intrusion in a series of raucous cries that echo interminably throughout the hills. "Damn!" our hero whispers to himself. "Every deer in the world will know I'm here!" After getting no results, apparently, the blue jay flutters off, still shrieking, until its cries fade away in the distance. By this time, the waiting hunter has a firmly entrenched case of nerves. And at this precise moment, deer will inevitably be headed toward his post.

Awaiting the Deer's Appearance

At first our hunter is not aware of their approach. He has heard numerous strange noises during his short wait, and none of them have culminated in a deer's appearance. The faint rattle of brush and tiny rustle of leaves that presage the appearance fail to inflict themselves upon his senses. So far he has gathered himself into a tight knot at every new sound, but now he resolves to wait for the buck to appear before again getting into such a funk. Therefore, the sudden appearance of a sleek pair of does directly in front of his stand gives him, to put it mildly, quite a turn. As his eyes first come to rest on the deer a mighty hand clutches at his heart, giving it a quick, thorough squeeze, sending a tingling fluid — hardly blood — through every nerve and muscle within his body. His mouth flies open as he clutches for more breath and, deep within this oral cavity, his ticker clicks with increasing tempo, like a recalcitrant metronome.

Vainly he looks for antlers and, as the graceful does float by, he glances down at his rifle to check it once again. He looks at the safety, and in his new terror cannot for the life of him remember if it is off or on. Again he tries it and, satisfied, he clicks it off and looks up once more. As his eyes adjust themselves to the new focus, he finds himself staring into a face wearing a high rack of gleaming antlers. Now he is in a fix. Directly before him, head high, ears erect, stands the object of sleepless nights; of many day dreams; of many weeks of preparation and endless planning. Trees and saplings obscure most of the buck from his view. Only the proudly erect head and white throat patch appear vividly before his gaze. The rest of the sleek body is buried behind natural barriers.

Does our hero bring his rifle slowly to rest against his shoulder, carefully cheeking the stock and bringing the front sight up to the gleaming white throat patch, gently squeezing off the shot that will anchor his prize in a flurry of flailing hoofs? No, he does not. Instead, a new fantastic fear freezes his blood — not enough of the deer is visible for him to hit. His palsied hands can never direct the front sight to that white throat target. His fevered brain now knows his shooting ability is not that good, and with each fleeting second the buck is nearer to flight. In sheer desperation he throws up the rifle, only to have it catch under his arm, before coming to shoulder. Damn it! He'd forgotten to try the rifle when he had the new hunting coat on. But with the first quick movement, the deer is away, bounding down through the tall white birch, white flag flying defiantly. Hurriedly the sights are put together, but in the early morning light the front sight seems dim.

A shift of the head brings the front sight into clear view. Now the rifle is poked ahead of the running deer and the shot blasts out, followed by repeated reports until the deer is out of sight. Shaking and weak, the hunter comes slowly back to earth, to the grim realization his deer is still bouncing brightly along, with never a hair disturbed and suffering only the indignities of hurried retreat.

Is There no Cure?

This is the classic example of the seizure known universally as "buck fever." Many times it is evidenced in different ways. The hunter might fail to fire even a shot at the deer, or he might pump every cartridge through his rifle action without firing a single one. But in all cases the result is the same: The buck escapes. From a purely selfish viewpoint, this is an excellent state of affairs. If buck fever and buck ague were nonexistent

maladies, few bucks would be left for the rest of us. Without this affliction, almost every hunter who saw his deer would be shortly carrying it
home, to the distinct alarm of conservation officials. However, nothing
that this writer, or any other, can say on the subject will change the condition. My observations are purely rhetorical.

Any man who spends the greater part of his life hunting whitetails is
bound by the law of averages to encounter some humorous situations,
with buck fever a principal underlying cause. Most failures with hunters
so afflicted result from ignorance in handling their guns, and their
normal human desire to grasp and retain that which is not yet rightfully
theirs. Only by careful pre-seasonal preparation can a hunter overcome
the ravaging effects of the nervous palsy or rigidity induced by buck fever.
Deer hunters must be guided by a great singleness of purpose, a firm
resolve to match physical qualifications with emotional stability.

On at least one occasion I obtained firsthand information on the influence of buck fever. One might say I was in the middle of the situation.
Here is how it came about:

Slow Reaction Times

For several days, my group of hunting pals had been trying to drive a
big buck out of a valley swamp. Early in the season, one of the boys had
missed this buck and since that day we were convinced it hid away in the
recesses of the swamp. Cover was good and the surrounding ridges were
densely thatched with laurel, scrub oak and jack pine. It was difficult to
drive out the deer to a stander, for its path could cover any one of many
routes, all of them through thick terrain. Our group was limited in
numbers, so we were required to stand three men and drive only two. On
the morning I have in mind, three of us had taken stands along a wood
road that paralleled the swamp edge a few hundred yards above the
swamp on a little ridge. The two drivers worked through the low ground,
then came up the ridge through tangled cat-briers and laurel clumps, but
without starting any deer.

We had made this drive early in the morning, and because the season
was well advanced, the boys weren't in any sweat to make the next drive.
Accordingly, we agreed to go back to camp about a quarter-mile away,
and have a fresh cup of coffee before beginning the next drive. The two
drivers started off for camp, leaving my two companions and me standing
in the wood road. For several minutes we talked together in hushed tones,
planning new strategy to kill this swamp buck. Then we, too, made off for
camp. Quietly we moved along the wood road, one young lad leading the
way, another bringing up the rear.

As we passed some thick clumps of white birch and cat-brier, the man
ahead suddenly stopped, pointing down into the white birch through
which the drivers had just come. Almost at the same instant the lad
behind me whispered, "It's a buck!" At the moment my view of the deer
was obscured by a clump of big oak trees, but I took one step backward
and peered down into the heavy stand of white birch. True enough, there
stood a buck, quartering away, with his head turned over his shoulder and
looking directly toward us. With a single movement, I unslung the short-

barreled Krag, swung it up and, as the front sight appeared through the rear peep against the buck's flank, I squeezed off the shot. At once the deer floundered to the ground, and as I was about to send in a finishing shot, both my companions jumped over the stone wall, directly in the line of fire, toward the deer. Meanwhile, the buck had risen from the ground, but only moved a few feet before expiring. This was indeed luck, for I would never have had another shot at him without risking the life of either one of the two men with me.

At any rate, after we had the buck in camp, both of the boys who had been with me began to lay me out for not giving them a chance at the deer. This was absurd, for both had seen this buck several moments before I had, yet they seemed frozen at the sight. It has always been my aim to kill a buck as quickly as the opportunity presents itself, but evidently my companions had suffered a slight touch of buck fever at the quick wraith-like appearance of a buck where deer had no logical right to be.

Do You Belong?

Such experiences are common in every deer-hunting territory. There is no way to counteract the thrill attendant on first sighting a white-tailed buck, nor should there be. Such a thrill is the primary reason for hunting deer, and without it, a man might better sit home by the fire and recount the experiences of youth, when heart-stopping thrills were still a part of his existence. Any sportsman who can kill his deer without the tingling spine, the quick clutch at his heart, the delicious trembling of nerve fibers when the game is finally down, has no place in the deer woods.

CHAPTER 13

The Archer Deer Hunter

Scattered throughout our broad expanse of deer-hunting territory is a select group of highest-quality sportsmen. In singles, pairs or small groups they take to the woods each year, garbed in conventional woods garments but carrying the primitive weapons of a bygone age.

Around each hunter hangs the traditional aura of Robin Hood and the American Indian, for these are the modern-day archers who prefer to take their game under the most exacting of all hunting conditions and with weapons, that, although wholly adequate, are certainly not a most efficient method of destruction.

The Archer's Place in Deer Hunting

It might be difficult for the nonhunter to visualize the reasons for bow-and-arrow hunting; but for men who love the outdoors, the sweeping roll of timbered ridges, the stark-white stands of birch and the quiet gray halls of beech, the bow and its silent but deadly missile might become a logical choice. Certainly it will never be the weapon for a man who must kill every buck he sees; neither will it be the choice of the hunter who cannot bear the ridicule of his hunting partners or friends. No, far from this, the bow and broadhead shaft are the weapons of the true nature lover, the hunter who above all things dislikes the discordant crash of gunpowder rending apart the holy silence of the forest.

Then, too, the man who takes his buck with the longbow and feathered shaft feels a far greater physical intimacy in the act than the hunter who squeezes a trigger, thereby releasing the storehouse of energy which lies within the brass cylinder in his rifle chamber. The killing force of the arrow is the direct result of the archer's muscular effort in compressing the bow, then releasing this force to speed toward the quarry.

Any man who takes up the bow as the weapon for bagging his white-tailed buck will realize full well the great handicap under which he will hunt. For many hunters who are surfeited with killing deer with the rifle, archery offers a welcome change in values and results. The kills will be few in number, but the experiences will far outweigh those of the rifle shooter. Successful deer hunting with the bow demands by far the greatest skill in woodcraft and stalking, plus the most intimate knowledge of the personal habits and characteristics of the game.

The great, widespread increase in archery deer hunting is a heartwarming indication of the greater sporting trend of a new generation of hunters. The archer hunts not for meat, not for the trophy, but for the sheer, pure joy of matching wits and endurance with that clever animal, the white-tailed buck. It is apparently the renewal of the dauntless pioneer spirit, the heritage of Americanism, that prompts this new crop of archers to meet the challenge offered in taking deer with the bow and arrow.

Many states, recognizing this new surge of aesthetic endeavor, have gone along with the archer in establishing special seasons or setting aside hunting preserves for archery alone. Here he will be in company of his own choosing and will enjoy a greater feeling of comradeship and sympathy with his fellow hunters. No archer likes to think his already slim chance of bagging a buck will be unfavorably influenced by the presence of rifle-toting sportsmen in his hunting grounds.

Leaders in the movement to promote archery hunting have been Michigan and Wisconsin. In Michigan, the entire state was open in 1946 for taking antlered deer from Oct. 1 to Nov. 5 inclusive[1], and in Allegan County deer of either sex could be taken. In 1946, the state commission set the special Allegan County season to extend from Oct. 1 through Dec. 15. This liberal archery deer season was excellent for weekend hunters throughout autumn. The warm weather hunters had their chance to bag a deer when the air was balmy, and the more serious hunters were able to take their hunting trips when the deer were moving in cold weather and on snow. Experience shows that in Allegan County, the best period for archers is during the first two weeks in November.

Wisconsin's archers have done a creditable job, not only in promoting the sport, but in really taking deer. The 1945 season was one of the most successful in the entire country. Roughly 3,500 archers took to the field and bagged 160 deer with the bow and arrow — 69 bucks and 91 does.[2] The state's special archery provisions are highly favorable for the archer-hunters. In 1945, they were permitted to hunt throughout a 45-day period in 49 counties, and during this period one deer of either sex, over yearling size, could be taken. The outstanding archery preserve is the Necedah Wildlife Refuge, 40,000 acres in Juneau County, which was opened to archery hunting in 1945 after being closed to all hunting for six years.

Wisconsin also is unique in that it publishes a complete report in its conservation bulletin on the deer taken the preceding year, giving sex and weight of deer, county in which taken, weight of bow used, whether the shot was running or standing and how far the deer traveled after being hit.[3]

As far back, comparatively speaking, as 1938, Wisconsin had a keen interest in the archer-hunter. The commission's report for that year shows about 600 archery permits issued, with only six hunters bagging their bucks. This low average of success in those early years of archery hunting indicates it was even rougher going than today to kill a deer with the bow and arrow.

In deference to these "pioneers" in archery hunting and for the further interest of new archers, the author is listing the circumstances of each

[1]*In 1999, as in the years leading up to the current day, Michigan's archery season ran Oct. 1 through Jan. 1 statewide.*

[2]*In 1999 in Wisconsin, 252,431 archers killed 91,937 deer.*

[3]*The Wisconsin Department of Natural Resources still publishes an annual harvest report, breaking the kills down by sex, county and management unit.*

1938 kill as published by the Wisconsin Game Commission:

1. Howard L. Thrapp,
215 N. Allen St., Madison
Date: Oct. 15, at 11:30 a.m.
Location: Columbia County
Shot: Deer standing at 66 feet
Weight: 191 pounds dressed
Points: 10
Bow: Osage orange, rawhide back,
72-pound draw
Arrow: Birch, 26½-inch barbless broadhead
Fall: Deer traveled 30 yards after shot

2. Walter O. Widner,
928 Humboldt, La Crosse
Date: Oct. 15, 2 p.m.
Location: Buffalo County
Shot: Deer standing at 60 feet
Weight: 278 pounds dressed
Points: 10
Bow: Lemonwood, 45-pound pull
Arrow: 28-inch barbless broadhead
Fall: Deer traveled only 30 feet after shot

3. Clayton M. Sweo,
609 Allen St., Rhinelander
Date: Oct. 15, 5 p.m.
Location: Iron County
Shot: Deer standing at 90 feet
Weight: 190 pounds dressed
Points: 8
Bow: Osage orange, 65-pound pull
Arrow: 28-inch barbed broadhead
Fall: Deer traveled 400 yards after shot

4. Lester Shore,
1314 Hoven Court, Madison
Date: Nov. 1, 11:30 a.m.
Location: Columbia County
Shot: Deer running at 60 feet
Weight: 200 pounds dressed
Points. 10
Bow: Cuban lemonwood,
75-pound pull
Arrow: 28-inch birch barbless broadhead
Fall: Deer traveled 500 yards after shot

5. Frank J. Parker,
2560 N. Eighth St., Milwaukee
Date: Nov. 5, 10 a.m.
Location: Columbia County
Shot: Deer running at 45 feet
Weight: 245 pounds dressed
Points: 8
Bow: Lemonwood, 55-pound pull
Arrow: 26-inch barbless broadhead
Fall: Deer traveled 100 yards after shot

6. Wallace J. Bowman,
Madison
Date: Nov. 12, 11:55 a.m.
Location: Columbia County
Shot: Deer turning at 60 feet
Weight: 125 pounds dressed
Points: 4
Bow: Yew, 60-pound pull
Arrow: Cedar, 28-inch barbless broadhead
Fall: Deer traveled 150 yards after shot

Each of those six deer were killed with a single shaft. In addition, no deer were lost that year by archery hunters because of failure of the arrow to kill. However, two or three of these archers had a fairly long chase to recover their buck.

Seventeen states, at this writing in 1948, provide special archery preserves, special seasons for archers, or both. New York state legalized longbow hunting in 1929, but did little to promote archery throughout the state other than opening Westchester County, just outside New York City's limits, to the archery deer hunter. During the 1945 season, just over 30 deer were taken by archers almost within sight of Manhattan's skyline. There is, however, a movement underway to open additional and more desirable areas to deer-hunting archers for coming seasons in New York state.[4]

Limitations of Archery Equipment

To become a good deer-hunting archer, not only must a sportsman change his mental attitude to be in tune with the clan of successful bow-and-arrow men, but he must prepare to spend months in patient practice with the primitive weapons before he steps into deer country. Even then he must reconcile himself to going deerless for a few seasons, unless

[4]*By the early 1950s, New York archers were killing more than 1,000 deer annually, and throughout the 1990s, New York archers annually killed between 15,000 and 25,000 deer.*

exceptional luck is on his side. The archer, by the nature of his weapon, will never become a threat to our supply of deer, but his rewards in satisfaction, thrills and excitement will be far greater when he does connect than any that ever come to the rifle-hunter.

An archer need not be the world's best shot in order to kill his deer. It is a rare buck that is killed at a distance as great as 50 yards, even though a normal individual with good equipment can score regularly on a deer target at this range with lots of practice. There are many more important deterring factors in shooting deer than the archer's ability to hit his target. Every man who has hunted whitetails knows how seldom it is that a fairly open shot can be had, and what we usually term an "open" shot in rifle shooting can still be an impossible chance for an archer. An arrow needs only to touch a twig, either at its head or anywhere along its length, to be deflected far off its course. And the chance of hitting such overhanging twigs and branches is high in white-tailed deer cover.

With the rifle, a hunter needs only a small opening, say about 4 inches in diameter, through which he can poke his bullet and nail his buck. At deer-hunting ranges the trajectory of the bullet will seldom show a curve greater than 1 inch above or below the line of sight. With the bow and arrow, this curve is greatly exaggerated; and the lighter the bow weight the greater the curve in the line of flight as the arrow travels to the target, even at fairly short range. Therefore, the archer must have a nominally high vertical clearance in order to direct his shaft above the target that it will carry up to the desired range.

Then we must have sufficient horizontal clearance as well, for when the arrow leaves the bow it "flirts," weaving from side to side at the feathered end until it stabilizes itself in flight. This amount of "flirt" or "whip" varies with the stiffness of the shaft, the cast of the bow, the width and length of the fletching. The larger the feathers, the less this tendency is evident; but there is a limit to the size of fletching that can be used, and it cannot be fully corrected.

This is the archer's greatest hunting problem: to find his deer through a large enough opening and to be able to drive the arrow through to the target. Just the slightest touch from an intervening branch in the path of the arrow will cause a dismal miss and often a lost arrow as well as a lost deer. Much of this high arching trajectory can be lessened by use of a heavy, fast bow as strong as a man can pull, and arrows that are stiff enough to withstand the shock of the release with a minimum of "flirt."

The Killing Effect of Broadheads

The layman, and many deer hunters as well, ridicule the killing effect of a broadhead arrow driven from a heavy hunting bow. A number of years ago, I was making up a hickory-backed Osage orange hunting bow when one of my deer-hunting pals dropped into the shop. I was tillering up the bow and shaping up the bends in each limb when my friend made a remark about my coming into a second childhood, seeing that I was playing with toys. It so happened that a chestnut board, about 6 feet long, 10 inches wide and an inch thick stood against the rear wall of the shop, so I decided to demonstrate that modern bows could hardly be called toys. I picked up an old handmade broadhead shaft from the workbench, nocked it and let drive at the chestnut board. By sheer luck the broadhead blade struck close to the center, with the blade upright, and the plank promptly split full length into two halves, each piece rattling to the floor. When my friend's hair had uncurled, I walked over and after five minutes' work with a pair of pliers, managed to get the shaft free of the wall, which it had penetrated freely after splitting the long plank. This, of course, did not demonstrate any effective killing power, but I am certain my friend never again thought of an archer as carrying toys.

It has been demonstrated over many years that the broadhead shaft, driven from a hunting bow, has remarkable powers of penetration on even the largest game. The late Arthur Young killed every species of North American game, including the tremendous Alaskan brown bear, with single shafts from his 90-pound bow. Modern archers who kill game the size of deer find that just as often as not the arrow will pass cleanly through the animal on broadside shots even with the 1-inch-wide steel broadhead.

The broadhead, of course, unlike the rifle bullet, kills by hemorrhage rather than shock. But any deer solidly hit anywhere in the body area has little chance to escape. The bleeding effect of arrow wounds is prodigious; usually a hit anywhere in the body cavity will bleed the animal to death within a few minutes. A keen-edged broadhead shaft will sever every nerve and blood vessel in its path, giving virtually the effect of a broadsword pushed through the body. The trailing of arrow-wounded deer at once becomes a simple thing; bleeding is not only extremely free, but the shaft within the wound prevents its closing to shut off the blood trail.

A hunting arrow simply has no shocking effect, unless by chance it strikes a nerve center within the spinal column. But a heart-shot buck will invariably come to earth quicker with a broadhead wound than if he were struck with a standard .30-caliber soft-point bullet. Rifle bullets have a tendency to mangle tissue, contributing to quick clotting of blood and the cessation of a blood trail, unless the hit is highly mortal. With the broadhead blade, nerves, tissues and blood vessels are severed cleanly and thoroughly, making a wound that fails to clot up. Even in lung-shot deer the arrow will cause a more quickly fatal wound than the rifle bullet; for with the entry of the shaft, air reaches the lung areas and both lungs collapse as a pricked balloon.

My experiences with the bow are not extensive enough to prove of any value, but my first buck was struck in the left flank as he quartered away, the shaft passing through the diaphragm and emerging behind the right shoulder. The arrow penetrated beyond the feathers, out of sight in the flank, and as the buck made off through the white birch, the forward end of the shaft snapped off against the trees.

When I came up to the buck 100 yards away, there was no sign of an arrow visible, so I concluded the shaft had passed through. However, when I dressed him out, my fingers soon found the shaft, lying diagonally within the body cavity and almost through the center of the diaphragm tissue. This buck bled out most thoroughly within 100 yards of being hit. When I turned him over after making the belly incision, what seemed like a water-pail of blood poured out. I have never seen a more completely drained buck nor one that expired more quickly to a raking shot from the rear with conventional deer rifles.

Selection of Equipment

In selecting his hunting equipment, the archer will be wise to get the fastest wood in the heaviest bow he can handle. This means either laminated split bamboo or Osage orange; yew is a wonderful bow wood but it is so soft it damages readily under hunting conditions. The bow should be short, for easy handling; backed with some tough material like silk, nylon or fiber for both increased cast and strength and protection to the bow wood itself.

This backing should be dark in color, otherwise any buck will be alarmed at the light flashes when the bow is raised for the shot. However, in selecting the hunting bow it is not wise to go overboard in drawing weights; many men cannot pull, hold and smoothly release a shaft from a bow pulling in excess of 60 pounds. A 50-pound bow certainly has enough power for penetration, but it has a slightly higher trajectory than bows of heavier weight and quicker cast. Therefore, as in all other hunting problems, a happy medium must be chosen.

Arrows must be carefully matched with the bow. Heavier, faster bows will require a heavy arrow shaft for stiffness. Usually a bow pulling more than 60 pounds will require a ⅜-inch shaft to prevent buckling or "whipping" at the release. Lighter bows, down to 50 pounds, will be best-suited with smaller shafts, about 1½-inch in diameter. Feathers should be large enough to support the shaft in flight; probably a minimum size for hunting would be 4 inches long and ½-inch wide. Large-diameter shafts with heavy broadheads will require even larger feathers than this.

In any event, the fletching on a broadhead arrow should be slightly spiraled on the shaft, or the head will cause planing through the air. If the arrow spins in flight, in a way similar to the rotational spin of a rifle bullet, little, if any, of this planing effect will show. Few archers, however, will begin the hunting game by making their own arrows, so when hunting arrows are ordered from the manufacturer the bow length, weight and material should be specified.

Broadheads are still the subject of much discussion and experiment. Roughly speaking, the head should be barbless, three times as long as it is wide, and made of light spring steel. The barbed head does nothing the barbless cannot do to kill game. Furthermore, from the conservationist's viewpoint, it is not as desirable for it will not work out of the wound should a light hit be made. Another thing, the barbed heads continually catch on the top of a quiver as they are withdrawn, and often will jab an archer's finger if he makes a full, quick draw.

Practice Methods for Hunting

The most important problem for the inexperienced hunting archer is how to get the right kind of shooting practice for deer hunting. Orthodox target shooting will teach a hunter the proper methods of holding, aiming and releasing, and these fundamentals should be first well-established on the target range. For hunting, however, a different technique is required. The lessons learned in target shooting at specified ranges and with target arrows will be of little benefit in the hunting field. First of all, the switch from light, slender target arrows with pile heads and tiny feathers to the solid, thick hunting shaft with its long fletching and broadhead point will throw the archer's point of aim way low and at the same time will show a much higher trajectory curve over the usual hunting ranges, that is, up to 50 yards. To get sensible practice at hunting ranges and with arrows that will shoot exactly like the hunting shafts, the archer should order with his hunting broadheads a matching set of roving arrows, preferably with hardwood footings. Then with these arrows he can spend some time on the target range, learning the new holds for the different trajectory at various ranges.

With this knowledge fixed in mind, he will spend some time in the field, just wandering, shooting at random targets such as tufts of grass, rotted stumps or anything that comes to his fancy, all at various unknown ranges. Only in this way will he prepare his shooting skill for the deer-hunting season. No rule can be laid down for trajectories and sighting for the archer, as there can be for the rifle shooter; each man, each bow and each set of arrows is a law unto itself and the archer must work out the problem under the best simulated hunting conditions.

It is advisable to perfect a somewhat different draw for the roving and hunting field than is used by the target shooter. Almost every target shooter holds a draw low under the chin and either sights well below the gold over the tip of the arrow, or uses a properly adjusted bow sight to correct for this low draw. But with the heavy hunting bow and the premium on accurate work at unknown ranges up to 50 yards, the line of the arrow's flight must be held as close to the eye as possible. This offers the least change in holding at unknown ranges up to the limit of the bow's point-blank range.

Today's best field archers draw to the corner of the mouth or to the angle of the jawbone, rather than under the chin, tipping the bow slightly to the right and inclining the head in the same direction. This brings the arrow more or less in line with the shooting eye and brings the nock end close to the line of sight. Practice with this method in the field at odd ranges will soon prove its worth over the conventional head-erect, low-under-chin draw found on the target range. When the archer has developed a degree of shooting skill that holds most of his arrows within the red ring of a regulation target at 40 yards, he is ready to take to the deer woods with the knowledge that should a fair chance at a buck present itself, he will at least have the necessary know-how to connect.

How to hunt with the bow and arrow is much more of a problem than it is with the rifle. Orthodox still-hunting methods will seldom get an archer a sufficiently close shot to score. The best method seems to be patient watching on runways at the edge of heavy cover, where the deer will approach the archer's stand close enough to afford a shot. Best of all, if the archer has the opportunity, he may stand a regulation deer drive.

Organized group hunting will give him his best chance at a buck, but human nature being what it is, archers are seldom welcome among the ranks of rifle-shooting groups. All in all, the archer has a tough row to hoe in the deer-hunting field, but to a man who loves the sport this will never be a deterrent.

The Archer's Future in Deer Hunting

The best course for a man who feels the blithe spirit of the archer in his veins is to seek until he finds a stout-hearted companion of kindred spirit. Only the most rugged individualist can follow the archer's way of life alone. But with the understanding and sympathy of a friend or two, archery in the deer-hunting field can be and is one of the most exciting, satisfying and spiritually gratifying sports that a hunter can pursue.

New legislation will foster and nourish the growing sport until within the next decade archery will assume a major place in the deer-hunting field. For as one of our modern pioneer archers has said, "So long as the new moon returns to the heavens a bent, beautiful bow, so long will the fascination of archery keep hold of the hearts of men."

CHAPTER 14

Venison for the Table

Many years before the Catskill deer herd approached its 1940s proportions, one of the nuclei herds in the Southern area was enclosed within the relatively narrow limits of the Chapin estate in Sullivan County's Mongaup Valley. As this herd increased in leaps and bounds, the overflow spread throughout this area of the county. Deer hunting at that time was just beginning to come into its own for Eastern hunters.

What Makes Good Meat?

Of this time and locale, Bert Sauer tells a story in connection with venison. Bert and his gang had been hunting their deer along the fringes of Chapin's estate. They had no organized club or camp buildings — just a few interested hunters who would get together each year for the short open season, staying at a nearby farmhouse. Each year their farmer-host would raise a young bull calf, fatten it well and slaughter it about two weeks before opening day. When the gang arrived, he would have a well-seasoned, tender young beef for filling stomachs emptied by long hours in the woods.

But one year, with chores and other things keeping him busy, he had forgotten to slaughter his calf in time for proper aging of the meat. In the last-minute rush, he disposed of the job only the day before the gang arrived, bringing with them two young tenderfoot hunters. That night when the gang had assembled around the poker table for the usual deer hunter's bull session, their host called Bert aside and explained the situation. He suspected there might be a complaint or two after the first few mouthfuls of young bull were consumed, so he decided it best to anticipate the reaction. Bert laughed it off, then suddenly was taken with an idea: Why not let the two greenhorns get first crack at the new beef?

Next morning, in the blackness of pre-dawn, breakfast was under way. The host's eldest daughter, in on the plot, sneaked out to the woodshed and sliced two long, tough, stringy slabs of meat, right off the shank. These two choice morsels were thrown into the big skillet and fried as rapidly as the huge, wood-burning kitchen range could turn them out. Slyly, yet casually, the two big plates of beef, piled-high home-fries and thickly sliced home-baked bread were slipped onto the table before the two new men.

We must credit them with rugged determination. For many minutes each one bravely sought to hack off a mouthful. This accomplished, more minutes were spent in vain mastication, until in desperation the lump was swallowed whole. Bert noticed that after each had manfully disposed of several mouthfuls, the remainder was left severely alone. Each lad tackled the potatoes and bread, but no more of that meat!

Breakfast over, Bert collared the pair. "What's the matter with you boys? Didn't you like that venison? I didn't see you eatin' much of it."

"Gosh, Bert," spoke up the older of the two, "we didn't know that was venison. You can bet if we'd 'a' known about it we'd have et a lot more of it!"

Where Does Venison Rank?

This story accurately sums up the layman's opinion of venison as a food. And until recent times we could include a great proportion of deer hunters in this category. Better legislation and wider education in meat handling have done much to improve this picture with 1940s hunters. Not so long ago, most states made it illegal to possess venison for any appreciable length of time after the season closed. Extensions of possession time could sometimes be had by applying for, and paying for, a special permit. This was too much trouble for many hunters. They would eat it all or give it away before the end of the short grace period. Such venison had barely time to cool properly, to say nothing of aging. Normally, such meat, whether venison or not, is hardly ready for the table. Our best packing-house meats are all well-aged, sometimes for several months, before coming to our tables. Why not give our venison similar treatment if we would really enjoy it?

It is decidedly unfair to venison as a food to compare it with best grades of beef. Top-grade beef is the result of many years of carefully selective breeding for the best meat types, careful feeding from infancy and grain fattening before slaughter. Directly before slaughtering, every effort is made to keep the animals quiet and comfortable. And, of course, the slaughtering and butchering is done under conditions that create complete blood drainage and no damaged meat. Likewise, good beef is slaughtered at certain periods when the animals are in the best physical condition. Then, rigid inspections allow only the best beef to reach the market. This is not an apology for venison, merely a small explanation to mark the distinction between beef and deer meat, often compared unfavorably with the flesh of a prime steer.

To eat good venison, hunters must treat this meat special. They must be able to discern the good from the poorer animals, and make the necessary adjustments to produce tasty venison dishes. It is perhaps unfortunate that hunters have little choice in taking their venison. They usually take the first antlered deer to come before their sights and merit plenty of praise for making a clean kill. As a matter of fact, there is no way to determine how well a buck will eat until it is killed and dressed. I have killed spikes and forkhorns — apparently the best eating of male deer — and have found one or two that had less prime meat than a heavy old buck of many summers.

An unavoidable fact of the 1940s is that virtually all bucks are hunted after the rutting season has passed, or at least well under way. This factor produces lean venison, and lean meat of any kind cannot be as tender as that which is well-larded with fat. All other things being equal, the fattest deer produce the finest venison, both in quality and flavor. This has nothing to do with the buck's age. Young bucks that should be good eating will often run off all their fat during the rut. When the mating fever is full in their blood, they neither rest nor eat to any extent until this fire has subsided. A young buck taken just after this period will show the ravages of the reproductive urge in lean hips and protruding ribs.

A fat, senile old buck, passing his prime of vitality, will retain a large proportion of his premating good condition and almost always will be tender and well-flavored. Two of the best-eating bucks ever to grace my table were such deer. Heavy in body, with wide-spreading antlers, each was the "hermit" type, feeding cautiously after dark, hiding away in daylight hours and, so far as I could tell, never associating with the does. Both bucks were blanketed in layers of fat, with thin layers marbling the flesh. Venison of the best!

Conditions under which the buck is taken decidedly influence meat quality. Deer that were horribly wounded and then trailed for miles before being recovered show the effects of such killing. The meat will be darkened with diffused blood, and much of it will be blood settled near the wound. These parts can be discarded in the butchering, but the flavor of the venison throughout will be impaired by such unconventional slaughtering. Any buck so killed will never compare with deer taken by a clean, quick kill.

In any case, we must make the best of what we have. Seldom will any buck be in such poor condition that proper handling cannot procure good venison. But hunters must be able to discern these qualities in their game and take the necessary steps to condition it.

Hanging and Aging Venison

Let's assume you have a nice little forkhorn buck. When you dressed him out in the woods, you noticed strings of fat clinging to his intestines. His kidneys were buried in fat strips, clinging to each rib. Plenty of this same fat could be seen lying under the hide along the flanks and over the chest. With such a prime specimen, you can strip off the hide, cut a steak and throw it on the broiler as soon as the body heat has cooled, and you'll have good eating. The same goes for a big deer or a small one. If the fat is there, the venison will be tender. Not too often, though, do we kill such prime deer. The run of the mill buck will be somewhat leaner, perhaps much leaner. These are the problem deer, the deer that should be hung in the hide for 10 days, three weeks or a month.

No fast rule should be made in regard to handling deer. Each must be treated as an individual. Almost every deer will be improved in flavor, if not in tenderness, by hanging it in a refrigerated cooler or in a protected building if the weather is uniformly cold. Ideal temperatures for aging venison are somewhere between 36 and 42 degrees, but not freezing. Freezing your buck will not age him, for freezing hinders the breakdown of the muscle cells. It's proper to freeze your venison after butchering and after it has been aged, but not before.

The exact period of time for aging venison is by no means fixed. A prime fat buck need hang in the cooler no more than a week. Lean, rangy deer, impoverished by the ravages of the rut, can hang well for a month. A light coating of fuzzy mold will form inside the body cavity after a week or more, but this is of no concern. It can be easily wiped off and the meat below will be mellow and tender. Any deer in the hide, properly cooled after dressing, will remain edible a long time in a cooler, provided the temperature is kept constant. Any "high" odor that develops will be from the flank meat or thin edges of the abdominal cavity. When this is cut away, the remainder will be sweet and tender.

A buck hung in the hide will cure well and rapidly, not drying out in the process. If the carcass is skinned, then allowed to hang, the whole outer surface will harden like rock, and in time will get some of this "high" odor. This does not mean the meat is spoiled. Simply slicing off this hard "case" will reveal good venison below, but these air-dried deer are never as palatable as venison cured in the hide.

It's true that some curing will be gained by skinning out your buck, butchering it into the proper cuts, and then quick-freezing and storing it in the locker. This is fine for prime venison, but for the less-fat animals, such treatment stops far short of proper aging. Only a prolonged period in a refrigerator cooler at about 40 degrees will make such deer tender and flavorful. After the curing process, if you still want your deer to hang a bit more, it can be hung in a freezing compartment and frozen solid. Needless to say, any buck so frozen will remain in good eating condition almost indefinitely until ready for skinning and butchering.

Skinning and Butchering Deer

When your buck is ready for eating, get it home from the locker plant and allow yourself a full evening for skinning and butchering. If you plan to have the meat processed and stored in a locker, get the proper wrappings from your locker owner. If you'll make venison sausage — and by all means, do — get a dozen 1-quart ice-cream containers from your locker plant or the drugstore. Have your small-bladed skinning knife sharp, and borrow a meat saw from your butcher. Together with a short piece of manila rope, your oilstone, an old sheet of oilcloth, and a short, heavy club, you're ready to get your venison out.

Bring your deer into the woodshed or down into the cellar, anywhere there's a solid beam for hanging it. If the carcass is frozen, you'll need to wait until the juices begin to flow inside the body cavity before you can get the hide started. First, disjoint or saw off all the legs, then slip a short piece of rope through the gambrel of each hind leg. Throw your rope over the beam and pull up the deer while someone gives you a hand to get the carcass off the floor. Tie this one leg fast, then make the initial cut from the shank right down to the straddle. Make fast the other leg-rope at a point two or three feet from the first tie, spreading the hindquarters to make the skinning points more accessible at the beginning. Now make the second cut, down the inside of the other leg, meeting the end of the first cut in the straddle.

Pull the skin down on each leg, using the knife only to separate the tissues, until the tail can be skinned out. Run your knife underside the tail from its root to a point halfway to the tip of the tailbone, and peel down the skin until you can get your fingers between the tail-bone and the hide. Then with a sharp, downward pull, slip the tail-bone right out of the tail.

If you plan to mount the head, now is the time to mark the hide all around the shoulders and across the brisket, bringing the cut over the top of the withers. It will be much easier to determine where the hide should be cut while it still is on the buck, then no mistakes will be made after the hide is off the deer. Also at this point, the cut should be made from the top of the shoulders to the midway point between the ears. This greatly eases removal of the neck skin, rather than trying to pull it down over the neck as a tube. For some reason, the neck skin clings tightly to the flesh, and if the hide is not slit at the top of the neck line the skinning job will be lengthened.

From this point, getting the hide off is merely a task of strength. The hide is pulled down, rather than cut loose from the carcass. The knife will be needed only to keep the separation going and at tight places along the sides and the middle of the back. Much of the hide can be pounded loose with the short club, your fist or the butt of the skinning knife. Considerable weight will be exerted on the hide to get it loose, so be certain the deer is solidly hung close to the beam with a strong rope. When the forelegs are reached, make the same cuts from the shank end, down the inside of each leg and meeting behind the point of the brisket. If you have made the preliminary marking cuts for mounting the head, the foreleg cuts can be brought out to meet these cuts just behind the brisket.

Of course, it is not necessary to remove this much hide for mounting the head unless a shoulder mount is desired, but even for a neck mount, better be safe and allow plenty. If the head is not to be saved, an opening cut can be made from the junction point of the ribs, through the brisket and up the underside of the neck to the lower jaw, thus opening up the neck for easier skinning.

When the skinning progresses to a point just behind the buck's ears, feel for the axial joint with your fingers or by inserting the knife point. This joint marks the connection with the skull and spinal column. Cut through the flesh completely around this point, then simply twist off the head. It is never necessary to saw or chop off a deer's head to get it free.

Now with the butcher's saw, begin to cut the carcass in half, first cutting out the tail to clear the path for the saw. Facing the deer's body cavity, start the cut and continue down through the straddle, taking all pains to keep to the center of the spine. It will facilitate making a straight cut if the flesh down the middle of the back is parted first with your knife. Continue the cut right down through the entire spinal column, sawing through the rib cartilage, until the entire carcass is split in two equal halves. Take one half of the carcass down from the beam, and lay it on your oilcloth-covered table, keeping the body cavity side down.

With your knife and meat saw, divide each of the deer halves. Wrap each portion separately in the locker paper or in wax paper. If you steak the hindquarters, wrap each steak separately. In any case, do a neat workmanlike job, cutting off all scraps and pulling or cutting off external tissues. You can now quick-freeze all the better cuts for roasts, steaks and chops, saving the less desirable portions — shanks, flank and neck — for making stew, mincemeat, venison sausage or meat balls.

Making Full Use of Venison

As far as I can see, there is not one part of the animal that should be wasted. There are many ways to make use of each portion. Shoulders, loin, saddle, rump and ham all make good roasts, chops and steaks. Even the neck of a fat deer, boned out and rolled, makes a fine pot roast. In fact, the toughest part of a tough deer will be tasty and flavorful if the buck has been well aged, with the less choice portions stewed or pot-roasted in a pressure cooker.

But for greatest utility of these portions, give me venison sausage every time. Nothing in pork sausage compares with it, either for flavor or texture. Here is how I make it, and it's always good:

1. Take the two front leg shanks, and bone them and strip out the tendons. Do the same with the shank end of the haunch, after steaks have been cut.
2. Throw in the flank meat after making certain none of this has a "high" odor. If any of this meat has this odor, don't use it for sausage or anything else.
3. Now remove most of the excess fat, if any, and if you want a large batch of sausage, put in some of the lower shoulder or neck meat. Cut all of this into cubes small enough for grinding.
4. Take this to a butcher shop, weigh it and have your butcher add one-third this amount of pork fat-back. Have him grind the whole works twice, but not too fine.
5. Add sausage seasoning and one teaspoonful of powdered ginger for each 5 pounds of the sausage. Mix well, adding just enough water to free the sausage from your fingers while mixing.

This can now be packed in your containers, quick-frozen and stored in the locker, but first try some the next morning for breakfast with buckwheats!

Beef Recipes Will Work

In preparing any of the choicer cuts, much the same procedure is followed as with beef. There are two noticeable differences, however. The meat is somewhat drier, though fine in texture, and the fat is similar in characteristics to lamb fat, almost like tallow. When venison is oven-roasted it should be well-larded with fat bacon or salt pork, inserted into slits cut into the meat, or skewered fast with toothpicks. Basting the roast occasionally with red wine does no harm either! And when serving venison, it is nothing less than sacrilege to serve it on a cold plate, so warm the dinner plates well if you would keep your gravy liquid.

Almost any beef recipe will serve for preparing venison. Steaks should be sliced thick, seared on a hot broiler quickly, then broiled rare. The chops correspond to rib steaks in beef, and can just as easily be broiled, basting occasionally with melted fat. In any case, use your favorite beef recipes, but cook the venison for somewhat less time.

In camp we would take a haunch of venison from a young spike buck, skewer to it long strips of salt pork, then hang it in front of the big open fireplace about two feet from the heavy oak log fire. At noon when the gang came in for lunch, they would turn the leg around, attach more salt pork, and throw another log on the fire. After sunset, with a tired, hungry bunch of hunters sitting around the table, that roast leg of venison disappeared like fog in a breeze. Of course, hungry hunters will eat almost anything, but I often drool at the thought of those crispy brown, open-hearth haunch roasts.

Certain recipes have become traditional for preparing venison. Among these is a venison sauerbraten, a famous venison party dish:

1. Take a solid chunk of the rump and immerse it in the following sauer-pickle for 48 hours:
2. Mix 2 parts (at least) water to 1 part vinegar.
3. Sweeten with brown sugar to remove the vinegar bite, tasting as you mix the ingredients.
4. Add several slices of lemon and raw onion, sliced clove of garlic, two tablespoons of mixed pickling spice, and a stick of cinnamon. (The bath should be just enough to cover the meat, and the meat must be turned frequently during the process.)
5. When pickled, brown the meat in a heavy Dutch oven in hot fat. After browning, cover and pot-roast slowly, allowing 30 minutes per pound, but not over four hours total. During the roasting, baste frequently with the pickling liquid.
6. When the piece is done, make gravy, using the pickling liquid instead of water. Add to the gravy a half-pint of cream.
7. Simmer.
8. Serve with potato dumplings and sauer red cabbage.

Among the author's pet recipes for venison is pan-roasted venison chops:
1. Take four or five rib chops, sliced thick (one to a rib).
2. Roll in seasoned flour and brown quickly in a heavy iron pan.
3. When browned, lay a strip of bacon on each chop, baste with Burgundy or Claret and cover.
4. Simmer 30 minutes.
5. Thicken gravy with flour and add Worcestershire sauce.

Endless Ways to Prepare Venison
The number of ways in which venison can be prepared is endless. Each region of the country has a favorite recipe, be it venison stew, venison and spaghetti, venison Swiss steak, venison paprika or hundreds of others. The author could list many more recipes for venison cookery, but in the end would add but little to what might be found in household cookbooks. The only points to bear always in mind are the natural dryness of the meat and its richer flavor. There is no magic in preparing properly handled and cured venison, but it does require a magician to serve appetizing venison dishes if the animal was not properly treated from the moment of its taking — through hog-dressing, cooling, curing and proper butchering. For only through the most careful, intelligent handling will venison be meat fit for the banquet table.

In camp, the successful hunter will want to eat some part of his deer almost immediately. Bear in mind, the meat should never be eaten until the body heat has thoroughly cooled out. Usually this will be a matter of 12 or more hours, for the heavy hair forms a most effective insulation for retaining this heat. However, two parts of the animal are fit for almost immediate consumption: the liver and the tenderloins or "backstraps." The liver should be sliced carefully, not too thick, not too thin, roughly about ⅜-inch thick. Fry it quickly in good bacon fat until the blood just ceases to ooze. The backstraps are the choicest tidbits in the deer. These long tender strips of meat lie along the backbone on the inside of the body cavity, just above the kidneys. Most of the time they can be pulled right out with the fingers. Slice these across the grain in thick chunks for pan-frying, or leave whole for broiling. In even the leanest, stringiest buck these backstraps will be tender no matter how prepared.

Sometimes liver flukes — liver worms — will be found in a deer's liver. These don't harm the liver in the least if it's properly cooked. Simply remove them and cook as usual. Both the heart and kidneys are saved and eaten by venison-hungry hunters. The heart should be split, tissues removed, parboiled for 15 minutes, then fried. Kidneys should be split, washed thoroughly or soaked in weak bicarbonate solution, then broiled or fried. All of these parts can be eaten almost as soon as the hunter returns to camp with his deer, but for the rest of the venison, proper aging in the cooler produces the best meat.

Clayton B. Seagears, director of New York State Conservation Education, has a simple recipe for an unusually good and different venison ham. Here it is, just as he has put it down:

1. Take your haunch of venison and carefully separate the muscles so the connective tissue or membranes can be stripped off. This will allow the "curing paste" to come in direct contact with the meat.
2. Now mix about 2 lbs. of salt with 5 tablespoons of ground cinnamon (some use allspice), and the same amount of black pepper. Plaster the meat with this. If it won't stick, wipe meat with salt brine.
3. Next, hang the coated raw chunks outdoors on hooks or string under a shelter so that rain will never touch them. The wind and sun will do the rest.
4. In about 4 or 5 weeks, cut off some thin slices and holler for your doubting pals.

Long-Term Storage of Venison

Venison can be pickled, smoked, dried and canned. For hunters who have no access to commercial refrigeration, all meat can be preserved those ways. For pickling, cut the meat into long strips, and soak it 24 hours in a salt brine heavy enough to float an egg. Remove from the brine and hang to dry. When dripping ceases, lay strips on a board or tray and dry in a slow oven.

Smoked venison is delicious and easy to prepare: Soak long strips in salt water for an hour or two, drain and hang on a wooden slat over a slow fire of green wood or corncobs. Sawdust also will create a good heavy smoke. An old barrel makes a good smokehouse for this job. If it's made of metal, the fire can be built right in the middle. In a wooden barrel, build a tiny fire on a sheet of metal or an old washing tin placed in the bottom. The fire should be kept low and small. Only a little heat should be generated, but it should produce plenty of smoke. After four or five days of intermittent smoking, the venison is ready. For dried venison, hang the strips over a low fire away from the smoke and flame. No presalting is necessary for dried venison.

Canning is perhaps the most commonly used method of preserving venison if refrigeration is lacking. The methods used are almost identical with home-canning vegetables. Meat can be cold-packed or it can be cooked and then packed. The latter method produces the tastiest venison. The first step is to remove the bones and all excess fat and stringy tissues, cutting meat into pieces conveniently sized to fit into the canning jars. Pan-broil the meat in salt pork or bacon fat, seasoning with salt and pepper while cooking. When nicely browned, pack in sterilized jars to within an inch of the top. Add a few spoonfuls of drippings to each jar, then screw on the lids tightly, wipe off tops and place in pressure cooker. Cook at 15 pounds pressure for about an hour. Such canned venison makes excellent Swiss steak and venison stews.

Venison can also be kept in other ways if commercial cold storage lockers aren't available. The meat can be wrapped in individual sections for cooking, then frozen in the freezing compartment of the household refrigerator. Then it can be packed in a barrel of sawdust and left outdoors or in an unheated building. Such packing will keep the meat in good condition throughout normal late fall or winter weather. Better still, the meat can be frozen and packed in a barrel with cracked ice and sawdust, storing it outdoors in a spot protected from the elements and never touched by the sun.

Another important precaution to remember is not to allow once-frozen meat to thaw until ready for use. Thawing and refreezing adds nothing to meat quality, and will usually hasten spoilage.

The Supple Deer Hide

Of all the useful portions of a buck's body, none is more abused than the hide. Most hunters discard the hide or give it away. In the city near where I spent most of my life, tons of deer hides were thrown into the dump to be eaten by hordes of rats infesting those places. That was a disgraceful waste of prospective buckskin, a wonderful leather for garments, surpassed by no other for beauty of texture, softness and durability. If any hunter doesn't use his deer hide, he should at least give it to someone who will. Beautiful gloves, shirts, jackets and other garments can be made from a few deer hides at a fraction of their usual cost — if the hunter supplies the hides.

In fact, it's simple to tan your own buckskin. Once tanned, garments can be cut to standard patterns and sewed by a shoemaker or by any dressmaker who uses a heavy machine. To tan a deer hide, the hair is first removed. Some hunters will have a hide or two tanned with the hair on, but this makes a messy skin, useful only for a wall ornament. It can never be used for a rug. The hollow, strawlike hair continually breaks off, and in time the rug will be an eyesore in the room. There are many ways to remove hair from a prospective buckskin. What follows are two simple methods.

For the first method, start by soaking the green hide in a strong solution of milk of lime. Leave it in a short time, then pull on the hair. The solution frees the hair from the hide so it can be pulled out easily. Another method: Pour two gallons water, one quart slaked lime and one quart wood ashes into a wooden tub or crock. Immerse the hide and leave for 24 hours or more until hair slips and can be pulled out. After either of these treatments, the hide must be thoroughly rinsed, to remove all traces of the solution.

To make the buckskin, start with these ingredients:

- ✓ 5 gallons of water
- ✓ 3 pounds of salt
- ✓ 1 pound of alum dissolved in hot water

Now put the salt in the water, add the alum solution and stir until all is dissolved. When the solution is quite cold, immerse the hide and allow it to remain in the bath for a week, stirring it daily. At the end of the first day, take the hide out and hang it to dry. When still moist, go over the entire flesh side with a dull knife or scraper, removing all flesh and fat, then place back in the solution for the remainder of the tanning period. (The salt and alum solution is perfectly safe, even if the hide is left in it longer than the prescribed time. It can safely remain for several weeks without danger of overtanning.)

Now remove the hide and rinse it thoroughly, first in a weak washing soda solution, then in clear water until all traces of salt are gone. (Taste it to check this.) Hang the skin a few hours to drain completely, then roll up for overnight. Next day, begin to work the skin by pulling and stretching it. If it has dried too hard, dampen lightly with warm water. Put a short length of thin board in a bench vise and work the skin over this until it softens appreciably.

At this point, the skin is ready for oiling. Oil lightly with neatsfoot oil, lard, cottonseed oil, bacon grease or any animal oil. Indians oiled the skin with the brains. Whatever the oil used, apply warm to the flesh side of the hide and rub it in well. Let it hang after oiling for a day or two, then soak it in a bath of strong soapy water for a few days. Again take out the hide and work it over your board, pulling and stretching until it is completely "broken." This part of the job is hard work, but it requires only time and effort. During this "breaking" process, keep the hide moist, not dripping, and permit it to dry between times. Finally, the hide will reach a point where it will no longer stiffen after drying. It is now finished buckskin.

However, to do a real job and make the hide almost waterproof, close the pores by smoking it over a slow fire of green hardwood.

This smoking does wonders for the hide, making it a better leather for outdoor wear and at the same time turning it to a pleasant dark gray color. It is now ready to be cut up and made into durable garments or gloves, any of which are a joy to own and a pleasure to wear: velvety to the touch, yielding to every movement of the body, quiet in the woods and almost impervious to wind and water. Truly ideal garments for the woodsman!

Let none of your buck be wasted. Eat the venison, tan the hide, tie bucktail lures from the soft tail hair, bass fly-rod lures from the coarse, hollow body hair. Mount the head for your den, make a hat rack or gun rack from the hoofs. Make or have made a pair of gloves, a new buckskin shirt or a pair of moccasins. Yes, brother hunter, the white-tailed deer is a magnificently bountiful creature.

PART 2

The Mechanics of Deer Hunting

CHAPTER 15

The Weapon and the Load

Any writer, however well-informed and widely experienced in the hunting field, approaches such an important chapter as this with deep humility. That, in a deer book, such a chapter must be written is self-evident, but the problems facing me are of great breadth and subject to many qualifications. Many deer hunters, given such an opportunity, would rise to the occasion with high enthusiasm, leaping into the discussion with little regard for the tender toes of the existing millions of deer hunters.

The selection of the deer hunter's weapon has always been, and will ever be, a never-ending source of argument and discussion, theory and superstition. No one — writer, gun editor, gunsmith or clairvoyant — can hope to pick a rifle for the experienced hunter, and it would be presumptuous of me to make such attempts.

Specific Requirements of a Deer Rifle

Experienced hunters have their rifles. They have made successful kills year after year, and they handle their guns with the ease born of long familiarity. No one needs to advise such hunters on the selection of the proper firearm. This they know, and know thoroughly. On this note, we can leave experienced hunters and turn attention to the many thousands who have not yet killed their first deer and to those who might have killed one or two deer and have missed or lost all the rest. This latter group of hunters is the most inclined to change rifles after each unsuccessful season. These hunters flounder in a welter of confusion, becoming more discouraged with passing seasons.

I will not launch into lengthy discussion of various calibers and types of actions, citing hundreds of instances to prove the efficiency of outstanding deer rifles. Such information has already been made public through hundreds of thousands of words printed in books and sporting magazines since deer hunting first became the sport of the common man. Rehashing such information simply adds to the confusion in the minds and hearts of many hunters who take to the woods each year. Rather, we'll approach the subject from a little different angle — the capabilities of the shooters themselves, not the high degree of excellence of certain cartridges and rifle actions.

Let's admit that at the beginning there is no best rifle for white-tailed deer hunting. All centerfire rifles, ranging from the tiny .22 Hornet through the multitude of increasingly larger calibers and loads to the mighty .405 Winchester and .375 Magnum, can be and are good deer rifles in the hands of the right person — the hunter who, by years of training, study of deer anatomy and physical temperament — can extract from any selected caliber its most efficient performance on game.

During the 1930s and '40s, I've been fortunate to have hunted deer throughout a wide area in the Eastern states. I've spent much of this same period behind the gun counter as salesman, gunsmith and firearms mentor to many thousands of deer hunters in the most heavily hunted section of New York state. The sum total of these experiences indicates that most hunters select a gun by the record and reports of other successful hunters, and not by examining their own qualifications to handle such a firearm. It's wise, of course, to pick a rifle that performs well in the hands of your friends, but such a selection is not conclusive. Many variable personal factors fit the gun to the hunter.

By and large, today's deer hunter is not a skilled hunting rifleman. I say "hunting rifleman" to distinguish between the hunter and target shooter, for there is a marked difference. If we glance at the records of licenses issued to deer hunters in 1948 and compare them with a year, two or even three years ago, we require no Holmes to deduce that hundreds of thousands of new hunters have been added to the growing ranks in a short time. Most of these new hunters are not hunting riflemen of any marked degree of rifle skill even after a lifetime of deer hunting. These new hunters, then, are most in need of advice in selecting a rifle to match their own hunting skill and psychological make-up.

It would be simple indeed if we could pick one type of rifle action and caliber, fitted with a fixed setup of sights and loaded with one type and weight of bullet, then place it in the hands of all beginning deer hunters, saying to them: "This is the one and only deer rifle. It is the best for every range and every type of shot you'll get, whether it be broadside, head-on or quartering away, whether your deer is at 20 yards in heavy laurel or 200 yards off in a pasture. It will kill your deer at the first shot no matter where you hit him, and the sights are so efficient you will forever be able to see them against the game at any legal hunting time of day, in sunlight, rain or snow and in any kind of cover. The cartridges are loaded with just the right design and weight of bullet to shoot through heavy timber and screens of evergreens, carrying true to your aim. When the deer is struck the bullet will penetrate completely and expand just enough so that it will not pass through, but will lie against the hide on the far side of the animal."

Ah! Utopia, you say, and you would be right, but no such rifle, cartridge, bullet design or sighting combination now exists or can ever exist. Yet I have many deer-hunting friends who are convinced they own such a rifle, and fearlessly recommend it to the new hunter searching for the ideal gun.

Back in the 1920s, when I first took to the deer woods at a tender age, deer hunting was limited to certain small groups of hunters. At that time we enjoyed no such widespread distribution of white-tailed deer as we do today. In order to hunt deer, hunters joined deer-hunting clubs. Most of the hunting was done on private lands, heavily posted and club-owned. In the more exclusive outfits with limited membership, a new prospective member had to wait several years for a member to drop out or die before the new hunter could gain entry. Under these conditions, new deer hunters had somewhat easier going in weapon selection than today. They were in immediate contact with men of good hunting experience who were well able to give the fundamental advice requisite to killing their buck. Again, the choice of weapons was not quite as wide as it is today, tending to lessen the confusion somewhat when the greenhorn picked out his rifle. He took the Winchester carbine in .30-30 or .32 special; the Savage 99 in .30-30, .303 or .250-3000; or the Remington 8 or 14 in .30, .32 or .35-caliber. He then stuck with it until he could handle it well. The deer he killed in successive seasons would be a clear criterion of the increase in his own hunting and shooting skill.

Likewise, such new hunters, in the constant company of men who were killing deer season after season, would gain helpful firsthand observations on the performance of various rifles and cartridges. There is no substitute for on-the-spot observations of rifle performance in building a hunter's confidence in the efficiency of his own gun. Such bolstered confidence goes a long way to improve a new hunter's faith in his rifle. Psychologically, this is of the greatest importance to deer-hunting success, as far as the weapon itself enters the picture.

Today's new hunters begin their search for a deer rifle under somewhat different circumstances. Most often they have neither the time, money nor inclination to join an established club. Deer hunting today is of great scope. No longer is it limited to the private lands of limited forest areas. Deer today are everywhere, in farmlands, near metropolitan areas, and in every part of the land where cover and food exist. New hunters today can find deer within easy driving distance of their homes. Gone is the necessity to join a club and spend a week or two each year hunting the same grounds season after season. Today's deer hunters can seek new fields each year if they so desire. There is no limitation other than the time at their disposal.

Thus it is that today's new hunters often lack the comprehensive guidance of old and tried deer-hunting pals. They often hunt with a small group of friends, many of whom are hardly more experienced than themselves. They must depend on the wealth of controversial literature extolling the virtues of this or that rifle over the balance of the wide field of firearms, and then try to make an intelligent selection.

But often, perhaps most often, the friendly guidance of friends is not enough. New hunters must search their own background of shooting experience, their emotional stability or lack of it, and their general knowledge of deer anatomy if they are to make a suitable compromise in gun selection. I'll try to point out some of the factors affecting a new hunter's reactions in handling a rifle, and from these perhaps reveal some glimmer of light to implant or restore confidence in one's selection of the means to take from the woods the prize of the hunt.

The Five Groups of Deer Hunters

To establish a starting point for self-classification, I will divide deer hunters into five large groups, all of whom face similar hunting problems and shooting backgrounds. The groups line up something like this, but not necessarily in order of skill:

Group 1 comprises new hunters with no experience in the shooting field, other than some .22 plinking or an occasional foray after rabbits with the scattergun. It might seem strange to establish such a group as a member of the deer-hunting clan, but this group offers a large potential increase in deer hunters each year. To this group, deer hunting is not yet a way of life, but it offers sufficient glamour for many hunters who have never hunted before to now be seeking deer. Whitetails are large enough to be highly desirable as a trophy and for food value, and are now well enough distributed to be accessible to large numbers of hunters.

Group 2 comprises the many new deer hunters who have a wide background in small-game hunting with the shotgun, but who have only in the past year or two hunted deer. Many in this group have had indifferent success with the rifle, even though they possess a good grade of shotgun shooting skill and general hunting ability.

Group 3 would include that substantial number of city-bound men who have a good background of deer-hunting experience but little time or opportunity to practice with their pet rifle. Most of this group clean their guns a day or two before the season opens and pack them away in the hall closet the day after the season ends. This group usually has a majority of small-game shotgun shooters in the ranks.

Group 4 is the simon-pure target shooter who might be a member of a metropolitan rifle club. He is an excellent shot on inanimate targets, well-versed in ballistics and firearms technicalities, and lacks only the acquisition of woodcraft and deer-hunting experience to bring him into the expert class.

Group 5 is the last select, highly skilled group of hunters, small in percentage numbers, who possess an intimate knowledge of woodcraft, an abundance of hunting skill, the ability to hit deer in the proper spot, and the general groundwork in all types of shooting that makes them deadly with almost any type of rifle. These hunters invariably have a wide experience in shooting from early childhood. They have a deep affection for their favorite rifle and treat it as a warm, personal friend.

Problems and Recommendations for Each Group

I'm primarily concerned with the first three groups. The two latter groups can give most sporting writers cards and spades, and still come out top men on a deer hunt.

To clarify a situation so controversial as selecting a deer rifle, I want to first state that the gun I have in mind will be used only for white-tailed deer hunting in normal Eastern covers. The same rifle would be equally correct for hunting in Michigan, Wisconsin, Minnesota or any other region in North America where the cover so limits the hunter's vision that shots longer than 100 yards are rare. This is not to say that whitetails are always killed at such ranges. There are always some exceptions. Occasionally we hear of hunters who shoot their deer from a platform high in a lone pine tree that overlooks a wide expanse of scrub oak or low laurel. And in some sections of Pennsylvania, deer hunters sit the ridgetops in rocky, low-brush areas. Their shooting will be at deer moving along adjacent ridges. But this type of long-range shooting is somewhat special in whitetail hunting and cannot be considered an important factor to Eastern deer hunters. Hunters who go for this long-range work will equip themselves with a flat trajectory, high-energy bolt-action rifle and mount it with the best hunting riflescope they can afford. Likewise, we will not mention rifles that are a compromise between deer hunting and vermin shooting. Such rifles are, at best, a compromise and are not best suited for hunting whitetails. Deer hunting has assumed such status that the rifle should be selected with deer only in mind. No one in his right mind would pick a shotgun for duck shooting and then use it for woodcock shooting. Neither should we select a weapon for deer and expect it to perform properly on woodchucks, coyotes and crows. It is just as illogical to select a deer rifle when we have moose, elk or mountain sheep in mind. A deer hunter who might someday make an expensive trip for any or all of these larger animals might better wait until the day arrives and then buy a weapon suited to this type of hunting. The added cost of the new rifle will be but a small percentage of the whole outlay for the big-game hunt.

The hunters in Group 1 — new deer hunters — are faced with the toughest problem of gun selection. Many of them do not yet own a rifle. When deer-hunting time nears, they beg or borrow an old hog-leg .38-55, a beaten-up, rusty old Krag, or even worse a "souvenir" German Mauser or Japanese Arisaka shipped home by G.I. Joe. New hunters carrying such a rifle have two strikes on them before seeing deer country. First, they unconsciously fear the rifle, knowing they'll get a belt in the jaw when touching it off. Secondly, the sights on these rifles are usually the poorest in the shooting field, hardly discernible in good light and hopeless in deer country. Add to this the fact these hunters have no background of mechanically fixed shooting skill, and no knowledge of exactly where to hold to hit a deer. If a shot at a buck presents itself, they usually miss. If they're lucky enough to hit a deer, it will be most often struck through the "biggest part" — right through the paunch. If the deer goes down to this shot, it gets right up and our hapless hunters fumble with the action, failing to reload in time for a finishing shot. Or they might manage to reload but cannot put their sights on the moving deer in time. Thus we add another lost buck to the Conservation Department's headaches.

There is no quick solution to finding the right deer rifle for rank beginners. They tend to consult more experienced friends, where they find no two hunters using the same type of action or caliber. This adds to the indecision. Then they avidly read every magazine article and book on the subject and decide to buy a rifle with sufficient power to kill a deer if they can manage to plant a bullet anywhere in the deer's body. Secretly, they realize their lack of shooting skill and are hazy on placing a shot in the most lethal spot.

These shooters often decide on a .30-06 or .270 bolt-action, a .300 Savage or Remington, a .348 Winchester or .35 Remington. With the new rifle in hand, oozing confidence in its excess of power for killing deer, they drive to the outlying districts or nearest rifle range. At first they stand up on their two hind legs and try to hold the wandering front sight on the target. Perhaps they fire a shot or two, resulting in clean misses. They then decide the prone position will be steadier, so they take a few shots from just above ground level. If their will power has been good, the first shot should be satisfactorily near the middle of the bull's eye, but for some unaccountable reason succeeding shots wander all over the target, even missing the backstop now and then. They now decide the ammo is too costly and hard to get for this kind of practice, so they cart home the new rifle, their confidence severely shaken.

In almost every instance these new shooters are highly sensitive to recoil and muzzle blast. The .30-06 and .348 are just too much gun, the .300 and the .35 not much easier on jaw and shoulder. The .270 isn't too tough on the shoulder and jaw, but the muzzle blast scares the devil out of people every time they touch it off. Just a bit of this treatment builds up a deeply implanted fear of the rifle's potency in the beginners' minds, and they are never able to shoot these rifles with any skill and confidence.

Hunting experts stoutly maintain a hunter never feels the rifle's recoil when shooting at game. I agree — if we're talking about experts, but experts are sadly too rare in the deer woods. I believe recoil is the weightiest factor in choosing the beginner's deer rifle. No hunters willingly admit, even to themselves, that they fear their rifle's recoil. Once stuck with one of these heavy rifles they will cling to it year after year, afraid to admit to themselves or their friends that they're flinchers and will never become a fine rifleman. Unconsciously, they always hope that what the experts say is true: that under the excitement of seeing and shooting at a buck they will overcome the tendency to flinch at the shot, making another clean miss or a "fluke" hit.

That is the wrong approach to becoming a good hunter rifleman. The only solution is practice with a small rimfire, shooting week after week at small targets and big targets, tin cans, matchbooks, anything that can be seen well enough to hold on clearly. Only then will the vital importance of trigger squeeze become paramount in the shooter's mind, to the end that they summon all their will power to control their nervous muscular reaction until the bullet is on its way.

New hunters must first seek proficiency in shooting with the small rimfire before trying to use the bigger rifle. Even then, if their temperament shows a tendency toward nervous reaction to the blast and bump of a high-powered rifle, they should choose a lighter caliber — still adequate for deer — and a rifle action selected for its heavier weight, the better to absorb recoil. Going from a 24-inch barrel .30-06 sporter to a .30-30 short-barreled lever-action carbine will not give sufficient relief to sensitive shooters. Better to choose a lighter caliber, but let it be in a rifle action of good weight. As an example, the .250 Savage in Model 99 R or RS. This rifle has normally light recoil, little blast and is heavy enough in barrel and stock to make comfortable shooting.

Hunters who have not yet killed their first deer must be primarily concerned with their ability to hit the deer in a vital area, rather than carry a rifle with an overabundance of killing power that scares hell out of them to shoot. No amount of power in a rifle will kill deer unless it is delivered into the game with a well-directed shot.

The .30-30 Rifle Group

Rifles of the .30-30 class (.250-3000, .32 Special, .303 Savage, .30 Remington, .32 Remington) all have sufficient power to kill white-tailed deer and are more comfortable to shoot than the heavier calibers. It is possible to carry lack of recoil too far, however. No one could sincerely recommend a new hunter use a .22 Hornet, .25-20, .32-20 or .38-40 simply because these cartridges have virtually no recoil. This latter group of cartridges are effective only in the hands of the best hunter riflemen; and then only under favorable conditions, that is, short range and a favorable angle for making a vital hit.

Beginning deer hunters will have no mental commitments regarding the best type of action. Remington's Model 81 autoloader in .30 or .32 Remington caliber is good, but the autoloader is not the ideal type of action for a beginner. It contributes to hasty, unaimed firing in the hopes at least one shot will hit the deer. Better is the smooth-functioning, rapid-action Remington Model 141 in the same calibers. New shooters might also like the feel of the Savage 99 EG or 99 R in .250 Savage, the Winchester Model 65, or perhaps the Marlin Model 36 — all lever-actions. These models function well and are rapid enough for additional shooting after the first shot is away. The autoloading actions are only slightly faster than the pump. Recoil throws the sights off the target anyway, and during this period the hunter learns to throw the slide or lever so little, if any, shooting time is lost. It's unfortunate, however, that hunters with autoloaders tend to machine-gun shots at deer, usually with little effect.

Bolt-action rifles are not the best choice for new deer hunters, much expert opinion to the contrary. However, there is a nationwide tendency among deer hunters to regard bolt-actions as purely military rifles or a long-range affair for plains shooting or potting vermin. This prejudice unconsciously reflects itself in the beginner's choice of a rifle, and I believe it's better for beginners to bypass this mental barrier rather than try to use a bolt-action rifle in spite of it. Expert hunters are wedded firmly to the bolt-action; first because of its positive functioning under tough conditions, and second, for its better adaptation to modern cartridges. It is inherently more accurate than any other type of action, but in deer hunting this is of little consequence. All of our current rifles and cartridges are sufficiently accurate for any white-tailed deer hunting.

Speed of fire is of only secondary importance in killing your buck. It seldom happens that a deer is killed readily after being missed by the first shot. The first shot is almost always the best, and every effort must be made to make the first shot count the most. After witnessing rapid-fire matches at deer, I've often thought the sport would be farther ahead for both the hunter and conservationist if we were required to use single-shot rifles for hunting deer. There would be fewer silly misses at close range, and undoubtedly fewer deer escaping to die a lingering death. With the single-shot rifle, none of us would be tempted to take an odds-on chance at a flash-shot. We would be more patient in waiting until the deer moved into a better position for a clean kill. When a decent shot did come, we would be doubly careful to pick the right spot for a lightning kill and would be more careful to hit that spot. Let every deer hunter — beginner or not — concentrate on placing that first shot, and there will be little need to worry about how fast he can fire a magazine at the deer.

For hunters in Group 1, there is but one solution to success in killing their buck. Select a rifle of ample power in the .30-30 class, picking the action that feels best in the hands, and a model one happens to like. New hunters at the shooting game will form a liking for a certain type of rifle. Perhaps it is a carryover from childhood, when they admired the lever-action hammer guns used in the Western "horse operas." Maybe they owned a Daisy "pump-action" repeater air rifle and developed an affinity for this type of action. Subconsciously, this will be reflected in their liking a present-day high-power arms. By all means, let them follow this tendency, for no one handles a rifle at its best unless they have a sincere liking for it. When hunters talk about it, it's a "doll-baby" or "some gun." From this point onward, the hunters should handle their new rifle at every opportunity until it becomes as comfortable to their touch as a pair of old gloves.

At the same time that they pick a high-powered rifle, they should order a .22 rifle in its counterpart. If they pick the Model 141 Remington, then also buy the 121 Remington. If they select a Winchester, Savage or Marlin lever-action high-power, then match it with the Marlin 39 lever-action .22 rifle. If they decide on the Model 81 Remington autoloader in a high-power, they will do well to buy with it the smaller Remington .22-caliber autoloader Model 241, or the Winchester Model 63.

New hunters should then consider proper sighting equipment. The factory sights on their high-powered rifle will no doubt need some changes — perhaps a larger front sight and a good receiver sight with large aperture for the rear. Whatever the choice, duplicate it also in the .22-caliber model. To complete the job to its final finish, have a gunsmith add weight to stock and forearm of the lighter rifle, bringing both arms into the same weight and balance. The same gunsmith can, at the same time, adjust the trigger pulls to a similar weight and crispness.

All this might seem like a bit of trouble and undoubtedly it is, not to mention the expense involved. But for hunters who seriously desire to kill a deer next season and for seasons thereafter, it might be the only solution. With the .22 rifle they can enjoy cheap rifle-shooting practice in almost any community. The recoil is no factor, and after a few months of practice they will be able to pick up their high-powered rifle and shoot it with the same skill as its smaller brother.

Don't underestimate the need for this background of shooting skill in hunting. A fundamental requisite in killing game is for hunters to have a background of training that precludes the necessity of remembering the mechanics of shooting and operating the rifle for successive shots. It must be done by rote, without conscious thought. At this stage of the chase, their full faculties are devoted to keeping the game in sight and deciding at just what point they should make their shot.

It's not necessary for a deer hunter to be a highly accurate shot on game or targets. The definite requirement to kill deer is that they be able to keep all their shots within an 8-inch circle at 50 yards, irrespective of stance or position with regard to the target. Of far greater importance is that they be able to pick up their rifle, mount it to the shoulder smoothly yet rapidly, and touch off the first, second and third shots quickly and within this limit of accuracy. Never should they look at the rifle to determine whether its safety is on or off, nor should they look directly at any part of the action or sights. Their gaze must be kept always directly on the target, and the other operations of shooting must fall into line.

Hunting experts will be inclined to scoff at such elementary advice, yet every hunter who has gained any proficiency has, in the beginning, passed through almost this exact procedure. It takes time to achieve smoothness and facility in simply aligning sights, and even more time to inure the nervous system to the blasting "pow!" and jerk of recoil as the cartridge explodes. And until this stage has been passed, a new hunter should not go deer hunting. It not only might mean a heartbreaking trip, but might result in a badly wounded deer left to die, unrecovered.

Roots in Farm Country

I was fortunate to spend almost all of my boyhood on a farm, in good small-game country, although at that time deer had not yet been seen in any numbers. My parents were both city born and bred, and were horrified at the idea of my wanting a rifle. But somehow, along about age 9 or 10, I got hold of a little single-shot Remington .22 — a Model 6 I believe — with a flat, folding tang peep-sight. In a short time I could knock a starling off the barn ridge without too many misses. By the time I reached my middle teens, I owned a Stevens drop-block .25-20 single-shot with a vernier tang peep sight. This outfit was tough medicine for gray squirrels, not to mention the hundreds of woodchucks that fell before the little 86-grain soft-point bullet.

One fall, about the time I was 16, I decided I must hunt deer. My dad cooperated to the extent that he furnished transportation to the nearest deer woods, but there the cooperation ended. Undaunted, I sneaked into the woods on an old woodsroad, using the same methods I had used to stalk gray squirrels feeding on fallen hickory nuts. I hadn't yet seen a deer, either in the woods or on a game preserve, but I was certain I would recognize one if I bumped into it.

With the confidence of youth and inexperience, I walked the trail quietly for about a mile. Suddenly, I heard a slight noise to my left — a crackling of twigs and rustling of brush and leaves. Thinking it must be another hunter, I waited for him to show himself. Instead, out into the small white-birch grove walked a nice, fat little buck. He stopped to look me over, turned his head away just once, then as his eyes swept back to me my little .25-20 bullet ripped through his neck. To be sure, my knees shook horribly and my heart thumped so loudly I was sure the deer could have heard it, but my rifle training kept my mind and hands coordinated up to the moment of the kill. There was no magic in killing this deer, which my parents seemed to think. It simply was the result of early, thorough training in rifle shooting. So it must be with every hunter who would kill a deer quickly and neatly.

The Shotgun-Trained Deer Hunter

The foregoing more or less sums up the major problems facing Group 1 deer hunters. Hunters in Group 2 show much the same tendencies, but are not quite as sensitive to recoil, because this group hunts small game with shotguns. They lack the primitive fear of the high-powered rifle, but they, too, through constant use of shotguns, have acquired a habit of jerking their shots. The reason for flinching might not be the same, but it results in just as many misses on deer. Hunters in this group, as a whole, are not rifle-trained. Most of their failures in deer hunting rest with the trigger-jerking habit or lack of familiarity with the strange rifle. In fact, it's seldom that we find an expert with the shotgun who is also an expert rifleman. The two shooting methods are so widely opposed, not only in a mechanical sense but as they affect the shooter's temperament. Good wing-shooting with a shotgun requires the gunner to determine at once — before the first movement to throw the gun is made — just what line of flight the flushed bird will take. With that fixed in his mind, the gun is thrown to the shoulder while taking this line of flight, and the muzzle is pointed to swing under and past the target. Then when the eye signals the brain that proper lead has been established, the trigger is abruptly jerked and the follow-through continued.

The rifle shooter must be much more deliberate. When the target is in a favorable position for the shot, the rifle is brought smoothly to shoulder, and the cheek pressed firmly to the comb to steady the eye in relation to the rear sight. The front sight is aligned on the target and in the same semiconscious movement aligned with the rear sight. Then the shooter stops all movement momentarily as the shot is squeezed off, with the sights held as nearly as possible in the desired spot.

Of course, there is much more detail to rifle shooting, but I merely wish to emphasize the difference in movement between the two types of shooting. Shotgun shooting is a picture of rapid movement, lightning calculation, instant action with the slight inaccuracy caused by jerking the shot, which is lost in the pattern spread and short range. The premium here is on speed and accuracy in determining the lead and angle of target, and then blended to the rhythmic action of pointing the gun.

The premium in rifle shooting is on pinpoint aiming precision, a momentary hold when all movement stops, and the smooth trigger squeeze, holding everything until recoil blots out the picture.

Shotgun shooters must meet the challenge offered by this change of pace in rifle shooting and conquer it, if they're to kill deer. The quick transition from wing-shooter to deer hunter with rifle often finds the hunters unfamiliar with their new weapon and still shotgun shooters in mind and reflexes. Many times, faced with the sudden, startling appearance of a white-tailed buck, they handle and shoot their rifle as though it were a shotgun. They throw the rifle to shoulder, point at the game and slam off their shot — following the same action pattern they use on a rising woodcock over alder tips.

Particularly noticeable is their reacting to the rifle as though it were their more familiar pet shotgun when they try for a second shot, if they miss or fail to down the deer with the first. Here again the stress of excitement leads them to try to operate their rifle as though they were holding their favorite scattergun.

I recall an incident that illustrates this tendency. In the late 1930s, one of my new deer-hunting buddies was on a watch next to mine during a drive at the feet of the Shawangunk Mountains in lower Sullivan County. We were about 60 yards apart, both facing a short, narrow swale. This lowlands was spongy with peat moss and piled with tangled cat-briers, rhododendron and blown-down rotting tree trunks. Shortly before we took these stands, one of our gang jumped three deer off the ridge behind us and took a snap at a buck just before the deer disappeared into the swamp. We decided to drive the swamp in hopes the deer might still be hiding there.

Taking my partner figuratively by the hand, I placed him in a favorable spot at the base of a huge red oak at the swamp's edge and near the crossing, which headed up the ridge. He was carrying a new Winchester Model 55 in .30-30, with visible hammer and lever action. At that time I had no idea regarding his experience as a rifleman, though I knew he often hunted small game. This, however, was his first deer hunt.

Shortly after I walked to my stand farther along the swamp-edge, I glanced over and saw him raise his rifle, pointing it into the heavy briers and blowdowns. I waited breathlessly for him to shoot, but he took his time, following the progress of the deer as they worked toward the crossing. Just as they came into my view on his far side, he shot once. With a great crashing, the deer turned back into the swamp, out of my sight at once. My partner feverishly pointed his rifle after them and, making strange movements with his right hand, followed with a series of metallic clicks. I finally realized he was cocking the hammer and snapping it on the fired cartridge, not once but many times.

At last he lowered his rifle, having fired only the one shot. I walked over, wondering what could have happened to the rifle. At first I thought the empty case might have expanded tightly in the chamber, locking the action. I asked what in the devil was the matter with him. I could see he had the action open and was dumping the cartridges onto the ground.

"Brother," he said, "I never thought I'd live to see the day I'd do a fool thing like that. Two bucks — not one, but two — walk out right in front of me at easy range and what do I do but miss the first shot."

"Yeah, I know," I shot back at him, "but how about the rest of that gunload? You've got six more shells in that gun and you should have had a good crack at 'em going through that swamp!"

"Right!" he says. "But do you know what I did? I kept cocking the hammer and snapping it on the empty. Ask me why and I can't tell you. Guess I must have thought I had my old double-barrel hammer gun with me."

This is exactly what had happened. He had hunted for years with a double-barreled hammer shotgun and had always carried the hammers down. If he missed his first shot, he would reach up and cock the second barrel for a follow-up. In the excitement of shooting at his first deer, he fell back into the old habit, forgetting the gun in his hands was a lever-action repeater.

I can recall many such experiences among my friends and deer-hunting acquaintances. All of the incidents point to a general unfamiliarity with the hunting rifle. There is no obvious solution nor concrete recommendation to cover an entire group of shooters. Each individual must evaluate his reactions or probable reactions when getting his first chance at the white-tailed buck.

Many times a large front sight, mounted on a ramp, and a large aperture rear sight, will so simplify sighting that shotgunners can more readily change their instinctive style of gun-pointing into more precise aiming. Perhaps of greater importance is selecting a deer rifle that most nearly resembles their shotgun in shape and function. If they regularly use a pump-action shotgun, then the Remington slide-action high-powered rifle is a wise choice for deer. And hunters who like autoloading guns for bird shooting will have fewer functioning troubles with an autoloading rifle.

In each of our first three groups, a general unfamiliarity with rifles is the greatest cause of failure. Even Group 3 deer hunters, those of considerable hunting experience, seldom spend much time with their firearms aside from the hunting season. They might take a quick trip into the countryside on a Saturday afternoon, and then take a shot or two at a target or woodchuck to ensure it's lined up. On the way home, they rub their jaws, knead their shoulders a bit, and wonder why Ol' Betsy kicked so much harder than she did last year.

Such hunters most handicap themselves if they use a heavy-caliber rifle for deer. The instinct to flinch at the shot and jerk the trigger is well implanted, primarily through infrequent practice and lack of contact with the rifle year-round.

Never Underestimate Recoil

Perhaps the reader believes I place too much emphasis on recoil. But it's been my impression for many years that not enough emphasis is placed on this highly controlling factor in deer hunting. During my years in the sporting goods and gunsmithing business, I fired every make, model and caliber of high-powered rifle to appear on the North American hunting scene since the 1890s — and to this we can add several foreign arms. In the course of mounting hundreds of rifles with new iron and riflescope sights, I was required to shoot them on the range.

Customers often returned with their newly equipped rifle, after I had adjusted the sights, to complain that their shooting didn't seem to improve. So off we would go to the rifle range to take turns trying out their pet. I would watch their shoulder and arm muscles carefully as they let off each shot, watching for telltale evidence of a flinch. If, after their shots had wandered all over the target and past the backstop, I accused them of flinching, they would emphatically deny it. Perhaps they weren't aware of it, I would think, so I'd load their rifle again, carefully mixing in two or three "dummies," new cartridges prepared by pulling the bullet, dumping the powder, exploding the primer and reinserting the bullet. It's often difficult to detect flinching in a shooter firing a high-power rifle, because the blast and rifle jerk so closely follow the flinch as to appear like a single movement. But the dummies solved this problem, both to my satisfaction and the shooter's.

Only a day or two ago I was discussing deer rifles with Ed Buckley, an Adirondacks deer hunter of deep experience with high-powered rifles. Ed has killed many deer and shot many different rifles. He's a fine pistol shot as well. He mentioned that he had been shooting a service Springfield the previous autumn with the M1, 172-grain boattail bullet — a pretty hot load, incidentally. He confided that after shooting about a dozen of these loads in the prone position, he'd had enough. He couldn't keep his shots in the bull. He explained — a little sheepishly — that he hadn't shot the "old girl" in so long that she'd taken him by surprise. Shooting it made him so jumpy that he called it quits for the day. This from a deer-hunting rifleman with worlds of shooting experience. It can and does happen to the best men if they lay off the rifle shooting for a while.

It's equally true that among deer hunters we find plenty of men with sufficient willpower or stolid temperament that recoil has little effect on their shooting. They can and do handle heavier calibers with deadly effect, but their numbers are small. In the final analysis, only the shooter can recognize the existence or lack of these qualities within himself, and must choose a firearm on that basis.

Regarding specific rifle choices for each of the three groups, I hesitate to crawl out on that controversial limb. Group 1 new hunters will enjoy good hunting results with any of the following: Remington's Model 141 and 81 in .30 or .32 Remington calibers; Savage's 99 EG, R or RS in .250-3000 with the 100-grain bullet; Winchester's Model 65 in .30 Winchester (.30-30) or .32 Special; Marlin's Model 36 in .30-30. I hesitate to recommend any of the carbines in the Savage, Winchester or Marlin lines. I think the lighter weight and shorter barrel increase recoil and muzzle blast.

For Group 2 hunters, all of the above are satisfactory, and to them I add the .35 Remington caliber in Remington's Model 141 and 81 and the .300-caliber in the Model 81 only. To the Savage list I add the .300-caliber in each of the models listed. These added calibers are in the "just-to-make-sure" category. Many hunters prefer them for their added shocking power — but watch out for that recoil!

Hunters in Group 3 will be guided solely by their personal evaluation of their qualifications. They will not go wrong with any of the above calibers or rifles listed. They might prefer the bolt-action arm. If so, the Model 70 Winchester stands at the head of the list. Suitable calibers are the .300 Savage, .30-06, .250 Savage, .257 Winchester Roberts, and 7 mm.

That is about as far as I'll go in making specific recommendations.

Any rifle choice must be tempered by its user's personality and sensitivity. Making a definite selection involves a search of the hunter's shooting experience, mechanical aptitude, favorite sights, preferences for action types, psychological reactions to strange situations, age, weight, hair color, grandmother's maiden name, and so on.

The .30-06 as a Deer Rifle

Competent deer hunters unconsciously resent any implication that their rifle might be inadequate for the job. During the late 1920s and early 1930s, deer hunters were subjected to a huge wave of books and magazine articles extolling the virtues of the .30-06 Springfield cartridge and bolt-action rifle. Many deer hunters seriously began doubting their judgment in keeping the .30-30, .303, .37 Special, .38-55 or whatever happened to be their pet caliber or rifle. Most such information indicated these rifles were inadequate for deer hunting except at ridiculously close range or if the animal happened, by chance, to be struck in the head or spine.

For several years, writers went overboard condemning rifles in the .30-30 class as deer killers — insisting that good results couldn't be expected unless the .30-06 or rifles of similar power were used. I remember reading an article by the late Captain E.C. Crossman discussing the merits of various deer rifles. Crossman said, in effect, that the .30-06 was far too much gun for a "flea-bitten white-tailed buck weighing not over 125 pounds." He added that the .30-06 had been used on African lions by his friend Stewart Edward White with much success. This fact might impress deer hunters. He stated, with typical Crossman humor, that there is much similarity between the African lion and the Eastern white-tailed buck: each had a leg on the same corner. But there, he thought, the similarity ended.

Perhaps no man in the country better understood the .30-06 than Crossman. Certainly no one had more respect and admiration for its accuracy, smashing power and all-around versatility. Witness his excellent volume *The Book of the Springfield*. He was a widely experienced big-game hunter, an expert ballistician and, perhaps more than anything, a down-to-earth practical realist in the hunting field. As much as he admired the .30-06, he believed this cartridge was too much for whitetails.

Experiences with the .250 Savage

I followed Crossman's writings for years, right up to the time of his death. Purely on the strength of his recommendations, I bought a .250 Savage lever-action rifle. This rifle was my first "high-powered" job, and it has always been a wonderful rifle for taking whitetails. When I first began hunting with the .250, my friends gave me the raspberry. The rifle was too small, its bullet too fast. It would blow up on the first twig it touched. To top it off, it was hardly big enough to more than scare a deer.

Strangely enough, I killed the first three bucks I shot at with this rifle. One buck was struck in the neck, the others through the chest cavity. All three dropped as though struck by lightning. Shortly after this, I joined a deer-hunting club and meanwhile I had picked up another .250 Savage, the neat, trim little Model 20 bolt-action, at that time the lightest-weight high-powered rifle on the market.

My fellow club members were the big-gun type. Most used the .35 Remington, a few carried the .300 Savage, and one had a .38-55. The advent of a new young hunter with a small-caliber deer rifle came as a shock. I had broken tradition with my pea-shooter. The gang instantly decided I would contribute little to the pile of venison "whacked-up" at season's end. Nevertheless, I killed the first deer driven to my stand — by a neck shot, I'll admit — but still a thoroughly dead deer. The next season I again was fortunate enough to get a shot and again dropped my buck. By this time, the .250 and I were accepted by the gang. Never again were any remarks made concerning the infantile appearance of my little rifle.

Somewhere during this time I sold my original .250 Savage to Bert Sauer. Bert is a grand old-time deer hunter, a charter member of one of the first Sullivan County deer-hunting outfits, and a thoroughly experienced woodsman and rifleman. For many years Bert killed his deer with a .303 Savage, but on the eve of opening day of deer season, some kind-hearted sportsman stole Bert's pet rifle from his car. Bert knew I had an extra rifle, so he offered to buy it rather than borrow it. I favored the Model 20 over the 99G, so I didn't hesitate to let Bert take it. But after he discovered it was a .250-3000, he cooled off a bit. I reassured him by saying I had killed three deer with it, and hadn't had much difficulty in the killing, so he decided to "take a chance."

As he left, he said, "I can always unload it next year if I don't like it." That was probably true enough, but I believe Bert still owns and uses this same little .250 Savage. The first four years he owned it he killed four bucks with a total of six cartridges. "Missed one," he explained a little sheepishly, "and I had to finish off another one with a second shot. But man, I never saw a deer killed any quicker than with that little .250. I never had such good luck with the old .303."

For many years the .250 has been a stepchild. Born of the genius for cartridge design that was Charles Newton's, the cartridge was years ahead of its time, as were most of Newton's designs. It came into being just before World War I when riflemen were not yet used to thinking in terms of high velocity and the tremendous shocking effect from high velocities. Unfortunately, Newton made extravagant claims for all of his cartridges. Some were justified, many were not. Sportsmen were urged to use these light-bullet, high-velocity cartridges on elk, bears and moose. Big-game hunters all over the nation were soon condemning Newton's claims for these cartridges, among them the .250. Logically, such a cartridge is not adequate for these large animals. As a result, the .250 gathered unto itself a big black eye, which it has not yet eradicated.

It is a fine killer of white-tailed deer when loaded with the 100-grain bullet. It is even better when hand-loaded with the 117-grain bullet in a 10-inch twist barrel, using increased powder charges. But such a combination is not suited to the average deer hunter, and it is not available commercially. Suffice to say, any hunter using the .250 Savage 100-grain load owns a mighty efficient rifle for whitetails. It is a cartridge admirably suited to those who might be sensitive to recoil and excessive muzzle blast. Of all the calibers suited to deer hunting, the .250 Savage is without doubt one of the most pleasant to shoot. It is highly accurate, even in lever-actions. It has a very flat trajectory, light report and little recoil effect — altogether a highly versatile cartridge for deer.

Much has been said about the .250's tendency to blow up in heavy brush and timber. Perhaps with the original 87-grain soft-point bullet, that might have been true to some extent. But I've killed many deer with this cartridge in the little Model 20 Savage under all hunting conditions. Never have I detected such tendencies with this cartridge's 100-grain bullet; at least no greater blow-up effect than with any of the other normally acceptable deer-hunting calibers.

For six years I left the rifle with "Sherry" Schuerholz for the Pennsylvania deer season. In this same period, he and other members of his gang killed nine deer with the rifle without a lost buck while hunting in the heavy Pike County covers. If there were any defect in the cartridge's performance, surely some tangible evidence should have come forth during those years of deer hunting in Sullivan County's laurel thickets and Pike County's scrub oak and heavy timber.

CHAPTER 16

Brush Guns and Other Deer Hunting Firearms

One topic that will forever generate debate and unsubstantiated claims among deer hunters is bullet performance on its way to the target. In my opinion, much of this talk about bullets blowing up and deflecting on brush can be charged off with many other deer-hunting alibis.

Years ago when low-velocity, heavyweight bullets were the only cartridges available, the heavy bullets would easily deflect or "ricochet." But today's lighter bullets and stepped-up velocities create a different effect. The bullet's fast drive keeps it steadily on course — even while ripping and tearing through leaves, twigs and grass — until its force is spent in the target, on masses of vegetation, or inside some solid object. It's difficult to turn a high-velocity bullet from its intended path. The bullet destroys itself or blows up in the process, but this involves tearing a path through many yards of heavy thickets or scrub brush.

Experiments in Bullet Deflection

It's true, however, that bullets of the highest velocities like the .220 Swift and the 110-grain .30-06 will blow up after passing through small saplings or branches. The force involved is imparted by the high rotational spin of the bullet itself — centrifugal force. When the bullet's balance is disturbed by passing through any object that tends to change the bullet's shape, centrifugal energy within literally tears the bullet apart as it wobbles through the air. To a lesser degree, this is true of cartridges of lower velocity, but modern bullet designs with their heavier jackets tend to keep the bullet from shattering itself.

Several years ago I got a bit of firsthand information on bullet deflections and "blow-up." To reproduce hunting conditions as closely as possible, I carted my props into deer country; up into the laurel, scrub and birch thicket behind our deer camp. For a target backstop I used an 8-by-4-foot sheet of "Celotex" board, on which I had painted a black cross. The target was a regulation 100-yard, 8-inch bull's-eye at the center of the cross. I placed the backstop inside the heaviest cover I could find, and then moved away until I could no longer see the target but could determine its location by plotting the intersection of the wide black bands on the backstop. For the test, I used rifles in six calibers: the .250 Savage, .30-30, .300 Savage, .35 Remington, .30-06 Springfield and

.38-55, with as much variety in bullet weights as I had on hand. The firing point was at a paced-off range of 80 yards from the target, shooting through the heaviest portion of brush I could select. I fired 10 shots of each caliber and load, each held in the same way to strike center on the target. I recorded the results in my notebook and, to say the least, I found them surprising.

This is the report, just as recorded, in the order of shooting:

.250 Savage, 87-grain pointed soft-point. 2 clean hits in target; 3 hits in target slightly keyholed; 2 hits just off target to the right, in backstop; 2 hits low in backdrop slightly keyholed; 1 bullet missed entirely. Group size 14 inches at greatest spread.

.250 Savage, 100-grain open-point expanding. 6 clean hits in target; 2 in bull; 2 keyholed in target; 2 hits just under target in backstop. Group size 18 inches, maximum, all shots in group.

.30-30 Winchester, 150-grain open-point expanding. 5 hits in target; 3 just below target; 1 just above target; 1 shot missing. Group size 15 inches maximum.

.30-30 Winchester, 170-grain soft-point. 2 hits in target; 7 hits scattered in backstop, making group 40 inches maximum. 1 shot badly keyholed, high and right at 2 o'clock, 42 inches from target center.

.300 Savage, 180-grain soft-point. 3 hits in target; 7 scattered right, left and low in backstop; group size 22 inches, maximum. 3 shots slightly keyholed.

.35 Remington, 200-grain Express Mushroom, 2 shots in target; group size in backstop 22 inches excepting a wide left shot, which was 28 inches from center of target, badly keyholed.

.30-06, 110-grain Hi-Speed Mushroom. 7 hits in target; 1 just above target; 2 missing. Target perforated with bits of bullet jacket and lead, either from one or both of the missing bullets. Group size of bullet holes 10½ inches maximum.

.30-06, 180-grain Western soft-point. 8 hits in target; 2 low in backstop. Group size 15 inches maximum. One of these shots cut off a small poplar sapling about 1 inch in diameter 50 feet from target.

.38-55, 255-grain soft-point. 2 shots in target, both low; 8 hits scattered in backstop, 3 badly keyholed, one high, the rest low. Group size 30 inches maximum.

Of the 60 shots fired, only four failed to hit the 8-by-4 backstop. Presumably, these blew up on some brush. When I analyzed my results, I found that about 90 percent of the shots stayed within 10 inches of the point-of-aim — and this at 80 yards through the heaviest kind of deer cover. Also, there is no doubt in my mind that some of the groups would have been smaller if I could have been certain of holding on the target. At best, I could only guess about the location by checking the intersection of the guide lines on the backstop. My holding probably had an error of 4 or 5 inches at this range. After firing each group of 10 shots, I shifted my aiming point just a bit to give the next string a new path. Needless to say, the passage of 60 bullets inflicted many scars on vegetation involved in the test.

Such a performance, however, is not conclusive. Rather, it strikes a balance between reality and imagination. Many shooters who have exaggerated ideas about bullet deflection and blow-up could learn much about the problems if they conducted such a test themselves. The indications, supported by my own observation, are that slower, heavier bullets plow through brush and saplings better than lighter, faster bullets, but are more likely to stray from the original sight line. But this wandering is not as great as many deer hunters believe. In my test, I fired bullets through more brush and small trees than any hunter would do if actually shooting at a deer, for at no time in this test could I see the target. Even so, if I had been shooting at a deer at this 80-yard range, nine shots of each 10 fired would more than likely have hit the deer.

I do not suggest, obviously, that deer hunters shoot blindly through heavy cover at a buck without making the simplest effort to find an opening. My point is that many deer hunters overwork the bullet-deflection alibi as a substitute for better shooting.

Rifle Actions and Preferred Calibers

Any selection of a deer rifle is closely knit with the cartridge desired. Many recent new cartridge developments are available only in bolt-action rifles. Most of the older, rimmed-head numbers are confined to lever-actions. Selecting the proper cartridge, then, has immediate bearing on the rifle action to be chosen. Deer hunters with a new rifle in mind tend to pore over ballistics tables to find a cartridge of just the right performance to meet their ideas. Unfortunately, such study has little value. Many factors affect cartridge performance on game other than the factory-estimated figures of muzzle velocity, energy and trajectories. The bullet's sectional density and rate of expansion are by far the most important factors in cartridge performance.

For example, suppose we select a cartridge in the .30-06 category, the 220-grain bullet with short exposed lead point, or the 220-grain Express Mushroom. Here we find a velocity of about 2,300 feet per second and striking energy of 2,800 foot-pounds, depending on which manufacturer's tables we read. We compare this with the .257 Roberts and find a 100-grain bullet driven at 2,900 fps with a striking energy of 1,860 foot-pounds. The conclusion, based on the figures alone, is that the 220-grain .30-06 bullet is a much better choice as a deer killer. Actually, the .257 Roberts with the 100-grain bullet would be much more effective, because the bullet design would transmit more of the available energy to the game.

The heavier 220-grain .30-06 bullet is designed for game heavier than deer. The bullet's expansion is delayed by its thick jacket design so great penetration is achieved before expansion occurs, making it a desirable load for moose, grizzly bear and other large game. Such a bullet would zip through the whitetail's comparatively small carcass with little or no expansion unless the deer were shot end to end. The greatest part of the bullet's energy would be spent in the terrain on the deer's far side after passing through. Such expended energy does little to kill your buck.

On the other hand, the lighter, higher-speed 100-grain bullet of the .257 Roberts will seldom pass through a buck, even on broadside hits. Its open-cavity, thin-jacket design permits it to expand almost as soon as it enters the body cavity, tearing a terrific wound channel and expending all of its available energy within the carcass. It is this salient feature of all the lighter-bullet, high-velocity cartridges that makes them deadly on deer.

Hunters who select their new rifle must consider all the elements involved in deer hunting. They must sacrifice some desirable characteristics of high-velocity cartridges to obtain sufficient bullet weight to give good penetration on raking or angle shots, and to carry through scrub oak, laurel and other hazards involved in shooting whitetails. The cartridge elected should have a bullet of sufficient weight, be of such design that expansion takes place readily, and yet not be so heavy that it induces flinching from recoil. Many such cartridges are in the field, giving shooters a wide choice.

Generally speaking, if we can say there is consensus on such a controversial matter, a cartridge should have these characteristics: It should be roughly .30 caliber; shoot a bullet weighing between 150 and 180 grains at a velocity somewhere between 2,200 fps and 2,700 fps; have a bullet designed for fast, high expansion in its forward end; and a bullet jacket thick enough to hold the bullet's rear portion together for greater penetration. Any cartridge conforming to these specifications will perform well on whitetails.

I recall a deer shot by one of my fellow club members. This chap had a new Winchester 54 in .30-06. He had traded in his .32 Special carbine, which he had carried many seasons. He had killed many deer with the little carbine, but he had lost a deer the year before. He concluded he needed a more powerful rifle, hence the .30-06. On one of our drives, he took a stand next-man to mine, but about 200 yards below me on the slope. During the drive, a fine 10-point buck came quartering up the ridge, eventually passing directly before him. With supreme confidence he waited for the best shot, finally driving a bullet through the buck's broadside chest cavity. The buck dropped, but at once gained his hoofs. Again my friend plowed one through the shoulders, and the deer again came up for more, this time quartering away. My friend's third and last shot took the buck far back, but this time it didn't down him.

The moment these three shots resounded sharply through the peaceful serenity of the Oakland Valley, echoing back and forth across the Neversink River, I shifted my stance toward my partner's post. Seconds later I could see a deer heading my way, hobbling slowly and painfully through the birches. I knew at once the deer was badly hit, even though I could not yet see antlers. He stopped momentarily in a clump of birches, then loped ahead, stopping within 30 yards of me near a large beech tree. To my amazement, the buck leaned heavily against the tree for support, blood trickling down its foreleg. I quickly dispatched it with a neck shot.

After the drive came through, my partner walked up to my stand and we looked over the deer. Two holes pierced its left side halfway up and just behind the shoulder. The third shot had entered far back in the flank. We turned the buck over and found two neat holes on the other side of the forequarters, and the third hole behind the last rib. None of the exit wounds showed signs of any great expansion. When we opened the deer its vital organs were, remarkably, in good condition with the exception of the holes through its lungs and paunch. We found no evidence of the great rupturing effect usually seen in the chest cavities of deer I killed with the .250 Savage.

Naturally, I wondered what load he had used, so I asked to see a few of his cartridges. He handed me several loaded with a long bullet tipped with a tiny bit of lead. I guessed they might be Western's 220-grain short exposed point. My friend didn't know the bullet weight. He had "just bought a box of .30-06s." Sure enough, when we made camp he found the box, and they were 220-

grain heavy-jacket, delayed-expansion bullets designed for really heavy game. Therefore, the bullets passed cleanly through, distributing little shock. Fortunately, he had gotten three shots into this buck, which soon would have dropped even had I not finished it off. I have little doubt we would have had a long chase if the buck had been hit only once with those heavy, slowly expanding '06 loads. If better deer loads had been used — the 150- or 180-grain bronze-points, mushroom or open-point expanding — the first shot would have likely produced a quick kill.

Bullet Design and its Effect on Deer

Bullet design is one of the most important controlling factors in selecting a deer rifle for deer. During the 1940s we saw new bullet types engineered to provide maximum in killing effect. Some of the light-bullet, high-velocity cartridges were improved immeasurably by the Core-Lokt Remington and Western Silvertip loads, particularly the .250 Savage and .257 Roberts. A stock complaint with users of these calibers is that they blow up so readily that penetration is poor. In the older Spitzer soft-points and the Hi-Speed Mushroom, this tendency was evident. But with the controlled-expansion Core-Lokt, Silvertip and similar designs, much of this objection has been removed. These bullets expand beautifully at all whitetail ranges, yet the jacket design prevents disintegration of the bullet within the animal. The same improvements have occurred in the old .30-30 and .32 Special flat-point soft-nose, using the long, exposed point. The new bullet gives uniformly good expansion in front, yet restrains the rear half for follow-through punch.

The ultimate ideal in bullet design for whitetails is one in which, when the bullet is fired from a rifle of good power (the .30-30 class or a bit heavier), complete penetration of the vital organs is achieved in all reasonably taken body shots, with the bullet stopping against the far-side hide or some little distance short of this. This means the bullet drove past the middle of the deer, "where he lives," and delivered the full force of the rifle's striking energy to the animal's nervous system. No bullet design can achieve that result every time. For example, a bullet designed to blow up on side or short-angle body shots will not penetrate the vitals if the deer is hit from behind. Such a bullet stops before the vital areas are reached. Even though the wound will eventually prove fatal, it won't drop the deer quickly. To make intelligent bullet selections, hunters must make some sort of compromise. If they select an efficient design for quick expansion, they must forgo rear-end shots in order to make a clean kill. No one in command of his faculties will choose a deep-penetrating bullet on the odd chance of having to shoot lengthwise through a deer to kill it. Yet every year hunters carry rifles loaded with that type of ammunition.

One of the most satisfactory loads in this respect, for my use at any rate, has been the 180-grain Remington Core-Lokt bullet in the .30-40 Krag cartridge. I've killed five deer with this cartridge in which the bullet passed through the body cavity and lodged against the hide on the far side, dropping out when I skinned the buck. All of these bullets expanded to about three times their diameter at the forward end, leaving roughly half the bullet remaining to carry through. Some of the bullet's forward end disintegrated in the process, but that indicates desirable shocking effect, which dropped each deer virtually in its tracks. No doubt the .300 Savage with the same bullet weight and design would have performed similarly, because these two cartridges are almost identical ballistically.

Today's deer hunters have many bullet types from which to select the best loads for their pet rifles. The list includes regular soft-points, Hi-Speed Mushroom, open-point expanding, bronze-point, Protected Point, Peters Belted Bullet, Remington Core-Lokt and Western Silvertip. The latter three are all controlled-expansion bullets. Deer hunters often vacillate in choosing between the open-point and soft-point, ultimately shying away from the open-point. Many stories in circulation claim open-point bullets don't expand readily enough on deer, but the country's best big-game hunters believe no bullet design is better, provided it's driven with sufficient velocity. Most open-point bullets depend on the compression trapped air in the cavity to force the bullet's sides apart, thus upsetting the balance. This blows the jacket's forward end to pieces, thus making a high-shocking wound.

To achieve this desired effect, the bullet must be driven at a fairly high velocity, something faster than 2,000 fps when it strikes the game, not when it leaves the muzzle. Hunters tend to think of velocity in terms of muzzle velocity — when they think about it at all — forgetting the loss in velocity involved in the bullet's flight to the deer. With some cartridges, velocity loss is extremely high the first 200 yards of the bullet's flight, but for deer shooting, long-range velocity losses are not important. Also, open-point bullets are not efficient at velocities slower than 2,000 fps, so bear this in mind when choosing a load. For example, the .35 Remington load with a 200-grain bullet starts at about 2,200 fps. By the time it reaches 100 yards, it has slowed to about 1,850 fps; and at 200 yards it has slowed another 100 fps or more. Beyond 100 yards then, the open-point 200-grain load cannot entirely be depended on to open rapidly inside a deer. It will, of course, open up at these ranges on heavier game, but for deer there could be failures.

With these fairly low-velocity cartridges and loads, the long soft-point bullet is the most dependable. Above the critical velocities, no bullet design performs any better than the open-point type. Variables in jacket thickness between manufacturers tend to change the bullets' expansion rates, but in general, this rule is good.

The Shotgun for Deer Hunting

Traditionally, when we think of firearms for deer, the rifle at once comes to mind. In some regions, however, rifles are barred. I have always been confused by the legislative logic that bars rifles in one state or county, and then mandates use of the shotgun with its heavy slug or round-ball. Both of those projectiles tend to ricochet more than a rifle bullet and are certainly as dangerous, if not more so, at short range in crop field hunting situations. Further baffling, in some other regions adjoining those in which rifle hunting is permitted, only buckshot is legal. These are highly paradoxical situations that do little to conserve game and ensure safety.

At best, the shotgun is an inadequate firearm in the hands of a deer hunter. True, in Southern states where deer are hunted with hounds, the shotgun and buckshot are the only practical combination. Vegetation is dense, shooting ranges are short, and most shooting is at hard-running deer. In most deer hunting areas, however, shotgunners are at a definite disadvantage whether using rifled slugs or buckshot. Legislation being what it is, however, many thousands of hunters must use shotguns if they want to hunt deer in their home state or county. My home county permits only the shotgun and slug or single ball, but we solve this problem by hunting adjoining counties where none of this foolish legislation enforces use of an inadequate firearm.

Granted, the slug load in any shotgun larger than the .410 is deadly if the slug is placed somewhere in the deer's vital area. But with the shotgun, this can be a serious problem: Shotguns lack any sighting equipment but the most rudimentary front sight, making sight elevations largely guesswork. Then too, double-guns tend to cross their patterns, making the right barrel shoot the slug to the left and the left barrel to the right.

On single-barrel guns, pumps, autoloaders and over-unders, hunting accuracy can be vastly improved by mounting a pair of simple rifle sights. I've fitted several guns this way, with sights easily removable, so the gun was not changed for small-game hunting. Judging from the way most shotguns shoot or fail to shoot, rifle sights are the only satisfactory way to make shotguns adequate for deer hunting. Shotguns are designed and built to throw shot, not rifled slugs. Consequently, there is no attempt to make the gun perform with slugs. Likewise, rifled slugs shoot most accurately from a barrel with a minimum of choke or no choke, and such guns are seldom found in the field.

The Rifled-Slug Load

Good hunting accuracy, however, can be had with the rifled slug. I have test-targeted many shotguns with slugs after fitting rifle-type sights, and have been surprised at the accuracy of certain guns. One Winchester Model 12 in 20-gauge, for example, consistently shot 5-inch groups of five shots at 60 yards — the recommended point-blank range. I have also shot some groups at this range that measured less than 4 inches. This is exceptional accuracy from a smoothbore, certainly good enough for deer hunting. After putting several hundred of these slugs through at least 50 shotguns, I concluded that all of them would shoot groups of less than 10 inches at 50 yards. Undoubtedly, there is good hunting accuracy in slugs. The problem for deer hunters is to bring it out. That is best done by fitting the shotgun with good sights and then practicing at the target range to determine the gun's peculiarities. Adjust the sights to be dead-on at 50 to 60 yards.

As far as trajectory and energy are concerned, both characteristics are well-embodied in slug loads for whitetails, at least for ranges up to 75 yards. The figures are something like this:

Gauge	Muzzle Energy	100-yard energy	Slug Weight
12-gauge	1,995 foot-pounds	1,165 foot-pounds	1-oz.
16-gauge	1,600 foot-pounds	940 foot-pounds	⅞-oz.
20-gauge	1,245 foot-pounds	720 foot-pounds	⅝-oz.

Gauge	Trajectory 50 yards	Trajectory 100 yards
12-gauge	+½ inch	-2½ inches
16-gauge	+½ inch	-2¾ inches
20-gauge	+½ inch	-2¾ inches

Shotgun slugs travel quite flat over the 100-yard range, certainly flat enough to eliminate holding over at normal hunting ranges. Rifled slugs don't expand much after striking deer, but their large size gives them terrific smashing effect, certainly enough to down any deer hit in a vital area. Paunch shots are taboo, though, with rifled slugs. These shots take a heavy toll of deer that are never recovered by hunters. In general, the shotgun and slug load should be effective on deer at normal hunting ranges, but the missing factor in the hunting field is accurate sights.

A novel, effective addition to a shotgun for shooting slugs is the so-called 1-power (actually, no power) scope. These scopes provide quick sighting through a wide field of view, and they have the additional advantage of placing the target and sighting dot in the same focus.

Buckshot for Deer

The shotgun paired with buckshot is a different story, and, in my opinion, a mighty sad one. Buckshot's limitations as a deer killer are understood by only a handful of deer hunters. Unfortunately, many sportsmen must use this load if they want to hunt deer in their home states or counties. It's true that buckshot is deadly in areas where cover is so thick a deer cannot be seen past 35 or 40 yards. In fact, any shotgun load at close range is deadly. For many years, African hunters used a big-bore double shotgun to back up their rifles against charging, dangerous game.

The major drawbacks in buckshot loads are their failure to retain lethal striking force for any considerable range, and rapid dispersion of the pellets, which precludes putting enough shot into the game to kill through shock. And the shotgun, to be effective, must kill by shock. Individual pellets cause little bleeding unless by chance they sever large arteries. There's no apparent pellet expansion in flesh and no tearing lacerations and ruptured tissue, which make rifle bullets so deadly. To kill a buck neatly with buckshot, then, hunters must put a large part of the original load into the deer, inflicting enough shock to kill.

Unfortunately, when we take our favorite scattergun to the range for pattern tests, we're due for a shock. We might have a fine full-choke gun capable of putting 70 percent of its No. 6 shot load into a 30-inch circle at 40 yards, which is highly efficient on ducks or wide-flushing ringnecks. But let's say we fire a load of 00 buckshot at a 4-foot square paper at 25 yards. Checking the results, we should find a fairly good pattern, bunched in small groups, but with all nine shot within a 24-inch circle. This, we think, should kill any deer it hits. Then we move back to the 40-yard mark and fire another 00 load at the paper. Here is where we get the shock. The same load that produced a well-grouped killing pattern at 25 yards has now spread all over the paper, with perhaps two or three shot missing entirely. Shot-holes will be unevenly grouped, leaving wide gaps in the pattern. This 00 buck load at 40 yards will often throw shot in little bunches, two in one corner that can be covered with the hand, then far over in another corner a group of three equally clustered. But it's the gaps in between, plus the wide dispersal of the pattern as a whole, that make buckshot a poor killer at longer, ranges. The whitetail's vital area is not large, roughly 12 by 18 inches; and the neck and head area is somewhat smaller. To kill a buck and still recover it, most of the buckshot load must hit this area. If we lay a 12-

by-18-inch rectangle on a pattern board and fire at it beyond 40 yards, we'll be lucky to get more than four shots into this area at every try. We need more than this to ensure a clean kill, unless chance's guiding hand puts two or three through the heart or spine.

With the single 0 buckshot load, we have three more shot to give an effective pattern. The single 0 buckshot load also gives somewhat better patterns with less tendency to group in small bunches and fewer fliers. But even with this better-balanced load, patterns are not good beyond 40 yards. Full-choke guns do not produce patterns as well as those from modified or more open chokes. The swedging effect of tighter chokes deforms the shot as it passes through, causing shot to wander from the pattern's center.

Either of the above loads will kill deer, but it's up to hunters to pattern both loads at ranges up to 50 yards. Only then can they decide whether to use the heavier pellets of the 00 load or the somewhat fuller pattern of the single 0 buckshot.

Buckshot shooters sometimes experiment with many methods to produce tighter buckshot patterns. One of these methods is to remove the top wad and pour hot paraffin wax over the shot, then replace the top wad. Thus far, I've heard of no remarkable results from this experiment. Ballistically speaking, I fail to see its merit. A more practical method is to split each shot open, string them onto a silk line, and crimp each shot over the line about four inches apart. Then pack the shot back into the shell, usually leaving out a shot or two to make room for the line. These loads are reputed to shoot much tighter patterns than the same load before doctoring. Some of my New Jersey friends use them exclusively. They say the much closer grouping is worth the trouble it takes to doctor the load. In fact, this load is marketed commercially by a Southern outfit that custom-loads them to order. It's certainly a step in the right direction, for hunters who must use buckshot are severely handicapped in taking their deer. Now and then we hear of a freak kill made with buckshot at long ranges, even up to 100 yards. Not many hunters will have the phenomenal luck to bag a deer at such range with a shotgun, but I suppose it's that 1-in-a-million chance that will forever urge buckshot slingers to shoot at deer far outside the shotgun's effective range.

New Developments in Deer Firearms

I began preparing this chapter on deer-hunting loads and firearms just before Pearl Harbor hit us with such tremendous force that everything else was forgotten in the interest of the nation's defense. As World War II rolled along with its developments in weapons and firepower, I envisioned a changed postwar era for deer hunting. However, as I write this, there has been little in firearms developments to arouse interest from hunters. The big gun plants are crowding out as many of the prewar rifle models as production capacity will allow. The demand for firearms is so great that there seems little need to spend money to create demand for new designs in hunting rifles. The arms plants are concentrating production in the few models most suited to supply the greatest need. Stevens-Savage has announced a new light bolt-action .30-30 in the low-priced field, modeled on the older Savage 40 bolt-action. The new rifle is a bit more graceful in appearance than the 40, with a flush magazine holding three cartridges, making, a four-shot rifle in all. It looks and handles as a deer rifle should, and will make a highly suitable deer rifle for young hunters, especially the ex-GI trained in the use of bolt-action arms.

Remington's latest contribution to postwar firearms is an interesting low-priced bolt-action high-power rifle with several new features. This new Model 721A is faintly reminiscent of the old Model 30 Express, which was designed on the 1917 Enfield action. However, this new model comes in several attractive calibers: .30-06 Springfield, .270 Winchester, both with 24-inch barrel; and the .300 Magnum with 26-inch barrel.

A shorter-action design of the above, called the 722A, is built in .257 Roberts or .300 Savage calibers. The 722A has a shorter bolt-throw and a bit less weight than the 721A, otherwise both rifles are identical.

The racy stock design with a nice, full pistol grip will appeal to deer hunters who like bolt-action rifles, as will its comparatively light weight. The 721A rifle weighs about 7.4 pounds, the 722A a few ounces less. The design of this new rifle keeps the scope shooter well in mind. Its safety is on the side, where it can't interfere with the low mounting of any scope; and the bolt handle doesn't turn up to interfere with the sight line. In addition, its receiver ring and bridge are drilled and tapped for standard scope mounts.

Remington has provided in this rifle an adjustable-tension trigger without double-draw pull. It also has an encased bolt head that surrounds the cartridge head, giving the shooter maximum protection. With these new features and a fairly low price, this rifle should be an excellent addition to Remington's top deer-hunting favorites: the models 141 and 81.

Winchester is concentrating its production on the Model 70, the .94 Carbine, the .64 Deer Rifle, and the .348-caliber Model 71. Remington, of course, is turning out the slide-action 141 and the autoloading Model 181, both highly effective deer rifles. However, the demands are so great and distribution so thin that many hunters will be without a new rifle when deer season opens.

Selecting the Used Rifle

This lack of new deer rifles will force many hunters to buy a used rifle, if they're fortunate enough to locate a good one. Most used rifles of American make that are now available are good buys. Rifles bearing Winchester, Savage, Remington and Marlin trademarks are built to perform satisfactorily for the hunter's lifetime. Most will function properly for many more years if they're kept clean and rust-free. Aside from dents and scratches in the stock and worn spots in the bluing, any of these arms might be just as good as a new rifle. However, you should check out a few points before buying any used rifle. This is a good time to point them out.

First, the rifle should show evidence of having had reasonably good care from its previous owner. The most obvious sign of abuse is rust pits on the barrel or action. Such rust can be removed by polishing with steel wool, but the pits will forever remain as evidence the former owner didn't spend much time looking after his rifle.

Second, be sure ammunition can be easily obtained for the rifle in question. Many calibers are no longer loaded by ammo-makers, nor do they intend to load many of these in the future: 6.5 Mannlicher, 6 mm Lee Navy, .256 Newton, .25-36 Marlin (the .25-35 Winchester and Marlin rifles are no longer made, but ammunition will probably be loaded for years), .30 Newton, .32 Winchester self-loading, .33 Winchester, .35 Winchester S.L.R., .35 Newton, .40-60, .40-82 and similar old-style black-powder cartridges. Likewise, prospective used-gun purchasers must be sure they are not picking up a "wild-cat" caliber — such as a .250 Varminter, .25 Niedner, .280 Dubiel, .35 Whelen[1] or .400 Whelen — unless fully aware they must hand-load their own stuff or buy it from a commercial hand-loader. That's not the cheapest way to buy ammunition, incidentally.

Sometimes, a good American-made rifle will be offered in otherwise good condition but have a small part missing: a hammer, firing pin, extractor or ejector. Unless the rifle is more than 50 years old, its maker should be able to supply parts for it out of stock. But this is true only of American-made arms and gunmakers still in business. For example, the Standard Arms Co. of Wilmington, Del., built a number of gas-operated and slide-action rifles built for the Remington rimless .30, .32 and .35 cartridges. Because this company has been out of business for years, replacement parts don't exist. This is also true of most foreign arms, with the exception of the '98 German Mauser and British Enfield. Our own Krag, Springfield and 1917 Enfield can be supplied with parts right out of the National Rifle Association's service department.

The Remodeled Military Rifle

Once these points are cleared up, inspect the rifle's mechanical parts. Wipe the barrel dry before the inspection. A light film of oil or grease in the bore will make a badly worn and pitted bore look pretty good, and a barrel filled with dust and lint will look much worse than it might be. Hold the gun up to indirect light for inspection. If the lands are badly rounded, not sharp-edged in any sense, and the grooves rough and black, the rifle has likely seen all of its useful life. If the lands seem somewhat distinct and the grooves fairly clean, the barrel will likely still produce enough accuracy for hunting. This is particularly true if the upper half of the barrel is in good condition right up to the muzzle. No rifle will shoot accurately if the muzzle end of the rifling is worn smooth or damaged. Considerable wear at the chamber end is permissible. It's fairly easy to inspect the bores of take-down arms and bolt-action rifles, but solid-frame lever-actions won't permit an easy look through the bore. To inspect these, insert a bit of white paper into the opened action, and hold this to reflect the light.

Of course, the best test of the rifle's accuracy is its performance on the range. If this is permissible, fire the rifle at a paper target at any range up to 100 yards. Use a padded rest for the forearm and shoot in the prone position. If all the holes in the paper appear round with no tendency toward an oval shape, this indicates the barrel is still good enough to spin the bullets properly. Should the holes show any tendency to enter sideways or "keyholed," discard the rifle at once. Likewise, the group size will show some measure of the rifle's accuracy, but it's not conclusive unless the tester is a skilled rifleman.

Examine the sights on a used rifle for damaged or bent front sights or missing screws. Any of these items can be repaired, but this must be considered in the deal. Check the action to make certain it locks fairly tight. The extractor and ejector should be in place and in working order, and be sure the extractor hook is not broken out. With the rifle fully cocked, test the safety for positive

[1]The .35 Whelen became a commercial cartridge in 1988 through the Remington Arms Co. Remington also offered its annual Model 700 Classic that year in the .35 Whelen. It also introduced the Model 7600 slide-action in the cartridge in '88, but discontinued the chambering in that rifle in December 1994. From 1989 through 1994 the chambering was available in various versions of the Model 700. The .35 Whelen was also available in the Model 7400 autoloader from 1993 through 1995. The Model 700 KS Mountain Rifle remains available in .35 Whelen through Remington's custom shop. Remington and Federal still offer the load in their ammunition.

functioning by forcing the hammer or cocking piece forward with some pressure. This will determine the margin of safety in the sear surfaces. Used guns have often been tinkered with by their former owners, and the trigger mechanism is the usual sufferer. Lightening trigger pulls is a delicate job — not in the lightening alone but in the preservation of the flat contact surfaces. Rounding these surfaces can cause an accidental discharge if the hammer or cocking piece is struck or shoved with enough violence to push the cocking sear over the trigger sear. This should be carefully checked in a used rifle.

A dented or otherwise marred stock should not deter hunters from buying a rifle that's otherwise sound. A cracked stock, particularly one cracked through the grip, is not so good, but any stock damaged only by the usual scratches and dents incurred in hunting can readily be refinished. The dents can be steamed up, scratches sanded off, and the whole job done over with an oil finish. The cost will be in labor only, and besides, it's good fun for long winter evenings.

The foreign military arms of World War II are far too numerous to mention in detail. The country is now flooded with all types — German, Belgian, Czech, Austrian, Italian and Japanese. Most of these are, and should forever be, merely souvenir weapons. Many are good for deer hunting, but the hunter is seldom qualified to separate the wheat from the chaff. Unless such rifles can be examined and checked by competent gunsmiths, the entire category should be discarded for American hunting.

Our own new military rifles of World War II, the Garand and the M1 carbine, are not suited to hunting nor available to hunters. The Garand is a highly efficient military weapon of great firepower in .30-06 caliber, but it's a clumsy, poorly balanced arm unsuited to sporting conversion. The little carbine with its pitifully inadequate cartridge can never be a deer rifle. Some deer will be killed with it, but for each one recovered 10 will stagger off to die miserably.

In Europe, many commanding officers sensibly barred use of the carbine to soldiers shooting European deer for food, permitting only the Garand. This carbine cartridge compares unfavorably with our old loadings in the .32-20, never a deer killer except in the hands of the best hunter riflemen. Many hunters have had visions of picking up a wartime Garand or M1 carbine for little money, planning to use these for deer. However, (in the late 1940s) it is illegal for private citizens to possess either of these arms. Furthermore, ammunition manufacturers are forbidden to offer the .30-caliber carbine ammunition for civilian sales. It's conceivable the Garand could be offered for civilian sale, but I doubt any hunter will seriously consider this rifle after reviewing all of today's sporting rifles.

Rifles for Women

Strangely enough, the female hunter is appearing with greater frequency in deer country each season. At Northville in the Adirondacks last season, I noted a sizable number of red-capped and red-coated Dianas. It was inevitable that this should be so, for deer hunting comes within the reach of more people each year. The wider distribution of deer, easier hunting methods, and the glamour of taking a white-tailed buck should all appeal to the huntress.

The perfect deer rifle for women would be the Savage lightweight 99 T in

.250-3000. No rifle of ample power for deer will be more pleasant for her to shoot. Perhaps a heavier caliber will be more in line with her ideas. If so, her rifle can be fitted with a muzzle brake, a highly efficient device for hunters sensitive to recoil. These brakes increase muzzle flash and blast, however, so consider that in making a decision.

The True Custom Rifle

Each year, as hunters and riflemen become more discriminating in their choice of rifles, the truly custom-built rifle is more in demand. These rifles should never be confused with the sporting-conversion of military rifles now offered by many companies. Conversions are justly popular with many hunters, and in most cases are well-designed and serviceable. The usual practice in converting these rifles for hunters is to take standard military arms — the Springfield, Enfield and Mauser — remove the military sights, shorten the barrel (if necessary), polish the barrel, fit ramp front sights and aperture rear, and then fit the rifle with a machine-turned and inletted stock designed by the individual maker. Some handwork is required in final stock fitting and finishing, and then the action and barrel are reblued. Some models, particularly the Enfield conversion, require additional machine work to remove the rear-sight base and fit the magazine to flush outlines.

All of those jobs make excellent sporting rifles at no higher price than similar rifles of standard design. They fill a need at the present time, when gun plants are far behind deliveries. However, the great proportion of these sporter conversions offers little more than shooters can have with Remington and Winchester high-power bolt-action rifles.

The custom gun lies in a special field of gunsmithing. It is designed individually for the shooter for whom it is built. Such a rifle is expensive, being built by a skilled craftsman, but it is only in such a rifle that discriminating hunter-riflemen can incorporate their own ideas. Fine wood can be obtained in the custom-gun stock, designed according to the hunter's personal needs — correct drop at heel and comb, Monte Carlo comb, desired pitch and length of butt plate, suitable shape and fit of cheek piece, special sighting equipment, more comfortable pistol grip, a pleasingly artistic checkering design, and a fine finish. Perhaps the shooter wishes a new barrel of a special caliber not available in the action type he chooses. This the custom gunsmith can supply.

Rifles of this type should be, and usually are, purchased by hunters who have been in the shooting field long enough to have well-established ideas about their requirements. A hunter of abnormal build, or with physical disabilities preventing use of a standard rifle can many times be fitted with a suitable rifle by a custom gunmaker. Hunters should not spend money on one of these costly arms unless they need special work. Most hunters have no fixed ideas of gun design. They will be suited well with standard arms, and at much less cost.

True custom-gun work is limited to a comparative handful of gunsmiths across the country. It's difficult for hunters to select the right man for the job, but to save money and spare themselves disappointment, they must pick a skilled, reliable man to perform the work.

Most custom rifles are built on bolt-action or single-shot rifles. For deer hunting, the Krag, Springfield, Mauser and Enfield are all good actions for a basic start. However, there's no reason why any of the lever-actions, autoloaders and slide-actions cannot be built to custom specifications. A sturdy action such as the 99 Savage, built with special cheekpiece stock, suitable forearm design, top-shelf sighting equipment and other refinements, can well take its place beside the best bolt-action, custom-built sporters. The emphasis in custom rifles, however, is on bolt-action arms. These are best suited to rebarreling with special calibers, and are more adaptable to drastic changes in stock design.

Whatever the hunter's choice of action for the custom job might be, let him first fix in his mind the principal design and specifications before placing his order. Consult the gunsmith commissioned to do the work on any of the points that might be hazy. Most gunsmiths will perform work exactly as outlined, even though it might be against their better judgment. In any case, smart hunters will get their gunsmith's advice, recognizing that the gunmaker's wider experience will temper radical design to more practical lines.

During World War II, I was associated with Eric "Pop" Johnson and Bob Owen in manufacturing the .50-caliber Browning machine gun. Both of these gunsmiths, world-famous in stock work and barrel making, confided that their biggest headache in custom-gun work was their customers' "screwball ideas" or that many didn't supply enough accurate information to intelligently build the rifle.

Custom rifles will never be a choice for the masses. They take up where regular manufacturers stop. But they're the only answer for the hunter-riflemen who must have a rifle "tailor made" to conform to his advanced ideas. Perhaps best of all, they answer every hunter's craving for something different, a rifle of beautifully graceful lines, artistically executed by a master gun-craftsman whose love of firearms is apparent in his work. In other words, a rifle to cherish, to fondle, to hold close to one's heart as a warm friend and dependable companion in the woods.

Trust in Confidence, Reliability

In these past two chapters, I deliberately avoided firearms technicalities. I wrote these chapters in the hope that the new or less-experienced hunters might find some hints to explain some of their failures. No one hunter can find sufficient experience, even in a lifetime of deer hunting, to become the sage adviser whose words are the criterion by which deer hunters must, forever after, live. I'm merely another deer hunter who has had, through fortuitous circumstance, a bit more firearms experience than the average hunter who signs a deer license each year.

It should forever be fixed in a hunter's mind that the caliber and design of a firearm are of far less importance than his ability to handle it. With a well-made reliable rifle in hand, hunters must climb the mental, physical and emotional steps up the ladder of experience, until at last their ability matches the accuracy, killing power and reliability of their rifle. If their confidence then matches their ability, they should, with the favorable smile of Old Lady Luck, kill their deer.

CHAPTER 17

Sights: Open, Peep and Riflescope

The connecting links between deer hunters' rifles and their bucks are gun sights. Widely discussed among all shooters, and always controversial with big-game hunters, metallic rifle sights have made less progress in development from 1900 through the late 1940s than any other part of a firearm. The accuracy of any rifle strictly depends on its sighting equipment, yet many thousands of wonderfully accurate rifles are handicapped with obsolete sighting equipment.

When Decent Sights are Lacking

It seems silly to find a rifle as highly accurate as any good .30-06 equipped with a plain metal bead or blade for a front sight and a notch for a rear sight. Such equipment would not deliver better than fair accuracy, even in an expert's hands. This same .30-06, with hunting ammunition, can easily put all of its shots into a 6-inch circle at 200 yards, but crude sights make holding as close as that physically impossible. Look through the lineup of any American rifle manufacturer and you'll find new models, even those chambered and bored for the most modern cartridges, turned loose on hunters with sights that were old stuff during the Civil War.

There can be only one reason for such neglect: manufacturing costs. A dollar or less in saved manufacturing costs will make the consumer's final price much more attractive. It's also possible that riflemakers believe many shooters will change the sights to their liking anyway, so why jack up the retail price with sights that will be discarded? This latter might be a pleasant thought, but it doesn't happen often.

If these gunmakers realized how badly these poor sights make their latest rifle and cartridge perform, I would almost bet a quick change would evolve in factory sight equipment. During the 1940s, some manufacturers released two or three models with receiver or tang peep sights as standard equipment, but these few models don't amount to more than 10 percent of the entire line of American-made deer rifles.

There is nothing really new in the recent entire line of metallic hunting sights. Many hunters think peep or aperture sights are a recent fad, but their use dates to the days of crossbows hundreds of years ago. The tang peep of Lyman and Marble type has been in use longer than 100 years. In fact, the Lyman tang sight is today virtually the same as the Lyman of a century ago. Why, then, don't more shooters use good sights — I can't call them "modern" sights, because they're not — instead of worrying along for years with poor equipment? I blame the riflemakers for not educating shooters and supplying them with good sights, either through negligence or deliberate intent.

Metallic rifle sights fall into two classifications: the open or "notch" type and the aperture or "peep" style. With both of these rear-sight designs, the same front sight can be used, so let's go into the front sight situation first, because it's highly important. No matter what type of rear sight your rifle carries, if the front sight can't be readily seen, you might as well not have sights.

Front Sights for Whitetail Shooting

The term "front sight" covers a multitude of types for widely varying purposes: small-game hunting, simon-pure target work, "plinking," long-range big-game hunting and quick, accurate work at short range in heavy cover. In deer hunting, we can shortcut through all these styles right to the last mentioned. That's because most whitetail shooting is done at ranges less than 100 yards, and in close cover where backgrounds do not provide good visibility. For this hunting, we need a front sight easily seen in any light and durable enough to stand hard knocks. It must also allow a fair degree of accuracy in a hurry, for snap-shooting at moving targets.

First, let's discuss the size of a front sight. Regardless of the sight style or material used in its makeup, a front sight for whitetail shooting should be large. The only possible reason for using a small front sight under any shooting condition is to obtain greater accuracy on small targets. By no stretch of the imagination can a white-tailed buck be called a "small target" at normal hunting ranges.

In some instances, the rifle's barrel length will determine the best size for the front sight. It's self-evident that a 3/32-inch bead will look larger on a 20-inch carbine barrel than on a 26- or 28-inch rifle barrel. If we can make any definite statement about a minimum front-sight dimension for deer shooting, it would be this 3/32-inch size. Under some conditions of poor visibility and deficient vision on the hunter's part, a 1/8-inch bead is a big advantage. Sights this size are sometimes listed by the makers as "semi-jack" sights, but don't be fooled into thinking they're for night shooting. These big sights are highly accurate on deer at all hunting ranges, and are a necessity under all bad sighting conditions.

The medium beads, measuring about 1/16 inch, with which most rifles are factory equipped, are a bit too small for good results on whitetails. These sights are intended as a compromise, to be used on game and targets of all sizes from woodchucks to big game. But if deer hunters want a front sight for deer hunting only, they're better off with these larger sizes.

Now let's discuss the shape of front sights. The round bead is almost universally used, and is conceded to be as good as any for all hunting purposes. Some hunters trained in shooting at targets prefer the military type square-top post, and for some eyes this sight will give better holding for elevation. The squarely cut off top of the post makes a clear line of demarcation against any target. That feature eliminates the tendency of top sights to blend into the background, which sometimes happens with the round bead. I prefer the square-topped sight for all deer hunting for this reason, because there is never doubt about the position of the front sight's top in reference to the target. This is drawing the point a bit too fine for deer hunting, though, and we can consider it of minor importance for whitetail hunting.

One point about the shape of the front sight that is important, however, is to have the bead face perfectly flat. Many round beads have round or almost round faces. With this type of sight we encounter the condition known as "shooting away from the light," caused by light reflection distorting the shooter's view of the bead. Sunlight striking this bead from the side causes that side to look larger than the other, throwing the bead center out of line, or "away from the light." This objectionable feature is particularly noticeable with large front sights. To correct or prevent it, use nothing but a flat-faced bead. The flat face reflects light uniformly and gives true holding under all angles of light reflection.

A front hunting sight made by King called the "Reflector front sight" was developed to provide better illumination by using light reflection. This sight incorporates a built-in chromium reflector in its base, which picks up overhead light and throws it on the bead. The principle is good, certainly it is quite new, and it makes this sight outstanding for hunting under poor light conditions.

Materials of many kinds have been used to make front sights: pure gold or silver, "German silver," copper, bronze, ivory and various plastics in different shades. Selecting the best material for a front sight, which determines the color, is largely a matter of backgrounds and cover to be encountered, as well as time of year. The clear, dead-white of an ivory bead is fine for all conditions except when snow covers the ground. Then it might be hard to find, just when you need it most. It stands out well against the green of spruce and laurel or the brown and black of late-fall hardwood covers. The silver bead is equally good under these conditions, but neither should be used if the ground is likely to be snow-covered. Some deer hunters will compromise on a gold bead, because this can be seen well against any background. It also has the outstanding virtue, common to metal beads, of durability. Probably the best bead color for any condition is red. It stands out sharply against evergreens, dead leaves, tree trunks and snow, not to mention the gray-brown of a deer.

The only weak point in plastic or ivory beads is their fragility. Sometimes a mere touch against a stone, tree trunk or frozen ground will crack them off. The hunter is out of luck for the rest of the trip, or for that day at least. The smart thing for deer hunters to do, if they're at all prone to breaking off ivory sights almost every season, is to use a silver or gold bead for strength. Then, if encountering snow during the season, they can blacken the front sight by smoking it with a match, and resmoking it as often as it rubs off. When the snow melts, the original gold or silver can be renewed by polishing the bead with fine steel wool. Don't try to smoke an ivory or plastic sight, because you might be surprised to learn it's made of celluloid. Before you know it, you'll need a new front sight. Ivory sights that have yellowed with age can be bleached to their original whiteness by exposure to sunlight. But if they've been smoked in any way, they'll never again be white.

The Front-Sight Ramp

No discussion of front sights is complete without mentioning the front-sight ramp. Hunters who follow the latest trends of riflemakers have probably noted that almost all new models carry a special type of front-sight base, called a ramp, in which the front sight is mounted. Some are an integral part of the barrel and others are made separately and attached by bands, screws or sweating to the barrel.

Ramps are not a new flight of fancy with riflemakers. Rather, they serve two definite purposes: quicker sighting and greater strength. Not only that, but they have an artistic appearance. These ramps rapidly guide the eye upward along the incline toward the front sight, throwing the shooter's eye to this sight at once. Many older rifles, especially military rifles, have very high front sights (out of necessity), leaving the front-sight bead perched atop a narrow stem. This narrow stem gives no guide to the shooter's eye, slightly slowing the sighting process.

These high front sights are also easily bent out of alignment and, in appearance, add nothing to the rifle's graceful lines. Using the long ramp as a base for sights makes it possible to mount a low sight that is much less subject to damage. This also enhances the rifle's appearance. In addition, most ramp sights provide a hood or sight cover, which is great protection to the sight in transportation. Of course, the hood should be removed for deer hunting to allow all possible light to reach the sight.

Front sights are made in a tremendous variety of shapes and sizes, each adapted to special conditions. Globe sights, combination sights, reversible sights and aperture sights all have a place in rifle-shooting, but certainly not for whitetail hunting. What deer hunters need most is a rugged sight, clearly visible against all backgrounds and in poor light. Once a sight is properly mounted and adjusted, it will stay that way for seasons to come.

The "Open" Rear Sights

Open rear sights have always been a touchy subject with me, but as long as manufacturers keep putting them on rifles, they must be considered. Many open sights consist merely of a flat-topped bar with a small V- or U-shaped notch to center the front sights. Of all the many styles of open rear sights, this type seems the lesser evil. It's fairly quick to catch and obscures little of the target. However, the so-called "buckhorn," "semi-buckhorn" and Rocky Mountain types found on thousands of hunting rifles are the worst sights for hunting whitetails. Of all standard factory sights, these are the slowest to use, the most difficult to see and the least accurate. For quick shooting and shots at running deer, they invariably cause shooters to throw their bullets high because the front sight is not pulled down low enough in the notch.

With the flat-topped sight, some of this high-shooting tendency is prevented, but even then the notch is fuzzy and indistinct, especially in the poor light of deer woods. I think there is only one good open rear sight regularly supplied for deer rifles. This sight has a slightly concave-top rear sight with a vertical white line in the face's center. It has no notch. To align this sight properly, you simply catch the front bead over the top of the rear sight in line with the vertical white line, and the hold is right. There's little chance to hold too high, because the bead just rests atop the rear sight. Windage alignment is quickly made with the center line. There is no notch to "fuzz" and no possibility of holding "too fine" or "too coarse" unintentionally. This rear sight is listed by Savage Arms Corp., and is regularly supplied on the 99 T model in connection with a red bead front sight, making as good a set of open sights as can be had for deer hunting. The red on the front sight contrasts starkly with the rear sight's white line, giving rapid, positive sight alignment. These sights can be had on any of Savage's regular models if specified, and can also be adapted to many other makes of rifles.

Redfield makes a flat-top replacement rear sight using the white line principle in connection with a notch. Marble's and King also make similar rear sights, using a white diamond in place of the line, with the point of the diamond ending at the bottom of the notch. In these three different makes of rear sights, the notches and white line, or diamond, are made up as a separate insert, giving shooters the choice of V-shaped or U-shaped notches by simply reversing the insert. In addition to the flat-topped style of sight, all these manufacturers make similar sights in semi-buckhorn and buckhorn styles, but the flat top is by far the best for all shooting.

Any and all types of open rear sights create certain sighting difficulties. They must be mounted at least 14 or 15 inches away from the eye, for optical reasons, to be seen clearly, thus shortening the rifle's sighting radius, which increases sighting errors. At this distance, the eye is slow to pick it up. For quick shooting, or when the light is poor, shooters won't take time to pull the front sight down in the rear notch, or they won't be able to see it if they do get it down where it belongs. In either case, the shot will go high, and if they're using a buckhorn type, the high "ears" on each side of the notch will further induce this high-shooting tendency. In addition, the rear sight's outline obscures much of the target, making such open sights hopelessly inefficient.

Hunters can make small changes in their sights to aid efficiency in the woods. If a rifle has a rear notch with high sides, they can be filed flush with the top of the notch. Shooters who like the visibility of the ivory bead can make an effective substitute with a drop of white lacquer on the face of the regular bead. Lacquer can be carried in a small bottle in a recess in the stock under the butt plate, and applied with a pin or matchstick. To remove it when there's snow, simply scratch it off with a fingernail or a knife blade. Filing the rear sight, of course, leaves the metal bright, so it should be reblued to avoid rust and light reflection. Front sights with a rounded or oval-faced bead can be filed flat to eliminate the "shooting away from the light" fault, but it requires care to keep the surface square.

The Peep Sight

Many times since the mid-1930s I've gone out on a limb in recommending peep sights to deer hunters — seasoned veterans and novices alike. With only one exception, each of these new peep-sight users has been better satisfied than with the open sights he had used formerly. The lone unhappy hunter had to be fitted with a good riflescope before finding satisfaction.

I've always found it a deep mystery why there is such prejudice among deer hunters against peep, or aperture, rear sights. The peep sight is infinitely more accurate, faster to use, and easier to see than any other metallic sight, yet not more than one deer hunter in 10 is willing to give it a tryout. The optical advantages of a peep are self-evident: longer sighting radius, rear sight closer to the eye, and better view of the target. There is better sighting under poor light conditions, and no necessary focusing on the rear sight, nor the possibility of holding the front sight high in relation to the rear sight.

Using the peep sight is ridiculously simple; so simple, in fact, that shooters are not conscious of it when shooting. The peep hole is an open window through which we see the front sight and target clearly. No effort should be made to see the rear peep ring, much less to try to focus on it. A major reason for mounting the peep close to the eye is to discourage the shooter from focusing an eye on the peep ring. With the ring so close to the eye, it's impossible to focus on it, which is just as it should be.

To clarify the confusion in using the peep sight in hunting, let's compare its sighting processes with open sights. With open sights, shooters first bring the front sight into their line of vision, then settle it in the rear notch, carefully centering it in the notch neither too high nor too low. This process takes a certain amount of time and concentration, even though it might be unconscious. Shooters must then swing the front sight on the target in the proper spot and squeeze off the shot. The peep-sight user must only look through the peephole at the front sight, swing the front sight onto the target and fire when the sight rests in the right place. Of course, trained riflemen in either case do not look directly at their sights. They keep their gaze focused on the target and let the sights fall into line as they will, even though they're somewhat out of focus.

It's an optical truth that our eye can focus at only one distance at any given time. The peep necessitates concentrating on only two points, the front sight and the target. With open sights, some attention must be paid to the rear sight in addition to the front sight and target. It seems the benefits of peep sights would be of obvious advantage to new hunters, who must pay more attention to sight alignment than the skilled shooter. Good shooters know almost unconsciously when their sights are in the correct relative position. They can then concentrate on the target exclusively.

Beginners have the bad habit of looking directly at their sights, first the front, then the rear. Finally, they shift their vision to the target. We all know the eye cannot change its point of focus abruptly. It takes a fraction of a second for our vision to clear up on the target after we've been watching the sights. In that brief instant, the buck might disappear or shift position, requiring an entire sighting procedure all over again. With experienced hunters, this is not a major point. They can shift their aim readily and quickly as occasions demand. But for the uninitiated, this slower sighting process often means failure to make a kill or a hit.

This, then, is the major advantage of peep sights in deer hunting: They require less concentration in sighting than open sights, and leave shooters free to watch their game directly. The aperture is usually large enough so the entire target can be seen within it. None of it is obscured by the high sides or flat bar of rear sights on open sights. The front sight stands out clearly and alone in the aperture's center, and gives shooters greater latitude in holding.

Peeps are More Accurate

Why, then, the prejudice against the peep sight? Frankly, it rests in ignorance and inexperience among hunters, and a reluctance to try something new. Deer hunters usually say they're "use" to the rear sight of open sights, and that they can't quickly find the front sight through the peephole. They don't realize that the less attention they pay to the rear peep, the more natural and rapid their sighting will be. Complaint No. 2 is that they can't center the front sight in the peep, whereas it's difficult to hold it anywhere in the peep ring except the center. Our eye, normally and naturally, will align and hold the front sight in the center or approximate center without any effort. Merely looking through the peep in the natural act of sighting gives precise alignment for windage and elevation.

I might add that, under hunting conditions, there is no crying need to center the front sight exactly. Slight errors in holding the front sight in relation to the rear peep will not make any appreciable difference at the target. The rear peephole, although relatively small, appears extremely large to the shooter because of its close position to the eye. Therefore, any error in centering the sight large enough to cause great inaccuracy is instantly detected and corrected unconsciously by the eye because of this magnification in appearance.

Some years ago I made a practical test under hunting conditions to find how much this "off-center" influence has in throwing bullets off line. I used a Springfield sporter mounted with a receiver peep, whose disk was a ⅛-inch hunting-style aperture. At 75 yards, shooting in the prone position with a padded rest, I fired four groups of three shots each, holding each group with the front sight held as far off-center of the peephole as I could and still clearly see the sight. I held Group 1 to the top of the circle, Group 2 at the bottom, and groups 3 and 4 to the right and left of the peep ring. Those holdings should show the maximum amount of error to expect.

The results were gratifying. I made a more-or-less square group with a maximum spread of 12 inches, measuring between the widest shots. This indicates that as long as the front sight could be seen in the peep ring, the bullet would strike not more than six inches from the point of aim at 75 yards. Few hunters who roam the deer woods each fall can hold any better than this in the normal offhand hunting position. And then, for most all deer hunting, we can shorten this 75 yards by half, giving the effect of not more than 3-inch inaccuracy in any direction. Even when deliberately keeping the sights as far out of alignment as possible, the results remained in the effective "killing circle" at whitetail ranges. This is convincing testimony to the accuracy of the rear-aperture sight.

I don't want to give the impression that only peep sights are effective on deer. Many more deer are killed each year by hunters using open sights than are taken with peep-sighted rifles. But the fact remains that peep sights of the right kind will materially aid novice hunters and even the veteran whose vision might be failing. To a few deer hunters, sights are not at all important. They can kill their buck almost without seeing sights. Years of constant practice and use of the same rifle have made them so familiar with the feel of the stock against their cheek that they can shoot well enough to kill deer without paying much attention to the sights.

Satisfied Peep-Sight Users

A white-haired old hunter came into the shop one year with a .351 caliber autoloading Winchester that was equipped with factory sights. He confided that his shooting had been falling off lately, and he had missed a deer or two because he couldn't make out where the sights were anymore. His problem was poor vision, and I recommended a good riflescope. My idea didn't seem in accord with his ideas, though. He wanted me to mount a straight shotgun rib on the barrel in place of the regular sights. He was certain the rib would be all he needed to kill a buck, so I did as he wished, and mounted a rib on his rifle.

The next spring he was back again, looking for suggestions on different sighting equipment — but he didn't want "one of those newfangled telescopes." The only alternative for the old-timer was a set of peep sights, so I mounted a quarter-inch ivory bead on the front and a tang peep rear equipped with a hunting disk of ½-inch outside diameter with ⅛-aperture. After we had sighted up his rifle properly, the old-timer used it for 'chuck hunting that summer and then proceeded to kill his buck with it that fall. He has used the outfit "as is" ever since. Needless to say, the combination suited him well. Regretfully, I must add, he has since passed on to the Happy Hunting Grounds, where sights are no problem.

About five years ago I fitted up a friend with a set of peep sights, but only because I had been hammering at him for a couple of seasons to give them a tryout, knowing they would improve his shooting. We were members of the same hunting club, and I had seen his shooting effectiveness on deer. He missed many easy shots. His eyes were normal enough, but he never seemed to take time enough to line up his sights properly. The instant the rifle touched his shoulder he would start throwing lead, most of it high over the buck. He was using factory sights, a plain bead front sight, and a semi-buckhorn rear. I was convinced after hunting with him long enough that his trouble was sights. He was a fair enough shot to kill deer with little trouble.

After plenty of persuasion, he allowed me to mount a good rear peep on his rifle and a good-sized red bead front sight. He used this setup throughout the summer with good results. In fact, he almost doubled his average on woodchucks. But just a few days before the deer season opener, he developed a bad case of cold feet. He rushed to the shop with his rifle and asked me to put on an open rear sight similar to the original factory job, simply because he was afraid to take the peep sights into the deer woods. It so happened I couldn't supply him from my stock on hand, so I wired at once for the sight. It arrived too late to catch the first day of deer season, but I called him that night after his first day's hunting to give him the news. You can imagine my surprise when he told me that he'd just that day killed a dandy buck with his outfit and he wouldn't change sights again for anything. He used those same sights ever since, and to date has a pretty good record of bucks killed.

Three Types of Peeps

Of the aperture sights suitable for hunting, three head the list: the tang sight, the receiver sight and the cocking-piece sight. The cocking-piece sight is little known and not in general use. Lyman makes one for various bolt-action rifles including the Krag, Springfield, Newton and Mauser. It is mounted on the end of the cocking piece or bolt, placing the sight relatively close to the eye, which is its only advantage. This type is difficult to mount properly, it has no adjustment for windage, and its weight often slows down lock speed, causing misfires. To remedy this latter condition, a heavier mainspring must be installed. Altogether, the cocking-piece sights have little merit, so we can eliminate them from this discussion.

The tang peep has two distinct advantages: Its position is close to the eye, making for quick sighting, and it is easily mounted on hunting rifles. Almost all lever, slide and autoloading rifles of American make are drilled and tapped to take some type of tang peep sight. These holes are filled with dummy screws by the factory. In most cases, all that's necessary to mount them is to remove the dummy screws and screw the sight base into position using screws furnished with the sight. In the Winchester lever-actions, you'll find two screws in the "tang" — the metal strip in the rear of the action atop the grip. The rear screw of these two is an action screw that fastens the action to the stock. The front screw is a dummy. Furnished with tang sights for these rifles is one long action screw and the regular forward-sight base screw. It's simple to remove the action screw and mount the sight in place. Savage lever-actions have two dummy screws in the top tang just behind the hammer indicator. The Remington slide-action has two of these dummies in the rear of the action placed side by side. In the Remington autoloader, the single dummy screw is in the middle of the upper tang just behind the receiver wall. Lyman and Marble's make tang sights to fit all these rifles. The Lyman line of tang sights is made in two styles. The No. 1 has a built-in turn-down peep, making two sizes of aperture readily available. The No. 2 series is used with disks of any size that suit the hunter's fancy. The No. 1 style cannot be used with a disk, because it is not drilled and tapped for it. Therefore, for best all-round purposes, the No. 2 style is probably the better of the two, as various disk sizes and apertures make the sight more adaptable to shooting conditions.

Of the three types of rear aperture sight, I prefer the receiver sight, which is rigidly mounted on the rifle receiver and features good windage and elevation adjustments. During the 1940s, design and manufacturing have devoted more attention to this type of sight than to any other metallic sight. And with good reason. Receiver sights, properly mounted, become almost a part of the rifle. They are seldom knocked out of adjustment by a hard blow and they're easily sighted-in at any hunting ranges. They're the best type of aperture rear sight adapted to bolt-action arms, and are equally adapted to lever, slide and autoloading actions. In all respects except one, they're superior to the tang type of sight. That one point is that they cannot be mounted quite as close to the eye as the tang sight. This is but a minor detail and is far outweighed by the receiver sight's ruggedness for hunting.

All types of receiver sights are, of course, mounted on the receiver, usually necessitating the drilling and tapping of two holes, sometimes three. Many rifles come from the manufacturer already drilled and tapped for receiver sights exactly the same as for tang peeps. Among these are the Winchester models 54 and 70, the Savage models 40 and 45 and the Remington Model 30 Express. On the whole, though, many rifles can be fitted with tang sights instead of receiver sights by simply attaching the sights to holes already placed there by the manufacturer. Winchester, Marlin and Savage lever-actions must all be drilled and tapped for receiver sights, either by the shooter or by a gunsmith. The chapter on gunsmithing will give details on this job, because in most cases it's within the capabilities of the hunter himself.

Windage and Elevation Adjustments

In any type of rear aperture sight, it's important to have adjustments for elevation and windage that can be securely locked after the rifle is sighted in at the proper range. Without locking features, your rifle is constantly subject to subtle sight changes in the hands of well-meaning friends or hunting partners. Many of these individuals simply must fiddle around with sight adjustment screws every time they pick up a strange rifle, and if you happen to be the victim, your next shot at a buck might be three feet away from your holding, all through no fault of your own. This then, is one of the strong points in favor of the receiver sight over the tang sight. Almost every model has some means of securely locking windage and elevation adjustments so they can't be moved with prying fingers. Neither will a hard knock move them.

This feature of easy adjustments for elevation and windage is also more or less true of receiver sights. Few tang sights have any adjustment for windage and if so, they can't be locked in position. Elevation with the tang sight is obtained by turning a knurled sleeve, which is threaded to the stem, raising it or lowering it as desired, but such adjustments are coarse. Add to this the lack of windage adjustment in these tang sights, and we can appreciate that these sights are not easy to adjust. The receiver sight incorporates a movable slide for elevation, with definite graduations marked and with a graduated windage scale. This makes sighting-in simple, and adjusting sights for different loads and ranges equally simple.

For all deer-hunting conditions, though, rifles should be adjusted with one type of ammunition and one definite range. The sights should then be locked in that position and severely left alone. Why then the need for accurate adjustments? In the first place, the initial sighting-in is simplified and the sights can be adjusted accurately. There is no need to fiddle with paper shims and hammering the front sight this way and that before a satisfactory adjustment is reached — at a colossal waste of ammunition. Shooters are often tempted, in desperation, to let it go as "good enough," even though the sights might not be quite as they should be. With good adjustments, there is no excuse for this practice. Secondly, deer hunters like to change front sights occasionally, or change the bullet weight in the cartridge they're using. With sights easily adjustable, this little task is a pleasure, but with the tang type of peep having no windage adjustments or a coarse, nonlocking elevation adjustment, it's too much trouble for most hunters.

Choosing a Receiver Sight

In making your decision on a receiver sight, you can choose from Lyman, Pacific, Redfield and others. Of all these various makes, Redfield has some outstanding features. Most Redfield sights are designed so little wood, if any, must be cut out of the stock to inlet the base, and several of their designs enable the shooter to attach the sight without drilling and tapping additional holes. Their windage adjustment is of the opposing screw type, permitting accurate and easy adjustments and, perhaps best of all, complete adjustments for elevation and windage can be made with a coin or washer. There is no need to carry a screwdriver.

Choosing the best type of receiver sight usually means going through all the manufacturers' catalogs, and selecting from each the model and design of sight that best applies to your make of rifle. Look for rugged design, which will add to your rifle's appearance. Make sure it has good windage and elevation adjustments, and make certain these adjustments can be positively locked after all sight adjustments are made.

One additional point regarding the aperture rear sight: If you find the use of the peep disk, even with a large aperture, seems to slow down your sighting, remove the disk and use the stem hole only for sighting. This might seem to be a wide peep hole at first glance, but accurate shooting, and very fast shooting, can be done with the peephole only, without disk. The peep outline will seem fuzzy and indistinct, and the hole so large that the entire front sight, sight base and forward end of the barrel can be seen through the peep, but if you look through this ring, not at it, and hold your front sight on the target, you'll hit your game.

It seems hardly necessary to point out that when peep rear sights are used, you must remove the middle open, or barrel, sight. Every now and then we run across a rifle mounted with a good peep sight but still having the rigid open sight in place — something like trying to walk with an extra leg. The peep rear and front sight are the only two points needed for accurate alignment. The middle sight is just in the way, slowing down sighting speed and obscuring half of the target. There is a good point in using a folding middle sight in place of the regular open sight, but this should be kept folded down out of the way when the peep is used. If any need arises to check the alignment of the peep sight, the folding sight can be snapped up and the check made by glancing through all three to make certain they line up. A folding sight is especially useful when a tang peep is used, because these tangs are subject to slight changes caused by falls or hard knocks. The folding sight affords an instant checkup and a means of realigning the peep sight, if it should be out of adjustment, without the necessity of shooting the rifle in on the range.

Rifle Sights on Shotguns

Recent developments in the rifled shotgun slug, plus legislation prohibiting rifles in certain states and some areas in other states, have brought renewed interest in shotguns for deer hunting. Rifled-slug loads are remarkably accurate in all gauge shotguns for deer hunting at normal ranges, meaning from 50 to 75 yards. The rifled-slug load will group closely enough to the point of aim to make vital hits certain at these ranges. All that remains is to equip the shotgun with suitable sights to bring out this accuracy and make close holding a possibility. Good sights, even the simplest type, will make a shotgun effective for most deer-hunting conditions, and some hunters use them today rather than going to the expense of a new rifle just for deer hunting. Many hunters can only spend a few days in the deer woods each year, and some believe this hardly warrants the purchase of a high-powered rifle, if the shotgun can do the job.

Of course, any shotgun can be used as is, with the regular front bead and no rear sight, but we can't bring out the slug's accuracy with such crude sights. Each year many deer are killed with such equipment, but much better results can be had with good sights. Any gunsmith can adapt rifle sights to most shotguns, using screws for attaching them. This makes it possible to remove the sights after deer season and go back to small game.

On double-guns, I mount a standard front sight of low height just behind the regular factory sight, screwing the sight base to the rib with small fillister head screws. I first sweat the sight base to a thin steel block, and then drill this block with a bit large enough to just permit passage of the 6-48 screws. Then I spot and drill the rib with a No. 31 drill and tapped with a 6-48 tap. After screwing the sight and its base into position, I select a low folding leaf sight for the rear with a dovetail filed in a quarter-inch piece of steel. The steel is of a width that suits the rib. I then fit the sight base into place. Next, I drill and screw the steel block into position that will place it about 14 inches from the shooter's eye. The gun can then be tried on the range, and the rear sight can be adjusted by moving it sideways in the dovetail. Elevation on the first trial will probably be too high, so the base should be filed off and tried again on the range, repeating this until the sight is aligned.

This setup permits easy removal of the sights at any time, and the holes can be filled with dummy screws. It requires only five minutes to mount them again when the shooter is ready to use slugs. Many variations in sights can be selected for shotgun use. Even receiver sights and tang peeps can be adapted to repeating shotguns with good results, but if a rear sight is fitted, either open or peep, a new front sight must also be mounted. That's because the regular front sight will be much too low to be used with the new rear sight.

CHAPTER 18

Sighting In for Deer Hunting

Every hunter has heard the term "point-blank range." Some hunters know what it means, but most don't. The idea most often circulated among deer hunters is that point-blank range is the greatest range at which a rifle will "shoot flat." As a matter of fact, no rifle shoots flat, but many have flatter trajectories than others. This is particularly true of modern high-velocity cartridges whose trajectories over a 200-yard range are so low that the bullets seem not to drop.

What is Point-Blank Range?

Generally speaking, a rifle's point-blank range is the exact range at which the bullet strikes the line of sight on the target. For example, if we're shooting a .30-06 Springfield, it's customary when deer hunting to adjust the sights so the bullet strikes at the point of aim at 100 yards. Then, at 50 or 60 yards the point of impact will be an inch or less above the line of sight. At 200 yards, the bullet will strike about five inches below the point of aim, using a 180-grain bullet. The point-blank range then, with this sight setting, is actually 100 yards, although it could be changed to 50 yards, 200 yards or even 300 yards, simply by changing the rear sight's elevation.

Under most hunting conditions, though, the term "point-blank range" means that particular sight setting for a rifle which will give the least error in impact over the greatest range without changing the hold on the target or changing the sight setting. With the .30-06 using the 180-grain bullet, this setting would be about 200 yards, because there will not be more than four inches variation from the point of aim at any range up to 250 yards. In other words, with the rifle sighted at 200 yards, the rise in bullet flight at 100 yards will be about two to three inches above the point of aim. At 250 yards, the bullet will still only drop four inches below the point of aim. So with a .30-06 rifle sighted at 200-yard point-blank range, hunters can hold on a buck's shoulder at any range from 25 yards up to 250 yards with a reasonable expectation of making a vital hit, even though making the same hold at any range.

For rifles with a higher trajectory than the .30-06, a shorter "point-blank range" must be used. Rifles in the .30-30 class should be sighted at 100 to 150 yards for best results over their effective range. If we sighted in a .30-30 at 200 yards the rise in bullet flight at 50 yards would be three inches and at 100 yards 4½ inches. On neck shots at deer, this would be enough variation to cause a high miss, so it's best to shorten the point-blank range for this caliber.

To obtain maximum efficiency with rifles in this class, the 150-yard range is most effective. Sighted-in at this range, the bullet rises no more than two inches at any range up to the point-blank distance, which is close enough for all practical hunting purposes.

Charts showing the trajectory curves of popular calibers will give shooters enough information to make their own choice in deciding the point-blank range of their rifles and cartridges. Such charts are readily available from most ammunition manufacturers.

Hunters who are at all interested in bettering their shooting performance have at some time pored over ballistics tables issued by ammunition makers. The information has little value to many hunters because they don't know how to apply it to their pet rifle. For instance, let's suppose we have a rifle using the .300 Savage caliber and we decide to use the 180-grain bullet for all purposes. Glancing over the trajectory table, we extract this information: mid-range height at 100 yards, .84 or about ¾ inch; at 200 yards, midrange height is 3.76, or about 3¾ inches; at 300 yards the height is 9.64 or about 9½ inches. This means that if we sight in our rifle to hit center at 300 yards, our bullet will strike almost 10 inches above the line of sight at 150 yards. This is entirely too high for hunting, unless most of the shooting is at ranges exceeding 200 yards.

With the rifle sighted in at 200 yards, the bullet strikes about four inches above the point of aim at 100 yards. This is much better, but for pinpoint work on small targets it will still be a bit high. We go on, then, to the figures on the 100-yard trajectory. At 50 yards, the height above the sight line is less than an inch. So for deer hunting, where ranges are almost always less than 100 yards, we sight the .300 Savage in at this range, knowing that at ranges up to 150 yards, our bullet will travel within two inches of our line of sight, disregarding any change in range.

What these trajectory tables don't tell the shooter is how much the bullet will drop beyond the 100-yard range, provided our rifle is sighted-in for that distance, or for any other range. They tell us how high our bullet will go above the sight line at 100, 200 or 300 yards, but not how far the bullet will drop below the sight line if we sight in our rifle at ranges less than 300 yards. This is another story, and it's difficult to make an explanation without showing trajectory curves to illustrate the point.

Perhaps I place too much emphasis on choosing the best point-blank range for the deer hunting rifle. It's true it won't have much bearing on a deer hunter's sighting, because most shooting is done at 40 to 60 yards. And if the country to be hunted is thick and heavily timbered, it's best to forget about long-range sighting and set the sights to shoot where the rifle is held at 50 yards. Then, if the occasion arises when a neck shot is realistic, the hunter will be in a better position to do so. However, when deer hunters want to use their rifles for varmint shooting to keep in practice, and much of this shooting is at 100 to 300 yards, it's important to know something about sight settings.

Sighting in the Deer Rifle

Strange as it might seem, most deer hunters know little about how to sight in their own rifles. This doesn't apply to all deer hunters, but it's true of a large portion of them. Many worry that their rifles are hopelessly out of sight adjustment, but year after year they make the most unaccountable misses on easy targets. Too many deer hunters use their rifles only during the deer season. They never take them afield or onto the range until they're ready to go hunting, but this is usually a bit too late.

Since about 1935, I've had occasion to do this little job for hundreds of hunters with every conceivable type and caliber of rifle; not to mention a multitude of sights, from the coarsest of military sights to the modern rifle-scope. In all but a few instances, the hunter could have done the job just as well as I had, perhaps better. Why? He would have the sights adjusted to his particular method of holding and his own peculiarities of vision.

It seems decidedly elementary to go into details about how sights should be moved to achieve desired results on the target, but few deer hunters are technical riflemen. It's second nature with experienced riflemen to check their sight alignment whenever they're ready to do any shooting, and to make necessary corrections. Deer hunters, on the whole, don't take the time to acquire the information, and even if they do, most hesitate to take a chance on putting it into effect.

I hunted for a couple of seasons with a bunch of old-time deer hunters, all of them wise in deer lore and skillful enough with rifles to bring home the bacon. During my third year with them, one of these men had some tough luck the first few days of the season. He missed three bucks cleanly, all at easy killing distance. After his third miss I had the temerity to suggest that his sights might be out of line, but he assured me they hadn't been touched for 10 years and he had always done good work with them before. Nevertheless, I persisted until he let me try out his pet — an old Winchester .38-55 with a long octagon barrel, fitted with plain bead front sight and a wide-V rear notch.

As I picked up the rifle and glanced over the barrel, it seemed that the rear sight was perched way out to the left, but I thought I'd shoot it before commenting. My only available target was a fair-sized white rock about 60 yards from the camp, so I fired one shot, holding for the center. This first shot passed left of the rock, missing my hold by at least a foot. I tapped the sight a bit to the right with a small hammer and tried again. This time I hit the rock, but still to the left. After more wallops with the hammer and some more shooting, I finally got the sight aligned. The rifle is still doing service in the deer woods. I'll never forget the look of amazement on the owner's face when I lined up the sights so easily just by tapping the rear sight with a hammer. He had this idea that adjusting sights was some dark mystery performed in the hallowed recesses of the gun factories, and should never be attempted by laymen. His rifle had likely been dropped or suffered a hard blow in transportation, just hard enough to move the rear sight in its dovetail slot.

Sighting in a rifle is simple. First, we must form a mental picture of the sight line and line of fire. Just visualize two imaginary lines, one running through the rear sight and over the center of the front sight to form the sight line; and another line running through the center of the rifle bore, following the exact path of the bullet's flight. Viewed from above and behind the rifle, the sight line should be superimposed on the line of fire, or exactly parallel to it. If we change the relative position of either line, the rifle will shoot to the right or left.

For sake of illustration, let's take a lever-action rifle fitted with regular open sights: a metal bead front and a notched rear sight. Assume also that the rifle is correctly sighted, with the sight line directly over the bore. To see what happens when we reposition the rear sight, take a heavy needle and scribe a tiny mark on the barrel and a corresponding mark on the rear sight base. Then take a small hammer and a copper drift punch and tap the rear sight to the left about ½-inch.

What has this adjustment done to our sight line? The rear of the line, starting at the rear notch, has been pushed to the left so the line of sight passing over the front sight now veers right of the line of fire, just below it. We fire the rifle at a target, being careful to hold just below the center of the bull's-eye. We find the shot has gone some distance left of the bull's-eye, indicating the rifle now looks to the left even though our line of sight was held directly for the center of the bull's-eye. Our problem is to bring the shot back into the bull's center, meaning the shot must be moved to the right. We must tap the rear sight to the right — in the same direction we want the shot to move — and keep firing at the target until the sight is moved the proper distance, bringing the point of impact into the target's center.

If our rear sight were moved to the right out of alignment, our shots would pass right of the target and we would have to move our rear sight left to bring our point of impact toward the left and into the bull's center. The only point to remember is that the rear sight must be moved in the same direction as we wish to move the point of impact.

We find a similar condition in changing sight adjustments for elevation or "range." If the rifle is shooting high, we must lower the rear sight. If it is shooting low, we must raise the rear sight. The same rule of directional movement is the same: The rear sight must be moved in the same direction we want the shot to go. Viewing this process from the side, we find a bit of difference in the line of sight and the line of fire. Our sight line is still a straight line, passing through the sights and to the target, but our line of fire is now curved, caused by the bullet's trajectory. These two lines are not parallel, nor can they ever be, because we must elevate the bore just enough so the bullet carries up and out to the point where the line of sight strikes the target's center at the desired range. In other words, even though our sight line might be level and parallel with the ground, the line of the bore will be lower at the rear than at the muzzle, giving the bore an upward tilt just enough to compensate for bullet drop. When the two lines are fixed in their proper relation to each other, so the bullet strikes exactly at the same point as the line of sight at the proper range, we will have "point-blank sighting."

To get a clearer picture of what happens when the sights are raised or lowered, we must visualize the raising of the rear sight as having the effect of dropping the bore's rear, further tilting the line of fire above the target and sending the shot high. Lowering the rear sight brings the rear ends of our two imaginary lines closer together, lifting the bore's rear, and tilting its angle of fire downward for a lower impact point.

That's all there is to adjusting sights, provided the rear sight can be adjusted. However, under some conditions — such as changing to a light-bullet, high-speed load — we will find our rifle still shoots high, even with the rear sight dropped to its lowest position. We must then change the front, or muzzle end of the bore line. Our problem is still to lower the bore end below the line of sight, dropping the bore angle to give us a lower shot. How do we change the front sight? Some hunters' first thought is to file off the front sight, but this makes a rifle shoot still higher. The answer is to mount a higher front sight, spreading the line of sight and the line of fire at the forward end of the rifle. The effect of this higher front sight is to throw the front or muzzle end of the rifle lower, dropping the angle of fire.

On rifles with open rear sights mounted in dovetail barrel slots, sight adjustments are not so easy as with rifles fitted with an aperture rear sight having definite graduations for windage and elevation. Under these conditions, we must first scratch a scribe line on the sight base and barrel and make the necessary adjustment for windage by tapping the sight in its slot left or right as required. The scribe line gives us a definite starting point. We can check it as we go along, using the "cut and try" method, tapping the sight a little, shooting at the target, checking the results and repeating the process until the windage is aligned.

With most open sights, elevation adjustments are made with a step — a notched piece of metal under the base of the rear sight notch. Sliding this step farther under the rear notch base raises the sight to the desired elevation. This method, however, is crude and often fails to give the exact elevation requirements. As we raise the step notch by notch, we'll finally reach the point where our last adjustment is too low and the next step too high. This can be remedied by filing off the step's bottom, trying it from time to time until reaching the correct elevation.

Sighting in is simplified with the receiver-aperture sight. This sight has a graduated windage scale, with each graduation moving the point of impact a definite amount. There is no need to use a hammer on this sight, because windage movement is usually obtained by screws. The same goes for elevation. After the rifle is properly sighted, the point-blank or "zero" screw can be tightened and the elevation slide locked into position.

The principles of sighting are simple and, when grasped by the shooter, always firmly in mind. Any problems involving different types of sights can be solved by applying the principles just outlined. Movements to obtain requisite adjustments are the same, regardless of the sights in question.

The Hunting Scope

This brings us to the hunting telescopic sight, the most accurate sighting instrument yet devised for deer rifles. Dozens of different riflescopes are made in this country, all with a definite place in the shooting picture. But only a small proportion of these are suited to white-tailed deer hunting.[1] For our deer-hunting purposes, a riflescope must meet rigid requirements, else it will be more of a hindrance than a help. The question most frequently asked by deer hunters is, "Do I need a scope for deer hunting?" Secondly, they ask, "What will a scope do for me that can't be done with regular iron sights?"

To answer the first question honestly, I must say that in most cases a riflescope is not a necessity, but it can be a big help. Only in those cases where a shooter's vision is extremely impaired is the scope a dire need. In these cases

[1]Today, of course, the white-tailed deer is a driving force in the design and manufacture of riflescopes, inspiring entire scope lines specifically targeting deer hunters. In addition, besides offering well-stocked lines for rifle-hunters, most companies now offer scopes designed specifically for deer hunters using shotguns, handguns and muzzleloaders.

it sometimes means the answer to whether someone shall or shall not hunt deer again.

The second question requires much explanation. Briefly, here is what a scope will do for your deer hunting. It eliminates all but a single sight, and that sight is contained in the scope itself. There is no worry as to whether two sights must be properly aligned on the target. With riflescopes, the target and sight are in exactly the same focus. Next, scopes allow good shooting under light conditions so poor that neither the target or iron sights can be seen. A scope also brings the target closer to the shooter with its magnification, allowing much more accurate shot placement. In heavy cover, when shots are often taken through timber and brush, a scope uncannily picks out obstructions that would stop or deflect the bullet, giving hunters a better opportunity to pick openings for the shot. Finally, hunters who use a good scope always know exactly what they're shooting at. Antlers can be readily seen on a buck, and sometimes the points can be counted before making the shot. Most important of all, no hunter equipped with a scope should ever kill or injure a fellow hunter by mistaking him for a deer.[2]

Understand, though, that not all riflescopes provide these benefits. Low-priced instruments with poor optical qualities and narrow fields of view are worse than nothing at all, so deer hunters who contemplate buying a scope must know what to look for. About 1935, I had an amusing experience that shows the need of selecting the right scope for hunting whitetails.

In early fall that year, an elderly gentleman I knew approached me over the gun counter to ask about a scope sight for his deer rifle. He confided that the old eyes were going bad on him, and the boys were starting to rib him about misses he had made the preceding year or two.

At the time there were few American-made scopes I could recommend for deer hunting. I happened to then be using a good quality imported scope, so I suggested he buy one of these and I would mount it on his rifle. The imported scope idea didn't hit him just right, so he passed it up for the time being. Not long after this he dropped in again waving a Lyman leaflet that extolled the virtues of a certain 5A telescope. It was his understanding that the 5A was the best scope Lyman made at the time, and it would be good enough for him. I tried to explain to him that this was a target scope and not designed for hunting, but he couldn't be swayed.

Following his wishes, I ordered the scope and mounted it on his rifle. Then, with a heavy feeling of remorse, I delivered it to his hands. I heard no more from him until after deer season was well past. One day he dropped in again. My first question was, "How did the scope work out?"

"Oh ——-!" He waved his hand. "That d——d thing. I knocked it off with a rock." He said two bucks had come to his stand during the first two days of the season. He shouldered his rifle and, try as he would, he couldn't find them in the field of view, so he never fired a shot at either buck. At an extreme moment, some time after the second buck walked off, he found a good-sized rock and calmly proceeded to knock the scope off his rifle. He finally killed his buck, using the front sight alone, because I had removed the rear sight when mounting the scope.

This 5A scope, while an excellent model for target shooting, had not a single feature to adapt it to deer hunting. Its 5-power magnification was too

[2]Although most shooting accidents during deer seasons in recent years are self-inflicted or involve "covering" another hunter while swinging on moving deer, some hunters continue to be shot after being mistaken for deer. While the popularity of riflescopes the past 30 years has helped reduce mistaken-for-deer accidents, most hunter safety experts believe "hunter" or "blaze" orange laws and mandatory hunter education training play larger roles.

high for the deer woods, and its field of view — about 18 feet at 100 yards — much too narrow. Its reticle was a fine cross-hair, and its light-gathering powers left plenty to be desired. It also came with fragile mounts having delicate adjustments, and was so mounted that the scope tube slid forward from the recoil during each shot, making it necessary to pull the scope back into shooting position after each shot. In other words, everything about it was wrong from a deer hunter's point of view.

Here are the points we must demand in a deer hunting riflescope:

It must have good light-gathering power or illumination, so that deer can be seen even under the worst sighting conditions encountered in heavy coniferous timber, and also at early morning or late afternoon.

Its field of view must be wide enough so running deer can be easily picked up by the hunter. This field of view is the amount of landscape that can be seen through the scope in normal shooting position at 100 yards. For example, Noske lists the field of view of one of its scopes as 38 feet, meaning if we sight through this scope at 100 yards, we'll see 19 feet to the target's right and left, as well as above and below it. This makes for quick sighting even at moving targets.

Another important feature in a deer hunting scope is a low power, for only with low power can we get good brilliance and wide field, and still keep the weight and length of the scope down to proper limits. It's only with a low-power glass that we can hold the rifle steady enough for offhand shooting, because the wobble of the shooter's hands is magnified in direct proportion to the scope's power. Even though the hunter is actually holding the rifle just as steady with a 10-power glass as with a 2½- or 3-power instrument, the psychological effect is so damaging that poor shooting results. A 3-power glass is the highest magnification that should be used in a hunting scope for whitetails, and less than this is better.

Still another necessity in the scope is long eye relief — the distance the shooter's eye must be held from the eyepiece to see the fullest field of view. In high-powered rifles, this eye relief should be long enough to prevent the scope from striking the hunter's skull during recoil. Add to this the danger of fogging the lens with breath during cold weather if the lens is too close to the hunter's face. A hunting scope should also have a "noncritical" eye relief. That is, shooters must be able to take a quick, clear sight even though their shooting eye is not in line with the exact center of the scope's tube. There should be a latitude in hunting scopes of about a quarter-inch, giving hunters accurate sighting anywhere within this radius. Then, when they hurriedly shoulder a rifle, they will be better able to see the target and scope sight immediately, without needing to reposition their head to see the scope's full field of view. To incorporate this feature, manufacturers list the scope's specifications on the exit pupil's size. The exit pupil controls, to a degree, the amount of light admitted through the scope as well as its noncritical eye-relief feature.

The choice of the sighting device within the scope, usually called "reticle," is also important. This should be heavy enough and coarse enough to stand out against any background and in dim light. Popular and efficient reticle styles include the sharp picket post and flat-top picket post, and either can be obtained with a single lateral cross-hair. Of the two styles, the flat-top picket gives the best definition for deer hunting because the cleanly cut-off top gives definite holding for elevation under all conditions. The lateral cross-hair, which is a single fine wire extending horizontally across the scope's field, crossing just below the top of the post, is a good check to prevent canting the rifle. Normally, though, it isn't necessary because it's easy to hold the wide post fairly upright, at least accurately enough for hunting purposes. Many other varieties of reticles are available in American and foreign-made scopes, but either of these perform properly for deer hunting. Cross-hair reticles, pin heads, narrow-taper posts and other target styles of reticle are not designed for whitetail hunting, so they should never be considered for this purpose.[3]

With scopes, windage and elevation adjustments must receive considerable emphasis. These should be internal, or contained within the scope tube, permitting a rigid, nonadjustable mount to be used. Adjustments in the mount itself are seldom satisfactory for hunting, because they will not hold their zero for long. The adjustments on hunting scopes need not be as fine as with target scopes, but they should be graduated to within an inch at 100 yards.[4] For the same reasons as outlined for receiver peep sights, they must be rigidly locked in place once sighted in at the required range.

Lastly, a hunting scope should be short, lightweight and rugged in construction. It should be fixed-focus and so streamlined that there will be few projections from its contours to catch in brush or clothing. The scope with its mount should add no more than 1 pound to the rifle's weight, particularly if the rifle is to be carried all day in rugged country.

A great wave of postwar development has made available to deer hunters a wide choice of suitable optical devices for hunting. Before World War II, we had a limited field of American-made scopes of high quality. The Lyman Alaskan and the Noske were the only two makes that could compare favorably with the best imported glasses. The Weaver line included the 330 and 29S, both excellent value in their price field, but lacking wide field and top light-gathering power.

As I write this in 1948, I know of at least 10 excellent makes of low-power scopes suited to whitetail hunting, and many more are in the development stage. All possess the qualifications required of a big-game scope to a greater or lesser degree, dependent on the price involved. Some of these scopes have features that set them apart, but in general, all will prove highly satisfactory to deer hunters.

To clarify some details involved in selecting a hunting scope, I made the following chart, listing each scope in order of price range, as this was written. I also listed some salient points of excellence to aid the choice.

[3]Variations of the cross-hair are by far the most popular reticle now available. In recent years, the duplex cross-hair — wide wires on the perimeter and tapering to a fine wire at the cross-hair — is the dominant reticle. Koller's favorites, the post and cross-hair models, are no longer available from most manufacturers, having never caught on with deer hunters.

[4]Most windage and elevation adjustments on modern riflescopes are ⅓ or ¼ inch per click at 100 yards.

Make of Scope	Power (Actual)	Field of View Feet at 100 yards	Exit Pupil Diameter Inches	Eye Relief
Lyman Alaskan	2.16	38	.36	4¾ inches
Noske	2.35	32	.30	4½ inches
Norman Ford Texan	2.0	42	.35	4¼ inches
Leupold	2.25	35	.30	3¾ inches
Bear Cub	2.25	35	.32	4 inches
Maxwell Smith G88	2.25	36	.29	4¼ inches
Maxwell Smith Zicon	2.50	34	.26	3½ inches

Weaver K 2.5	2.1	39	.38	5 inches
Maxwell Smith Vectra	2.6	32	.26	3¼ inches
Weaver J 2.5	2.1	33	.28	4¼ inches

All of these scopes have internal adjustments for windage and elevation, with the exception of the Bear Cub. This model has adjustments for elevation only and must have a mounting that permits windage adjustment.

There is no great variation in weights or lengths for these scopes. The Alaskan is the heaviest at 11 ounces, the Bear Cub the lightest at 5½ ounces. The longest model is the Bear Cub, measuring about 11¾ inches; the shortest is the Noske at 9⅝ inches. An interesting departure from convention can be noted in the Leupold. This model has no projecting knobs for sight adjustment. The entire tube is streamlined, with rotating sleeves for windage and elevation changes, making a smooth-looking job.

Hunters must bear in mind the important points in the hunting scope: wide field, good light-gathering power (large diameter exit pupil), and sufficient eye relief. Higher-priced models generally give most of the best. It's safe to say if deer hunters want the best in a hunting scope they will choose the Lyman Alaskan. If they want the most for their money, dollar for dollar, the Weaver J2.5 is without equal in this field.

Mounts for Deer-Rifle Scopes

Mounts for riflescopes have enjoyed greater development than scopes since the war. A truism is that any scope is worthless unless the mounting holds it firmly and rigidly, not only shot to shot but over long time periods. But we now have so many mount designs that deer hunters will be more confused than ever in making a good choice.

With few exceptions, there is no need to select a mount that gives windage or elevation. With the exception of the Bear Cub, no American-made glass for deer hunting needs such adjustment. This makes for rigidity and simplicity in design, for the mount can be made to become almost part of the rifle. With such a simple design in mind, hunters can decide whether they want a fixed, semi-fixed or quick-detachable model.

Among the fixed types are the Redfield Senior mount and the Weaver line of side and top mounts — the Type N, Type Q and Type U. The Redfield mount is desirable for use with a heavy scope on a rifle with heavy recoil. Many deer hunters, however, will not like the fixed mount because it is not removable and replaceable without resighting. Conditions sometimes make it necessary to remove the scope and go with iron sights. This is where the detachable mount proves its worth.

An old and tried favorite in this category is the Griffin and Howe double-lever mount. I've had one of these on a .256 Newton for more than 15 years, and have many times removed and replaced the scope with no apparent change in sighting. This mount also leaves the top of the rifle "clean" for use with open or aperture sights. The Redfield Junior is a popular light mount that is semi-fixed, and can be removed easily and retains its zero when reinstalled on the rifle. However, with this type, part of the base remains on the receiver bridge and interferes with aperture sights.

One of the best new mounts, at a low price, that allows easy removal for use with the iron sight is the Echo. This is a side mount that slides on a half-dovetail base that's firmly attached to the receiver, much the same as the Noske and G.H. Mount. It goes back on the rifle precisely to its original zero, and removes by unscrewing two knurled nuts. This mount is somewhat less costly than the other two mentioned, and so far works fully as well.

The Williams easy-detachable mount has great appeal to whitetail hunters. In this mount, we have a fixed base on the rifle that screws fast to the scope's mounting rings with two large knurled screws. The scope can be removed rapidly by unscrewing the mounts off the bases with your fingers, and a neat aperture sight installs instantly in the rear base. This makes a quick conversion job for hunters who encounter unfavorable scope-hunting conditions.

Hunters might also consider the swing-out mounts by Pachmayr and Burton. In each of these, the entire mount is hinged to permit the scope to be swung left and out of the way for using iron sights. However, these mounts place the scope low on the receiver, so for instant change-over in sighting, an open rear sight must be used.

Stith's mounts appeal to hunters who want to install their own mount and scope. These mounts go directly on the Winchesters 54 and 70, or the Savage 99S, without drilling additional holes. Also this mount is desirable for use with the Bear Cub scope, because it has excellent windage adjustments.

In selecting any mount, hunters must first decide which features they need for their hunting conditions. The best mount is one with a simple design that allows strong construction and no moving parts, which prevents tinkering by hunting partners. It's desirable, however, for deer hunters to have some means of changing over to iron sights conveniently, then back to scope sights without needing to resight.

Besides the mounts listed here, many others are now on the market and new designs constantly appear. Each has merit, but must be carefully examined in relation to whitetail hunting conditions. Once again, hunters must call upon their experiences to make a wise choice, but factors mentioned here should influence that decision.

Sights: A Deer Hunter's Vital Link

Thus we have covered, for deer hunters at least, the field of gun sights. Again, I must emphasize that sights are the link between hunters and their deer, and only by proper sight selection can they hope to enjoy good hunting. That means — first, last and always — not only hits, but clean kills. Only by experiment can hunters work out the selection challenge themselves. No two individuals are the same in vision, coordination or ability to handle their firearms. In gun sights, more than in any other branch of shooting, "one man's meat is another's poison." Sights must be chosen to fit the individual and, when once the happy combination is reached, the hunter should stick to it until physical or mental changes signal new experimentation.

CHAPTER 19

Gun Work for the Deer Hunter

All shooters can be roughly divided into two classes: those who should never attempt any repair or remodeling work on their firearms other than routine cleaning and oiling; and those who possess enough mechanical skill, ability with their hands, and an abundance of patience to perform the simpler gunsmithing jobs that can be done at home.

Usually, it's safe advice to sweepingly advise all shooters to leave their guns alone and trust incidental repairs and changes to a competent gunsmith. Many fine rifles have been almost irreparably damaged in the hands of their owners. Eventually, damaged rifles must be sent to the factory or a gunsmith, who must not only make the original repair but correct mistakes made by the owner — often a costly procedure.

Can You Handle Simple Gunsmithing Jobs?

On the other hand, many repairs and alterations can easily be made at home. Often it is inconvenient, sometimes impossible, to find a good gunsmith nearby. It might be equally inconvenient to send a rifle to the factory for repairs. In addition, many alterations desired by gun owners will not be handled by the factory. And finally, the shooter might not be able to afford professional charges for all the work desired. Add to this the fact that many in the shooting clan have a hidden but overpowering desire to tinker with their firearms, particularly on long winter evenings when there's nothing to do in connection with their sport but look ahead until next season, so far away.

Only individual shooters can properly classify themselves. They alone must decide whether to leave their pet rifle alone or — if willing to learn how to perform the desired job and whether to purchase the necessary tools and materials — patiently carry the work through to completion. Most hunters have the "hurry" complex. If they start a job, they want to rush it through because they can't wait to see how it will look when it's finished. Just a few months ago, I completed a restocking job for a friend on a bolt-action rifle. I used French walnut of good figure and applied a nice oil finish. I didn't do any checkering on the stock, however, because he thought this work would put the job's price somewhat above the limit of his pocketbook. A few weeks later, he dropped in to ask whether I thought he could do the checkering himself, if he had the tools. I encouraged him to try the job, but warned he needed to practice quite a bit on his old stock or scrap pieces of wood with a rounded surface. I also cautioned him to proceed slowly and carefully, taking at least three weeks for the job, which I believed was a safe minimum.

The next morning he was back to return my tools, telling me he had completed the whole works, pistol grip and forearm, the night before. He admitted, though, that he had stayed up a bit later than his usual bedtime to finish it. I didn't have the heart to ask how the job looked, but about a week later I saw the mess myself. The stock was ruined, at least in appearance. He had made little attempt to properly space the lines. The angle of the cross-lines was all wrong, and none of the lines were deep enough to be called checkering. The wood's surface on the grip and forearm was covered with a series of hideous scratches. To effect a repair on this job would mean the complete removal of the scratches, using scraper and sandpaper. Then it would need a complete refinishing of the grip and forearm and a new checkering job. This work would easily cost twice the price of checkering alone.

I'm satisfied this shooter had enough ability to perform the work properly, but he was so obsessed with completing it in a hurry that he rushed it through to the end, ruining a beautiful piece of wood.

What follows are some gunsmithing jobs that can easily be done at home by hunters possessing a certain degree of mechanical skill and an abundance of patience: fitting of new sights, stock changes for better fit, rebluing of metal parts, altering trigger pulls, applying wood finishes, fitting of sling swivels and slings, remodeling of military rifle stocks, and rebedding of rifle barrels for better accuracy. These jobs can be done with a minimum expenditure for simple tools and materials from hardware dealers. In this chapter, I'll outline some jobs that can be performed with simple tools, even though special tools would be more efficient but more difficult to obtain, and more expensive. I cannot consider the use of these special tools as a time-saver, for it's assumed the hunter will have ample time to perform any and all operations.

Fitting New Rifle Sights

Perhaps the most commonly attempted alteration of the deer rifle is adding new sights. As we've seen, factory sights are seldom satisfactory for discriminating deer hunters. Some changes are almost always in order to better suit a rifle to the owner's vision and the country to be hunted. We've already discussed selecting the correct sighting equipment, so we will deal only with fitting and adapting these sights to a rifle.

First, the front sight. Almost all factory rifles are fitted with front sights driven into dovetail slots. A few are mounted with the blade-type carbine sight, held in place with a pin or screw. It's simple to remove the old front sight from a dovetail slot by driving it out from the left side of the barrel to the right, using a drift punch of copper, brass, fiber or hard wood. The barrel should be held in the jaws of a substantial vise, padded with leather, lead or soft wood to prevent marring. Never try to drive out the sight with a hammer directly. This will not only deform the sight base, but it's possible the sight stem will be struck and bent out of shape, making it worthless for future use.

The new front sight must be selected not only to fit the slot, but it must be the same height as the old sight. Otherwise, the elevation will be changed, necessitating a change in the rear sight. If an aperture receiver or tang sight is also to be fitted, this is not so important. That's because accurate elevation adjustments can be made in the rear sight. But some attempt should be made to have the new front sight be the same approximate height as the old one.

Drive the new front sight into place, using the copper drift, from the right side to the left. Dovetail slots are all tapered for a tight fit, so this must be remembered in removing and replacing sights. The front sight should be centered as accurately as possible, using the eye alone. Then the rifle must be sighted in, following the suggestions in the previous chapter.

Blade-front sights are somewhat simpler to replace, because the position is fixed. With the new blade pinned or screwed into place, no further sighting in is needed — provided, of course, a sight of the correct height is chosen.

Open rear sights, fitting in barrel slots, are handled the same way, driving out the old sight from the left and driving in a new sight from the right. It helps in replacing the sight to scratch the barrel at the forward point of the old sight before removal. Then drive in the new sight until it aligns with the scratch mark. This can sometimes be done with enough accuracy for the rifle to need no further sight adjustments. If the rear sight is a bit too high, file the sight elevator step a bit on the bottom until reaching the correct adjustment.

Mounting a peep or aperture sight is a bit more detailed, but these can be mounted if reasonable care is used. Most American rifles other than bolt-actions come drilled and tapped for some type of tang peep sight. If your rifle is so equipped, remove the dummy screws and attach the sight with the screws furnished. Then check the alignment by glancing through the peep and aligning it with the front sight and middle barrel sight. If, as is almost always the case, the tang sight has no windage adjustment, it will be necessary to shim the base with paper or thin metal strips to bring it into proper alignment. Even better, remove the sight and carefully file the base to bring the stem into proper alignment. This gives close, permanent windage adjustment if the filing is done carefully.

With bolt-action rifles, and in cases when a receiver sight is to be mounted on other action types, the job is not simple. Some bolt-action models — notably Winchester's 54 and 70, the Remington 30 and Savage's 40 and 45 — are already drilled and tapped for standard receiver sights. On these rifles, mounting means merely attaching the sight with the screws furnished and inletting the sight base and/or slide into the stock.

To do this properly, the action should first be removed from the stock, the sight screwed into place, and the action placed in position in the stock. With a scriber or sharp pencil, mark the stock to the sight base's outlines, then measure down the side of the stock to the approximate depth of the base. Saw out this section with a fine-tooth saw or hacksaw, and remove the wood with a flat chisel. Coat the bottom of the sight base with a mixture of red oil tube colors and light oil. Place the action back into the stock and tap the sight base lightly with a wooden block; just enough to make an impression on the wood. Remove this wood until the base is in position, taking care not to make any gouges. With the base in place, relieve the cutout sides by removing wood with the chisel so there is a slight gap about the thickness of a playing card on each side of the base and the bottom. This clearance prevents the sight from loosening from recoil. No shims are necessary under the sight base to achieve alignment, because such adjustments are made in the windage adjustment itself.

Drilling and Tapping Receivers

Owners of the Krag, Springfield, Enfield, Newton and related foreign-made arms such as the Mauser and Mannlicher, must drill and tap the receivers for mounting these sights. This is also true of most American-made lever, slide and autoloading arms, if receiver sights are used. This shouldn't discourage owners of these rifles, because mounting such sights is simple, and perfect results can be expected if proper steps are followed.

If a receiver sight is to be mounted, the primary step is to order the proper size drill and tap with the sight. Most sight screws are not standard, and taps will not be available locally, so get these from the sight maker. (Most sights are mounted with a No. 31 drill and a 6-48 tap.) With the sight in hand, go to a hardware store and buy a drill that will just enter the holes in the base. A No. 29 is usually right, but there is often variation in base holes, so buy the size that will just pass snugly into the hole. This will be your spotting drill, used for locating the tap-drill holes in exact center.

Set up your action in a vise between padded jaws, then set the base on the receiver, aligned with the iron sights. Clamp the base in this position with a small C-clamp. With the spotting drill, drill into the receiver through one of the base holes just deeply enough to center the tap drill. Then with the tap drill, go right through the receiver, but be sure to change the spotting drill for the tap drill first. Many times a shooter forgets to change to the tap drill after spotting the hole, making an oversize hole through the receiver that cannot be tapped for his sight screw.

With the base still in position, start the tap, first wetting it with turpentine. Proceed gently, making a quarter-turn at a time, backing up the tap after each quarter-turn to free the chips. Now go right through with the tap, taking care to keep the shank properly centered in the base hole. Remove the tap carefully and screw the base down tightly with the sight screw. Repeat the operation with the other hole, still keeping the base in position. This is important, for the base acts as a drill jig, giving properly centered holes.

As an additional word of caution in mounting sights, make certain that base screws are kept tight at all times. When the sight base is screwed fast as tightly as it can be done by hand, set the screwdriver in the slot and tap it with a hammer. This often allows an extra quarter-turn to be made on the screw, setting it up tight.

On the Krag, Springfield, Enfield and other military rifles, the owner will often find case-hardened receivers. Case-hardening creates a hard outer shell, only a few thousandths-of-an-inch deep, caused by carbon absorption during heat treatments. It's too hard to drill, so this outer surface must be ground off on an emery wheel before the drill can be started. Mark through the base holes with the sight in position to determine the location, and grind two small spots, just large enough for the drill to go through. Then proceed with drilling and tapping. The job is completed by inletting the sight base into the stock as previously described.

In all cases where an aperture rear sight is mounted, the middle open sight should be removed. This slot can then be filled with a slot-blank or with a folding middle sight. If you don't care to go to the expense of either, make a blank from the old rear sight by filing off the sight and front projection, leaving only the base to fill the slot.

Mounting cocking-piece sights is a job for the factory or a skilled gunsmith. A gun-owner should not try to mount this type of rear sight, because it's necessary to anneal the cocking piece and mill in a dovetail slot at exactly the right angle.

With the great increase in telescope sighting equipment during the past few years, many riflemen will want to mount these themselves. However, I cannot conscientiously recommend this to any but the most experienced shooters and mechanics. It requires considerable skill and knowledge of sighting principles to properly apply a hunting scope to a high-powered rifle. This had best be left to the scopemaker or a reputable gunsmith.[1]

Stock Surgery on Military Rifles

The alteration, remodeling and refinishing of rifle stocks offers perhaps the best opportunity for shooters to make changes to better adapt the firearm to their needs. Unfortunately, most American rifles seem designed for the unhappily nonexistent individual, Mr. Average Man. The result is few factory stocks that actually fit many hunters. Not that these rifles cannot be properly handled, but many can be better adapted to individual requirements, making them more suitable. Slight changes in the shape or angle of the butt plate, size and height of the comb, and shape and position of the grip can make the rifle point more accurately. This is an important requisite for quick, accurate shooting.

Most work on gun stocks requires little equipment. A saw, a few chisels, a rasp, files and sandpaper will perform almost any stock alteration, even building a completely new stock. With these tools, pistol grips and higher combs can be inset, stocks shortened or lengthened, and pitch of the butt plate changed. Military rifles are good candidates for this, because almost every military rifle stock is wrong in most respects for hunting.

Let's suppose we have a Krag carbine, as issued, to be converted to better stock dimensions for improved fit and handling. The Krag has a low comb and no pistol grip, and the stock is a bit short for most hunters. The first step in raising the comb is to lay out on the sides of the old stock the proper lines for cutting off the comb. Start about one inch below the top of the grip. Then measure down from the top of the butt about 1½ inches. From this point, draw a line connecting it to the bottom of the first line drawn. Saw to these lines, which should make a right-angle cut atop the stock.

Now select a piece of walnut about 2 inches thick, giving enough surplus for finishing on the sides, and high enough to give enough height to the finished comb.

Square the ends of this block and plane the bottom to a true square surface. Rub this surface all over with carpenter's chalk, and spot it to the cutout on top of the stock, removing the impressions made on the old stock cutout with a chisel and flat file. When a good bearing has been obtained, and no light shows through the joint, we are ready for the gluing. For this, nothing works better than Casco waterproof glue.

Mix up a small quantity of glue and size both sides of the joint, letting it dry a few minutes before the final application. Coat the joint well with glue and place the two surfaces together, clamping tightly for about 12 hours. The comb can now be shaped to the desired form, first reducing it on top so the bolt will clear. Work down the heel to the proper drop, which is determined by individual preference. Work the sides down with plane, rasp or spokeshave until the

[1]*Mounting a riflescope today is far easier than it was in Koller's era, because of an impressive variety of mounts, rings and pre-drilled and tapped receiver holes. Even so, scope mounting is not a job for inexperienced deer hunters. If you have any doubts about your ability to solidly and precisely mount optics to a firearm, take the work to a gunsmith.*

outlines please the eye.

To inset a pistol grip, select a block of wood about 4 inches long, 3 inches deep and at least 2 inches wide. Saw an angle of about 20 degrees on each end, with one end slightly tapered. Lay this on the side of the stock in the desired position and mark the angles on the wood with a scriber or pencil. Saw out the dovetail and chisel out the wood to a perfectly square bottom. Start to set in the block, spotting as before with the carpenter's chalk until a good fit is obtained. During this operation, don't try to force the block into position or the wedge pressure might split the stock. Glue into place and clamp, and let stand 12 hours to set.

The fitting of both joints must be accurately made, or there will be unsightly gaps in the wood after the stock is worked to shape. After the glue has set, work on shaping the grip, first fitting the grip cap. For best outlines on a pistol grip, the forward end of the cap should be about 3½ inches from the trigger's center. With this measurement carefully held, other lines will fall into place as shaping progresses.

The butt angle can now be sawed to the correct pitch. The pitch is the angle of the butt plate to the line of sight, and is determined by placing the butt flat on the floor with the receiver against the wall, then measuring from the wall to the front sight. Four inches is a comfortable pitch angle, and suits many individuals of normal build.

The length of the Krag stock is just shy of 13 inches, and this will be too short in most cases. It can be lengthened several ways. Adding a recoil pad will give extra length, as will building up under the butt plate with several thicknesses of hard rubber. Most satisfactory is the addition of a matching piece of walnut, cutting the stock just enough to get under the oil-soaked wood, then gluing on a piece of walnut to give the required length for finishing. The butt plate can then be screwed and glued to the addition, and the whole completed by filing and sanding until ready for the final finishing.

These methods apply equally well to any sporting rifle. Any arm equipped with the curved, narrow and uncomfortable "rifletype" butt plate can be converted by sawing off the butt to the proper angle. Next, fit a better-designed plate, lengthening the stock if necessary by gluing on an addition. In fitting wood surfaces that must be glued, always use carpenter's chalk for spotting. Don't use a mixture containing oil, for oil prevents glue from adhering to the joint.

Refinishing Rifle Stocks

Work of this nature necessitates complete stock refinishing. Many hunters would like to refinish their rifle stocks, even if contemplating no other changes. Standard varnish or lacquer finishes found on factory firearms are not durable, and a few days in the woods finds such rifles covered with unsightly scratches that cannot be removed or easily covered. The solution is an oil finish, and nothing in gunwork is simpler than this, for it requires only linseed oil and hand rubbing.

The first step in refinishing is to remove the old varnish. This can be done by wetting the surface with paint remover, using an old cloth or a piece of cotton. Allow it to stand until the varnish begins to curl. It might require more than one application if the stock is old, but two or three applications will do the job. (Of course, for any work of this nature, the stock should be removed from the action to protect the metal parts.)

After scraping off the varnish, go over the stock with coarse sandpaper, then wet the wood to raise the grain. Dry the stock over a quick heat — a gas flame is about right — after which you'll note the grain has raised up in the form of tiny splinters. Cut these off with steel wool, then sand the stock with medium sandpaper. Continue these alternate wetting-and-dryings and sandings until the grain will no longer raise, then finish the stock with fine cabinetmaker's 6/0 paper, sanding always with the grain of the wood.

At this point, several tiny pits or depressions will be noticeable in the now-smooth surface. These are pores in the wood that are normally filled with sap in the living tree. In American black walnut, these pores are noticeable and should be filled before applying the finishing oil. In foreign walnuts, these pores are not so large, and can usually be filled by the action of the oil itself. Perhaps a more important point in using wood filler is to prevent oil penetration from darkening the stock to the point where all grain and figure becomes obliterated. In dark American walnut, this is an objectionable feature in oil finishing, but in lighter woods it adds beauty. Only the firearm's owner can decide which type of finish looks best, but it's advisable to use filler on all dark woods of attractive figure.

To achieve the darkening effect on light woods while using filler on the pores, first apply a mixture of turpentine and raw linseed oil to the bare wood. This penetrates and darkens the wood with each successive application until reaching the desired shade, whereupon the filler is applied.

Use a paste filler mixed with turpentine to the consistency of cream. It should be applied with a brush and rubbed in across the grain, and then allowed to set about an hour. Then rub off the excess across the grain, using a rough, heavy cloth like burlap. Apply several applications over several days, allowing each to dry thoroughly before putting on more. The final coat should be thinned with turpentine and allowed to dry very hard. It can then be sanded smooth with a fine cabinetmaker's paper.

The stock is now ready for the oil finish, which means applying raw linseed oil by hand. Apply only enough oil to make the rubbing easy. Rub until the stock becomes warm and dry to touch, then put it away to dry. This first coat will dry and harden in about a day. Then apply another coat and again put it away to dry. Do not oil the wood any more until the previous application has dried fully, or oxidized. Further rubbing will only remove what has already been applied. As the finish builds up, more time will be needed between applications. The final coats require a week or more to dry, depending on temperature and weather. After all slight blemishes are filled, and a heavy oil coat has been built to a dull lustrous finish, the stock can be rubbed with rottenstone and sweet oil, using a felt rubbing pad. This brings out a fine, smooth finish that's durable enough to last for the life of the gun, its luster improving with handling. Small scratches that occur from use can be rubbed out with a new application of raw oil, so the stock will always look new. This oil finish is waterproof, untouched by weather or temperature changes, and is the most beautiful finish that can be applied to a stock.

Rebluing Barrels and Actions

A vague mystery in every gun owner's mind is the process of applying dull blue or black finishes on metal parts. Many believe this is painted on the steel, somewhat like stain or lacquer, but rebluing is simply a chemical rusting process that produces a blue or black rust rather than the common red rust. It is a straight oxidation process, induced by action of the proper chemicals, and it's a simple process once the principles are outlined. Old rifles and shotguns, with bluing faded by years of handling and use (perhaps a little abuse), can be made to look new again with a little effort and expense.

The double purpose of bluing firearms is to protect them from destructive rust and to dull the metal surface sufficiently for light reflections not to scare away game. Originally, bluing was called "browning" and the old-time arms were all finished in the deep nut-brown stain we now see on only the "Damascus" barrel shotguns of the late 1800s. Some bluing processes still leave the metal a deep brown, which is subsequently changed to blue by applying linseed oil. Today, those old formulas are seldom used, because they require a bit of time to apply.

As in many other processes, the success of bluing depends on the metal preparation before the chemicals are applied. This means complete removal of all the old bluing using a fine grade of Aloxite or emery cloth. Barrel, receiver, trigger guard and all metal parts must be brought to a high polish with the abrasive cloths, for it is only with a high polish on these parts that a deep, rich blue can be had.

With the barrel and action polished, prepare two hardwood plugs for the barrel. The solution must be kept from entering the bore. Otherwise, it might be rusted beyond repair. Turn these plugs so they make a tight fit inside the bore, leaving enough of each plug projecting so it can be a handle for the work. During the bluing process, nothing can contact the barrel until the bluing is complete, so these handles are important.

Materials needed will be a tank of sheet metal for boiling the parts. This tank should be made of sheet iron, galvanized, about 6 inches wide, 6 inches deep and 40 inches long. It should be long enough to take the longest barrel, together with receiver, that will be reblued. You can have this made up by a tinsmith or you can buy the sheet metal yourself and bend it up, then solder the ends. At the same time, get a box of fine steel wool, and have your druggist make up the following formula:

> 250 grains (avoir.) potassium chlorate
> 300 grains (avoir.) potassium nitrate
> 100 grains (avoir.) sodium nitrate
> 100 grains (avoir.) bichloride of mercury
> 35 grains (avoir.) copper chloride (cupric)
> 75 grains (avoir.) iron chloride (ferric)
> 50 cc. niter (sweet spirits)

Bluing the Barrel

Heat 400 cc. of distilled water to about 125 degrees Fahrenheit, add all chemicals except niter, stirring thoroughly until all are dissolved. After the mixture is absolutely cool, add the sweet spirits of niter and pour all into a colored glass bottle. Let this stand a day or two before using, because the chemicals must amalgamate.

Now place about 2 inches of water in the tank and set it on the stove to boil. Immerse the barrel and action in the water together with the other metal parts — trigger guard, magazine and so on. These small parts should have wires attached so they can be handled easily. Now add a handful of lye to the water and bring it to a boil. Then boil the parts about five minutes. This dissolves all oil and grease, making the steel receptive to the bluing solution. After about five minutes, remove the barrel and lay it on a pair of wooden blocks, which you prepared for resting with the wooden plugs. The metal parts can be hung from a nail in the wall or beam to prevent them from touching anything that might dirty the surface.

Dump the lye out of the tank and wash thoroughly in hot water. Also wash the barrel and other parts in hot water, and use a clean cotton cloth to remove lye residue. Again pour about 2 inches of clean water into the tank and bring the parts to a boil. Now take a wide-mouthed glass jar, and wire it fast in one end of the bluing tank. Pour into the jar about 3 or 4 ounces of your bluing solution and let it heat with the water in the tank.

You're now ready to start bluing. Take a short piece of dowel and lace on a clean swab for applying the solution. Keep this in the solution during the bluing process, right up until the moment of application. Now take out your barrel and allow the heat of the parts to dry the metal. Remove small drops of water on the barrel by blowing on them. Apply the solution to the barrel in long, lengthwise strokes as though you were painting it. Cover the barrel and action with the solution, allowing them to dry from their own heat. Then place them back at once into the tank. Permit the barrel and action to boil about five minutes, then remove them from the tank and set them up on your wooden blocks.

Now the entire barrel and action is covered with a dark rust. Remove this gently by brushing with the steel wool. As soon as you have carded off the rust, place the barrel and action back into the tank to bring them to boiling temperature. Again remove them and coat the barrel with solution, then place them back into the tank and allow them to boil a few minutes. Repeat this process until obtaining the desired dark color. On ordnance and regular high-pressure steel, about eight applications is enough. For some nickel steels and other alloys, as many as 20 applications will be needed to produce the proper color.

Bluing Smaller Parts

When bluing the smaller parts, speed is essential. The solution takes best only on heated steel, so it's important to apply the solution the instant the part is removed from the tank and the water dries off. On thin pieces, such as stamped trigger guards and magazines, it helps to hold the piece over the heat source as soon as it's removed from the tank to dry off the water. Then, quickly apply the solution. It's equally important to allow the solution itself to dry, forming the rust, before placing it back into the tank. Drying the solution on the metal causes the required oxidation.

After applying the proper number of coats, brush off the final rust with the steel wool. Then, while all the parts are still hot, apply raw linseed oil liberally and allow them to cool a few minutes. Meanwhile, heat equal parts of turpentine and beeswax over the fire and rub down the barrel, action and all metal parts with this mixture. This brings out a high gloss, rubbing out all the linseed oil, which, if not removed, hardens on the metal to make a messy appearance.

Hunters will occasionally want to reblue small parts such as pins, screws, front sights, sling swivels and sight bases rather than a complete firearm. For this work, there is a much simpler process than the above, giving equally good results with much less labor.

Obtain these chemicals: 1 pound sodium nitrate, 1 pound potassium nitrate, ¼ pound manganese dioxide. Heat these together in a heavy iron pot until they melt together and begin bubbling. Prepare the parts by polishing as before, and remove oil and grease by washing with alcohol. Attach wires to the parts so they can be suspended in the solution off the bottom of the receptacle. Hang the parts in the pot, let them remain about 15 minutes, and then examine them for color. If not dark enough, place them back into the solution until they reach the proper color. Then remove the parts and place them in hot — but not boiling — water for a few minutes. Remove and dry them off in sawdust or with a cotton cloth. Then oil with a light oil, and allow the oil to remain until the parts are cool.

This nitrate bath attains a temperature of about 750 degrees during the bluing process, so take care not to drop any water or oil into it, because it might spatter badly. Do not blue springs or hardened parts by this method, because the heat attained is sufficient to affect the metal's temper.

This substantially covers all the bluing work a deer hunter will need in repair and remodeling work. Literally hundreds of formulas are in use. All are good, but none are simpler, quicker or more effective than the above. Many of the rusting processes of bluing cover a period of 10 days to three weeks, usually with no better results than this quick method. The solution will take on all kinds of steel, with the possible exception of case-hardened receivers. These require special treatment, as follows: All Krag rifles and early Springfields have case-hardened receivers, which are difficult to blue by any method. However, if the receivers are brought to a high polish and treated with raw nitric acid, the surface readily takes bluing. Simply take a splinter of wood, wind it with cotton cloth to use as a swab, and rub the raw acid over the metal surface until it sizzles and turns black. If the metal fails to respond, heat it over a gas flame, and then apply the acid as before, washing the parts in hot water before the bluing process.

At present, many commercial bluing preparations are on the market. These work well if you carefully follow the manufacturers' instructions. The important point to remember in all rebluing is to prepare the metal so it is physically and chemically clean. And keep it that way during the entire bluing process. Do not touch the parts with your fingers, woolen rags or any foreign object, for each of these will mark the surface. Likewise, steel wool used to brush off the rust should be kept in a dry, clean wooden box. If these points are religiously followed, perfect results should be obtained on your first attempt.

As a last thought: City water is sometimes treated with chemicals, which can streak the metal in the bluing process. If this happens, obtain spring or well water or, best of all, rainwater.

CHAPTER 20

Altering Military Rifles and Other Jobs

Various models of military rifles attracted much of the deer hunter's attention during the 1940s. This might be because of increased interest in the bolt-action type of repeater, a search for greater accuracy, demand for more powerful cartridges, or greater appreciation of the bolt-action's reliable functioning under bad conditions.

At any rate, this interest has been influenced greatly by manufacturers who are making it easier for hunters to convert a military rifle to a suitable sporting arm by themselves. Easily fitted ramp sights, good aperture rear sights, a variety of buttplates and other fittings, and — most importantly — rough-turned and rough-inletted sporting stocks, are readily obtained in sufficient variety to meet almost all needs.

Converting the Military Rifle

Converting military rifles gives deer hunters almost all the advantages of a truly custom-built gun at less cost than a standard factory-made repeater — provided the owner performs much of the work. The Krag, Enfields and Springfield all offer strong actions that, once rebuilt, provide the best in sporting rifles for deer hunting. All of the remodeling work can be performed nicely by the hunters themselves with minimal expense for tools, but it necessitates patience, care and time.

Let's assume we have a Krag rifle — the long-barreled variety, not the more popular carbine — that we want to convert to a sporting rifle. Unfortunately, Krag rifles are no longer available from government sources because the supply is exhausted. But during the mid-1930s, every hock shop and "Army-Navy" store sold them at prices varying from $2 to $5. However, plenty of these grand rifles are still available in the hands of hunters across the country. Their actions are without question one of the smoothest bolts ever manufactured, and they're the quickest and easiest of any repeater to load. Simply snap open the hinged magazine cover, dump in a handful of cartridges, bullets pointing forward, snap the cover shut and the rifle is loaded. It's speedy and simple, especially if fingers are half-frozen. The Krag's only drawbacks — from an ultramodern viewpoint — is that it's built to handle rimmed-head cases only, and the bolt has only one locking lug, which eliminates it from really up-to-date rifles. However, the action is more than strong enough for the .30-40 cartridge, itself well-suited ballistically to all whitetail hunting. I believe these rifles will become more sought by hunters as the years go by, for nothing we have now approaches its smooth operation and easy loading.

Shortening the Barrel

The first operation in converting the Krag to a sporter is to discard the stock and top hand guard, and remove the bayonet band and forearm band. The barrel, now 30 inches long, must also be cut to a length for quicker handling and better balance. Before cutting the barrel, however, we must decide which type of front sight to use. The most logical choice is the barrel-band style of ramp, which is obtainable from Lyman, Redfield, Pacific or others. The ramp slips over the end of the barrel, and is tapped into place and held in this position by a pin or pointed set screw. Don't cut the barrel to length until the ramp has been driven into place, because there is some variation in barrel diameters.

Before the ramp is finally set, it should be squared. Gunsmiths do this with a surface plate and proper gauges, but novices can obtain good results by setting the barrel squarely in a vise, and using a level on the bottom of the magazine from below. The ramp sides can then be squared by using the end of the level, and bringing it as closely as possible into true square with the eye. It is remarkable how this work can sometimes be accurately done with the eye alone. If it isn't absolutely square, don't worry about it. Proper adjustment of the rear sight corrects slight errors.

With the sight in place, mark the barrel about ¼-inch ahead of the ramp with a three-cornered file, then saw it off as accurately as possible with a hacksaw. In the shop, this work is done on a lathe, and the muzzle is crowned at the same time with a form tool. However, with reasonable care, this facing can be done with a flat mill file, testing for squareness with a steel square. We won't crown the muzzle on this job, for this is mostly a matter of appearance. It is necessary, however, to countersink the rifling at the muzzle. Do this by placing the barrel level in the vise and, with a rose countersink in a bit brace, carefully bevel the inside of the bore to a depth of about ³⁄₃₂ inch, keeping the brace centered with the line of the bore. The barrel, as now finished, might not come out to an even number of inches because of the ramp's position. This is of no consequence, however, if it's about the right length — 24 inches is the accepted standard.

To obtain the required accuracy of the muzzle, it must be "lapped in" perfectly square with the bore. To do this, get a small brass ball from a hardware dealer, the type used in valve ball seats. Sweat this with soft solder to the end of a short piece of ¼-inch cold rolled steel. Plug the barrel's bore just below the muzzle with a wad of cloth. Coat the end of the ball with lapping compound or valve-grinding paste, and with your bit brace begin to lap in the end of the bore. Making a perfectly true seat requires a lot of labor, but it's vitally important to achieving top-flight accuracy. This operation can be easily and rapidly done with a crowning tool in the lathe, but lacking a lathe, we must use the ball method.

If a receiver sight is to be used, now is the time to mount it. For this job, the No. 102-K Redfield is admirable because it requires no drilling and tapping of the receiver. If an open sight is desired, a base must be filed out and drilled to fit screw holes in the barrel. The required rear sight is then fitted to this base. The aperture sight, however, is infinitely more satisfactory on a sporter. In this case, the screw-holes in the barrel should be filled. We can use the regular sight-base screws, cutting them off just above the barrel surface. They should then be peened down flush and filed smooth.

Fitting the Rough-Cut Stock

With the barrel cut and sights mounted, we turn to the stock. Rough-turned and rough-inletted replacements are available from several companies that advertise in sporting magazines. Write for catalogs and compare designs until you find one that matches your ideas on sporting stocks. All of these stocks are made somewhat oversize, so they can usually be worked down to individual measurements. The features that most influence your choice will be the shape and style of cheekpiece, drop at the heel, and height and shape of the comb. By all means, order the cheekpiece style of stock. If you decide later you don't want it, just shave it off with a draw knife.

The choice of wood depends on your pocketbook. Plain American walnut is the cheapest, plain French walnut next, crotch- and feather-grain walnuts are higher in price, and so on. Plain walnut stocks can be had for all conversion purposes for about $7. For a first attempt, it's wise to use this type of blank.

With a blank in hand, remove the bolt, magazine box and trigger mechanism from the action. Set the blank firmly in the padded vise jaws and prepare a mixture of red or black oil tube color and a light oil for your spotting-in work. Don't use linseed oil, for it will harden on the action and cause inaccurate fitting. It will also be difficult to remove.

First, compare the new blank with the old stock, noticing the cutouts for magazine, receiver, barrel and trigger guard. Now set the action in the stock and note where it touches the wood. Chances are it won't even start down into the inletted portion. Remove the action and note the impressions left on the wood by the red fitting paste. Carefully remove these portions with a flat chisel, being sure not to remove more wood than is needed.

From now on the work is simply "cut and try." The action must be frequently coated with the red paste to determine contact points. These are removed with the chisel and the process repeated. Particular attention must be paid to the cutout at the rear of the magazine box. This is the recoil shoulder, and a perfect bearing must be held against this throughout the entire inletting. If this isn't cut perfectly, recoil will force the action back into the stock, possibly splitting it beyond repair.

As the barrel begins to enter the groove, coat it with the spotting mixture and remove the contact points with a wide flat chisel. Make these cuts straight down and parallel with the sides of the barrel. If only a small amount of wood is to be removed from the channel, use a half-round file for all this work. Again, remove only as much wood as is indicated by the impressions. Keep a perfect bearing at all times along the full length of the barrel. The receiver also must have a perfect bearing on all sides and the bottom.

When the receiver and barrel have been inletted to half their depth in the stock, assemble the trigger mechanism and magazine box. Inlet these as before, taking care to leave no unsightly gaps in the wood that will show when the stock is completed. Relieve the trigger cutout on the inside so the mechanism works freely.

As the action begins to enter the blank, it's advisable to set in the trigger guard screws from below, catching them in the proper holes before tapping the action down to make the spotting-in impressions. This keeps the action properly centered in the stock, and keeps it at right angles with the blank's sides. If this is not carefully watched during the inletting work, the guard screws won't meet the holes in the action during the final stages.

If you're satisfied the action is in place or nearly so, begin inletting the trigger guard using the guard screws to keep it centered. Apply your fitting paste on the bottom of the guard and tap it lightly to secure the outlines. Remove this wood carefully, and as the guard enters the cutout, coat the sides and bottom to secure the side bearing. Be careful when fitting the guard not to go too deeply with the mortise or you won't be able to pull the action up tight with the guard screws.

In this work, proceed very slowly and carefully. Don't rush it, otherwise you might make a serious or unsightly mistake. Resign yourself to removing only as much wood as indicated by impressions made with the fitting paste. Strive for perfect bearing at all points, particularly along the sides of the barrel and around the receiver. Proper barrel bedding is critical to your rifle's accuracy and its ability to hold its zero, so spend as much time as necessary to achieve the best possible results. Many types of tools can be used for this inletting job, but the only real necessities are flat chisels of different widths and half-round or round bastard-cut files. Small gouges will help make the various radii, for example, at the ends of the trigger guard, but they're not essential to a careful workman.

After all parts are in place, trigger guard and guard screws properly fastened, and receiver and barrel inletted to half their diameters, the final step is relieving the wood at the tang or extreme rear point of the action. A tight fit here will force the action back during recoil, causing a wedge effect. This eventually splits the stock through the grip. With a radius gouge or half-round file, remove the wood behind the tang, leaving a gap not less than the thickness of a playing card. Slightly more might be better, depending on how accurately the rest of the fitting was done.

Shaping the outside of the stock can now begin. Start by measuring from the trigger to the center of the butt, marking off somewhere between 13 and 14 inches, allowing for the buttplate's thickness. The angle of the buttplate, or pitch, should be determined with the line of sight, and this line laid out on the sides of the buttstock. For the first cut, it's best to make the stock a bit longer than necessary. If too long, it can be shortened after trial. Cut down the comb so the bolt will just clear it, and mark off your drop at heel, which should be somewhere between 2½ and 3 inches. Draw a line connecting these points and plane this flat, to the line. Lay out now for the pistol grip, measuring first from the top of the comb down to rear edge of the grip, which should be about 3 inches. Measure now from the center of the trigger to the front edge of the grip, which should be between 3½ and 3¾ inches. Using the standard length of 1⅞ inches for the length of the grip-cap, the bottom of the grip can be determined by shifting these measurements to coincide. The butt should be at least 5 inches from heel to toe, so by connecting this toe measurement with the rear of the grip-cap we obtain the buttstock's outlines. The point of the comb should be about 2½ inches from the end of the tang to give good outlines. With these measurements made, the stock can now be worked to shape, using a draw-knife, spokeshave, rasp and coarse files.

During all this shaping, the stock should be brought to the shoulder frequently to determine its fit and feel. Fit the buttplate before work has progressed to the final stage, because this might influence the final finishing. The forearm can be shaped while the work is proceeding on the butt. Any length or style can be used, depending only on the owner's tastes. Strive for graceful lines, blending in with the outlines of the action and the buttstock. A good length for the forearm is 11 inches from the front of the receiver, although this again will be determined by personal tastes.

Unfortunately, we're limited in dimensions by rough-turned stocks, but most can be properly worked down to good proportions with a little forethought. The buttplate, as indicated, should be wide and rather deep, either perfectly flat or slightly concaved, because this style helps distribute recoil over a wider shoulder area, lessening its effect.

After final shaping is completed, the stock should receive a thorough sanding to remove all toolmarks, sanding always in the direction of the grain. Finish this with medium paper, and prepare the stock for the oil finish as outlined in the previous chapter.

Before final finishing occurs, some means must be provided for fastening the forearm to the barrel. This can be done in two ways. The first choice is to obtain a barrel band with a stud and screw, which passes through the forearm and secures the barrel tightly to the wood. The second choice is to use the original stock band that held the military stock to the barrel, fitting it during the shaping operation. This should be made a tight wedge fit, and it can be held in place by a small pin driven into the forearm just in front of it. The barrel band and stud is much neater in appearance, however, which is why it's preferred.

Refining the Trigger Pull

With the major remodeling work now complete — with the exception of rebluing — we now must refine the trigger pull, because this is directly related to accurate shooting. A hard, creepy pull with three or four "bumps" in it is not conducive to good shooting. Hunters with some experience using military rifles have probably noticed their long-creep or "double-draw" pull. To fire these rifles, the long slack must be taken up before feeling the final stage of the trigger let-off. This double-draw slack is out of place in a deer rifle and must be eliminated. Primarily, we must prevent the trigger sear from returning to its high position in front of the cocking-piece sear. In other words, we must prevent the trigger from coming forward too far when it's released after each shot.

Several methods can be used to block the sear into the proper position. The simplest and most positive is to drill and tap a hole for a small screw in front of the trigger guard. Drill this hole about a quarter inch from the front end of the trigger slot so a small plate can be screwed into position. This is set so the trigger rests against it, thus being blocked in its forward travel. To obtain proper adjustment, the plate should be drilled with four holes of the screw size, set in line to touch each other, then filed out to make an elongated slot. Then, by shifting the plate's position against the trigger and tightening down with the screw, the trigger can be blocked in the proper position to remove the double-draw pull. The trigger should stop just as the hard part of the trigger pull is felt. The plate need be only about ⅜ inches wide, ¾ inches long and not over 1/16 inch thick.

Some shooters suggest grinding off the top of the sear, shortening it enough to eliminate the slack, but this is unsafe. In most cases when this is done the shooter forgets a great deal of motion is lost in these rifles' cocking pieces. When the rifle is cocked, it can be fired simply by pulling up on the cocking piece, allowing the sear to ride over the top of the trigger sear. This one treatment has caused several shooting accidents every year. Better leave it alone.

Of course, when such a plate is used in removing the double-draw pull, it must be inletted into the stock under the trigger guard. This can be done any time during final operations on the rifle.

This brings us to the problem of trigger pull itself. Almost every high-powered rifle made, with the exception of the Winchester Model 70, comes through now and then with a hard, rough pull. Military rifles are especially annoying in this respect. Most hunters will do their best work with pulls of 4 to 5 pounds, and these are entirely safe. Factory rifles many times are turned out with pulls of 8, 10, even 12 pounds, none of which help hunters hit deer. The only thing lacking in these factory arms to produce good pulls is hand labor and time necessary to perform the job. We must admit, though, that in the hands of certain hunters, such pulls are not safe enough. But hunters who appreciate the niceties of good-shooting qualities in firearms will want to make some changes in their rifles.

The only tools needed are properly shaped slip-stones. Only two oil stones are essential: one three-square stone and one double knife-edge stone in ¼-inch diameter and medium grit. Add to these the same size and shape of stones in the "Hard Arkansas" type for final polishing. Hardware stores will get these for you on short notice.

The first step is inspecting the contact surfaces on the trigger sear, and hammer or cocking-piece sear. You'll likely find an uneven contact on both seats, with a few ridges showing on the surface. This causes a rough pull. Carefully stone both surfaces perfectly smooth and flat until good contact is made. It helps to hold the parts in a small vise to prevent "rocking" the stone, which causes a rounded surface. With surfaces smooth, assemble the action and test for even pull. You'll find a big improvement already. The pull will still be a bit too hard, so dissemble the action and begin to stone a small radius on the nose of the trigger sear. For testing the pull during this operation, it's handy to have a small spring scale that weighs by ¼-pound increments. The scale's regular hook can be removed and replaced with a long piece of thin drill rod hooked to the proper angle to contact the trigger.

The lightening operation requires many trials before the required pull is obtained, but a clean, sharp pull on your rifle is worth far more than the little time spent obtaining it. The main points to remember are to keep the contact surfaces square to prevent creep in the pull, and stone carefully to prevent lightening the pull too much all at once.

On bolt-action rifles, after the contact surfaces are stoned square and smooth, the pull will still be too hard. To reduce this, stone a small angle on the cocking-piece sear on the inside, that is, so the angle slopes toward the rear, shortening the contact surface. In most cases this will lighten the pull, but sometimes the angle must be stoned to slope back and down toward the outside of the sear rather than the inside. This will depend on the trigger sear's shape, and can be determined only by trials. If you have difficulty determining the contact surfaces, coat each with a bit of Prussian blue before testing the pull. High spots will instantly show up.

On hammer guns, where the hammer travel is an arc with the hammer pivoting on a fixed stud rather than traveling in a straight line as in bolt-action rifles, stoning sears is a bit different. In these actions, the trigger sear comes to a sharp point and engages in a deep notch. Trigger pressure causes a slight camming action against the spring's tension, causing the heavy pull. To eliminate this camming action, both sears must be stoned to an angle at right angles to the radius of the hammer fall.

After the pull is smooth and reduced to the required weight, stone all contact surfaces carefully with the "Hard Arkansas" stones. These stones are used only for final polishing because they do little, if any, cutting of metal. In trigger-stoning operations, great care must be used to keep surfaces square, otherwise a hard blow or knock can cause an accidental discharge. Proceed slowly, trying the trigger after each step to gauge how the work is progressing. Rapid, roughshod stoning might ruin the parts, necessitating replacement before the rifle can again be used.

On certain rifles, it is inadvisable to try removing the double-draw pull. These are models that use the trigger sear as a bolt stop, preventing the bolt from being withdrawn from the receiver at the rear of the bolt throw. A few such models are the Winchester 54, Savage Model 20, models 40 and 45, and the low-power centerfire models 23 B, C and D. In such actions, the sear's high position is quite necessary. Removing any of this slack will allow the bolt to be jerked from the bolt channel during rapid fire. Fairly good pulls can be stoned into these actions using the suggestions for bolt-action pulls, but the long preliminary creep must remain.

Fitting sling swivels completes remodeling work on the Krag. As with many other gunsmithing operations, the method of attachment lies with the owner's tastes, but for simplicity's sake I'll outline two methods for the Krag.

If a barrel band and stud are used for the forearm attachment, it's only necessary to use a swivel-attaching screw in place of the regular forearm screw. The swivel now serves the double purpose of fastening the forearm and holding the sling. If you're considering a sling for the converting job, order the barrel band, stud and front swivel bow as a single unit. If this is not done, or if the military stock band is used as a forearm attachment, buy a swivel bow equipped with an escutcheon. This is a round, fluted nut inletted into the inside of the forearm for taking the swivel screw. In either case, mount the butt swivel the same. Drill a hole at right angles to the bottom line of the stock and about three inches from the toe. Screw in the butt swivel tightly. The standard width for deer-rifle sling swivels is ⅞ inch, but if the regular army sling is used, 1¼-inch swivels are required.

Polishing the bolt and oil-finishing the stock completes the Krag's remodeling work. Bolts can be nicely polished with fine Aloxite cloth, saving the almost worn-out pieces for the final high finish. Or you might want to blue the bolt during the rebluing operation. If so, the bolt must be polished anyway, so it's only a matter of deciding whether a polished bolt or blued bolt is more attractive. As a word of caution in polishing bolts — don't polish the locking lugs in any shape, manner or form. Any removal of metal from the lugs, however slight, might cause uneven distribution of pressure or excess headspace. Correct headspace is a matter of two or three thousandths of an inch, so even lightly polishing the lugs can affect the rifle's safety or accuracy.

Tips for Other Military Rifles

The suggestions for converting the Krag rifle also apply to the Springfield, Enfield and others. However, the magazine on these rifles is centrally located and should be inletted with the trigger guard from the bottom of the blank, because it tapers in that direction. Take great care in this operation to ensure the magazine enters the well on the action's underside. This is a tight fit, so be sure to keep the magazine square with the sides of the blank while holding its relative fore-and-aft position in the stock. This is the only difficult operation in inletting these actions, so some care and forethought must be given before making the cutouts. It helps, before beginning the work, to assemble the action with the magazine in position and screwed up tightly with the guard screws, without the stock, of course, so the situation can be studied thoroughly to avoid mistakes. On these actions the recoil shoulder is in front of the magazine, and located in a little well inside the stock. Keep a tight bearing on the wood at the rear of this flat portion during all the inletting work. By doing so, you'll have no future fears of the stock splitting from recoil. In these, as in all high-powered bolt-actions, the tang must be relieved, just as outlined for the Krag.

To illustrate the importance of this recoil shoulder in stock construction, let me tell of a little incident that happened during the 1947 season. A young chap brought a nicely remodeled Enfield to my shop. It carried a well-figured stock, carefully checkered and finished, but split from the tang through the grip and into the comb. I disassembled the stock and noted the complete absence of a recoil shoulder. He had inletted the stock himself, and had removed that portion of the blank that formed the recoil shoulder. His excuse was that he didn't have a narrow enough chisel to get down into the cutout that formed the recoil shoulder. He thought it didn't matter anyway, so he had just chiseled it out. On the first half-dozen shots, the stock split because recoil drove the action back into the stock, wedging the tang into the grip with enough force to split it.

To repair the stock, I inserted a new recoil shoulder using screws and glue, then refitted the metal to make a firm bearing. I also forced open the stock itself at the split and forced Casco glue into the break. Then I made a stock-bolt to pass through the stock between the rear of the magazine and the trigger cutout. I next binded and firmly clamped the parts together. After the glue dried, I counterbored the stock-bolt head and nut, glued inlays into the holes, and then refinished the sides of the stock. The man's mistake had been costly, but we restored the stock to good shooting condition.

Owners of Enfield rifles should remove the rear-sight base on the receiver's rear bridge. This can be done by hacksawing, grinding and filing it to a nice contour, leaving a wall thickness over the bolt channel of about $\frac{3}{32}$ inch. A receiver sight can then be mounted on the right side, as with the Springfield. The Enfield action is identical to the Remington Model 30 sporting rifle, so if you can examine one of these in a dealer's shop, you'll get some ideas in shaping the contour of the rear receiver bridge. The Enfield has a barrel that's a bit long for deer hunting, so this should be cut off and faced, as with the Krag, after placing the ramp sight.

Springfield barrels are the right length as issued, so a ramp can be installed without cutting the barrel. If you don't want a ramp, a sporting front sight can be fitted using the standard front base. Redfield makes a nice model for this, called the "Full Block" sight. It's furnished in round or square gold bead, or round ivory beads, in $\frac{1}{16}$-inch and $\frac{3}{32}$-inch sizes.

Hunters who contemplate buying a military rifle for conversion should be aware of the comparative excellence of various models. Any of the Krags, Enfields and Springfields are good. Some Enfields have barrels slightly over bore diameter, but this won't greatly affect hunting accuracy. Other excellent rifles are the German Mauser Model 1898, the British Lee-Enfield, the Canadian Ross, the Austrian Mannlicher, Spanish Mauser, Belgian Mannlicher and others, but rough-turned and rough-inletted stocks are not generally available for these arms, other than the Mauser, so I cannot recommend them for conversion by a novice.

Each of these military rifles has its good and bad points. The Krag has a smooth bolt and a magazine that's easy to load, but its action is not as strong as the others designed for rimless cases. The Springfield — a modified Mauser action — and the Mauser itself are distinctly high-quality arms, making up into the best of sporters. The Enfield is a bit heavy, but it has a handy safety on the right side and permits low mounting of scope sights without altering the bolt handle — a necessary change in the Mauser and Springfield. The Enfield can also be procured at a low price, making it suitable for a beginner's experiments.

I can think of many other repair and alteration jobs hunters might be called on to do: repair broken stocks, and make replacement parts, pins, screws and so on. Unfortunately, space prohibits any further explanations of this work in one chapter. Hunters interested in these jobs can find complete books on this subject that deal with many technical details that are so much a part of the gunsmith's work.

Attaching Sling Swivels

One of the simpler additions deer hunters might want to make to their rifles is a set of sling swivels. Slings are becoming more popular each year, and for a good reason. Slinging the rifle over the shoulder now and then during the hunt relieves the cramped sensation caused by carrying the rifle for hours at a time. If the country is rough and steep ravines and hillsides must be climbed frequently, it's a great help to have both hands available. The sling also permits hunters to carry their rifle while using both hands to bring out their trophy. Some hunters, while liking the sling for those reasons, believe it encumbers the rifle in heavy brush and scrub oak by catching on every other branch. A solution is the quick detachable sling swivel, which allows the sling to be removed instantly and carried in the hunting coat. These are attached the same as standard swivels, but are more expensive.

On factory-made arms, the rear butt swivel is attached simply by drilling the proper-size hole, which should not be larger than the screw's base diameter. This is the thickness of the screw, less the threads, or the threads will strip the hole. I'm most concerned with the forward sling swivel, because it offers many problems.

In rifles with ample wood in the forearms, the escutcheon type of attachment can be used, inletting it into the inside of the forearm just behind the tip, and then catching the swivel into the threaded escutcheon and pulling it up tight. All bolt-action rifles can be fitted this way, as can some of the Savage lever-action models.

Savage lever-actions with short, thin forearms must be handled differently. The best approach is to find a block of half-inch cold-rolled steel, filing in the barrel radius with a round or half-round file, and spotting it to the barrel for fit with Prussian blue. Then place the block on the barrel in the desired position, scribe its outline on the barrel, and use a small file to remove the bluing from this enclosed area on the barrel. Next, tin this bare spot with solder after coating it with "No-Ko-Rode" soldering paste or zinc chloride. Give the same treatment to the block, and clamp the two together and heat them with a blow torch or over a gas flame until the solder melts, forming a perfectly sweated joint. Now drill the block and tap it to take the swivel screw, probably an 8-32, and make the swivel tight. If desired, you can drill and tap the block before soldering to eliminate any possibility of drilling into the barrel.

Winchester and Marlin lever-actions can be handled the same way by sweating the block to the magazine tube, but there is another way this can be done with less labor. Remove the metal cap over the forend tip, drill it with a hole to tightly take the forearm swivel screw, and then insert the screw in this hole and mark it about ¹⁄₁₆-inch above the hole.

Cut this off with a hacksaw, and then again insert it in the hole and rivet it solidly from the inside, resting the swivel on an anvil or heavy vise jaw. Replace the forearm cap, removing just enough wood from the underside of the forearm to allow the riveted end to pass.

The Model 8 Remington autoloader should be handled like the Savage lever-action, by sweating on a base block. However, the slide-action models 14 and 141 present a problem. They have no means of attaching a swivel other than the magazine band, as the magazine tube moves with the slide handle, so an attachment there would be unsatisfactory. A logical solution is to drill or bore out a block, file it open at the upper end, slip it over the magazine band, and then sweat it into place as outlined for other models.

I've given quite a few details on the work of attaching swivels, because many hunters carry rifles while wishing unconsciously for a sling. They lack a sling only because they don't know which type of swivels to use or how to attach them to their rifle. In recent years, much emphasis has been placed on using slings with bolt-action rifles, but little attention has been devoted to other types of actions, for which slings are just as desirable. This is unfortunate, because there are many, many more lever-, slide- and self-loading actions in use than there are bolts.

Care and Restoration of Rifle Bores

Finally, we come to the last task of gun ownership, which does not concern the owner's abilities of craftsmanship or patience. This task involves duty: properly cleaning firearms. "What?" you say. "Why, there's hardly any need to clean a gun now that we use noncorrosive ammunition!" To that I must say that's not so. Deer hunters have every obligation to clean their firearms. The difference with noncorrosive ammunition is that the process can be delayed, without causing damage. But regardless of claims of the noncorrosive qualities of modern ammunition, most of which are true, we still have moisture in our atmosphere. And we have some metal fouling from jacketed bullets.

A good solid steel cleaning rod is the most essential tool for keeping a rifle bore in good shape. With modern ammunition, cleaning the rifle can be deferred until after a hunting trip, so jointed, more portable rods are not necessary. Get a substantial steel rod, not brass, and keep it in the workshop or gun cabinet. Add to this some patches of Canton flannel, purchased already cut for your rifle's caliber, or cut them yourself from a yard of the material.

The first step in cleaning is to remove loose powder solvent. Push this out first with a clean dry cloth, not too tight. Next, powder and primer residue should be dissolved. The best way is to get hot water through the barrel. Hot water is a universal solvent and it works as effectively on powder residue as any commercial preparation. Unfortunately, it can only be used conveniently in rifles that can be cleaned from the breech. To do this, insert a fairly tight patch into the bore from the breech end and set the muzzle end in a pan of boiling water on the floor. Now pump up water into the barrel, using the cleaning rod as a suction pump, then expel the water by pushing the patch down to the muzzle. Repeat this until the barrel becomes warm, but be careful not to withdraw the patch completely from the chamber end. If you do, the action will be flooded with water. Now dry the bore at once with a couple of dry patches, and examine it for traces of fouling. If it looks bright and clean, run through a patch spotted with a standard gun oil.

Solid-frame lever-action rifles that cannot be cleaned from the breech should be cleaned with a commercial powder solvent. For this, use a bristle brush, with which the bore can be thoroughly scrubbed. Now wipe it dry with clean patches and oil as before.

If you note any lumps or patches in the bore after the solvent is wiped out, metal fouling is indicated. Usually this can be removed by brisk scrubbing with a brass or steel brush. If this fails, thread a wad of fine steel wool through the slotted wiper and scrub the bore. Heavily fouled barrels won't respond to this treatment. In these cases, the rifle should be taken to a gunsmith for an application of an ammonia solution. I don't recommend this treatment be done by a gun owner, because barrels and actions can be badly rusted if the solution is not handled intelligently.

By exclusively using modern ammunition in rifle barrels in good condition, few hunters will have much fouling trouble. If it occurs, the brush-and-steel-wool treatments will remove it safely. Rusted barrels are another matter, and require special treatment. If you can see rust in the bore, don't waste time with oils, hot water or powder solvents. Attack the bore at once with steel wool. If this doesn't remove it, take an old brush and wrap it with a cloth soaked in a mixture of flour of emery and sweet oil. Scrub the barrel thoroughly with this, then clean as usual. Unless the barrel is far gone, this will restore most of the original brightness.

For badly rusted barrels, only a lapping operation with a lead lap will put the rifle in shooting condition. This work is also the domain of a gunsmith, because it requires a special lapping rod and a good knowledge of rifle barrels. If you have a pet rifle with a badly rusted bore, don't junk it until a good gunsmith laps it out. If this won't give enough accuracy for hunting, either buy a new barrel or discard the entire arm.

Give some consideration to choosing the best solvents and lubricating oils. Stay away from commercial preparations that claim to be both solvent and lubricant. Each fluid serves a different purpose and the liquid consistency of each must be different. A powder solvent, to penetrate all points of the bore into the corners of the rifling and under metal fouling, must have a water-thin consistency. Such an oil cannot lubricate properly nor will it serve as a rust preventative because it tends to flow off metal. Lubricating oil and rust preventative must be the opposite. It must leave a thin, permanent oil film on contact surfaces, remaining there an indefinite time without flowing off, gumming or evaporating. If you must use commercial oils, put it up in handy cans. By all means use an oil made and advertised for guns, rather than the multi-purpose household oils. A single 2- or 3-ounce can of oil will serve a hunter for at least a year, unless it's used on the lawn mower or squeaky car-doors. Buy a can of regular gun oil and use it only for your rifle.

To protect the bore's inside during normal humidity, regular gun oil will do the job, but it must be renewed about once a month. In hot, humid climates, a heavier, semi-liquid grease is required. This is also recommended when the rifle is stored for a long time. Many deer rifles aren't used between seasons. To protect the bores, thoroughly clean them after each season and cover them with a regular gun grease. Never plug the muzzle with a cork or rag, because this causes condensation inside the barrel, soon rusting it. Likewise, don't use the so-called "anti-rust ropes." If they remain in the bore any length of time, the oil evaporates and the rope will rust solidly into the bore. This either ruins the bore or plugs it so the barrel might be ruined by its removal.

Care of External Parts and the Action

External portions of a rifle require little care. If small rust spots form at any time, brush them off with steel wool, not an abrasive cloth or compound, because this also removes the bluing. Before a hunting trip, if wet weather is anticipated, rub the metal parts with furniture wax or a melted beeswax and turpentine mixture. Either will protect against moisture. If your rifle's action gets soaked during a heavy rain, tie it muzzle down to the back of a chair, and set it close to a hot fire to dry out quickly. Then oil it with gun oil. The best insurance against rust on external parts is an oil-soaked chamois kept in a glass jar in the gun cabinet. Every time the firearm is used or handled, go over it once lightly with the chamois, and the gun will never rust.

When hunting in very cold weather, use only a little light oil for lubricating the action. Otherwise it might freeze tight or, at least, the firing pin's travel might be so slowed to cause a misfire. The best bet for all cold-weather hunting is to use no oil whatever on the action. Simply flush it out well with gasoline from a squirt-can. A clean action almost always functions perfectly even without lubrication. At any rate, it is much the lesser of the two evils. If the action is new and stiff, lubricate it with kerosene and you'll have no action troubles, even in sub-zero weather.

If your stock is varnished or lacquered, as most factory jobs are, nothing can be done to remove scratches. Furniture wax might help its appearance, but a new oil finish is the best solution. Oil-finished stocks can quickly be brought to their original condition by rubbing in more raw linseed oil. Age and use merely increase the beauty of oil finishes. Hunters who value the appearance and serviceability of their pet guns will do well to apply one.

In this chapter, I gave few technical details about gun repair. It's not my purpose to write a book on gun work. Many such books already on the market delve thoroughly into such work, and are far beyond my abilities. I've tried to discuss points of most interest to hunters who love their firearms, and who take pride in their ability to create things with their hands. Much work on firearms is the result of personal fancy, so don't hesitate to carry out ideas that might seem practical to better suit the gun for your own use. The suggestions I've outlined merely show the way for individuals with initiative and patience.

In stock work, particularly, only a few principles need to be followed. The rest will be dictated by personal needs and taste. I've made no mention of special branches of gunmaking that require unique knowledge and specialized tools. All of the work outlined in this book can be completed, albeit more slowly, with tools from the carpenter's box or on the garage workbench. Most of the necessary materials can be obtained locally. Arm yourself with several catalogs from various shooting-supply houses, decide the job you want most to do, and jump into it with the resolve to work slowly and patiently with forethought. If you do so, the results will always exceed your expectations.

CHAPTER 21

Mounting the Trophy

Editor's note: *Several of the taxidermy techniques Koller describes in this chapter have changed immeasurably since 1948. Rather than write footnotes for the myriad changes — such as using high-density foam for forms instead of layered wet paper and papier-maché — we've left most of the text intact to better understand this art as it was practiced in Koller's era.*

The culmination of all successful deer hunts is preparing and preserving the trophy. Any representative whitetail head, gracefully mounted and hung properly on the wall of an office or den, serves ever to renew the pleasure and thrill of that red-letter day when the Red Gods smiled favorably on the hunter. As I write this final chapter, there hangs on the wall near me, looking out over my left shoulder, the head and huge antlers of the biggest buck it has ever been my good luck to bring to earth. Almost every time I glance that way I can see again the flashing gleam of his 2-foot spread bobbing through the pines and over scrub oak in his last desperate dash for safety. These are the memories that make hunting so worthwhile. The trophy itself serves amply to keep bright the thrilling moment the years might try to dim.

Deer-Head Mounting is Easy

Few hunters think of mounting their own deer heads, and fewer still attempt it. Yet deer-head taxidermy is remarkably simple. Modern methods of commercial taxidermists have eliminated much of the messiness and reduced the skill requirements to the point where little real craftsmanship is required to turn out a creditable job. Taxidermy remains one of the fine creative arts, but much deer-head work is now out of this classification. All the skilled workmanship formerly required in modeling, shaping and posing the mount is now performed by artists who manufacture commercial supplies. Hunters can buy these products at low prices. With proper materials at hand — forms, eyes, panels and ear liners — almost anyone can prepare and mount a deer head with little expenditure of time and effort.

Mounting game birds and animals has always been shrouded in mystery. Taxidermists jealously guarded their methods from the public and their professional brethren. This secrecy obscured hunters' knowledge of the craft, and did nothing to encourage them to prepare and preserve their trophies. There is so much pleasure and satisfaction in this work, however, that it's only fitting to outline the details for those who want to perform the work as a large part of their outdoors hobby.

Pre-Mounting Care for Deer Heads

Mounting a deer head requires only a small amount of room, just a corner in the attic or basement. There will be no ripe odors to permeate the household, and little debris to clutter the floors. A garage or workshop is ideal for the work, but it's not necessary. The work can easily be done in the home without too much objection from family members.

The first step in preparation, whether you want to mount the head yourself or take it to a taxidermist, is to properly care for the head before transporting or skinning it. If the weather is cold or if the head can be express-shipped to reach the taxidermist in a couple of days, there is no need to skin out the head. It can be shipped whole and the taxidermist can take the necessary measurements before skinning.

The usual precautionary measures must be observed: Don't cut the deer's throat or make any incision in the neck skin. Next, when severing the head and neck skin from the hide, leave plenty of skin. Cut it off well behind the shoulders and brisket to give the taxidermist plenty of hide to work with. I've seen some mighty fine heads ruined by cutting the neck skin off too short. The only possible solution is to use a whole new scalp, or skin, from another deer, but the taxidermist is forced to make an extra charge. In addition, the head will not have its original skin, although this is not so important because hides look pretty much alike.

If you're going to mount the head yourself, or if you're worried the head will spoil in transit to the taxidermist's shop, you must take measurements and then skin out the head. The accompanying drawings show which measurements are needed to ensure a form of correct size is selected for the final mounting. It's best to take all the head measurements indicated, because some taxidermy supply houses have different requirements than others. The measurements indicated take care of all needs.

Taking the Right Measurements

To determine the head-size of the form, measure the distance from nose to eye corner, and from nose to point of skull. The circumference around the neck determines the size of the neck, which varies considerably with different supply houses. When measuring the skull, feel behind the antlers on the back of the skull for a bump. It is to this point that the skull measurement should be taken. In measuring neck circumference, pull the tape measure tight, otherwise the reading, taken over hide and hair, will result in a larger form than necessary.

The measurements to antler burr and antler points are essential for correct placement of the antlers on the form. Few taxidermists use these measurements, but they save a lot of guesswork in preparing the form. By this method, the position of the antlers in relation to the head is definitely established. Measure from the tip of the nose to the base of the antler, or burr, and to the tip of each antler from the nose. These are all the measurements necessary for correct mounting of the head, so keep them in a notebook as a permanent record.

Head and antler measurements before skinning.

To give novices an idea about which measurements they can expect to obtain, here is a complete set taken from a medium-sized Northern white-tailed buck, with a medium-sized, 8-point set of antlers:

✓ nose to eye corner, 6¾ inches;
✓ nose to skull point, 12 inches;
✓ circumference around neck behind ears, 17 inches;
✓ nose to antler burr, 9½ inches;
✓ nose to right antler point, 14 inches;
✓ nose to left antler point, 14¾ inches.

Skinning Out the Head

With measurements taken and recorded, begin skinning the head. I use a surgeon's scalpel with a 2-inch blade and a screwdriver with a dull, fairly broad blade. A small pocketknife can serve in place of the scalpel, but it must be keenly sharp. To keep it razor-sharp while skinning, keep an oil stone handy on the bench.

If the full hide is not yet separated from the neck skin, do this now by laying the hide flat on the bench and folded along the center of the back line. Cut the hide well behind the withers — or top of the shoulders — and brisket, making the cut straight down from the top through the foreleg skin, cutting both sides as they're held together flat on the bench. This gives enough hide to make a full shoulder mount if desired, and it gives us enough extra skin for a margin of safety. Now, place the head upright on the bench and, working from behind, start the knife-point into the skin directly between the ears in the center of the top of the neck. Slice through the skin from this point straight through to the top of the shoulders. This line is easy to follow even if the neck has been skinned out, because there is a line of dark hair running down the top of the neck to between the shoulders.

Next, start the knife-point directly behind the base of an antler and cut through to the beginning of the first line. Repeat with the other antler, forming a Y-shaped cut atop the skull. Begin separating the skin between the ears, widening the cut until the base of each ear is seen on the sides of the skull. If the neck has not been skinned out before, this must be done before the ear bases can be reached. When skinning, take pains not to cut into or through the hide. Rather, take some of the flesh with the hide, because it can be removed easily after the skin is salted.

When the ear bases can be seen, cut these off from above by slicing straight down with the knife, keeping close to the skull. This leaves the ear attached to the hide to be skinned out later. Be careful in cutting off the ears not to cut the hide when reaching the bottom of the cut, but proceed gently. Work the hide around the back of the jaw bones until the ear bases can be severed close to the skull without any danger of cutting the hide. The next step is to free the skin from around the antler bases, beneath the burr. Don't use the knife for this job, except to make the starting incision. Pry the skin off carefully with the screwdriver. If the head has dried to any degree, this process will be slow, but continue until the skin is completely freed from under the antler burrs.

Continue skinning out all around the head until reaching the eyes, and then skin these out properly. This is done by placing a finger in the eye socket under the back of the eyelid, and lifting it up and out so the blade can slice between the eyelid and skull. Be careful not to cut the eyelid in any way. When reaching the front eye corner, we find the skin here is attached firmly to the skull. Hard gristle makes for tricky skinning at this point, but normal care will preserve the eyelids and corners. Directly in front of the eye corner, the skin grows down into a depression, or pit, in the skull. This is the tear duct, and it requires special care to avoid being torn while separating it from the skull. Again, insert a finger under the skin and lift up and out while working the knife-point down into the skull pit, cutting all around under the skin, freeing it from this depression. The tear-duct skin is thin and hair-free, so it's important that no cuts be made through it, because they will show in the finished mount.

The next task is to peel down the skin until reaching the back corners of the mouth. Again, insert a finger or two to lift the lips away from the jaw and slice through the flesh, leaving the lips on the hide. Follow around the jaw line in this manner, cutting close to the jawbone, until the skin of the lower jaw is removed.

The nose and nostrils are now the only skin attached to the head, so remove the hide the rest of the way as follows: Insert a finger into a nostril until cartilage in the nasal passage can be lifted slightly at a point about two inches above the nose. Cut straight down to the skull at this point behind each nostril, leaving the cartilage attached to the nose skin. Continue down to the nose, cutting this off close to the upper jaw and leaving all the flesh and lips attached. The head is now skinned and ready for salting, but first saw out the antlers so the head and skull can be disposed of before they start decomposing.

The diagram shows how to make this cut. Place the skull in an upright position on the workbench, with the nose to the left and antlers at right angles to the bench's edge. Take a handsaw (any old carpenter's cross-cut saw will work) and start cutting at the rear of the skull, just under the skull point. Angle the cut so it will emerge at the top edge of the eye sockets, being careful to keep the saw level as it cuts through the skull. After the antlers are freed with their patch of skull, scrape or shake out the small quantity of brains that clings to the top of the brain pan. Next, wash the skull and antlers thoroughly with hot water, and trim off any loose flesh. The skull and antlers can now be set aside to dry out.

Next, start skinning the ears by turning them inside out. Notice the base cartilage of each ear is surrounded by flesh, so remove this. Start at the back side of the ear and trim it off close to the cartilage, leaving all the cartilage attached to the ear. After removing the flesh, reverse the ear by working your fingers up into the pocket between the ear cartilage and the skin on the back of the ear. This is sometimes a tough job because the cartilage grows tightly to the skin. Don't use the knife for this operation. Persevere with your fingers and the end of your blunt screwdriver until the cartilage breaks loose from the ear all along the back. Little attaching tendons here can be cut, but other than this the knife should not be used. Professionals use "ear-opener pliers" for this operation, which greatly speeds up the work, but it can be done just as outlined.

When the cartilage is loosened about halfway up the back of the ear, start turning the ear inside out. Work it carefully, separating the cartilage from the skin down to the edges of the ear and out to the tip, being careful not to tear the skin at the edges of the ear. It's vitally important to break the cartilage loose

Pry off

Cut

Head skinning method

out to ear's edges, otherwise the ear liner will not reach to the full outline of the ear in mounting, and the edges will wrinkle and curl in drying, making a messy-looking mount. It's a good idea, after the ear is reversed almost entirely, to turn it back again to its original position so the edges of the ear can be opened up from the cartilage. To do this, insert your finger and push it against the edge until reaching the outline of the ear.

Salting and Tanning the Hide

With the ears reversed and cartilage showing, we're ready to salt the scalp. Spread it out flat and sprinkle it liberally with table salt, rubbing it in well around the eyes, nostrils and lips. Fold it over and roll it up, and then lay it overnight in a cool place. The next day you'll note certain juices have formed overnight, so hang it up outdoors to drain, then resalt it and lay it out as before for another day.

By this time the salt will have sufficiently hardened the loose flesh and fat on the hide so it can be fleshed out, at least partially. Take your small knife and a heavy-bladed hunting knife and trim or scrape off flesh and fat clinging to the hide, paying attention to the areas around the eyes, nostrils and lips. It's likely you won't be able to remove all the flesh from the area around the nose and nostrils at this time, because the salt will not have affected flesh right next to the skin. Leave this temporarily and start on the lips. Split the lips with the knife almost to their edges and pare the flesh down closely, but the lips must not be cut off at the mouth's edge. After splitting the lips and removing some of the flesh, apply salt liberally to the lips and nostrils and lay it out for 24 hours, or until the flesh toughens from the action of the salt.

As an extra precaution, don't allow the first salting to remain on the skin unless it's frequently inspected. In this first salting, the flesh is not completely cured next to the skin, and the skin might start spoiling in the areas around the eyes, nostrils and mouth. When the hide is placed in the tanning solution, the hair will slip off the hide around these areas, making an irreparable blemish. However, after the hide is partially fleshed and more salt applied, the salt strikes down through to the hide, preserving it for a year or more.

Final fleshing should involve only the paring of the flesh to the lips skin, and around the nostrils and eye sockets. In final fleshing of the nostrils, the nasal cartilage should be removed and the nostrils skin preserved intact at least for an inch or slightly more, because the nostrils skin will show in the finished mount. The flesh must be painstakingly shaved from the nose, or the nose will wrinkle when the head is mounted and dried.

The skin is now ready to be tanned, so prepare a tanning solution. First, obtain a wooden or earthenware tub (not metal), and pour about 4 gallons of tanning liquor into it. The solution is made up of this formula:

1 quart common salt (NaC_1)
1 gallon water (H_2O)
1 ounce by volume sulfuric acid (H_2SO_4)

Dissolve salt in warm water and gradually add acid to prevent an explosion. After the solution cools, the scalp should be immersed and kept submerged by placing a block of wood on it. Move the hide around in the solution every few days for at least two weeks. It is then completely tanned and ready to mount.

Choosing the Right Form

In the interim, while the scalp is tanning, go through the classified advertising sections of outdoor magazines and send for a few catalogs from various supply houses. All that remains is picking out the style and size of mount that suits your fancy. All the big supply houses carry head forms for white-tailed deer in various styles: neck mounts, straight, right or left turn; shoulder mounts, straight, right or left turn; sneak mounts in the same order, and shoulder sneaks likewise. Pick a mount that is turned in some way, right or left, whichever is suited to its proposed location in your home. A turned mount is much more expressive of life than the regular straight mount.

After you've picked a mount, review your measurements and the manufacturer's specifications, picking a form that closely meets your requirements. If there is any doubt about your selection when measurements do not coincide with your record, always choose the next smaller size. A hide will shrink nicely without wrinkling, even if the form is a little small, but never order an oversized form. You'll be able to stretch the scalp to fit it without too much trouble, but when it dries, watch out! The stitches can break up the back, the skin might pull away from the antler bases, and the eyes will pop out.

With the form, you must order ear liners of the correct size, matching them to the size of the head form: small form, small ear liners; large form, large ear liners, and so on. If there is any doubt, get the ear liners large. They can be trimmed to fit the ear, but this is seldom necessary.

Perhaps a word here about the construction of the forms is in order. Commercial head forms and ear liners are made of paper. Layer on layer of wet paper is glued together inside a hollow form or cast, built up to a thickness of ¼-inch or more, making a strong, lightweight mount for the hide. Inside the top of the form is a block of wood for the antler screws. It's held there by gluing over it more layers of heavy paper. Ear liners are made the same way, except that they're not built to the same thickness. These forms are permanent. They will never sag or lose their shape, and they're correctly modeled to the proper outlines. They require only that the skin be stretched over them and sewed. No building up is necessary, as each detail is properly worked out in the form itself.

Here are a few points to consider when selecting your form. Choose the type in which the top of the head, where the antlers are to be placed, is flat. Some forms are made with a notched top to take the skull section, but these are not easy for novices to use. The eye sockets should be molded in the form, even to the high crown over the eye, eliminating any necessity to build up these points. The nostrils and nose should be well modeled, and the outlines of the jaw reproduced. As an added point, be sure the form is fitted with a neck board at the factory. Sometimes there is a small extra charge made for fitting neck boards into the form's base, but it's worth it.

Other Important Materials

Ear liners should be bought with the bases or butts already formed as an integral part of the ear liner. That eliminates the necessity of building up the ear base with plastic compounds, which must be done when a short ear liner is used. The short liner simply fills the pocket between the back of the ear and the cartilage. It does not fill the space left when the flesh is removed from the ear base.

Perhaps the most important point in the mounted head is the eyes. On them depends the lifelike expression found in some mounts but lacking in many others. They must be lustrous and correct in color and shape, truly "the windows of the soul." The highest quality eyes are the concave convex, which are hemispherical in shape and hand-painted. They're also the most costly. For deer-head work, the imitation concave convex are suitable. They're just a little flatter in front and flat in back, and they're also hand-colored. The workmanship on these eyes equals that of the genuine convex eyes, but the construction is not as expensive. They're somewhat better suited for use with paper forms, because their flat back sets them back farther in the socket, preventing to great extent the pop-eyed expression of many mounts.

Additional materials that must be ordered with the forms and eyes are needles, papier-mâché, a panel or shield, and a plate hanger for this. Any other incidentals can be purchased as needed. Two needles, usually termed "scalp needles," are required. These are curved, about 3½ inches long, and have three cutting edges. Papier-mâché can be purchased in the dry form to be mixed with water, or already prepared in an airtight can. About a pound is sufficient for one head. The panel or shield depends on the hunter's taste. It's important, though, to have it large enough. For medium-sized neck mounts, the shield should be at least 13-by-17 inches; for medium shoulder mounts, the shield should be 15-by-20 inches or larger. Black walnut and oak are good panel woods. They look nice and aren't too costly. Fir is less expensive, but it doesn't present the rich appearance of oak or black walnut.

Incidental materials include oil colors, paraffin, beeswax, linen thread, spring clothespins, camel's-hair brush, and 18-gauge wire brads. Some of the items are available around the house or shop, but if not, their cost is slight.

Mounting the Deer Head

When the necessary supplies are assembled, it's time to start mounting the head. The scalp, after its two weeks in the tanning solution, is well cured, so prepare it by beaming it down a bit to thin the skin at the proper places. Remove the scalp from the tanning liquor and wash it thoroughly in warm water after adding a double handful of washing soda. This softens the hide, making it more pliable. The soda also neutralizes the action of the tanning solution. Hang it up about an hour, letting the water drain off, leaving the hide moist but not slippery. Now prepare a small fleshing beam to facilitate thinning the hide. Take a 2-foot piece of 2-by-4 lumber and, with a plane or drawknife, round off one of the wide sides so it presents a fairly smooth-crowned surface. Bolt this to the bench so the end projects 12 or 14 inches past the edge, with the rounded surface facing up.

Now slip the scalp over the beam's end, flesh side out and nose snug against the end of the beam. Take a heavy hunting knife or drawknife, and pare the skin down around the eyes, nostrils, under-jaw, top of the head and along the lips. Shave the hide so it is thin enough to conform easily to the head form's contours. Take care shaving the lips so they will not be cut off at the hairline. Thin the hide around the antler burrs, which will prevent shrinkage at this point. After the hide is thinned properly, it can be returned to the tanning solution until the head form is ready.

Hang the head form by boring a hole in the upper portion of the neck board, and setting it on a large-headed wood screw or lag screw, fastened to the wall or a beam. It should be hung at a height to place the form's nose at about chest level.

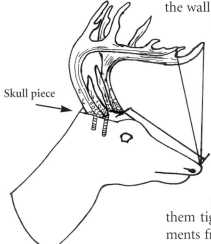

Skull piece

Placing rack on form

With a ¼-inch drill, bore three holes through the top of the skull carrying the antlers. These should be placed so there are two holes in the front, just between and in front of the antler bases. The rear hole is drilled in the skull's center just behind the antler bases, making a triangle with the apex pointing toward the back of the head. Countersink the screw holes with a rose countersink or a larger drill so the anchoring screws will be almost flush with the top of the skull.

Take your measurements chart and place the antlers atop the form with the antler bases at the given distances. Fasten them in this position with three 2½-inch No. 10 galvanized wood screws, setting them tightly enough so the antlers will be in position. Check the measurements from nose to antler points with a ruler. This measurement will usually be too great, indicating the antlers must be tipped forward. To do this, loosen the screws and insert a small block of wood under the rear of the skull. Then screw the skull down once again and check the measurement. You might have to change the block's thickness several times before it comes out right. If the antlers angle too far forward, use cardboard shims under the front of the skull piece until matching the measurements.

After the antlers are in place, you might notice small gaps between the skull and form. The skull's contour will also show a gap between the forward end of the skull and the beginning of the flat portion atop the form. These must be filled in and built up with the papier-mâché composition, following the form's outlines. Just under the antler burr is a hollow that must be filled with papier-mâché because flesh was removed here in cleaning the skull and it must be replaced. If this step is neglected, the hide will shrink into this hollow in drying and pull the skin away from the antler burrs, baring an expanse of bone. When the papier-mâché has dried hard, the form is ready for trying on the skin.

Remove the scalp from the tanning solution and hang it to drain off a bit before trying it on the form. It's not necessary to wash it until it has been fit to the form. Place the scalp, hair side out, over the form in the position it will assume when mounted. Slide the nose skin up over the form's nose and pull the scalp up to the antler burrs. Then fold the skin around the neck, estimating at this point whether the skin will go around the neck. If so, hold it in this position with one hand and with the other slide the nose skin down over the nose on the form, checking the position of the eye-holes in relation to the form's eye sockets. If you ordered the correct form, all these points will be in line. Sometimes, however, the skin, because of handling on the fleshing beam and washing, is stretched out of shape. If so, it won't go around the form completely or fails to come out right over the eyes. Not to worry. Wet buckskin stretches a great deal, and by working it over the fleshing beam or the edge of a board in a vise, it can be stretched enough in any direction to cover the form.

Washing and Poisoning the Hide

Once a good fit has been made, the hide should be washed and cleaned for mounting. Do this by immersing the hide in warm water with washing soda added. Then wash well in soapy water and rinse in clean warm water. Press out the excess water, but don't wring out the skin. Rather, lay it on a wide board to drain a bit.

Next, poison the hide to protect it from moths and dermestids. Arsenical soap can be painted on the hide's flesh side, but the following solution gives better results with no danger of infecting the operator:

Protective Solution
2 gallons water
1 lb. borax
1 oz. carbolic acid
1 oz. spirits of camphor
Boil water to dissolve borax, then add acid and camphor.

Now, immerse the still-damp hide in this solution for about 24 hours to thoroughly poison it. The scalp should then be removed, excess water pressed out, and laid flat to drain before it's ready for the final mounting.

The poisoning solution can be poured into the tub that was used for the tanning solution. The tanning solution should have been dumped out, because it has no further use. Arsenical soap is, of course, widely used in mounting work, including deer heads, but because it is highly poisonous, do not handle a treated skin if you have any small cuts or abrasions on your fingers or hands. Rubber gloves give adequate protection against arsenic, but the poison solution given above is more satisfactory.

As a matter of interest, however, here is the formula for arsenical soap:

Arsenical Soap
1 pound white soap (Ivory)
1 pound white arsenic
6 ounces spirits of camphor (by volume)

The soap should be sliced thin and melted over a slow fire, adding a little water. When it's melted, add the arsenic, stirring constantly, then add the camphor. Let it simmer until it becomes thick, and then pour it into a glass jar labeled poison. To use, mix a small quantity with water, and paint it on the hide with a brush.

After the scalp is poisoned, the ears should again be turned right side out and the ear liners fitted. First enlarge the ear pocket's openings by stretching them with your fingers. Pull hard, because there's no danger of tearing the hide. Now, insert the liners into the ear pocket. If they still go in hard, apply a little soap along the edges to help the process along. With the liners in place, press the cartilage back against them into position and note how they fit. They should come out to the ear tip and flush along the edges. If the cartilage bulges, the liner must be trimmed to make a fit. Do this with a heavy shears, tin-snips or sharp knife.

With the liners fitted, mix a little Casco glue and cover the liner and inside of the ear pocket. Again insert the liners and hold them in place by clamping all along the edges of the ear with spring clothespins. Cartilage at the base of the ear should be trimmed, as should the base of the liner, if necessary, permitting the cartilage to be pulled back into the liner's base.

Final Mounting and Finishing

The scalp and form are now ready for final mounting. Once final mounting begins, it must be completed while the skin is still wet, so leave plenty of time for this task. If a head is left half-finished to remain overnight, the scalp will be so dried out that it's impossible to make the necessary manipulations for setting the eyes, ears and nostrils.

To begin: Take the two scalp needles and thread them with a double thickness of heavy linen shoemaker's thread, previously waxed with beeswax. Remove the form from the wall and fit the scalp into position. Then lay the head on the bench upright but facing away. Look at the areas on the skin that will surround the antler butts. They can be recognized by a ragged appearance at the edges, because this skin was pried loose from the skull, not cut with a knife. Start your first needle from the flesh side at one corner of the antler section. Do likewise with the other needle at the other corner. Then knot both stitches so each threaded needle will be firmly attached to the scalp. Now bring the scalp around the antler butt, and make your first stitch with each needle to the opposite side of the hide. Do this by inserting the point about ¼ inch down the edge from the first stitch, and then repeat with the other needle. Make about three stitches loosely with each needle, then pull both threads together, bringing the skin firmly around the antler bases just under the burrs. Continue sewing the incisions, using the two needles, one at a time, inserting the points from the hide's flesh side. (Sewing from the flesh side prevents hairs from being pulled through with the thread.)

When reaching the end of the first branch of the Y-cut, tie off the two threads by knotting them together with a square knot. Repeat the process with the other antler until reaching the end of the other Y-cut. Now, instead of knotting the threads at this point, continue to sew together the neck cut to a point about three inches behind the ears. Tie the ends together at this point, again using the square knot.

Next, take a lump of papier-maché and work it around the butts of the ear liners so they will be set in place when the mount dries. After filling around the bases, continue sewing the neck incision until the form has been covered all the way to the base board. Now, tie off the threads, but don't cut them off. Leave the ends with needles attached until the head is finished, because you might need to do more sewing after the ears are pulled up into place.

Place the form back on its wall hook, then look it over. The ears droop dismally, the eye sockets gape, the nose is lumpy, the lower jaw skin hangs down, and the entire scalp is wrinkled. This is just as things should be at this stage! Each point will be fixed in its order, quickly and easily.

First, the ears must be set. Stand in front of the mount and grasp an ear butt in each hand and pull them toward you. Bring them well up against the backs of the antlers in an erect or "alert" position, facing well forward and slightly out away from the head. They can be held in this position in two ways. The easier of the two methods is to loop a soft rope or strip of cloth around the back of each ear, passing the end around the base of one ear, then over the top of the skull in front of the antler burrs to the base of the other ear. Then bring it around this and again over the top of the skull just behind the eyes, tying the ends together atop the skull between the eyes and antlers. Pull this rope up tight, smoothing the hair down under it so it won't be ruffled after the mount dries. This will hold the ear butts forward and firmly in position.

The alternative method is to take two pieces of ⁵⁄₁₆-inch welding rod, each about 12 inches long, and sharpen an end on each. Then, holding the ear in position, drive this rod into the form through the inside of the ear base, being careful to choose the correct angle for the rod. Repeat the process with the other ear. With the ears in the approximately correct position, remove the clothespins from the ear edges, and cut a piece of stiff cardboard that will conform to the inside of the ear. Fit these by pressing them back against the inner ear and again clamp with the spring clothespins along the edge. The ear positions can now be adjusted by tying them to the antlers with twine.

Tying method for holding ears in place

Take your blunt screwdriver and lift the lower jaw's skin. Find the center of the lower jaw on the skin and tuck it into the form's lip slot in the exact center of the lower jaw on the form. Fasten it into position by tapping in a wire brad. Continue this operation along the lower jaw, tucking in the skin and fastening it with wire brads about an inch apart. Work from the front toward the back of the jaw on each side until reaching the extreme corner of the mouth. Fasten the corner with a brad. When tapping the brads into the form, don't drive them all the way in. Leave enough of the head showing so they can be removed with a pliers after the mount dries.

To prepare the upper jaw and nostrils for mounting, mix a small amount of Casco glue. Then, working from the inside under the skin, coat the upper half of the form as far up as the eye sockets, working the glue into the tear ducts and nostrils. Then pull down the nose skin over the form, and with the blunt screwdriver tuck the center of the upper lip around and under the form and up into the lip slot in the exact center of the nose. Fasten it with a brad. Repeat around each side of the upper lips, working toward the back as you did with the lower jaw and placing brads about an inch apart to hold the lips in place. When reaching the back corner of the mouth, you'll find a small fold of skin left with no place to put it. Fold it over and nail it into place with two or more brads. It will dry nicely in this position.

Peg method

The skin inside the nostril should now be tried in the form openings. If there's too much nostril skin left on the scalp, pull it out and trim it off with a knife or scissors until it just lines the form and no more, then fasten it into place with a brad at each upper corner.

Most forms from the supply houses have the lip slots already cut. It's a good idea, though, to examine the form when it arrives to make certain of this point. If this detail has not been done, it's up to you to cut the slot with a narrow wood chisel and hammer. Turn the form upside down and, with your chisel, cut straight down through the paper form directly between the upper and lower lips. Make the cut close to the sides of the lower jaw, keeping in mind that the cut must be vertical when the head is hung upright. It often helps when placing the lips to widen this slot a bit with the chisel or a knife, giving more room for the lip skin. Lip skin is very important to successful fashioning of the mouth, so again, be certain there is plenty left on the hide after the fleshing and beaming operations.

Setting the Eyes

Now we've reached the most important detail: setting the eyes. Take a small wad of papier-maché and line the eye socket for the eye to rest upon. Lift the upper eyelid and slip the imitation eye under the lid, then bring the lower lid around and over it. You'll note the pupils are a long oval, so place the eye so the oval's long axis is nearly horizontal, with the front end tipped down just a bit. Take a nail or some other fairly blunt tool and press the skin into the tear ducts in the same way they originally grew to the skull. Drive a brad into the bottom of this tear duct and set it permanently with a nail set. This brad will not be removed. Now take another brad and drive it into the eye's front corner and into the front corner of the eye socket. Place the other eye exactly the same way. It's best to place both eyes before trying to obtain the right expression, rather than setting one at a time.

Stand back from the head and look at each eye. One will probably be higher than the other, or one might protrude farther from the eyelid. From a position in front of the head, push each eye toward the rear of the socket, pushing the front corner of the eye in toward the skull. The back of the eye should be covered all around by the eyelid skin, but the front corner should show a small triangular piece of the papier-maché filling. Adjust both eyes together, bringing each into correct adjustment by sliding them and pressing them into the pliable papier-maché filling.

There is no given rule for setting eyes, because each mount is slightly different. In general, keep the eyes slanted slightly toward the front of the head, pupils tipped forward and down a little, with the focal point of the head's gaze at a point about 10 feet distant and just below the mount's eye level. Pull the upper lid well down over the top of the eye and pull the lower lid up to an almost flat line. When the head shrinks in drying, the eyelids shrink back away from the eye, creating the proper expression. If allowances aren't made for shrinkage, the eyes bulge or "pop," giving the mount a frightened expression. When properly set up before drying, the mount should have a "squint" or sleepy look. The eyes should project about ⅛ inch beyond the contour of the eye socket, and no more.

The head is now mounted except for arranging the skin and cleaning off loose glue or papier-maché. Sponge off the extraneous matter with a wet cloth, clean out the excess from around the eyes and nostrils, and comb out the hair on the head. Check the sewing at the back of the neck incision, make any extra stitches that might be needed, and then knot the threads together. With an awl or ice pick, arrange the skin on the form by sliding it back toward the neck board to remove wrinkles.

When the hide lies smooth and sleek on the form, use brads about two inches apart to nail the skin down along the rear of the form. Place the nails so they will pass through the hide, form and the edge of the neck board. Use a sharp knife to trim the hide off the edge of the form, leaving about ¼ inch extending past the edge. Place the form on the wall and spread out the hide and hair around the base of the neck so it's smooth.

Go over the entire mount with the brush, removing marks made by the comb. If the hide dries with these comb-marks, they might show up as streaks in the finished mount. After a bit more brushing of the ears and head, put the mount in a warm place to dry for about a week.

When the head is dry and hard, first remove all the brads around the mouth and nostrils with a pair of pliers. Remove the clamps and cardboard from the ears, and untie the ear butts and ears from the antlers. Then go over the entire mount with comb and brush, and lay the hair down with your hands. The skin around the eyes and nostrils appears pale after drying out, but this color will be restored with oil tube colors or colored wax. But first, use papier-maché to fill in any small gaps around the nostrils and the front corners of the eye, and allow to dry.

Final Touch-Up Tips

The proper oil colors for finishing the head are black, Vandyke brown and Alizarine crimson. They can be applied with the camel's hair brush directly, after being thinned with turpentine, but a neater job is possible by using colored wax. Take equal parts of paraffin and beeswax melted together, and add a small quantity of the color from the tube, stirring quickly to aid blending. While the brown mixture is hot, apply it to the eyelids and inside the nostrils, allowing it to run down into the tear duct. This covers the area of bare skin and gives it a natural color. Also make up a small amount of black wax and paint the nose. Apply it smoothly by keeping the wax hot and holding the brush in the solution until the moment of application. Finish with a small quantity of pink wax made of the crimson in a light tone. Apply just a touch to the inside front corner of the eye and inside the nostrils.

If the wax fails to flow right and does not present a smooth appearance, go over it gently with a pad of cloth wet with turpentine. This smooths out all lumps and ridges, making a neat job. However, good results will come by simply painting the parts mentioned, using the regular shades of oil colors thinned with turpentine. If you desire a high gloss on the nose and around the eyes, apply a thin coat of clear varnish after the colors dry.

If the work has been carefully done on the mouth and lips, no filling-in will be necessary. Under no circumstances should the lips and mouth edges be colored or varnished in any way, for this is unnatural. Neither should the antlers be varnished. Instead, give them a dull gloss by using a cloth to apply a polish made of equal parts turpentine and raw linseed oil.

The mount is now complete except for the hardwood panel. Prepare this by first drilling three holes about three inches apart and roughly triangular in setup, drilling from the front center of the panel with a ¼-inch drill. Countersink the holes in the back of the panel and attach the plate or hanger. Set up the head, well centered on the panel, and screw it down using 2½-inch No. 10 galvanized wood screws.

The job is finished. You now have as good a mount as can be turned out. It's a light, well-posed, durable trophy that is proof against moths and the ravages of wear for many years to come. Its graceful appearance will make it a constant source of delight to its owner.

Before trying any work on deer heads, the novice should study photographs and artists' drawings of deer. Outdoor magazines are a good source of supply.

If possible, visit a state or private game farm and study captive deer for realistic positions of ears, eyes and so on. This "homework" provides valuable points in expressions only live animals can give.

Hunters who have completed their first job of mounting their own trophy are entitled to a feeling of superiority over the average deer hunter. Yet there is no sound reason why any hunter capable of killing a white-tailed buck under fair-chase conditions cannot also mount his buck, in view of the simplicity of modern methods. Any trophy mounted by the hunter's own hands brings and keeps a pleasant feeling of satisfaction that is lacking in all other mounts.

Conclusion of *Shots at Whitetails*

With the mounting of the trophy, we reach the end of this volume on white-tailed deer; through life habits, hunting methods, caring for the prize of the hunt; through the mechanics of weapons, loads and sighting equipment. All of these points hang heavily on the scales of deer-hunting success. I hope that throughout each chapter you detected my sincerity. Certainly every paragraph in the text was done with this uppermost in my mind.

Any reader, whether hunter or not, after wading through this book might conclude that my sole ambition is to spend every waking moment in new plans for shooting more deer. Nothing could be further from the truth. No one has more admiration for these grand, graceful wilderness spirits than I do. Even as I write these concluding paragraphs there are, within two miles of my home, numerous wild white-tailed deer. How I envy them their carefree, peaceful existence; their perfect liberty to move when and where they please! It is true their lives are threatened now and then, but so are we all — not only for two weeks, but for 52 weeks in every year, to almost the same degree.

My aim in presenting this work is not only to help deer hunters take their trophy, but to implant in them some of my unbounded admiration for these wonderful animals. I hope this book helps you find success in a soul-filling sport whose rewards lie deeper in the heart than the filling of a license.

I shall forever wonder how close I came to the mark.

JUNE 2000

Acknowledgments

This third edition of *Shots at Whitetails* would not have been possible without the help and cooperation of Paul Koller, Lawrence R. Koller's youngest son and only surviving offspring. Without Paul's assistance and insights, this book might have forever remained out of print.

Interestingly enough, although Paul inherited his father's passion for fly-fishing, insect hatches and rising trout, he seldom caught the autumn fever that sent Larry Koller into New York's Catskill Mountains to hunt whitetails. Paul moved to Missoula, Mont., in 1986 at age 42 and opened the Missoulian Angler, which offers custom flies, fishing tackle and guided trout-fishing trips. His new home meshed perfectly with his love for trout fishing, and he often joked that he wouldn't return to the East unless he was in a pine box.

Even so, Paul had inherited his father's incredible shooting skills, and shot a few Catskills deer as a young man. As a frequent visitor and appointed deer driver at the Eden Falls Hunting and Fishing Club in New York's Sullivan County, Paul was well-acquainted with his father's love for hunting the white-tailed deer. And, as a result, Paul well appreciates the deep loyalty and affection thousands of deer hunters have for *Shots at Whitetails*.

During phone conversations and a memorable visit with club members at the new Eden Falls campsite in March 2000, Paul helped me better understand the sometimes troubling, sometimes endearing man who was Larry Koller. Paul also graciously arranged for me to bring his father's famous .30-40 Krag back to Wisconsin temporarily so we could photograph the rifle for this book. It's hard to fully appreciate such trust until realizing the Krag was one of the few keepsakes Paul inherited from his father. Paul told us that Larry Koller sporterized this military rifle at age 19, his first such effort. Again, Paul, thanks for everything. I hope this newest edition of *Shots at Whitetails* meets with your satisfaction.

The experience of bringing this book back into print would not have been as rewarding and gratifying without the help of current Eden Falls Hunting and Fishing Club members, especially the club's current president and historian, Chris Thiesing, and longtime member Gary Ziegler, whose fathers, Ernie and Bill, respectively, hunted often with Larry Koller. These men trustingly provided many historical photographs of Koller and his contemporaries.

Finally, a warm thanks to Jennifer Pillath, *Deer & Deer Hunting* magazine's associate editor, who spent much of her own time tracking down Paul. Jennifer succeeded on a tough job that frustrated and defeated many before her.

— PATRICK DURKIN

Editor, *Deer & Deer Hunting* magazine

June 2000

1948

Acknowledgments

To develop this book on white-tailed deer, it must be evident that a writer requires much more knowledge than that gained by a mere lifetime of deer hunting experiences. It is my good fortune to have been associated with some of the best of Eastern deer hunters throughout the past two decades. Each of them has made his valuable contribution to ease the tortures of indecision along the trying, though exciting, path to whitetail hunting success. I wish to express my never-ending gratitude to all these firm friends and sturdy companions through the years that have brought me the tangible rewards gained in following the trail of the whitetail.

It must be equally evident that comprehensive knowledge of deer studies and habits lie far from the grasp of a single hunter's experience. For the information on deer research, distribution and general life statistics, the author is deeply grateful to the conservation authorities of New York, Pennsylvania, Maine, Wisconsin and Michigan. Their full cooperation in furnishing concrete facts and figures from files of many years' study has been of greatest help in preparing the text.

Full credit, as well as much gratitude, must be given also to Ben Pearson Inc. for its aid in adding to my knowledge of beneficent archery legislation throughout the country.

Last, but by no means least, I express my deep appreciation to Clayton B. Seagears, a man who is a constant inspiration to all sportsmen who know him; a tireless conservationist, devoting his ample talents to bringing about a better understanding between the sportsman and those who hold the future of hunting and fishing within their hands.

It would be ungrateful of me not to express my gratitude to Mrs. Koller for her gentle tolerance of my pecking at the typewriter during odd hours, not to mention her firm-handed help in keeping from underfoot our curious offspring.

Were it not for the warm sympathy and cooperation of all these wonderful people, this, my first book, could never have been carried to a final curtain.

— Lawrence R. Koller
New York, 1948

About the Author

Larry Koller, 1912-1967, was born in Brooklyn, but from age 7 lived in Orange County, N.Y. He ran a sporting goods store in Middletown, N.Y., and worked during World War II as a barrel department foreman for two New Haven, Conn., gun manufacturers.

He was a Catskill Mountain guide, gunsmith and tackle-maker long before he became known as one of the country's leading outdoor writers and editors in the mid-1900s. He was later an outdoor editor of *Argosy*, editor-in-chief of *American Gun*, and at his death was a staff editor and columnist for *Guns and Ammunition*. Besides being best known for writing *Shots at Whitetails* in 1948, Koller later gained renown for writing *Fireside Book of Guns, Treasury of Hunting, Treasury of Angling, How to Shoot, Larry Koller's Complete Guide to Handguns* and *Golden Guide to Guns*.

When *Shots at Whitetails* was republished in 1970, it was described as "much more than a fine hunting book. ... Koller (had) that special touch for the wilds that other sportsmen value and admire. ... Koller's interest in hunting, as with all of his acquired skills, was primarily that of a man interested in nature and in the ways of the wild. It is this that gives *Shots at Whitetails* a value beyond its eminent practicality and makes it a classic of wilderness lore."

Also by the Author

Treasury of Hunting
How to Shoot
Larry Koller's Complete Guide to Handguns
Treasury of Angling
Golden Guide to Guns
Fireside Book of Guns